Contents

Preface		**ix**
Acknowledgments		**xi**
Chapter 1	**What's New in FoxPro 2.0**	**1**
	FoxPro 2.0, The Product	1
	Open Architecture	2
	Rushmore Technology	2
	Compiler and Project Management	3
	The External Routine APIs	4
	dBASE IV-Like Features	5
	SQL SELECT and RQBE	6
	FoxPro Screen and Menu Builder	7
	Macros and EVALUATE( )	8
	Template Language	9
	New and Enhanced READ/GET Commands and Functions	10
	Menuing Commands and Functions	12
	What's New with FoxReport	13
	Data Import and Export	14
	Arrays	14
	More on Windows	15
	Printer Drivers	16
	Other Enhancements	16
	Chapter Summary	17

Chapter 2 Database Design 19
The Eight Steps to Database Design 19
Creating Your FoxPro Database 25
The Relational Integrity Rules 26
Normalization 28
A Complete Example 34
Chapter Summary 42

Chapter 3 Data Dictionary 45
What Is a Data Dictionary? 46
Data Dictionary Advantages 47
Setting Up a Primitive FoxPro Dictionary 48
A Functional FoxPro Data Dictionary System 50
Data Dictionary Files 51
The Data Element Dictionary 55
Extending the Dictionary Concept 57
Data Dictionary Implementation in the Dbase Family 57
The Recital Data Dictionary Facility 58
Chapter Summary 59

Chapter 4 Designing and Customizing an Application 61
Calling Other Program Modules 61
Establishing a Set of Library Routines 66
Performing Data Validation 68
Implementing Your Own Help Facility 74
Error Handling 86
Debugging Facilities 86
Custom Configuration 94
Chapter Summary 99

Chapter 5 Template Language Processing 101
FoxPro 2.0 Template Language 101
Specifying the Target File 104
Outputting Generated Lines 104
Steps to Template Language Processing 105
Template Language Processing Applications 105
Lbx2Prg—Converting a Label Form into Source Code 108
Chapter Summary 115

Developing FoxPro® 2.0 Applications

Second Edition

P. L. Olympia and Kathy Cea

Addison-Wesley Publishing Company, Inc.

Reading, Massachusetts • Menlo Park, California • New York
Don Mills, Ontario • Wokingham, England • Amsterdam • Bonn
Sydney • Singapore • Tokyo • Madrid • San Juan
Paris • Seoul • Milan • Mexico City • Taipei

Many of the designations used by manufacturers and sellers to distinguish their products are claimed as trademarks. Where those designations appear in this book, and Addison-Wesley was aware of a trademark claim, the designations have been printed in initial capital letters or all capital letters.

The authors and publisher have taken care in preparation of this book, but make no expressed or implied warranty of any kind and assume no responsibility for errors or omissions. No liability is assumed for incidental or consequential damages in connection with or arising out of the use of the information or programs contained herein.

Library of Congress Cataloging-in-Publication Data

Olympia, P. L.
Developing FoxPro 2.0 applications / P. L. Olympia and Kathy Cea.—2nd ed.
p. cm.
Includes bibliographical references and index.
ISBN 0-201-56786-5
1. Data base management. 2. FoxPro (Computer program) I. Cea, Kathy. II. Title.
QA76.9.D30484 1991
005.75'65—dc20 91-22568
CIP

Cover design by Jean Seal
Set in 11-point Times Roman by Context Publishing Services

Sponsoring Editor: Julie Stillman
Project Editor: Elizabeth G. Rogalin

3 4 5 6 7 8 9-MW-95949392
Third printing, May 1992

Chapter 6 Handling Date and Time Data 117
Summary of Important FoxPro Date/Time Features 123
Date Operations 123
Date Comparisons 125
Date Formats 125
Null Date 127
Date Storage Format 128
FoxPro Base Date 129
Packing Date and Time 132
Random Numbers and the System Clock 133
Appending Date Data from a Delimited File 133
Averaging Dates 134
Indexing on Dates 134
Is It a Leap Year? 135
How Many Days Remain in a Month or Year? 136
Computing the Number of Workdays 137
Chapter Summary 139

Chapter 7 Memo Field Techniques 141
Why Use Memo Fields? 141
Summary of Memo Field Enhancements in FoxPro 142
Creating and Accessing Memo Fields 150
Other Ways to Display Memo Fields 152
Memo Field Length 153
.dbf and .fpt Files 154
Managing Memo Field Space 158
Importing and Exporting Memo Field Data 158
APPEND MEMO and the Phantom Record 164
Memo Fields as Filing Cabinets 165
Getting Around Missing Memo Files 167
Memo File Corruption 167
Chapter Summary 168

Chapter 8 Handling String and Character Data 171
Data Type Conversion 171
Searching Character Strings 173
Word Wrapping in a Character Field During Data Entry 176

	Comparing Strings	176
	String Comparisons in SQL	179
	Replacing Characters and Strings	180
	Encrypting and Decrypting Strings	182
	String Animation	184
	The REPLICATE( ) Function	185
	Chapter Summary	191
Chapter 9	**Array Techniques**	**193**
	Arrays in FoxPro	193
	Array Element Addressing	194
	Initializing Arrays	195
	FoxPro Arrays versus Clipper Arrays	196
	Passing Arrays to Procedures	197
	Built-in Array Functions	198
	FoxPro Commands Involving Arrays	202
	Moving Data to/from Arrays and Database Fields	204
	SCATTER/GATHER versus COPY/APPEND Commands	209
	Sorting Data	209
	Array Sorting Techniques	210
	Chapter Summary	218
Chapter 10	**Indexing and Sorting**	**221**
	Sorting	221
	Indexing	222
	Database Searches	229
	Formulating Index Expressions	236
	Opening Indexes and Index Order	239
	Reindexing	241
	Indexing in a Multiuser Environment	241
	Searching for Close Matches	242
	Chapter Summary	244
Chapter 11	**Report and Printing Techniques**	**245**
	FoxPro's Report Writing Facilities	245
	Summary of FoxReport Features	246
	Report Enhancements in FoxPro 2.0	248
	Including Percentages in a Report	249
	The FoxPro Report Form File	250

	Printing Memo Fields	250
	System Memory Variables	252
	Page Handler	252
	Mailmerge Reports	253
	Snaked Column Reports	259
	Sending Commands Directly to the Printer	261
	Sending Nulls to a Printer	262
	Redirecting Printer Output to a File	265
	Printing on a Network	265
	Printjob and Endprintjob	267
	Printer Drivers	268
	Chapter Summary	272
Chapter 12	**Relationality with SQL**	**275**
	Introduction to SQL	275
	The SELECT Command	276
	RQBE	290
	CREATE TABLE	291
	INSERT INTO	293
	Chapter Summary	294
Chapter 13	**Low-Level File I/O**	**297**
	Comparison with the C File I/O Functions	299
	Uses of the Low-Level File I/O	299
	Chapter Summary	318
Chapter 14	**Multiuser Procedures and Techniques**	**321**
	Shared Files	321
	FoxPro Implicit Locking	322
	Deleting Records on a Network	326
	Controlling Concurrent Updates	328
	Deadlock	339
	Chapter Summary	346
Chapter 15	**More Multiuser Techniques**	**347**
	Reporting	347
	Transaction Processing	351
	ON ERROR Processing	357
	Maintaining a System Audit Trail	359
	Other Multiuser Considerations	361
	Chapter Summary	366

Chapter 16	**Application Program Interface**	**367**
	FoxPro API Basics	367
	Compiling and Linking API Routines	370
	Obtaining Parameters From FoxPro	371
	Returning Results to FoxPro	375
	Summary of API Routines	376
	Example 1: A Bios API Library	378
	Example 2: An API Library Containing Novell Netware Services	381
	Additional Example	382
	Chapter Summary	384
Chapter 17	**Building and Distributing an Application**	**385**
	Project Management	385
	Using the ENCRYPT and NODEBUG Options	388
	Optimizing Performance	389
	Writing an Application Config.fp File	392
	Compressing Files for Distribution	393
	Installing Your Application	395
	Application Adhoc Reports and Database Security	396
	Chapter Summary	403
Appendix A	**FoxPro 2.0 New and Modified Commands and Functions**	**405**
Appendix B	**SET Commands**	**417**
Appendix C	**FoxPro Colors**	**427**
Appendix D	**API Library Routines**	**435**
Appendix E	**FoxPro Standard Index (.Idx) File Structure**	**451**
References		**455**
Index		**457**

Preface

This book begins where the FoxPro manuals end. Much of the material in this book is not covered by the FoxPro manuals or other books. In essence, this is a book about techniques—written by application developers primarily for those who want to develop FoxPro applications and who need the tools and information not readily available elsewhere. For example, we devote an entire chapter to the important subject of database design techniques. Being database developers ourselves, we learned quite some time ago the enormous value of spending the requisite time to plan and design databases carefully.

We also provide a detailed discussion of multiuser procedures and techniques. This is partly a reflection of the ever-increasing need for network database applications in today's market, and partly a reflection of our experience in FoxBASE+ and FoxPro applications development. Much of what we do entails large-scale database development for local area networks, including porting mainframe database systems to FoxPro applications on microcomputer-based LANs. Indeed, we began what may have been the first multiuser FoxPro application using the first beta copy of FoxPro single-user version. The chapters on multiuser techniques go into considerable detail on issues such as controlling concurrent updates and deadlock prevention, including techniques that take advantage of facilities provided by the LAN operating system. We also discuss transaction processing and various options for implementing transaction processing in a FoxPro application. These include the Novell NetWare TTS facility and two approaches of how you might write your own transaction tracking facility.

The book describes how to take maximum advantage of FoxPro's open architecture. We discuss how to extend FoxPro's language through its new Application Program Interface (API) facility, and show an example of how you would use Novell NetWare's own API facility to tap network services from a multiuser FoxPro application. We devote a chapter to FoxPro's template language, or text merge facility. With most data files in FoxPro 2.0 now in the familiar .dbf format, template language processing has eased code generation from screen, menu, report, and label forms. For instance, we show the power of the template language in converting a label form into a fully customizable FoxPro source program.

We discuss FoxPro's revolutionary Rushmore Technology for data retrieval, and how to cast queries to take advantage of it. We also devote a chapter to FoxPro's outstanding Structured Query Language (SQL) and Relational Query-By-Example facilities. A discussion of printer drivers, another new feature in FoxPro 2.0, is included in the Report and Printing chapter.

We devote several chapters to showing procedures and techniques for manipulating different types of FoxPro data including date, time, memo fields, arrays, and character data. The thrust of these discussions is to show novel uses of FoxPro features that you can use in your own development work, as well as to encourage you to explore additional uses of the facilities and power that FoxPro provides.

One of the many new features in FoxPro 2.0 that would interest you as a developer is its project building facility, including the generation of your production application as a standalone .exe. In the book's final chapter, we put everything together and discuss how you would go about assembling and distributing your FoxPro application.

Our clients look up to us as "experts," but if the truth be known, we are only experts to the extent that we have made a lot of mistakes and we have learned from them. In this book, we try to give you the benefit of our experience in order to save you the agony of our mistakes. Whenever possible we teach by example, providing you with a sample program or program fragment to illustrate the techniques under discussion. Programs described in this book, along with supplemental files and assorted utility programs, are available separately on a program disk.

Writing a book is always an intense exercise requiring many sacrifices. Writing a book about FoxPro is no exception, but we are happy to admit that we enjoyed writing this book because we learned a lot from the experience and because FoxPro is central to many of our current applications development activities. If any of the techniques we describe help you in your work and save you some time, then the book has met its objectives.

Acknowledgments

For every book that has ever been written there is always a group of people who, directly or indirectly, made its publication possible. This book is no exception and we take singular pleasure in acknowledging the help of the following individuals.

We thank Emmanuel Sigler for technical edits to the manuscript. We are grateful to Dr. David Fulton, Walter Kennamer, Chris Williams, Janet Walker, Gloria Pfeif, and the Fox Software technical staff for answering many technical questions, and for religiously keeping us up-to-date with FoxPro beta and production files and documentation. We also acknowledge the assistance provided by Julie Stillman and Elizabeth Rogalin of Addison-Wesley.

This book would not have been possible without the continued support and encouragement provided by Adonice Hereford.

Chapter 1

What's New in FoxPro 2.0

FoxPro 2.0 introduces a number of significant and unique enhancements to the Dbase language. In this chapter, we briefly discuss most of the new features of the product. In subsequent chapters, we go over these new capabilities in more detail. Appendix A summarizes all that are new and have changed in FoxPro 2.0.

FoxPro 2.0, The Product

Version 2.0, like version 1.x, comes either as a single-user or multiuser package. However, Fox Software now provides two versions in each package: standard and extended. Thus the single-user package consists of the programs FoxPro (standard) and FoxProX (extended), whereas the multiuser or LAN package consists of the programs FoxProL (standard) and FoxProLX (extended).

The standard version can be used on typical AT class machines with the usual 640K of conventional memory. The Extended Version is a true 32-bit program designed for machines that have extended memory and are based on at least the Intel 80386 chip. The Extended Version should be used when you are processing databases whose aggregate number of records exceeds half a million records, or when you need as many as 65,000 memory variables and 65,000 elements per array. The Extended Version uses all available extended memory, and memory permitting, sets no real limits on the number of indexes, windows, and Browse sessions. The maximum length of a string in the Extended Version is 2 gigabytes.

FoxPro 2.0 has a base memory footprint of about 280K RAM, considerably less than that of version 1.x. Consequently version 1.x applications that had trouble running on networks should work much better under version 2.0. When invoked, FoxPro 1.x always started out by creating a 400K file that was automatically deleted when the software was terminated normally. This presented quite a problem for network administrators since it meant providing enough disk space for each concurrent FoxPro user. Version 2.0 does not require the 400K startup file, so it can be started even if you are logged into a 360K floppy drive and pathed to 2.0 on the hard disk.

Version 2.0 uses a new memory management scheme—a segment loader—instead of the three small overlay areas of version 1.x. Since version 2.0 avoids the performance degradation resulting from code being swapped in and out of the overlay areas, FoxPro 2.0 applications run much faster particularly on a network.

Open Architecture

FoxPro 2.0 adopts an open architecture philosophy that is reflected in many of its new features. For example, developers have access to the FoxPro engine through the external routine APIs (Application Program Interface). The product also has new commands and functions that allow developers to manipulate its system windows and menus in order to build applications that look like FoxPro itself. Whereas version 1.x has files in inscrutable binary formats, most version 2.0 files are in the familiar .dbf format. For instance, FoxPro 1.x had the help file as a database, allowing you to easily create customizable help files for your applications. Now FoxPro 2.0 has report, menu, and screen formats in .dbf files as well, so you can manipulate them just like any other databases.

Rushmore Technology

FoxPro 2.0 uses a data access technique called Rushmore, which allows sets of database records to be retrieved at speeds comparable to those of mainframes. Rushmore permits a FoxPro application to handle million-record databases comfortably. It depends on the FOR clause expression for searching databases. To take advantage of Rushmore, the databases must be indexed and the FOR clause must contain a basic optimizable expression (BOE). A BOE can take the following form:

```
<index expr> <Boolean operator> <constant expr>
```

where <index expr> must match the expression on which the index was created. The index expression may not contain an alias. The index may be a regular (.idx) index or a compact index.

If the database contains the LastName, Street, City, Zip, and Comment fields and it is indexed on the first four, the following expressions are BOEs:

```
Lastname = "Hereford"
Zip <> "20878"
UPPER(City) = "POTOMAC"
```

The following expressions are not BOEs:

```
UPPER(COMMENT) = "NOTES"            && Not indexed on Comment
'208' $ Zip                         && $ is not a Boolean operator
SUBSTR(A->Street, 1, 4) = "Main"    && Contains an alias
```

BOEs may be combined with other BOEs using the AND, OR, or NOT logical operator to form complex FOR clause expressions that are also optimizable. BOEs may be combined with non-BOEs using the AND operator to yield partially optimizable expressions.

Rushmore technology is automatically used in the new SQL SELECT command. FoxPro disables Rushmore whenever a WHILE clause is included in a command (such as LIST, SCAN, and BROWSE) that would otherwise use Rushmore. Standard FoxPro cannot use Rushmore when the total number of records in open databases exceeds half a million records; in those cases, you should use the Extended Version.

You can disable Rushmore either by using the NOOPTIMIZE clause of a command that can use a FOR expression, or by using the SET OPTIMIZE OFF command. SET OPTIMIZE ON reenables Rushmore. You would want to disable Rushmore whenever a potentially optimizable command modifies the index key in the FOR clause. In such a situation, if you did not disable Rushmore, it would not have the most current information about the database.

Compiler and Project Management

FoxPro 2.0 has an .exe compiler making it possible for you to distribute applications without packaging them with the familiar FoxPro Runtime module. The compiler is really just one aspect of FoxPro's project management facility, which is similar to the Make facility of conventional programming languages such as C. A FoxPro project file is a special file that keeps track of all programs and data files required by an application, including programs, screens, menus, libraries, reports, labels, queries, format files, and all the connections and dependencies among the files.

When FoxPro compiles an application, the project file helps ensure that every compiled module in the application is based on the latest source code. The application created from a project file includes code generated from screens and menus. True to form, the project file itself is a FoxPro database (.pjx) with an associated memo file (.pjt).

You normally create a project interactively through a dialog invoked by using the CREATE/MODIFY PROJECT command. Alternatively you can create a project from the command line or in a program using the following command:

```
BUILD PROJECT <prjfile> [FROM <mainpgm> [,<pgm> | <lib>[,...]]]
```

FoxPro creates the project by processing one or more program and library files, and by searching references to other programs and libraries, which FoxPro processes as well.

You use the new EXTERNAL command to include files and to resolve undefined references in a project created by the project manager. The EXTERNAL command is also used to alert the project manager to a filename contained in an expression or macro as well as to array names that were created in another procedure or UDF.

With FoxPro's APIs, you can write your own functions and extensions to the language and have them assembled into an external library. The new SET LIBRARY TO <lib> command then makes the functions in the external library available to FoxPro and the application. External functions destined for inclusion in the library may be written in C or Assembler and then compiled into object files.

After you build a FoxPro project, you have the option of building an application (.fxp) for runtime distribution similar to what you have now in FoxPro 1.x, or you can build a standalone .exe that does not require the FoxPro Runtime module. To build the .exe requires just the BUILD EXE <exefile> FROM <prjfile> command. The complementary BUILD APP command creates the application in .fxp form.

The External Routine APIs

FoxPro's Application Program Interface permits you to extend the capabilities of the language and its user interface seamlessly. With it, you can perform advanced operations, including handling FoxPro events, processing FoxPro statements, and manipulating memory, memo files, databases, and FoxPro windows.

The API library contains an extensive set of routines, including routines to

- Create, release, and change the values of memvars.
- Tap the power of FoxPro's file engine to optimize file I/O.
- Access FoxPro's database engine, including rolling back a record to the last version read from disk.
- Allow event handlers to intercept FoxPro events.
- Control window and streaming output.
- Create or release pads and menus or change the system menus to, perhaps, create a new set of disk accessories.
- Intercept and report error conditions.

External routines receive one parameter from FoxPro—a pointer to the parameter block that contains the number of supplied parameters and the parameters themselves. Programs may pass parameters by reference or by value. Programs may return results to FoxPro using a variety of API routines, including one called _RetVal( ), which can be used to return a string with embedded nulls or to return any data type except memo.

To a FoxPro user, an external routine looks just like a built-in FoxPro function or command except that it cannot be abbreviated to four characters. What if an external routine has the same name as a FoxPro built-in function, a memory array, or a user-defined function (UDF)? The precedence of function/routine evaluation is such that an external routine has precedence over a similarly named UDF, but it does not have precedence over a built-in function or an array.

External routines may be coded only in either 8086 Assembler or Watcom C and are subject to strict rules of behavior regarding memory protection. They are either purgable or locked, depending on whether they are located in the overlay or the root segment.

dBASE IV-Like Features

One of the features of dBASE IV that users like is the multiple index facility where up to 47 index tags may be kept in one .mdx file. In dBASE IV, an .mdx file is either a production or nonproduction .mdx. A production .mdx has the same name as the database, and all its tags are automatically maintained so they never get out of sync with the data—a perennial problem with other Dbase products. FoxPro has the compound index (.cdx) file, which is the equivalent of dBASE IV's .mdx facility except that whereas an .mdx can have up to 47 tags, a .cdx has no limit on the number of tags. The "structural" .cdx is the functional equivalent of the dBASE IV production .mdx. A .cdx file automatically uses FoxPro 2.0's compact type of index.

The INDEX command such as the following:

```
INDEX ON <idx_expr> TAG <tagname> [OF <.cdx file>]
```

creates the indicated tag entry in the .cdx file. The index expression may now contain a user-defined function. In dBASE IV, only index tags in an .mdx may have the DESCENDING clause. In FoxPro 2.0, you don't even need to build a tag or new index file to get your data to appear in descending order. The SET ORDER TO <field or index> DESCENDING command gets you what you want. To support the new .cdx facility, version 2.0 has new functions and commands such as CDX( ), MDX( ), TAG( ), COPY TAG, and DELETE TAG.

Another dBASE IV feature that is new to FoxPro 2.0 is the SET SKIP TO command. In conjunction with the SET RELATION command, it links files when there are one-to-many or many-to-many relations between records in the parent and child files, allowing easy access to records in child files that match the relation key.

SQL SELECT and RQBE

Another new feature of FoxPro 2.0 is the SQL SELECT command (which should not be confused with the SELECT <workarea> command) used to retrieve data from one or more databases. SQL SELECT, a very powerful command, allows you to retrieve data without requiring you to know which databases in which work area contain the data. One SQL SELECT command replaces a whole series of FoxPro commands or procedure to gather, sort, and display the desired information.

Unlike dBASE IV, you don't need to first SET SQL ON to use SQL SELECT. Furthermore, if you don't want to formulate the full Select statement yourself in the command window or a program, you can retrieve the same set of data interactively using FoxPro's new Relational Query-By-Example (RQBE) facility. With RQBE you define the data you want from prompts, picklists, and check boxes. FoxPro then formulates the appropriate Select query for you and executes it. You can save queries to a .qpr file, and you can direct query results to a file, printer, or table.

FoxPro Screen and Menu Builder

As part of its open architecture philosophy, FoxPro 2.0 provides its users with all the user interface design and creation tools they need to create application screens and menus that look like FoxPro itself. One of these tools is the Screen Builder, which you can use to design custom screens with a mix of screen objects. FoxPro screen objects are listed in Table 1-1. Screen objects may be assigned a host of attributes, including colors and range and valid clauses. Figure 1-1 shows a prerelease example of the Screen Builder.

When you build a screen, you are really writing a portion of your application code. Instead of writing the code line by line to build the screen, the Screen Builder lets you just specify the objects and their attributes, including any "code snippets" to specify the object's properties. You can also include your own code snippets for the entire screen, including setup or cleanup codes. These code snippets are stored along with other screen object attributes as part of the screen file.

The Screen Builder can be invoked with the CREATE/MODIFY SCREEN command. All the information about the screen (including data about each object, screen layout, and file) is stored in a FoxPro database file with a corresponding memo file. These .scx/.sct files may be manipulated just like any other .dbf/.fpt files.

After you design the screen, you can use the data stored in the .scx database to generate the code that reconstructs the screen. The code produced by the screen generator includes all the object definitions and code snippets you defined.

Table 1-1. FoxPro Screen Painter Objects

Object	Description
Controls	Can be used to define how data and commands are entered into FoxPro. They include check boxes, menu popups, scrollable lists, text buttons, and radio buttons.
Field Objects	Include database fields, memory variables, and output data from UDFs and complex expressions.
Graphic Objects	Include lines and boxes.
Text Objects	Include any text.

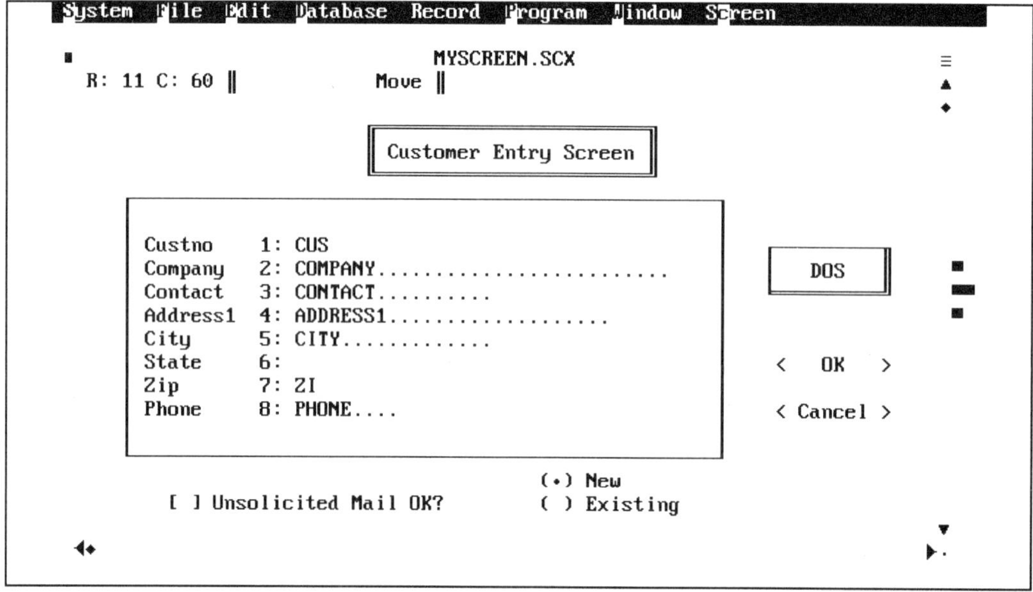

Figure 1-1. Sample Screen Builder screen from a pre-release version of FoxPro 2.0.

FoxPro 2.0 has a Menu Builder, which does for application menus what the Screen Builder does for application screens. With the Menu Builder, you assign commands or create procedures for the menu options. Again you may include custom code snippets for setup or cleanup in the menu system. Data you create with the Menu Builder is stored in a menu file with the .mnx extension, which is really a .dbf database, just like the screen (.scx) file.

A menu file is really a form of source code for the application in much the same way that the screen file can be considered part of your application code. The .mnx file stores all menu definitions and code snippets you create. The menu generator uses data stored in the menu file to generate the appropriate application code.

Macros and EVALUATE( )

Seasoned Dbase users know that macros, although convenient, can slow down a program significantly. In both dBASE IV and FoxPro 1.x, you can use indirect file reference instead of the macro function whenever you refer to a file. Thus, if the memvar Mfile contains the name of a database file, the USE (Mfile) command is much more efficient than USE &Mfile. FoxPro 2.0 has extended the concept beyond just filenames. With most commands that require a name, for example, database field, window, and menu bar names, you can now use indirect name references instead of macro substitutions. Therefore, a command such as DEFINE WINDOW (Wname) is completely valid where Wname is a memvar. Indirect name references are not supported in a few commands such as ?, LIST, DISPLAY (with a field name), and CALL.

With FoxPro 2.0, you may seldom use macro expressions because of the new and versatile EVALUATE( ) function. Like TYPE( ), this function evaluates a character expression, but instead of just returning the data type of the result, it actually returns the result of the expression. Thus, in an application where you would normally code an expression that uses a user-supplied value, for example,

```
LIST FOR &criteria
```

you can avoid the macro (and speed up your program) with the following equivalent code:

```
LIST FOR EVALUATE (criteria)
```

Template Language

FoxPro 1.x, like FoxBASE+, has template language and code generator tools in FoxView, FoxCode, and FoxGen. These tools are extremely useful, but like most code generator products, if you really need to be a master with them, you should be prepared to learn the ins and outs of the template language. Although you can still use the FoxPro 1.x template language tools in 2.0, you may not want to. Why? Because FoxPro 2.0's approach to template language processing excels in its simplicity.

In essence there really are no template language codes for you to remember. You write a seemingly ordinary FoxPro program that writes another FoxPro program or an entire application simply by using the new SET TEXTMERGE command facility and TEXTMERGE delimiters (by default, these are the angle brackets, << and >>) to enclose the expressions, functions, and memvars that you want the program to evaluate before writing the result to the generated application.

For instance, if a memvar called wname has the value MainMenu, the command

```
\ACTIVATE WINDOW <<wname>>
```

writes the code

```
ACTIVATE WINDOW MainMenu
```

as part of the generated program. In this example, the backslash tells FoxPro 2.0 that the line that follows is to be written to a file where the generated application is being recorded.

You only need to remember a few commands to produce generated code. For instance, if you want to create a complete application using one data entry screen, you would simply design the screen using the Screen Builder and then read the data stored in the .scx file using a program that uses SET TEXTMERGE and related commands to produce the application code. Chapter 5 discusses the FoxPro template language in detail.

New and Enhanced READ/GET Commands and Functions

To support the creation and display of design objects such as check boxes, FoxPro 2.0 has a host of new or enhanced commands related to READ and @...GET. For instance, CLEAR READ is a new command to terminate and exit the active READ; in FoxPro, READs can be nested up to four levels deep. The current READ level can be determined with the new RDLEVEL( ) function.

The familiar READ command now has several options, including CYCLE and OBJECT. With the CYCLE option, a READ does not terminate on the last GET. Instead, it recycles to the first GET. The cycle is terminated with Ctrl-W or Esc. The OBJECT clause specifies which GET field or object is initially selected during a READ. The new SHOW GET command redisplays GET fields or objects.

The @...GET command is used to create GET objects (Controls) including check boxes, text buttons, radio buttons, invisible buttons, popups, and scrollable lists. These terms are briefly defined in Table 1-2. The PICTURE or FUNCTION clause of the @...GET command dictates which object is created. For instance, the clause PICTURE "@*C" or the clause FUNCTION "*C" creates a check box. Table 1-3 lists the FUNCTION formats for the

Table 1-2. GET Objects (Controls) and What They Mean

GET Object	Description
Check Box	A "box" or small area on the screen or window that may or may not contain a check mark (an X) to indicate the state of a memvar or a database field.
Invisible Button	A selectable rectangular region of the window or screen underneath which may be placed any text or characters.
Popup	A rectangular region containing a list of options from which to choose.
Radio Button	A "box" or small area on the screen or window beside which may appear a bullet indicating that the button is the current choice.
Scrollable List	A list containing a set of options taken from a memory variable array or a popup definition.
Text Button	A region of the screen or window containing text surrounded by two pairs of angle brackets.

Table 1-3. FUNCTION Formats for Various GET Objects

GET Object	FUNCTION Format
Check Box	*C
Invisible Button	*I
Popup	^
Radio Button	*R
Scrollable List	Not applicable
Text Button	*

You may use the same formats in a PICTURE clause by preceding it with the @ symbol.

various objects. To use the same formats for a PICTURE clause, just precede the format with the @ symbol.

The @...GET command has the additional SIZE and ENABLE/DISABLE clause. On a check box, for example, SIZE dictates the width of the rectangle where you may click the mouse to choose the check box. The ENABLE clause activates the object for selection. A DISABLEd object displays in darkened color and cannot be selected or chosen.

With FoxPro 2.0, you can also create a rectangular text editing region for editing character expressions, database fields, and memo fields. You have access to standard editing features, including block operations and wordwrap. This facility should be embraced enthusiastically by many FoxPro 1.x users who want block operations while editing memo fields but without having to activate the system menu. The text editing region is created with the new @...EDIT command, which is similar to the @...GET command used to create the various design objects.

Menuing Commands and Functions

FoxPro 2.0 users have new means to control what appears in the System menu. An application can manipulate the various System menu pads and bars and return information about them. For instance, if you want to remove the Window pad of the System menu and the Filer option of the System pad, just issue the following commands:

```
RELEASE PAD _msm_windo OF _msysmenu
RELEASE BAR _mst_filer OF _msm_systm
```

There are several enhancements and additions to menu creation and display in FoxPro 2.0. Commands such as DEFINE BAR, DEFINE PAD, DEFINE MENU, and DEFINE POPUP all have optional KEY and MARK clauses. The KEY clause specifies the key or key combination needed to select the option and the key label string that displays next to the option. The MARK clause specifies the check mark character used to signify that the option is selected.

Additional optional clauses are provided with the various DEFINE commands. For instance, DEFINE BAR and DEFINE PAD have BEFORE/AFTER clauses to specify the location and activation order of a bar or pad. DEFINE POPUP now has the TITLE and FOOTER clauses to specify the strings to display at the top and bottom borders, respectively, of the popup.

Table 1-4 lists the new menuing commands, and Table 1-5 shows the new menuing functions.

Table 1-4. New Menuing Commands

Command	Function
MOVE POPUP	Move a menu popup to a new location.
ON BAR	Activate a menu popup or menu bar when a menu popup option is selected.
ON SELECTION BAR	Assign a routine to a menu popup option.
ON SELECTION MENU	Assign a routine to a menu bar.
SET MARK OF	Specify a menu pad or popup option check mark character.
SIZE POPUP	Change the size of a popup.

What's New with FoxReport

The .frx report file containing all the report definitions and data that FoxPro needs to create your reports is now simply a database just like .scx or .mnx. That means you can easily go back to a previously created custom report and modify its contents without having to engage in a FoxReport dialog. The REPORT FORM command (like LABEL FORM) also has a PREVIEW option.

Table 1-5. New Menuing Functions

Function	Returns
CNTBAR( )	Number of bars in a popup.
CNTPAD( )	Number of pads in a menu.
GETBAR( )	Name of a specified bar in a popup.
GETPAD( )	Name of a specified pad in a menu.
MRKBAR( )	.T. if a bar is marked.
MRKPAD( )	.T. if a pad is marked.
PRMBAR( )	Text from a menu popup option.
PRMPAD( )	Text from a menu pad option.

In previous versions of FoxPro, you were limited to one layout window. Version 2.0 lets you open as many layout windows as memory allows. The layout window also has a selection marquee that you can use to select multiple report objects. Furthermore the layout window now scrolls automatically when you stretch objects beyond the initial window. Additionally a report band can be of any size.

The Report menu popup has two new options: GROUP and UNGROUP. The GROUP option lets you take a collection of individual report objects and create a single object to facilitate the manipulation of a complex set of objects. The complementary UNGROUP option separates a grouped object back into the original individual objects.

In addition to the usual Sum, Average, and Count radio buttons for numeric fields in the Totaling Dialog of FoxReport, you now have radio buttons for descriptive statistics values such as standard deviation and variance for the same numeric fields.

Data Import and Export

FoxPro 2.0 can read and write an extended set of database and spreadsheet file formats. The new file types supported (listed in Table 1-6) can be included in the TYPE clause of the COPY TO and APPEND FROM commands. Version 2.0 also has new IMPORT and EXPORT commands that support these file types and facilitate data exchange with other database and spreadsheet software.

Arrays

FoxPro 2.0 has a whole new set of array functions similar to those available in Clipper. This includes ACOPY( ), ADEL( ), ADIR( ), AELEMENT( ), AFIELDS( ), AINS( ), ALEN( ), ASCAN( ), ASORT( ), and ASUBSCRIPT( ). Chapter 9 discusses these functions in detail.

AELEMENT( ) and ASUBSCRIPT( ) are new to Clipper users. FoxPro allows elements in a two-dimensional array to be referenced in two ways. One uses two subscripts that correspond to the row and column position of the desired array element. The other uses a single element number, which is the same number returned by the AELEMENT( ) function. ASUBSCRIPT( ) is the complementary function to AELEMENT( ), which returns the row or column position corresponding to an array element number. As we noted before, FoxPro's Extended Version allows up to 65,000 elements per array.

Table 1-6. New File Types Recognized by FoxPro 2.0 and Supported in COPY TO, APPEND FROM, IMPORT and EXPORT Commands

Format	Description
DIF	Standard Data Interchange format where vectors or columns become database fields and tuples or rows become database records.
FW2	Framework II spreadsheet file.
MOD	Microsoft Multiplan (version 4.x) binary file format document.
PDOX	Paradox database files.
RPD	Rapidfile database file.
SYLK	Symbolic Link interchange format used by some spreadsheet software, for example, Multiplan.
WK1	Lotus 1-2-3 Release 2.x spreadsheet format.
WK3	Lotus 1-2-3 Release 3.0 spreadsheet format.
WKS	Lotus 1-2-3 Release 1A spreadsheet format.
WR1	Symphony versions 1.1, 1.2, and 2.0 spreadsheet format.
WRK	Symphony versions 1.0 and 1.01 spreadsheet format.
XLS	Microsoft Excel version 2 spreadsheet format.

In a spreadsheet file type, the spreadsheet rows become database records, and the spreadsheet columns become database fields.

More on Windows

The DEFINE WINDOW command has three new clauses: FOOTER, FILL, and MINIMIZE. FOOTER specifies the string that displays at the bottom border of the window. FILL specifies the fill character for the window's background. MINIMIZE allows a window to be reduced to a minimum size; the window can then be docked at one corner of the screen, together with other MINIMIZEd windows, to give the active window more room.

You can change the size and location of System and user-defined windows with the new ZOOM command. These windows can be shrunk to a size that leaves only the window name or title visible, or enlarged to fill the entire screen.

In FoxPro, child windows may be created inside parent windows subject to rules of behavior imposed by the parent. For a forgetful parent, FoxPro 2.0 has a new WCHILD( ) function, which returns the number of child windows or their names. Similarly, the new WPARENT( ) function returns the name of a child window's parent window.

Printer Drivers

A printer driver provides the needed interface between your software and printer. In FoxPro 2.0 printer drivers are user-defined. They are simply programs or API routines, consisting of a set of specially named procedures which return values to FoxPro. Usually these values are your printer's control codes.

To create a printer driver, you write a program, say, Mydriver.prg, that contains procedures with names such as PDOBJST, PDOBJECT, PDOBJEND, and PDADVPRT. In the PDOBJST procedure you define the printer code sequence that you want FoxPro to use before printing each object (for example, text, fields, and boxes) in the Report Writer or by using the ?/?? commands. Similarly, in the PDADVPRT procedure you define how you want FoxPro to advance the printer head after printing an object.

You define your current printer driver simply by issuing the SET PDSETUP command, or by assigning the driver program's name to the _PDRIVER system memvar, for example,

```
_PDRIVER = Mydriver
```

You can also assign a default printer driver at startup by including a _PDSETUP statement in the Config.fp file. Chapter 11 discusses printer drivers in more detail.

Other Enhancements

In FoxPro 1.x, as in all other Dbase products, obsolete records in a memo file are never purged and continue to occupy valuable space even if you issue the PACK command. Heretofore the only way to clean the file was to issue a

COPY TO command. FoxPro 2.0's PACK command automatically removes obsolete data in both the database and memo files. It also includes two keywords: MEMO and DBF. Thus PACK MEMO removes outdated data only in the memo file, whereas PACK DBF packs only the database file. The new SYS(2012) function returns the memo field blocksize of a database.

The SET TALK command allows you to send talk (program line echo) to either a system window (using the SET TALK WINDOW command) or a user-defined window (using the SET TALK WINDOW <windowname> command). You can also direct talk from a window to the screen with the SET TALK NOWINDOW command.

FoxPro 2.0 now has context-sensitive help activated by the Alt-F1 key combination. The Help file database has a third field called CLASS which contains a category code for the help topic. A category code of wn means "What's New," whereas a command or function with a code of mu is a multiuser command or function.

The new SET HELPFILTER command displays a subset of help topics in the Help window. For instance,

```
SET HELPFILTER TO 'mu' $ class
```

lets you see only multiuser commands and functions.

You can now include a user-defined function in an index expression. With this facility you can easily show the progress of an indexing operation with the aid of a thermometer bar, or similar visual aid.

There are two new text buttons in the help dialog: LOOKUP and SEE ALSO. If you select a word in a help message and activate the LOOKUP button, FoxPro displays the appropriate help topic for the highlighted word. The SEE ALSO facility allows you to follow all the help topics connected to a command, function, or topic of interest.

Chapter Summary

FoxPro 2.0 introduces many significant enhancements to the Dbase language. It follows an open architecture policy, allowing developers to tap into FoxPro internals through the external API facility, and it uses the familiar .dbf format to keep most of its data. FoxPro 2.0 applications can be compiled as standalone .exes. Rushmore Technology is a data access technique that allows FoxPro to perform rapid data retrieval on indexed databases. FoxPro now supports multiple tags in a compound index file. Its compact index format generates small index files and helps speed up data searches.

The SQL SELECT command and RQBE facility allow complex data queries to be formulated by users with little or no experience in the FoxPro language. The new template language facility allows users to generate program code without learning an entirely different language.

FoxPro 2.0 has extensive enhancements in user interface areas, including screens, menus, and reports. It comes in both standard and Extended Versions. The Extended Version can be used to process very large databases or when the application requires no practical limits on the number of windows, memory variables, and array elements.

Chapter 2

Database Design

A good database design is quite possibly the most critical element in an application system, providing it flexibility and simplifying its maintenance. It is the groundwork you lay for your entire development effort. Even the best programming will not overcome a deficient design.

What factors should you consider when you start defining your database? This chapter answers this question with a set of steps you should follow to ensure a good design. It gives you some idea as to where to start and what questions to ask. We start out with the basics, then discuss more sophisticated design issues such as integrity rules and normalization of your database files, and finally look at how you implement these rules in a FoxPro application. Then we walk through a sample application to demonstrate how to implement each of the steps.

The Eight Steps to Database Design

The eight steps to a database design are shown in Figure 2-1.

Step 1: Complete a Thorough Requirements Analysis

First and foremost in any design effort is to complete a thorough requirements analysis. This means talking with your clients, managers as well as end users, to gain an understanding of the work process. The more you learn about what they do, the better equipped you are to start automating the process. Even if

8. Specify the Domain for Each Field
7. Build Your Data Network
6. Add Nonkey Fields to Your Database Files
5. Identify Foreign Keys
4. Define Primary Keys
3. Identify Relationships Among the Entities
2. Identify Entities
1. Complete a Thorough Requirements Analysis

Figure 2-1. The Eight Steps to Database Design.

certain aspects of the process will not be automated, it helps to define the procedures from beginning to end.

Clients do not necessarily have a complete idea of what the new application should look like. They usually do not know what is reasonable to expect from an automated system. Therefore, they do not know precisely what information you need to do the job. Start by gaining an understanding of the entire process from a high-level viewpoint. Ask enough questions to be sure you are not missing any of the big pieces. Then you can determine what details you need to design the system. In addition to talking to everyone involved in the process, read as many procedures manuals or other documentation as you can get your hands on. This can give you vital details that your client may have forgotten. In the end, your goal is to understand your client's work process as well as he or she does.

Step 2: Identify Entities

Once you understand the work process, you must define the entities with which you will be dealing. For example, an order processing system may have customers, orders, parts, and suppliers. Each entity represents a distinct object in the process. These entities may eventually be represented as tables in your database. Later you may add more tables or separate the entities into more than one table, but for now just make sure that everything is represented.

Step 3: Identify Relationships Among the Entities

Now that you know what entities you are working with, you must define the relationships that exist. For example, in an order processing system, each customer may have more than one order, but any given order belongs to just one customer. This is termed a one-to-many relationship. Each order may contain many items, and any given item will appear on numerous orders. This is called a many-to-many relationship. Finally, you may have a one-to-one relationship. For example, suppose that every item is produced by exactly one supplier, and every supplier provides exactly one item.

Identify all the relationships that exist among your entities, and the type of relationship (one-to-one, one-to-many, or many-to-many) in each case.

Step 4: Define Primary Keys

In each of your tables (entities) you need some identifier that distinguishes each record. Since one of the basic rules of good design is to not allow duplicate records, you must have a means of ensuring that each record is unique. The value that you use to distinguish your records is called the primary key. Later, we will discuss the requirement that no primary key be null (blank). For now, just identify the value you will use to differentiate among your records and to enforce the requirement that duplicates be rejected.

In some cases, the entity will already have a value that you can use as a primary key. For example, an Employee table could easily use employee social security number as the primary key. In other cases, your system may have to assign a value to be used as the key. For example, a Customer table may require that you assign a unique customer id to each record. It is important that you know how the client currently differentiates among occurrences of each entity. As part of Step 1, you should know whether unique customer ids are assigned as part of the current work process. Wherever possible, use "real" values, that is, values that are already in use and may have some meaning to your client. This means that you should use, for example, employee social security number rather than a system-assigned id.

If you have several choices for a unique key value, select the one that is most pertinent to the application. The primary key may be made up of more than one field value; this is called a composite key. It is perfectly acceptable to define such a primary key, but be sure that the composite value is irreducible. In other words, each field value making up the composite key must be required to ensure uniqueness. If not, drop that field from the primary key.

Finally, stay away from long character strings when defining the key. This is primarily to avoid confusion and errors when variable case and spacing is introduced to the character value. For example, Smith, J. and SMITH, J appear to be two different values. Some of the alternatives to using a character string are: find an abbreviation that retains the unique quality, use a numeric value associated with the record, or assign a unique number within your application. For example, when defining the unique key for a table of company departments, stay away from keys that look like this:

Accounting
Sales
Human Resources
Data Processing

Instead, either assign values (for example, 01, 02, 03, and 04) to the departments, or use easy-to-remember abbreviations such as:

ACCT
SALES
HR
DP

It is generally preferable to use codes in place of character strings where feasible.

Step 5: Identify Foreign Keys

C. J. Date (Date, 1987) defines a foreign key as an attribute (field), or attribute combination, in one table (T2) whose values are required to match those of the primary key of some table (T1). Tables T1 and T2 are not necessarily unique.

Consider our order processing example. The Order table will have a primary key of order number, perhaps generated by our application. In addition, each order must be traceable to the customer who placed it. We will include a field for customer id in each order. This customer id must match one of the (primary key) customer id values in the Customer table. This means that customer id is a foreign key in the Order table.

Essentially, the foreign key is used to associate a record with a value in another table. As another example, an Employee table may contain a department id field to indicate the department to which each employee is assigned.

Employee	**Department**
Emp_id	Dept_id
Dept_id	Dept_name

The Dept_id field in the Employee table links the employees with their departments, where the department information is stored in another table.

As discussed later in this chapter under the relational integrity rules, a foreign key must be either:

1. Equal to the value of a primary key in another table, or
2. Entirely null.

It is not usually desirable to allow a null foreign key. The problem with a null foreign key is obvious—it is impossible to link the record to a corresponding value in another table. This can be controlled within your application by requiring that the foreign key be provided (and validated) before permitting the record to be added. You may also have to ensure that the foreign key value is not deleted during a database update.

Step 6: Add Nonkey Fields to Your Database Files

Now that you have defined your entities and the primary and foreign keys for each, you must determine the remaining fields for each table. This is a critical step, resulting in the specification of each of your tables.

This is the time to decide on the field names for each table. You should adhere to some naming convention to facilitate your documentation and maintenance activities in the future. One good convention is to prefix each nonkey field name with the first two or three letters from the table name. Primary and foreign key field names should not have a prefix since they will appear in multiple tables. Of course your field names should be descriptive of the contents of the field. For example, a table named Order might consist of three fields: Order Id, Customer ID, and Order Date. Using our naming conventions, your field names might be:

OrdId (Primary key)
CusId (Foreign key)
Ord_OrdDt

The next consideration, and possibly the most important procedure in defining your database, is to normalize your tables. Normalization eliminates redundancy, keeps related data together, and ensures that you do not lose information when related information is deleted from the database. These points are explained in greater detail later in this chapter.

Step 7: Build Your Data Network

In this step, you simply map out what you have already defined. At this point, you know what tables you will be working with, as well as the primary and foreign keys for each table. Draw a simple diagram, displaying each table as a box and writing the primary and foreign key values in each box. Then draw lines to connect your primary keys and foreign keys. Figure 2-2 shows a sample data network for an order processing system.

This step does not add new information, but clarifies what you have already defined. Primarily, it serves to identify unnecessary tables in your database. If you see a table with no links to any other table, it is highly likely that you can eliminate the table from the database. Now is your chance to go back and redefine your tables so that you are satisfied with the "map" of your database.

Step 8: Specify the Domain for Each Field

During this step, you determine the most appropriate data type for each field. In other words, you determine the type of values the field will contain: numeric, character, date, and so on. Then you determine the acceptable range of values for each field. This is where you decide the length of a character field and the minimum and maximum values for a numeric field. Actually, you start determining much of your field validation criteria at this point. However, the validation procedures are not part of the FoxPro database design; you will incorporate your edit and validation routines into your application. When you have identified the domains, you are ready to create your tables in FoxPro.

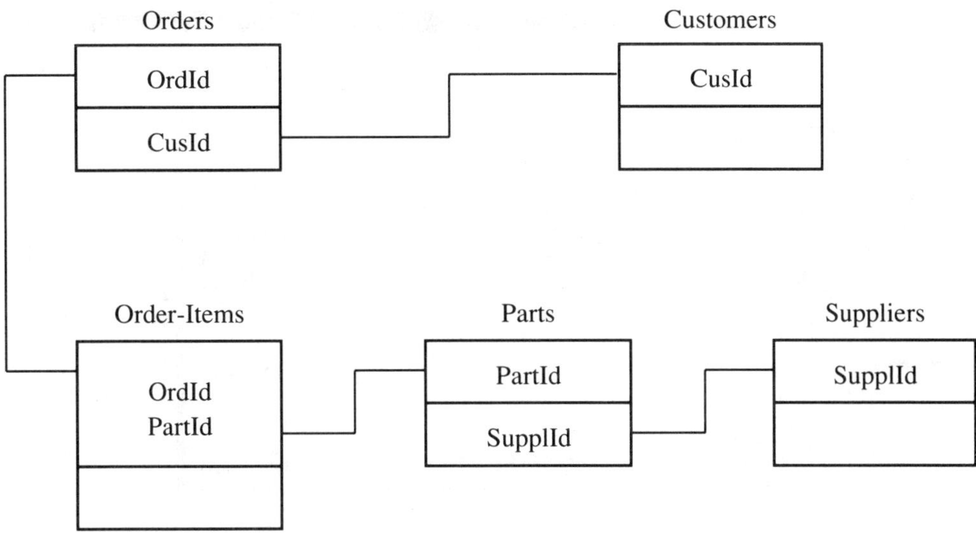

Figure 2-2. A sample data network diagram. Primary keys are shown in the top of each box and foreign keys are shown on the bottom.

Creating Your FoxPro Database

Once you have completed each of the eight steps, you know exactly what your database files (tables) should consist of. You are now ready to create your database in FoxPro.

Using the CREATE command, you create a database file for each table in your database. You have already identified the fields to be contained in each table, the names of the fields, and the field domains (numeric, character, and so on). Figure 2-3 shows a sample screen used to CREATE each file.

Of course, when you create your files, you have no means of indicating primary and foreign keys. In FoxPro, this must be controlled by your application when you start writing code. Once your files are built, you will usually want to create an index (or tag) with the primary key defined as the index expression. Of course, you may decide to build additional indexes to be used for reporting or other purposes as well. The creation of the index does not enforce the requirement that the primary key be unique and nonnull; you must enforce this through program code. The index does help you determine whether or not a record with the desired key already exists.

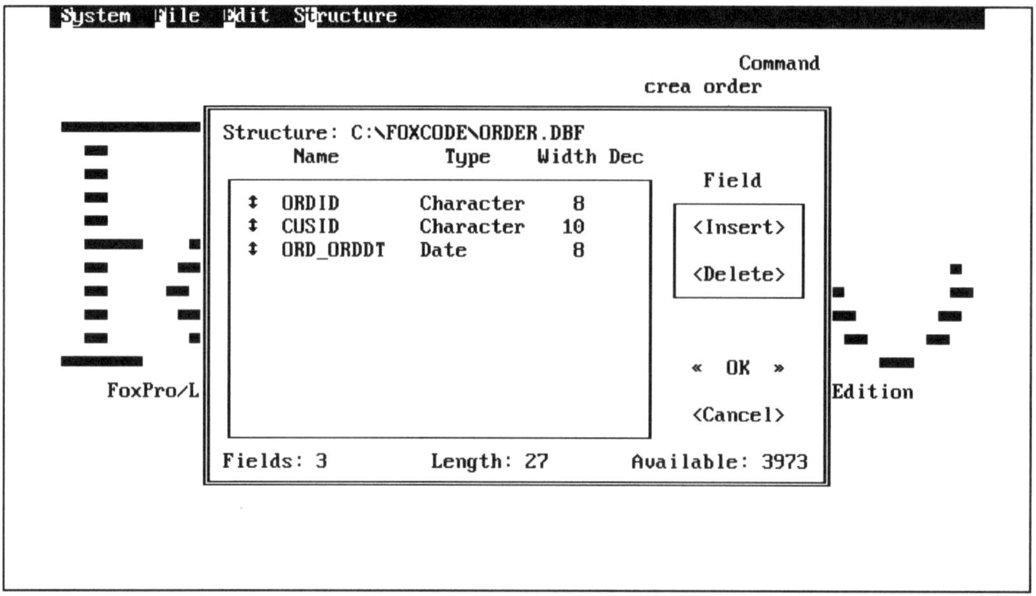

Figure 2-3. Sample FoxPro CREATE screen, used to define each database file.

How do you identify your foreign keys? Actually, you don't. There is no built-in facility for indicating which fields participate in a foreign key, or the link between foreign keys and their associated primary keys in another table. You have to handle the primary/foreign key relationships yourself in the program code, for example, with the SET RELATION TO command.

The Relational Integrity Rules

C. J. Date defined two integrity rules of the relational model. These rules, defined in terms we have been using, are as follows:

1. *Entity integrity* — No field participating in the primary key of a table may be null.
2. *Referential integrity* — If a table includes a foreign key (FK) matching the primary key (PK) of some table T, every value of FK must be either:
   a) Equal to the value of PK in some record in table T, or
   b) Entirely null.

Remember that a primary key is defined as a field (or combination of fields) that uniquely identifies each record in a table. If the primary key is a composite key (made up of more than one field), each of the fields must be required to ensure uniqueness.

We already mentioned these rules in Steps 4 and 5, where we defined the primary and foreign keys for our tables. The importance of these rules extends beyond just ensuring that our primary and foreign keys meet the listed criteria, however. We must ensure that the rules are met at all times. This means that you, as the application developer, must make sure that your system has addressed the following issues.

Null Foreign Keys

As previously mentioned, although the referential integrity rule allows foreign keys to be null, we do not recommend it. You must decide if you will allow null foreign keys in your application. In making this decision, consider the event that it represents. In other words, does it make sense within the context of your application that a foreign key might, even temporarily, contain a null value? The answer to this questions will in part determine the approach you take in designing your application.

Adhering to the Referential Integrity Rule

In ensuring that the referential integrity rule is always met, you should consider three operations: Inserts, Updates, and Deletes.

Inserts If a user attempts to insert a record with an invalid foreign key (that is, a value is entered for the foreign key that does not match any of the corresponding primary key values in the associated table), you can apply one of the following three rules:

1. Disallow the addition of the record and require the user to enter the primary key information into the corresponding table [DEPENDENT rule].
2. Automatically branch the user to another module where he or she can add the record with the required primary key [AUTOMATIC rule].
3. Accept the new record with a null foreign key value [NULLIFY rule]. (Applicable only if you accept null foreign keys.)

Deletes If a user attempts to delete a record containing a primary key that at least one table uses as a foreign key, the integrity rules can be enforced in three ways:

1. Automatically delete all records in all tables with the corresponding foreign key [CASCADE rule].
2. Allow the deletion only if there are no records with a foreign key matching the primary key about to be deleted [RESTRICT rule].
3. Nullify the foreign key values on all matching records [NULLIFY rule]. Of course, this option is valid only if you have decided to accept null foreign keys.

Updates You must also define how you will handle an attempt to modify a primary key that has related foreign keys. These three options are essentially the same as for delete operations.

1. Automatically update the matching foreign key values to the new value of the primary key [CASCADE rule].
2. Allow the update only if there are no records with matching foreign keys [RESTRICT rule].
3. Nullify the foreign key values on all matching records [NULLIFY rule]. Again, this option is valid only if you have decided to accept null foreign keys.

Normalization

Database normalization is a technique that simplifies the database structure and eliminates redundant data. As previously stated in Step 6 of database design, databases are normalized for the following reasons:

- To keep related data together.
- To eliminate redundancy.
- To ensure that information is not lost when related data is deleted from the database.

A normalized database is said to be in one of several normal forms. First, second, and third normal forms are the most common forms and the ones we will discuss. Refer to Date [Date, 1987] for information on fourth and fifth normal forms.

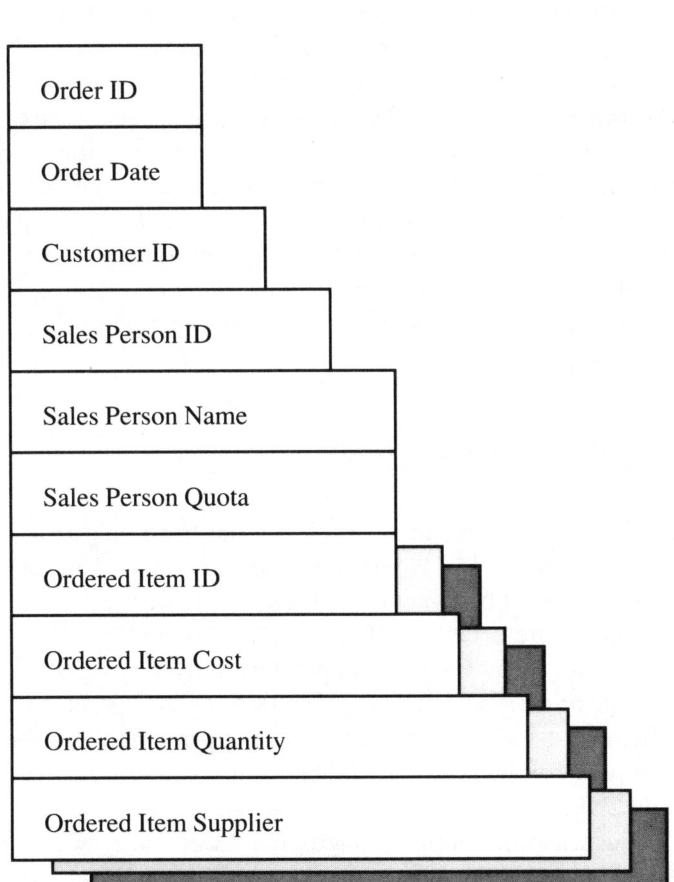

Figure 2-4(a). Unnormalized database.

First Normal Form (1NF)

A database is said to be in first normal form when all repeating groups have been put in separate tables. Figure 2-4(a) shows an example of a database that is not in 1NF. The Order table initially contains fields for Order ID, Order Date, Customer ID, Sales Person ID, Sales Person Name, and Sales Person Quota, and multiple occurrences of the Ordered Item ID, Ordered Item Cost, Ordered Item Quantity, and Ordered Item Supplier fields. Since an order may be made up of many ordered items, the item ids, costs, quantities, and suppliers are said to be repeating fields. The problem with this structure is that in order to store data about each ordered item, multiple Order records would be needed, which means the Order Date, Customer ID, Sales Person ID, Sales Person Name, and Sales Person Quota would be duplicated for each ordered item. This introduces a great deal of redundancy into the database.

To normalize this table, the repeating fields are removed to a separate table, with Order ID designated as the foreign key to link the ordered items to the order. Figure 2-4(b) shows the table after it has been normalized to 1NF; the Ordered Items have been moved out of the Order table and into their own Order-Item table. The primary keys are highlighted, and field dependencies are indicated with arrows. These tables are now said to be in first normal form. Note that we have eliminated the duplication of data by separating the table into two tables.

Second Normal Form (2NF)

A database can be cast into second normal form only if it is first in 1NF. In addition, every field in a table must be fully dependent on the primary key; otherwise, it must be removed to a separate table.

The Order-Item table in Figure 2-4(b) is not in 2NF because the Item Supplier and Item Cost are dependent only on the Item ID, not on the composite primary key of Order ID plus Item ID. Therefore, the Item Supplier and Item Cost should be pulled out to a separate table called Item-Data. The primary key for the Item-Data table is Item ID. Figure 2-4(c) shows the tables now in 2NF.

The justification for this change can be seen more clearly by looking at our table with sample data. The following example shows our Order-Item table before it is placed in 2NF:

Order-Item:

Order ID	**Item ID**	**Item Cost**	**Item Quantity**	**Item Supplier**
2378	A15	24.99	3	S234
2378	A48	12.50	8	S90
2379	A15	24.99	2	S234
2379	A23	41.25	4	S123
2380	A23	41.25	2	S123

As you can see, the Item Cost and Item Supplier information is duplicated. By separating this table into two, we eliminate the redundant data as follows:

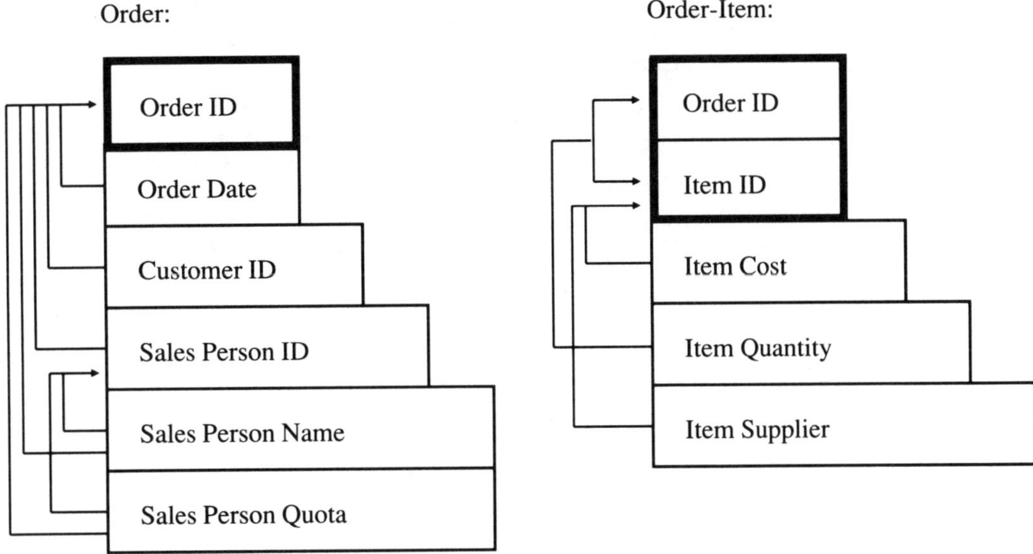

Figure 2-4(b). The same database in first normal form. Primary keys are highlighted, and field dependencies are shown with arrows.

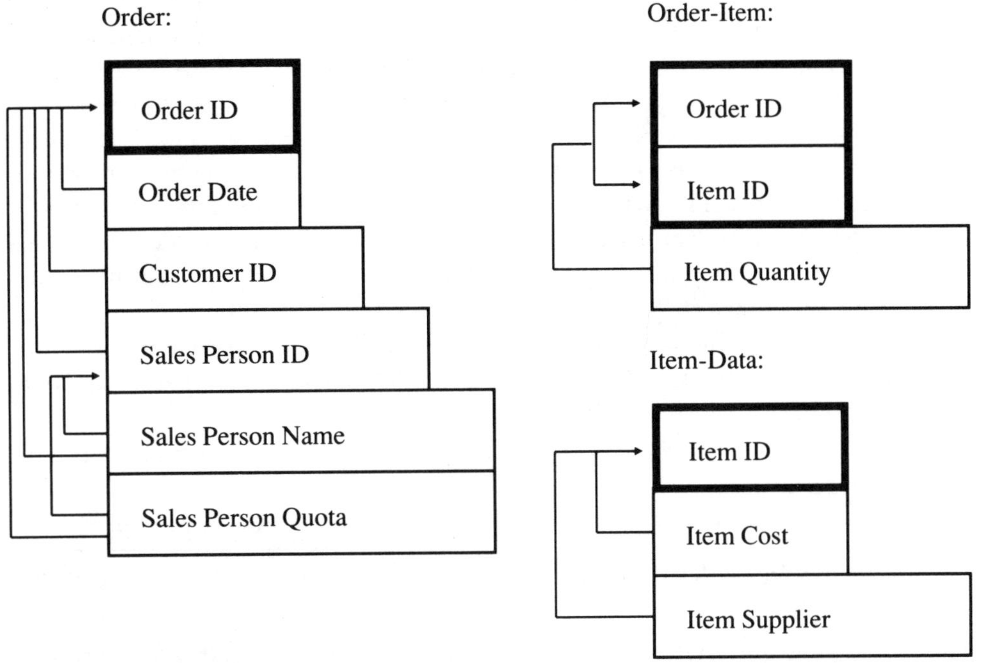

Figure 2-4(c). The same database in second normal form. Primary keys are highlighted, and field dependencies are shown with arrows.

Order-Item:

Order ID	Item ID	Item Quantity
2378	A15	3
2378	A48	8
2379	A15	2
2379	A23	4
2380	A23	2

Item Data:

Item ID	Item Cost	Item Supplier
A15	24.99	S234
A23	41.25	S123
A48	12.50	S90

Third Normal Form (3NF)

A table must be in 2NF before it can be cast into third normal form. In addition, every nonkey field in the table must be nontransitively dependent on the primary key. Fields that are transitively dependent on the primary key are removed to a separate table during this step. For example, in the Order table of Figure 2-4(c), the Sales Person Name and Sales Person Quota are dependent on Sales Person ID, which in turn is dependent on the primary key of Order ID. This is known as a transitive dependence. To put the table in 3NF, the Sales Person Name and Quota fields are moved to a separate table called Sales-Pers, as shown in Figure 2-4(d). The tables shown in this normalization example are now in 3NF.

Again, we demonstrate the advantage of 3NF with tables containing sample data. The following table shows the Order table before we separate the Sales Person data:

Order:

			Sales Person		
Order ID	**Order Date**	**Customer ID**	**ID**	**Name**	**Quota**
2378	02/12/90	C4990	S12	J. Jones	12000
2379	02/12/90	C3299	S13	M. Martin	14000
2380	02/14/90	C4163	S15	A. Smith	10000
2381	02/15/90	C2244	S12	J. Jones	12000

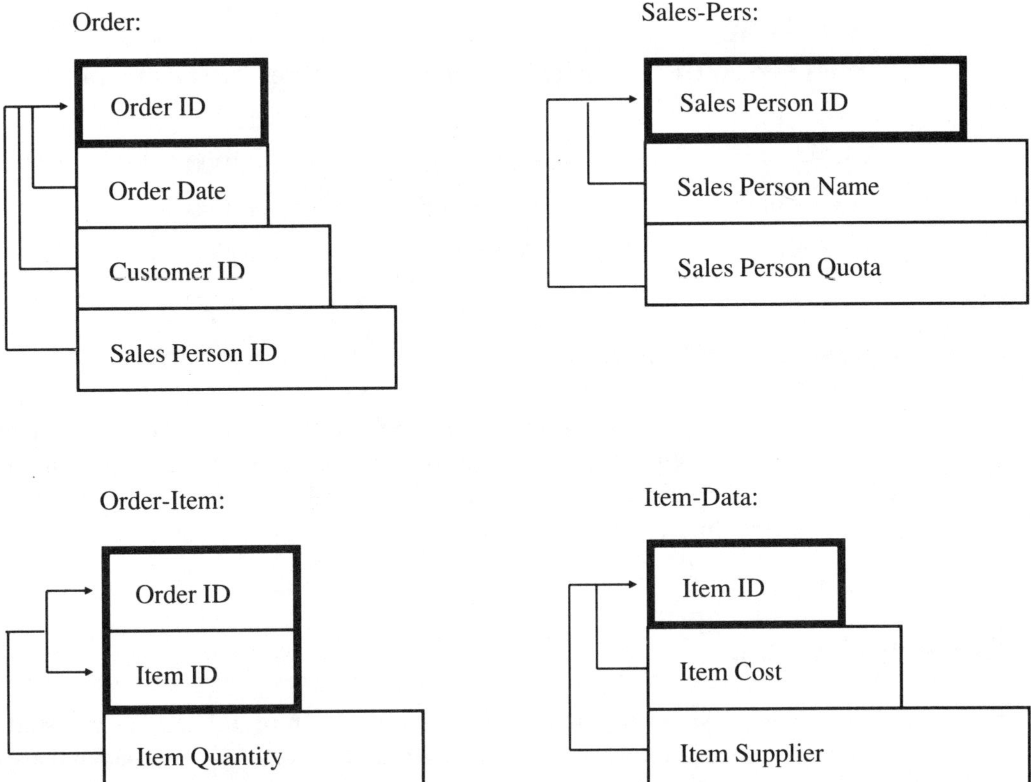

Figure 2-4(d). Third normal form. The results of normalization techniques applied to our order processing database. Primary keys are highlighted, and field dependencies are shown with arrows.

As this example demonstrates, the fields that are transitively dependent on Order ID (Sales Person Name and Sales Person Quota) contain redundant data. By separating these fields into a separate table, and thus placing the tables in 3NF, we eliminate the redundancy as follows:

Order:

Order ID	Order Date	Customer ID	Sales Person ID
2378	02/12/90	C4990	S12
2379	02/12/90	C3299	S13
2380	02/14/90	C4163	S15
2381	02/15/90	C2244	S12

Sales-Pers:

Sales Person ID	Sales Person Name	Sales Person Quota
S12	J. Jones	12000
S13	M. Martin	14000
S14	S. Harrison	11000
S15	A. Smith	10000

Normalization Results

After normalization, your database may look very different. You may have more tables, different tables, and/or different fields in each table. Only after you normalize the database do you have an accurate picture of the tables that will make up your system.

A Complete Example

In this section, we go through a step-by-step design of a database. We start with the results of a requirements analysis and show examples of the database tables as they evolve. In this way you can see how the database design starts, what decisions are made at each step, and what changes take place as we satisfy each of the rules. The example we are going to use is a common business application—the tracking of incoming correspondence as it passes through the various departments of a company, up through the time that a response/resolution is completed.

Step 1: Complete a Thorough Requirements Analysis

Assume that you have attended a series of meetings at your client's site. In addition, you have reviewed some existing procedures manuals, interviewed analysts, and examined typical types of documents currently received and processed. At the completion of this step, you have the following information:

- All correspondence is received in the company mailroom and stamped with a date of receipt. It is then routed to the receptionist, who opens each item, briefly reviews it, and determines where to route it next. The receptionist records the analyst to whom it is routed and the date it is passed to the analyst.

- Each analyst is a member of exactly one department.
- The analyst formulates a response and sends it out. Occasionally the document is routed to the wrong department and must be rerouted to an analyst in another department. When this happens, the receptionist's log book is corrected to show the new analyst and the date the document was passed to that analyst.
- Finally, the original document and a copy of the response is returned to the receptionist, who files both copies and updates his or her log with a close-out date.

The system you are to develop must replace the manual logging procedures. The most important aspect of the system is the ability to determine the status of a particular document at any given time and how it was resolved if it has been closed. The system should also provide management reports showing items not responded to within certain time frames. Management determines the specific time frames within which each document type must be responded to. For example, a request for literature must be answered within one week, a product order must be filled within two weeks, and a complaint must be answered within three days. Department managers also would like to be able to review the completed work of their analysts and be aware of which analysts have overdue items. Certain departments have specific needs, for example, the Customer Service department needs to know which issues generate the most customer complaints. With this information we are now ready to draft a database structure.

Step 2: Identify Entities

From our understanding of the work process at this point, we initially define the following entities for our system:

Documents
Responses
Analysts
Customers
Departments

Step 3: Identify Relationships Among the Entities

Now we are ready to define the relationships among the five entities we defined in Step 2. The relationships that are clear to us at this point are:

- Documents to Responses—A one-to-one relationship exists. Each document has one response, and each response corresponds to exactly one document.
- Documents to Analysts—A many-to-one relationship exists. Many documents are assigned to any given analyst, but a given document is assigned to only one analyst.
- Documents to Customers—A many-to-one relationship exists. A customer may write many letters, but each letter is written by only one customer.
- Documents to Departments—No relationship exists.
- Responses to Analysts—A many-to-one relationship exists. An analyst writes many responses, but each response is written by just one analyst.
- Responses to Customers—A many-to-one relationship exists. Each response is sent to exactly one customer, but each customer may receive several responses (if several letters are sent in by the same customer at different times).
- Responses to Departments—No relationship exists.
- Analysts to Customers—No relationship exists.
- Analysts to Departments—A many-to-one relationship exists. Each analyst is assigned to exactly one department, but each department has many analysts.
- Customers to Departments—No relationship exists.

Step 4: Define Primary Keys

For each of the five entities, we define a primary key. Again, the purpose of the primary key is to differentiate among the many occurrences of each entity (that is, to ensure uniqueness among our records in the table). We define primary keys as follows:

Entity	Primary Key	Description
Documents	DocId	A system-generated document id.
Responses	DocId	The document id of the original correspondence (same as above).

Entity	Primary Key	Description
Analysts	EmpId	Employee id.
Customers	CusId	First five digits of zip code plus last four digits of phone number plus one-digit sequence number used in case of duplicates.
Departments	DeptNum	A code assigned to each department.

Step 5: Identify Foreign Keys

The foreign keys indicate the relationships among the tables. We already indicated what types of relationships exist among the entities; now we must determine what field values we will use to associate a record with a corresponding primary key in another table.

Entity	Foreign Key	Description
Documents	EmpId	Associates the document with the responsible analyst.
	CusId	Links the document to the customer who sent it.
Responses	None.	We store the response data in the Document table, so no foreign key is required.
Analysts	DeptNum	Identifies the department to which the analyst belongs.
Customers	None.	There are no fields in the Customers table that depend on fields in other tables.
Departments	None.	There are no fields in the Departments table that depend on fields in other tables.

Step 6: Add Nonkey Fields to Your Database Files

First, we'll add the fields that seem to belong to each table. We will use a nonkey field naming convention of the first three letters of the table plus a descriptive field identifier that represents the data stored in the field. Key fields do not have the table name prefix since they appear in multiple tables. This convention helps us readily identify primary/foreign key relationships in our database. Figure 2-5(a) shows our tables before we have applied any normalization techniques.

When we normalize the database, we start by putting the database in 1NF. To do this, we examine each table and determine whether there are any repeating groups. Since we find no repeating groups in our initial database design, we determine that the database is already in 1NF.

Now we examine the database to determine what changes are required to satisfy the 2NF rules. For each table, every field must be fully dependent on the primary key. If we examine each table, we can see that our tables are already in 2NF, so no further changes are required at this point. By having already defined our entities, relationships, and key fields, we have started off with a database structure in 2NF. This demonstrates the value of going through each of the steps described so far before defining a database.

We still must ensure that the database is in 3NF. To satisfy the 3NF requirement, we eliminate any nontransitive dependencies. We find that there is one nontransitive dependency in our tables: the Doc_MaxDay field is dependent on CorrType, which in turn is dependent on DocId. We therefore remove the MaxDay field to a new table we call DayMax, as shown in Figure 2-5(b). The advantage to this change should be clear: we have eliminated a redundancy by storing the maximum days to respond in just one place, rather than for each document. Also, if management decides to change the requirements, the update is simply made to one record in one table. Finally, a subtle advantage is that we do not accidentally lose the maximum response time information for a particular document type in the event that all document records of that type are deleted.

Our database is now normalized to third normal form. The tables that make up our new database are shown in Figure 2-5(b).

Step 7: Build Your Data Network

Figure 2-6 displays our data network as we have currently defined it. We look at each table in our diagram and determine whether there is at least one relationship to another table by looking at the lines we have drawn to associate primary keys with foreign keys. In this case, every table is associated with at least one other table, so we decide that we do not have any frivolous tables and we leave the design as is.

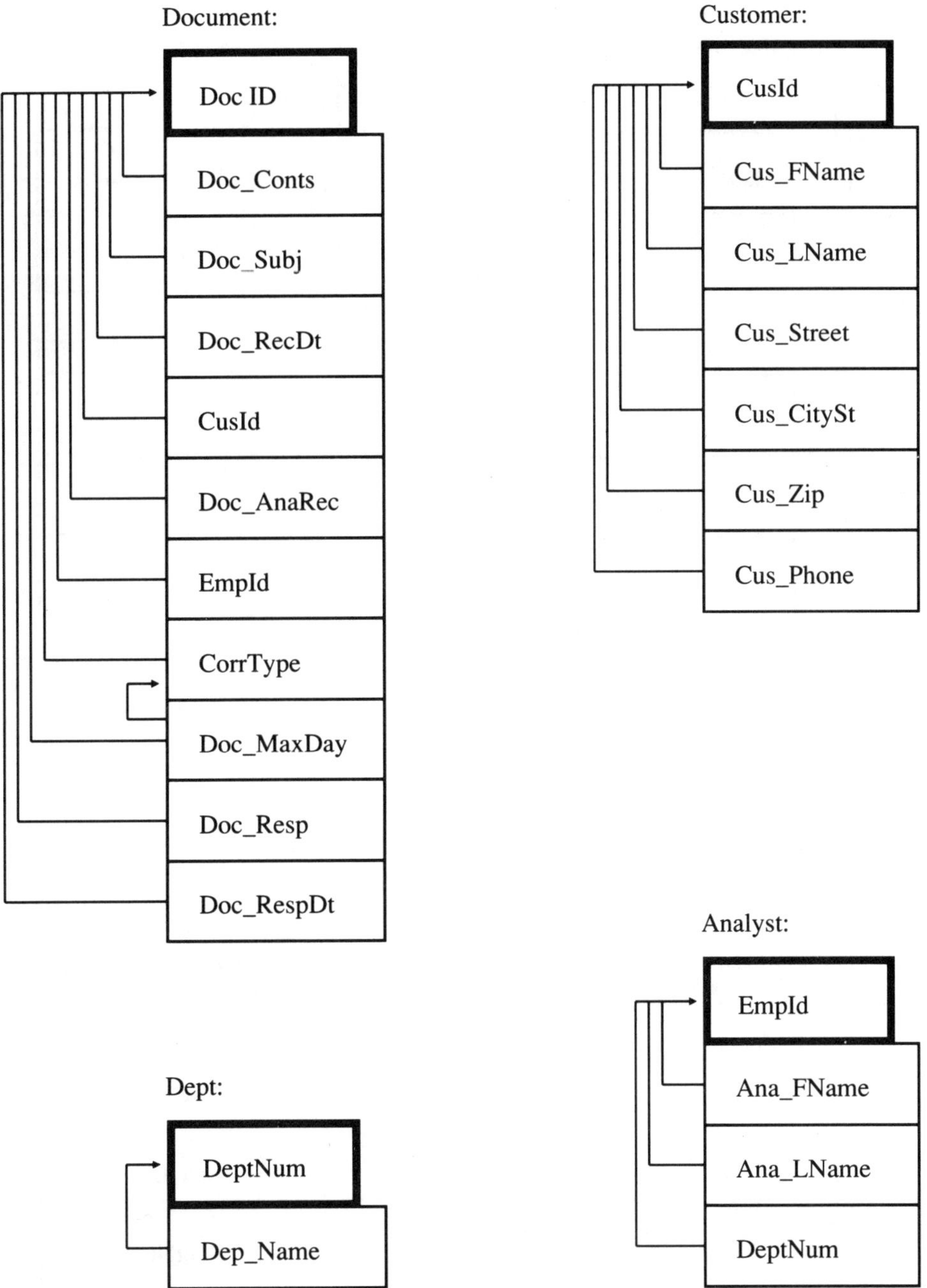

Figure 2-5(a). The correspondence tracking database before normalization techniques are applied. Primary keys are highlighted, and field dependencies are shown with arrows.

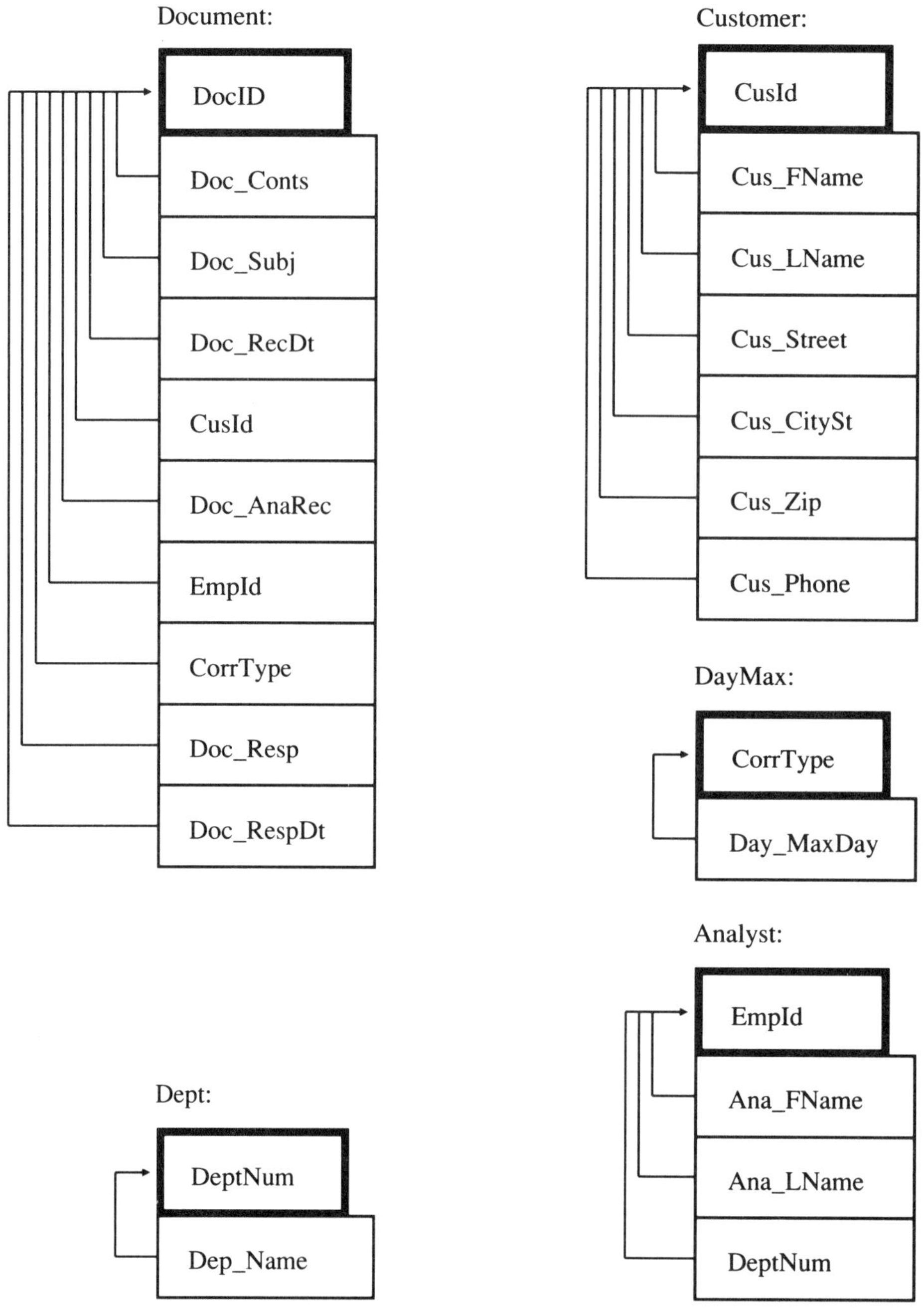

Figure 2-5(b). The results of normalization techniques applied to our correspondence tracking database. Primary keys are highlighted, and field dependencies are shown with arrows.

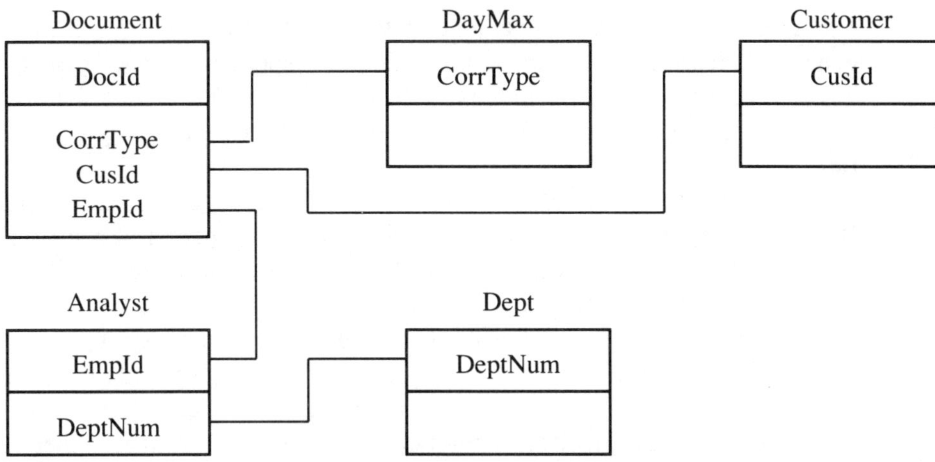

Figure 2-6. The data network diagram for the correspondence tracking database.

Looking at the data network diagram can also help point out flaws in the design; for example, you may notice that a critical element in the system is not addressed. You can always decide to back up to an earlier step, make the appropriate changes, and then pick up from there.

Step 8: Specify the Domain for Each Field

Now that we have defined all our tables and fields, we can determine the domain for each field. This means deciding the type of data to be stored in each field and the valid ranges.

FoxPro offers the following field types:

Character
Numeric
Floating
Logical
Date
Memo

As we look at each field, we should think in terms of these six data types and decide which is most appropriate. Then, for those fields defined as character, numeric, or floating, we will consider the valid range of values in order to determine the field size to be assigned.

For example, we may decide that the DocId field will be a system-generated character string made up of the correspondence type code (CorrType), received month and year (from Doc_RecDt), and an assigned sequence number. We therefore designate the field to be a 10-digit character field.

We assign a field type of memo to the contents (Doc_Conts) and response (Doc_Resp) fields since these fields will hold the contents of the original correspondence and the response. Not knowing how large these could be, a memo field is the best choice.

The CusId field is defined as the first five digits of zip code, the last four digits of phone number, and a one-digit identifier (used if several records have identical zip code/phone number combinations). For flexibility, we would like to be able to assign either a number or a letter to the identifier; therefore, we define the CusId field to be a character field of size 10.

Figure 2-7 shows our entire database with field types and sizes identified. It should be clear that the actual creation of our database in FoxPro is now very easy; we simply CREATE a .dbf file corresponding to each of our tables.

Chapter Summary

Database design is a critical step in the application development process. A good design ensures data integrity, eliminates redundancy, and facilitates system maintenance. Good programming practices cannot compensate for a poor database design.

In this chapter, we presented eight steps to designing a database. These steps are:

1. Complete a thorough requirements analysis.
2. Identify entities.
3. Identify relationships among the entities.
4. Define primary keys.
5. Identify foreign keys.
6. Add nonkey fields to your database files.
7. Build your data network.
8. Specify the domain for each field.

We also discussed the relational database integrity rules and techniques for normalizing a database, and how these rules and techniques apply in creating your FoxPro database. The Entity integrity and Referential integrity rules help

Document:

DocId	Character	10
Doc_Conts	Memo	
Doc_Subj	Character	12
Doc_RecDt	Date	
CusId	Character	10
Doc_AnaRec	Date	
EmpId	Numeric	9
CorrType	Character	2
Doc_Resp	Memo	
Doc_RespDt	Date	

DayMax:

CorrType	Character	2
Day_MaxDay	Numeric	3

Analyst:

EmpId	Numeric	9
Ana_FName	Character	10
Ana_LName	Character	15
DeptNum	Character	2

Customer:

CusId	Character	10
Cus_FName	Character	10
Cus_LName	Character	15
Cus_Street	Character	40
Cus_CitySt	Character	15
Cus_Zip	Character	10
Cus_Phone	Character	12

Dept:

DeptNum	Character	2
Dep_Name	Character	15

Figure 2-7. The correspondence tracking database field domains, defined specifically for our FoxPro application.

maintain accurate and consistent data. Normalization eliminates redundant data, keeps related data together, and ensures that data is not lost when related records are deleted from the database.

Finally, we looked at a sample application, a correspondence tracking system, and walked through each of the eight steps in order to design a logical database structure for the application.

Chapter 3

Data Dictionary

A typical business application consists of a large number of data elements in multiple data files, along with a substantial set of index files and reports. Many database development projects, particularly those involving a large team of programmers, analysts, and writers, can quickly run into trouble if no one bothers to ensure that data representation, even just a field naming convention, is consistent across all programs or system modules. Database normalization helps guarantee against data redundancy so that a nonkey field does not appear in more than one data file. However, without a systematic way of defining and maintaining data, the development team may well discover later on that a required field is unaccounted for in any of the data files, or that two fields in a file that earlier seemed different actually are the same.

One of the most glaring deficiencies of the Dbase product family, including FoxPro, is its inability to fully describe a data element, including the element's range of allowed values, picture clause, source, validation criteria, or even whether or not it is a required field. In Dbase's way of defining a database structure, all we have to work with is a 10-character field name that, in most cases, is hardly sufficient to describe the field, its data type, and its length (and number of decimal places for a numeric field).

Unfortunately, the term "data dictionary" is unknown to a generation of programmers and application developers whose first and only exposure to database management systems is the Dbase product family. Consequently, this generation's approach to data definition is backward—a collection of .dbf files is created before a complete and comprehensive set of all fields that the entire system requires is at hand. It is no wonder then that one of the most popular commands in the Dbase language, especially for beginners, is

MODIFY STRUCTURE. This is not a particularly attractive prospect given that changing data file definitions midway through the application development process is a wasteful exercise.

What Is a Data Dictionary?

A data dictionary may be defined as an organized system for uniformly defining and managing data elements, or fields. The dictionary acts as a central repository of information about each data element in a group of related systems. Its purpose is to facilitate access to, and control of, databases. The dictionary manages what is often referred to as metadata, that is, data about data. This metadata includes descriptive properties such as length, value range, validation criteria, or types of admissible data.

A data dictionary serves as a focal point for the development of standard data definitions and coding schemes. It can also serve as the primary tool for monitoring adherence to the organization's standards. Clearly, a fully developed data dictionary can serve as an organization's catalog of its data resources, fully documenting its data collection, processing, and dissemination activities. It is at once a tool for data resource management, data standardization, and system documentation.

In most cases, a data dictionary is itself an automated database system, although it does not have to be. It is intended to fully document all the fields and files that an application system requires. In some cases, the data dictionary is used to define all the data requirements of the entire organization, including programs and entire application systems.

A data dictionary may be manual or automated, standalone or dependent, active or passive. A standalone dictionary is self-contained, independent of the particular DBMS or other software with which it can interface. A dependent dictionary is usually a part of a standard DBMS and requires the facilities of that DBMS to perform its functions.

Depending on the degree of its integration with the database management system, a data dictionary may be considered either active or passive. An active dictionary becomes the sole source of data descriptions for all applications, including DBMS and language compilers. It is so tightly coupled with the DBMS it serves that the latter uses definitions from the dictionary at run time. To serve that function, an active dictionary clearly must contain current and accurate information that is shared by all software components of the system. One example of an active dictionary that is available for mainframes is the Integrated Data Dictionary by Cullinet Software. It serves a family of products that includes IDMS/R, IDBMS-DB, IDBMS-DC, Culprit, and Goldengate. In the Dbase world, the one product that implements what can be considered an active data dictionary (though far less active than Cullinet's) is Recital by Recital Corporation. Recital operates on Vax/VMS, UNIX, and Xenix machines.

A passive dictionary is used only to enter or retrieve entity descriptions. It is used and maintained independently of the DBMS, although the information it contains, for example, validation criteria for fields, may be the same information that the DBMS uses. An example of a passive dictionary used in mainframes is Datamanager by Manager Software Products. Datamanager does not depend on any specific DBMS, although it can be used to generate database definitions and source language statements. It has an interface with popular DBMS products such as Adabas, IDBMS, IMS, System 2000, and Total.

Although an active dictionary offers superior advantages in terms of ensuring the timeliness and accuracy of data, its use can entail significant processing overhead as the DBMS retrieves and updates information from this complex database. On the other hand, a truly passive dictionary has no processing overhead, but it has the serious disadvantage of possibly containing outdated information since it is maintained independent of the DBMS.

Data Dictionary Advantages

It is clear that an enterprise-wide data dictionary system permits centralized access and control of an organization's data. It provides the facility for fully documenting all data elements required by the organization and provides the mechanism for enforcing validation rules on those data elements. The desired result is that incorrect information never find its way to the organization's databases in the first place.

A data dictionary eliminates unnecessary data redundancy. A data element is defined once, even though it may appear on multiple databases. This ensures consistent definition of the field across all databases and across all applications. Any change in the field's properties, for example its validation rules, is instituted once—in the data dictionary—and the change is reflected on all the databases that use the field. A dictionary helps avoid the situation where two or more fields that look different are actually the same, subject to the same validation rules. Of course, the dictionary helps ensure that the text of the help prompts and/or error messages for a given field is consistent throughout all applications.

Programming teams, particularly those who work at remote sites, will find even a passive dictionary indispensable as the authoritative source of information for data element attributes (formats, codes, allowed values, and so on) that need to be enforced in application code. The dictionary is also a useful tool for communicating data element attributes among data users, programmers, and analysts.

Setting Up a Primitive FoxPro Dictionary

In the Dbase product family, we normally define a data file by using the CREATE command. This allows us to specify the name of the fields, their types (character, date, and so on), and field width, including the number of decimal places in the case of numeric fields. In reality, FoxPro (and other Dbase product family members) has a poorly documented facility that allows us to define much more information about the fields, including field description, picture clauses, or validation criteria. The additional information can be maintained as part of the system documentation, not as an integral part of an active dictionary system.

If we use a previously defined .dbf and then issue the COPY STRUCTURE EXTENDED command, the result is a new .dbf file with four fields and as many records as there were fields in the original file. For example, assume that we have a file called People.dbf, which has the following structure:

```
Structure for database : PEOPLE.DBF
Number of data records : 1
Date of last update    : 2/10/90
Field  Field Name  Type         Width     Dec    Index
    1  NAME        Character       25
    2  DOB         Date             8
    3  SALARY      Numeric         10       2
    4  CITYSTATE   Character       15
    5  NOTES       Memo            10
** Total **                        69
```

The following commands:

```
USE people
COPY STRUCTURE EXTENDED TO peoplex
```

produce the file called Peoplex.dbf with the four fields, Field_name, Field_type, Field_len, and Field_dec, and five records.

```
Structure for database : PEOPLEX.DBF
Number of data records : 5
Date of last update    : 2/10/90
Field  Field Name  Type        Width    Dec
    1  FIELD_NAME  Character      10
    2  FIELD_TYPE  Character       1
    3  FIELD_LEN   Numeric         3
    4  FIELD_DEC   Numeric         3
** Total **                       18
```

The first record has a Field_name value of Name, and the last record has a Field_name value of Notes. The philosophy behind an extended structure is to allow data files to be built from it using the FROM clause of the CREATE command. Thus, the command

```
CREATE people2 FROM peoplex
```

simply creates the file called People2.dbf with the same structure as People.dbf. However, what is not well documented is the fact that, we are free to add more records to an extended structure, in effect including more descriptive information about data fields. Adding records to an extended structure does not hinder CREATE FROM's ability to produce a perfectly usable .dbf file provided that we do not reorder the first four fields in the extended structure.

Therefore, we can modify the structure of Peoplex.dbf to our heart's content, adding fields such as Field_desc to more fully describe the field, Field_pict to document the field's default picture clause, Field_vald to record the field's validation criteria, and so on. This modified extended structure is clearly useful for documenting fields in a .dbf file and with additional work may be used as a core for building a passive data dictionary for an entire FoxPro application. In the following modified structure for Peoplex.dbf, we have added fields 5, 6, and 7. This file contains much more information about each field, but it can still be used to produce the structure of People.dbf.

```
Structure for database : PEOPLEX2.DBF
Number of data records : 5
Date of last update    : 2/10/90
Field  Field Name  Type        Width    Dec
    1  FIELD_NAME  Character      10
    2  FIELD_TYPE  Character       1
    3  FIELD_LEN   Numeric         3
```

```
    4  FIELD_DEC   Numeric       3
    5  FIELD_DESC  Character    65
    6  FIELD_PICT  Character    10
    7  FIELD_LOW   Character    10
** Total **                    103
```

A Functional FoxPro Data Dictionary System

A comprehensive data dictionary system that can serve the needs of an entire organization can be easily designed and implemented as a FoxPro application. We can make this dictionary much more useful than a regular passive one by including the following features:

- Each data element in the dictionary will have descriptive text of variable length that is implemented as a memo field. Then, in any application where a user is faced with a data entry or edit screen involving a given data element, the memo field data associated with that element can be made to pop up in a help window whenever the user presses the F1 key. This technique eliminates the need to create individual help screens for each field in each and every application. Moreover, any corporate policy changes that alter the definition or intent of the data element require changing only one source—the memo field data in the dictionary. Note that for the dictionary to be available in this way, the organization must adopt a standard that requires the dictionary .dbf to remain open in some agreed-on work area for all applications that require the services of the dictionary.
- The data dictionary is solely responsible for building .dbf files required by any or all applications. In effect, developers are not permitted to use the CREATE or MODIFY STRUCTURE commands in any application other than the dictionary system.
- Adding information such as field range values and edit or validation criteria for fields in the dictionary can be the basis for making the dictionary active at a later time by enforcing such rules in the application code.

Here are some of the steps we have followed to design and implement a corporate data dictionary:

1. Assemble a core group of people—a data dictionary committee—charged with the responsibility of defining all data elements required by the organization. This group should consist of representatives from

user and data processing organizations who have intimate knowledge of the organization's work processes, including data sources and paper forms. This group can also be very helpful in providing a first draft of the help text (memo field data) associated with a data element.

2. Define the structure of the data element dictionary. What information about data elements should be part of the dictionary? What other .dbf files should be part of the dictionary?
3. Adopt a field naming convention to ensure that a data element appears once and only once in the dictionary, and that we can easily tell from their names which nonkey fields belong to which .dbf files. Also, adopt a rule as to which work area, for example, FoxPro work area 25, to reserve for the dictionary in any application that requires its services.

One example of a field naming convention is that all nonkey fields must begin with the first three letters of the .dbf file to which they belong and that the fourth character in their names must be an underscore. For instance, Per_Dob, Per_City, and Per_State are nonkey fields in the Person.dbf file. Naturally, for this naming convention to work, no two data files in the system can have the same first three letters.

Since key fields may appear in multiple .dbf files (especially as foreign keys), they are not subject to the same rule. They may have an underscore in their names, but to minimize confusion, the organization should not allow it to be in the fourth position. Sample key field names are ProjectNo and Employ_Id.

Data Dictionary Files

To implement a FoxPro data dictionary system, we will probably require the following starter set of .dbf files:

- Fld_Dct.dbf
- Fil_Fld.dbf
- Dbf_Idx.dbf

Fld_Dct.dbf

This is the data element (field) dictionary. It includes all the attributes for each data element. We will discuss this file in more detail in the next section as it relates to the Fil_Fld.dbf data file.

Fil_Fld.dbf

This is a data file that associates which key fields belong to which .dbf file. It is used to create a .dbf file from its component fields. The files to which nonkey fields belong are already obvious from their names, so they don't have to be included here. The structure for this file is simply:

```
Structure for database : FIL_FLD.DBF
Number of data records : 5
Date of last update    : 2/20/90
Field  Field Name  Type        Width    Dec
    1  FILE_NAME   Character       8
    2  FIELD_NAME  Character      10
** Total **                       19
```

To build the required .dbf file (which happens to be the same as File_Name), we gather all the File_Name records from this file to capture all its key fields, and then we combine them with the nonkey fields obtained from Fld_Dct.dbf in an EXTENDED STRUCTURE ready to be CREATEd.

Listing 3-1 shows a sample routine to create a specified .dbf file from a data dictionary. The program first determines all the key fields in the .dbf as defined in the Fil_Fld.dbf file, and then looks up their attributes (for example, field_type) from Fld_Dct.dbf. Next, the program adds each key field as a record to Extend.dbf, which is just a file with an extended structure. The program then finds all of the file's nonkey fields from Fld_Dct, and once again adds each one as a record to Extend.dbf. Finally, the program creates the desired file with the single command:

```
CREATE (dbf) FROM Extend
```

The added advantage of creating .dbf structures this way is the ease with which we can enforce the rule that fields must appear in the structure in alphabetical order with key fields ahead of nonkey ones. This rule becomes very important with .dbf files that have many fields and at the early stages of data dictionary development when files are still in the process of being normalized. Arranging a long list of field names alphabetically clearly helps us locate a data element of interest even though the sequence of the fields is immaterial to FoxPro's CREATE command.

Periodically we may want to use this same .dbf generation scheme to ensure that all .dbf files used by an application are consistent with the current

Listing 3-1. Procedure BuildDbf is a sample routine to create a .dbf file out of its key and nonkey fields defined in a data dictionary.

```
PROCEDURE BuildDbf
************************************************************
* Program ...: BuildDbf.prg
* Author ....: P. L. Olympia & Kathy Cea
* Purpose....: Sample procedure to create a database file from
*            : a data dictionary. Key fields are obtained from
*            : Fil_Fld.Dbf, nonkey fields and all key parameters
*            : are obtained from Fld_Dct.Dbf.  Extend.Dbf is
*            : just a STRUCTURE EXTENDED .dbf for use by CREATE
*            : FROM
* Syntax ....: DO BuildDbf with Dbf
*            :  where Dbf is the name of the file to create.
************************************************************
PARAMETER dbf   && name of dbf to build
SET SAFETY OFF
USE Fld_Dct in 1 INDEX Fld_Dct       && index on Field_name
USE Fil_Fld in 2
USE Extend in 3      && some extended structure to be zapped
SELE Extend
ZAP

*-- Pick up key field names of desired .dbf from Fil_Fld
SELECT Fil_Fld
SET RELATION TO Field_Name INTO Fld_Dct
SCAN FOR Fil_Fld->File_Name = dbf
  DO AddField
ENDSCAN
SET RELATION TO
*-- Pick up nonkey field names from Fld_Dct
SELE Fld_Dct
SCAN FOR SUBSTR(Fld_Dct->Field_Name,1,3) = SUBSTR(dbf,1,3)
  DO AddField
ENDSCAN
USE IN 3
CREATE (dbf) FROM Extend     && One command builds the file
RETURN
```

(continued)

Listing 3-1. Continued

```
PROCEDURE AddField
  SELECT Extend
  APPEND BLANK
  REPLACE Extend->Field_Name WITH Fld_Dct->Field_Name, ;
    Extend->Field_Type WITH Fld_Dct->Field_Type, ;
    Extend->Field_Len  WITH Fld_Dct->Field_Len,  ;
    Extend->Field_Dec  WITH Fld_Dct->Field_Dec
RETURN
```

dictionary and are neither obsolete nor have been improperly modified by a programmer.

Dbf_Idx.dbf

This data file defines the key expression of each index file as well as which index files belong to which .dbf files. It is useful not only as an integral part of the system documentation but also for ensuring that all system indexes can be rebuilt correctly should they become corrupt. Note that the REINDEX command is useless if the index file header containing the key expression is itself damaged.

At a minimum, this data file has the following structure:

```
Structure for database : FIL_FLD.DBF
Number of data records : 5
Date of last update    : 2/20/90
Field  Field Name  Type        Width    Dec
    1  FILE_NAME   Character       8
    2  INDEX_NAME  Character       8
    3  INDEX_EXPN  Character     100
** Total **                      117
```

In Chapter 13, we introduce a facility for storing the .dbf name in the index file header area. We also demonstrate a way of extracting the .dbf name and the index expression for any index file and storing this information in a Dbf_Idx.Dbf file. The structure of the Dbf_Idx file we used for the examples is displayed in that chapter. We can use the sample programs to build and maintain our Dbf_Idx.dbf database file.

The Dbf_Idx.dbf file has the added benefit of guaranteeing that all index files associated with a .dbf file reflect current changes to the actual data file. Once an application opens a specified .dbf file, it looks to this file next to determine which index files should also be opened so they can be updated whenever necessary, ensuring that the index pointers always remain in sync with the data. In effect, such a procedure offers the same benefits provided by FoxPro 2.0's new compound index (.cdx) facility, which ensures that multiple tags in the index file reflect current data updates.

The Data Element Dictionary

What fields should the data element dictionary contain beyond the usual Field_Name, Field_Type, Field_Len, and Field_Dec? Largely it depends on the organization's requirements. Several of the fields included in popular data dictionary systems such as those provided by Recital and Wallsoft's UI2 Programmer are presented here.

Field Description

The data element dictionary needs a description field, say, Field_Desc, not only to fully describe the field, but also to use in a help window when a user presses the F1 key during a data entry or edit operation. Given the limitations in many Dbase dialects, this field often has been implemented in the past either as a single 254-character field or a series of, say, five 75-character fields called Desc1 through Desc5. However, the very nature of the information kept in this field, which would be extensive for some but skimpy in others, along with FoxPro's versatile memo field facility dictate that this should be a memo field in a FoxPro data dictionary. The contents of this field may then be popped easily through a memo window to a user during data entry.

Picture Clause

This field defines the display format of the data element, for example, @R 999-99-9999 in the case of Social Security Number. Both UI2 and Recital can automatically include the picture clause in the @...GET statement for the field.

Valid Clause and Range

A field range may be considered a subset of the Valid clause, although many data dictionaries include both. The Valid clause may specify an expression or function that an @...GET statement can use to determine if the user-supplied value for the data element is valid. This field may be implemented as a string that would be part of a Boolean expression, for example, "$ABCD" to indicate that only codes A, B, C, or D are valid for the data element. If the Valid clause is complex, this field can be implemented simply as the name of a user-defined function that is responsible for validating the data element's value.

A Range clause, like the Valid clause, specifies the domain of acceptable values for the data element, particularly for numeric and date fields. You may choose to implement this as two separate values, high and low, defining the ceiling and floor of the field.

An alternative to the Valid or Range clause is a Lookup clause that can be used to specify the name of an indexed table of allowed values for the desired data element.

Required Field

You may choose to include a required field attribute in your field dictionary. This attribute determines whether a user will be allowed to exit a data entry screen without entering a value for the field.

Default or Initial Value

Some data element dictionaries specify the default or initial values assigned to the field until the user modifies them.

Data Source

If your organization requires that the origin of the data element be documented, a dictionary entry for the field's data source may be in order. Data sources may refer to some standard government forms or company paper forms, surveys, questionnaires, or similar instruments.

Cross-Reference Field

For organizations that exchange data with other companies that use different data dictionaries, a cross-reference field in the dictionary keeps track of both the name of the field in the foreign dictionary and the data source of the field in the foreign system.

Extending the Dictionary Concept

Based on the contents of a data element dictionary, it is clear that its two major functions are to clarify or enforce field validation rules and to document the field as fully as possible for all users of the dictionary. We can extend the concept of the dictionary further by keeping track of which application module in the organization initializes, modifies, or simply reads each field in the dictionary. Such information is useful for establishing module dependencies because a module that uses or reads a field cannot precede one that initializes it. It is also useful (in the case of a passive dictionary implementation) in determining which modules will be affected by policy changes that necessitate modifying the validation rules for a field.

Data Dictionary Implementation in the Dbase Family

Since a data dictionary facility is largely ignored in the Dbase family of products, except in Recital, its enforcement or implementation is left to third-party products such as Wallsoft's UI2 or Symmetry Software's Symmetry IV. Note that the data dictionary implementation in these products is much narrower in scope than the enterprise-wide dictionary concept we've discussed thus far.

UI2 is primarily a screen and code generator of Dbase programs that use modifiable code templates. It allows you to define field characteristics that can become global default definitions for the field, which can then be stored in a central data dictionary. UI2 uses any validation rules you define for the field as part of the @...GET routine in the code it generates. Thus, it automatically takes care of initial value, picture, and valid or range clauses you attach to the field definition, just like an active dictionary would do. It also allows you to specify a display formula for the field so a user can better understand the screen prompt for the field. UI2 permits you to define up to three template-specific field attributes (called slots) to supplement standard field properties.

Symmetry IV's approach to a data dictionary is primarily for documentation only, which is in line with its principal focus of being a documenting and debugging tool for Dbase-type applications. You tell Symmetry the name of your top-level (main) program and where your .dbf and index files are, and it proceeds to read your entire application to produce summary and detailed data dictionary reports. In these reports, you provide the descriptive text for fields, data files, and index files. The database dictionary summary report lists all the .dbf files that the application used, along with the descriptions you supply. The field dictionary summary report shows the structure of each .dbf file, along with your supplied description for each field in the file. The field dictionary detail report lists the field attributes, including alias and range of values.

The Recital Data Dictionary Facility

In Recital you immediately notice that something is different because the CREATE command gives you a 25-character column in which to enter the field description. This descriptive text may be displayed automatically as part of the prompt for the field in full-screen system-generated forms such as those produced by APPEND, EDIT, or CHANGE. The SET DESCRIPTIONS OFF command disables the display of the text as a field prompt.

Recital can create an optional data dictionary file with a file type of .dbd. Field attributes that can be defined as part of the data dictionary are picture clause, valid clause, range values for dates and numerics, default initial value, calculation formula, and the following additional properties.

Property	**Description**
Error	Specifies the error message to display if validation for the field fails.

Property	Description
Help	Specifies the Field prompt to display in the message line.
Choices	Defines a popup list of choices for the field when the user presses the Help key.
Required	Specifies if the user must enter a value for the field.
Recalculate	Serves as a trigger causing all calculated fields to be recalculated and displayed whenever this field is modified in a form.

Recital automatically uses the field definition properties in the dictionary during data entry. For example, it attaches the defined picture, valid, or range clause to an @...GET statement for the field.

The Recital @...GET statement has options or qualifiers that may override, or be invalidated by, similar field attributes in the dictionary. For instance, the CALCULATE option cannot be used if the dictionary already has the property defined for the field. Similarly, any picture clause defined for the field in the dictionary cannot be overridden by a picture option in the @...GET command. On the other hand, the CHOICELIST option of the @...GET statement can override any Choices attribute for the field defined in the dictionary. Similarly, the HELP/MESSAGE option or the RANGE option of the @...GET statement may override the corresponding definitions in the dictionary for the field.

Chapter Summary

A data dictionary is an organized system for defining and managing data elements. It is at once a tool for data resource management, data standardization, and system documentation. A data dictionary may be manual or automated, standalone or dependent, active or passive.

In this chapter, we discussed some of the advantages offered by a data dictionary. Among the Dbase family of products, only Recital provides a dictionary facility. However, a comprehensive dictionary system can be easily implemented as a FoxPro application. At a minimum, such a system requires a file of data elements, a file associating database names with key fields, and a third file establishing index and .dbf relationships. Any required .dbf file may be generated from an EXTENDED STRUCTURE file using CREATE FROM.

We discussed the field attributes that are commonly included in a data field dictionary including picture, valid, range, and default values as well as text for prompts, helps, and error messages. We pointed out the advantages of using a memo field for storing descriptive text about data elements in the dictionary.

Finally, we described the data dictionary facility offered by Recital and by third-party Dbase products such as UI2 Programmer and Symmetry IV.

Chapter 4

Designing and Customizing an Application

Good programming practices dictate a modular approach to system design. This includes identifying commonly used routines and organizing them into separate procedures. Then, rather than have the same program code appear in many places, you have one routine that application programs can call as needed. The advantage to this approach is obvious—it simplifies maintenance and debugging and reduces the amount of code in the system. Structured program modules are designed to perform just one basic function (for example, add a record, modify a record, validate a user entry, or generate a report). When you take this approach, the result is a set of relatively small, understandable, and easy-to-maintain program modules that constitute your application.

Calling Other Program Modules

Once you have determined the modules you need in your system and their purposes, you need to think about how the modules are to be called. This is dictated in part by the purpose (and return values) of the module and in part by the language in which you are writing. Most, if not all, of your modules in a FoxPro application are written using the FoxPro language. These modules are written as procedures or user-defined functions (UDFs). Occasionally there is a need to perform some operating system–specific or low-level function that cannot be accomplished with the FoxPro programming language. In these cases, you can write a program in assembly language or C and convert it to a .bin (binary) file, which may be LOADed and CALLed from a

FoxPro procedure. You can also execute an external program with the RUN command. With FoxPro 2.0, you also have the option of integrating a C or assembly language routine into your application using FoxPro's APIs.

FoxPro Procedures

A typical FoxPro application contains many separate procedures. A procedure is a program or subprogram consisting of any number of FoxPro statements. Optionally a procedure can be called with parameters using the following syntax:

```
DO <procedure> WITH <parameter list>
```

Parameters are passed to procedures either by reference or value. When parameters are passed by reference, changes made to a parameter in the called procedure change the value of the parameter in the calling program as well. When passing parameters by value, a change made to a parameter's value from within a called procedure is known only to that procedure—the value of the parameter remains unchanged in the calling program. By default, FoxPro passes parameters to a procedure by reference. However, if a parameter is enclosed in parentheses when passed to a procedure, it is passed by value.

Procedures do not return a specific value to a calling procedure, although they can change the value of any parameters passed by reference or of any global variable.

A procedure is identified with the PROCEDURE <procedure name> statement as the first executable statement, although, as will be discussed later, it may be called as either a procedure or a function.

User-Defined Functions (UDFs)

A UDF is similar to a procedure in that it consists of a number of FoxPro commands or statements. It is identified with the FUNCTION <function name> statement as the first executable statement. It differs from a procedure in its calling syntax, return values, and its default use of parameters, however. A function is called with the following syntax:

```
<Function> ([<parameter list>])
```

where the parameter list is optional. A function always returns a value to the calling program. In FoxPro 2.0, a UDF is no longer required to return a value. If the RETURN is omitted, FoxPro automatically returns .T. (True) from the UDF. By default, parameters passed to a function are passed by value. You can SET UDFPARMS TO REFERENCE if you wish to pass parameters to functions by reference instead. The following example illustrates the difference between passing by reference and passing by value:

```
FUNCTION ChgParam

PARAMETERS x
x = x * 100
RETURN x
```

Example 1:

```
* Set UDFPARMS is VALUE by default
STORE 1 TO a
?a
?ChgParam(a)
?a
```

The results are:

```
1
100
1
```

Example 2:

```
SET UDFPARMS TO REFERENCE
STORE 1 TO a
?a
?ChgParam(a)
?a
```

The results are:

```
1
100
100
```

As this example demonstrates, changes made to a parameter are permanent only if parameters are passed by reference. As with procedures, a parameter that is enclosed in parentheses is passed by value, regardless of SET UDFPARMS. Since one set of parentheses is always required to call a function, an extra pair is needed for each parameter to be passed by value if SET UDFPARMS is REFERENCE. You can force a variable to be passed by reference, regardless of SET UDFPARMS, by preceding it with @. Again using the ChgParam function displayed in the preceding example, consider the following results:

```
SET UDFPARMS TO REFERENCE
STORE 1 TO a
?a
?ChgParam((a))
?a
```

The results are:

```
1
100
1
```

Although SET UDFPARMS is REFERENCE, the parameter *a* is passed by value since it is enclosed in parentheses.

Like a procedure, a UDF may be called as either a function or a procedure. If called as a procedure (with the DO <function> syntax), the function behaves like a procedure in that the return value is ignored and any parameters are passed by reference (unless enclosed in parentheses). Similarly, a procedure that is called as a function with the <procedure> ([<parameter list>]) syntax returns a value, and treats passed parameters according to the rules for functions. Thus the calling syntax actually determines whether a module is to behave like a procedure or a function.

Using LOAD, CALL, RUN, and APIs

For programs that are too difficult, too cumbersome, or altogether impossible to code in the FoxPro command language as procedures or UDFs, binary (.bin) files and APIs offer two attractive alternatives. Binary routines are most often coded in assembly language or in C and called within a FoxPro application. FoxPro treats .bin routines as though they were built-in procedures or functions except that they cannot be abbreviated to the first four characters. Examples of such routines that are popular in a multiuser application include those that redirect output to a variety of network printers as well as those that take advantage of the resources offered by the LAN operating system, for instance, transaction processing.

How do you create and use a .bin file? Normally, you would write the routine in assembly language, compile it, link it, and then convert the resulting .exe to a .bin file using DOS's EXE2BIN program. To use the routine, you must first load it into memory with the LOAD command. For instance, the FoxPro command

```
LOAD tts
```

fetches the Tts.bin file from disk and loads it into memory. You only need to load the routine once, no matter how many times you use it in the application.

When the application needs to use the services of the .bin routine, you invoke it with the CALL command, for example,

```
CALL tts [WITH <memvar>]
```

where the optional parameter may be a character expression or memory variable that allows you to pass data to and from the routine. If you no longer need the routine, you should free up the memory space it takes with the RELEASE MODULE command. Thus

```
RELEASE MODULE tts
```

releases the space occupied by Tts.bin. FoxPro allows up to 16 .bin files to be in memory at one time, so it is always a good idea to release those that your application no longer needs.

Binary routines are subject to a few rules. For instance, they cannot be larger than 32,000 bytes, they must originate at an offset of zero rather than at 100h, and they must never alter the length of the memvar passed to them as a parameter.

If you cannot convert an executable file to a binary file, you may still be able to execute the program from within your application. The RUN or equivalent ! command can be used to execute an external program, including DOS internal commands like COPY. If the program requires more memory than is available, you can issue the RUN command as follows:

```
RUN /n <command>
```

where *n* is the number of kilobytes required by <command>. If *n* is greater than the number of remaining kilobytes, FoxPro invokes FOXSWAP, a program that frees as much memory as is required by swapping the contents of memory to disk. To optimize performance, *n* should be set to the smallest number required for successful program execution, minimizing the amount of memory to be swapped to disk. If *n* is set to 0, the entire contents of memory are swapped to disk. RUN /0 should be used only when necessary to avoid the overhead incurred when swapping all of memory to disk and back.

APIs offer a more powerful alternative to extending the FoxPro language compared to .bin routines or the RUN command. Like .bin routines, functions coded using APIs appear to users as built-in functions. Unlike .bin routines, functions that use APIs can allocate or deallocate memory, and there are no artificial limits to the number of such functions that your applications can use at any one time. API-based functions also do not suffer from the disadvantage of the RUN command, which may require swapping portions of memory to disk depending on available memory. Normally, when FoxPro encounters a statement containing a string such as FUNC( ), it first checks to determine whether or not the reference is to a built-in function. If it is not, it next checks to see if FUNC( ) is an array. If that fails also, FoxPro next checks to see if the function is an external function coded with APIs. If you want FoxPro to bypass its precedence rule for function/array checking so that it uses your API-coded function directly, you should invoke the function with the CALL command, for instance:

```
CALL myfunc WITH parm1
```

Establishing a Set of Library Routines

We recommend that you establish a central location, that is, a dedicated directory, for all your standard routines. This will become your library. You must make your programming team aware of the existence and purpose of your library routines and provide them with the calling syntax of each routine. You must then require that all application programs call the library routines rather than duplicate code for those functions available in your library. The routines thus become "black boxes"; they accept a set of parameters and perform a specified function, possibly returning a value to the calling program.

What types of routines are likely candidates for a library? Generally any procedure or function that is needed by more than one program, or even that is needed by just one program in several different places. If your application is not designed yet, establishing a set of library routines is easy. Simply identify commonly performed operations and create procedures and functions to meet these needs. If your application already exists, you will have to evaluate your existing code in order to determine where identical or similar code appears in several places. If several programs contain similar, but not identical, code for a given purpose, a standard method must be agreed upon and implemented. This is why it is easier to design your library before you start coding. However, even if your application is already written, it is probably well worth your time to develop a set of common routines and modify the existing programs in order to simplify future maintenance activities.

Some typical candidates for library routines are as follows:

- Online help facilities
- Standard screen displays (color settings and placement of borders, boxes, and windows)
- Message placement
- Printer selection and control
- Data validation
- Opening and closing database and index files
- Error processing
- Multiuser functions (such as record and file locking)
- Naming of temporary work files
- Standard security measures such as validation of user id and password

Listing 4-1 demonstrates a simple routine that standardizes the presentation of error messages for an application. This routine, L_Msg, is called with the error message, which may contain from one to three characters strings, each a maximum of 40 characters. Later in this chapter, we discuss and provide sample code for online help routines, data validation routines (and presentation of error messages), and error processing.

You also need to establish a naming convention for library routines. This way, you can easily identify the library routines in your application. It also ensures that the program names for your library routines do not conflict with the names of the other application programs. The naming convention we use is to prefix the library routine names with "L_". For example, a routine to handle printer selection might be named L_Print. One of our applications, which provides a system maintenance subsystem for the network administrator, applies a prefix of "M_" to the routines designated for the maintenance programs. For example, a reindex routine might be M_Reindx. If you wish to distinguish functions from procedures, you could assign a prefix of "F_" to library UDFs.

Listing 4-1. L_Msg.prg, procedure to place a one- to three-line error message on the screen.

```
PROCEDURE L_Msg

*******************************************************************
* Program: L_Msg.prg
* Author : P.L. Olympia & Kathy Cea
* Purpose: Standard library routine to place error messages on
*        : the screen.
*        :
* Syntax : L_MSG ("line1","line2", "line3")
*        : where each line may contain up to 40 characters.
*        : "line2" and "line3" are optional.
*        :
*******************************************************************

PARAMETERS Msg1, Msg2, Msg3

mNumParm = PARAMETERS()

DEFINE WINDOW ErrMsg ;
        FROM 16,15 TO 23,65 ;
        TITLE "Error"

ACTIVATE WINDOW ErrMsg
mCnt = 1
DO WHILE mCnt <= mNumParm
        mCntStr = ALLTRIM(STR(mCnt))
        @(mCnt - 1),1 SAY PADC(Msg&mCntStr,WCOLS())
        mCnt = mCnt + 1
ENDDO
WAIT
DEACTIVATE WINDOW ErrMsg
```

Performing Data Validation

One of the most time-consuming programming activities is the coding and testing of edit and validation procedures for each application module. Furthermore, modifying validation criteria may well be the most common mainte-

```
Structure for database: C:\VALID.DBF
Number of data records:       12
Date of last update    : 02/28/90
Field  Field Name  Type        Width    Dec
    1  SCRNFLD     Character      12
    2  VALID_EXPR  Character     254
    3  ERRORMSG    Character      72
** Total **                      339
```

Figure 4-1. Sample .dbf structure to store validation expressions and error messages for screen fields.

nance activity in an application. A standard approach to data validation should help streamline these activities.

UDFs can be used in connection with the VALID option on an @...SAY/GET command to validate screen field entries. You can write a generic validation UDF to be used in connection with a .dbf containing your validation expressions, or you can write UDFs specific to each field. We provide examples of both in this chapter.

One way to standardize your validation procedures is to store your validation criteria in a .dbf. The .dbf contains one record for each field requiring validation. You can also store error messages in the validation .dbf. The advantage of this method is that a change in validation requirements (for example, a list of valid codes changes) does not require any program modifications. A sample .dbf structure containing field name, validation expression, and error message is shown in Figure 4-1. Note that the validation expression is limited to 254 characters since we are using a character field. If the validation expression requires more space, a memo field could be used in place of the character field.

Listing 4-2 presents a program "shell" that we will use for many of our examples in the remainder of this chapter. This program is designed to perform a simple product entry procedure for an order processing system. We will be including code fragments specific to the function we are discussing; these code fragments work in connection with the program shown in Listing 4-2 to perform the product entry function.

You can perform the validation from a standard UDF, as shown in Listing 4-3. The F_Valid function uses the VARREAD( ) function, which returns the name of the screen field being entered during a READ operation. It then searches the Valid.dbf file (indexed on UPPER(Scrnfld)) for a record that matches the results of the VARREAD( ) function. If found, the validation expression is evaluated, and if false, the error message is displayed. Note that

Listing 4-2. AddProd.prg, program "shell" to be used with sample code fragments that follow.

```
PROCEDURE AddProd
*********************************************************************
* Program: AddProd.prg
* Author : P.L. Olympia & Kathy Cea
* Purpose: Add a new product
*        :
* Syntax : DO AddProd
*        :
* Notes  : This is a program shell to be used with other examples
*********************************************************************
CLEAR
SET ECHO OFF
SET TALK OFF

*Initialize screen field values
mProdNum = SPACE(12)
mPro_Name = SPACE(20)
mPro_Cost = 0
mSupplId = SPACE(5)

*|                                                        |*
*|  Insert the appropriate AddProd code fragment here     |*
*|                                                        |*

READ

* Do other processing
```

if the expression is false, we return a value of zero rather than .F. This is required in order to suppress the FoxPro error message. This method has the added advantage of allowing the application to define the placement of the error message on the screen.

If you implement your own context-sensitive help facility (rather than the FoxPro SET HELP TO option), you can store your data validation in the same .dbf file with your help text. This method requires only one work area for the .dbf containing validation and help information. We discuss a custom help function that incorporates validation criteria in the next section.

Listing 4-3. F_Valid function to perform data validation from the Valid.dbf database.

```
*  AddProd.prg code fragment
*  This example uses the F_VALID() function to perform
*  screen field validation.

* Open the .dbf containing validation expressions
SELECT 25
USE Valid INDEX ScrnFld

* Define Error message window
DEFINE WINDOW ErrWind ;
        FROM 20,1 TO 23,78 ;
        TITLE "Invalid Product Entry"

* Display Add Product screen
@2,1 SAY PADC("-- Add Product Record --",WCOLS())
@3,1 TO 12,80 DOUBLE
@5,10 SAY "Product Number: " GET mProdNum VALID F_VALID()
@7,10 SAY "Product Name: " GET mPro_Name VALID F_VALID()
@9,10 SAY "Product Cost: " GET mPro_Cost;
       PICT "$99999.99" VALID F_VALID()
@9,45 SAY "Supplier Number: " GET mSupplId;
       PICT "@! ANNNN" VALID F_VALID()


FUNCTION F_VALID
*******************************************************************
* Program: F_Valid.prg
* Author : P.L. Olympia & Kathy Cea
* Purpose: Perform screen field validation, using Valid.dbf
*        :
* Syntax : VALID F_VALID()
*        : Returns .T. if user-entered data is valid
*        :
*******************************************************************

SELECT Valid
* Assumes that the .dbf containing validation criteria, Valid,
* is already opened in a work area
```

(continued)

Listing 4-3. Continued

```
* Determine screen field to be validated
SEEK VARREAD()

IF FOUND()
        Val_Expr = Valid->Valid_Expr
        IF EMPTY(Val_Expr)
                * If there is no validation clause, return .T.
                RETURN .T.
        ENDIF
        IF EVALUATE(Val_Expr)
                RETURN .T.
        ELSE
                ACTIVATE WINDOW ErrWind
                @1,1 SAY ErrorMsg
                WAIT
                DEACTIVATE WINDOW ErrWind
                * Return 0 instead of .F. to suppress the
                * Standard FoxPro error message
                RETURN 0
        ENDIF
ELSE
        * If screen field is not found in .dbf, return .T.
        RETURN .T.
ENDIF
```

You can also use the VALID option of the @...SAY/GET command with a UDF, without the validation .dbf file. In this case, you write one field-specific UDF for each screen field requiring validation. This method does require code modification and recompilation if a validation requirement changes, but it still has an advantage over placing the validation code in the calling program. At least your code modifications are limited to your validation UDFs, limiting the impact on the rest of your application. Listing 4-4 demonstrates a program segment that uses UDFs for field validation.

There is an advantage to using a field-specific UDF over a generic function that reads a validation .dbf. The VALID clause provides an option to determine the next GET field based on a numeric value returned from the validat-

Listing 4-4. Program segment showing the use of field-specific UDF validation procedures.

```
*  AddProd.prg code fragment
*  This example uses UDFs specific to each screen field to
*  perform field validation.
*  Note that only the F_PRDNUM function is shown in this example

* Define Error message window
DEFINE WINDOW ErrWind ;
        FROM 20,1 TO 23,78 ;
        TITLE "Invalid Product Entry"

* Display Add Product screen
@2,1 SAY PADC("-- Add Product Record --",WCOLS())
@3,1 TO 12,80 DOUBLE
@5,10 SAY "Product Number: " GET mProdNum VALID F_PRDNUM()
@7,10 SAY "Product Name: " GET mPro_Name VALID F_PRDNAM()
@9,10 SAY "Product Cost: " GET mPro_Cost PICT "$99999.99";
       VALID F_PRDCST()
@9,45 SAY "Supplier Number: " GET mSupplId PICT "@! ANNNN";
       VALID F_SUPPID()


FUNCTION F_PRDNUM
*******************************************************************
* Program: F_PrdNum.prg
* Author : P.L. Olympia & Kathy Cea
* Purpose: Validate the Product Number screen field
*        :
* Syntax : VALID F_PRDNUM()
*        :
*******************************************************************

IF EMPTY(mProdNum)
     ACTIVATE WINDOW ErrWind
     @1,1 SAY "Product Number is required"
     WAIT
     DEACTIVATE WINDOW ErrWind
    * Return 0 instead of .F. to suppress the
```

(continued)

Listing 4-4. Continued

```
     * Standard FoxPro error message
     RETURN 0
ELSE
     RETURN .T.
ENDIF


FUNCTION F_PRDNAM
* Validate the mPro_Name field
RETURN .T.

FUNCTION F_PRDCST
* Validate the mPro_Cost field
RETURN .T.

FUNCTION F_SUPPID
* Validate the mSupplId field
RETURN .T.
```

ing UDF. Thus, depending on the contents of the field, you can elect to return to a previous field or skip one or more fields. When the UDF returns a negative number, the READ command moves back that number of fields on the screen. If the number returned is positive, the READ moves forward the relative number of fields. Since the decision to move forward or backward normally depends on the field and its contents, you would not be able to use this feature in a generic validation UDF.

Implementing Your Own Help Facility

Using FoxPro's Built-in Help

FoxPro provides a complete online help facility. The help data is stored in the FoxHelp.dbf file and contains the most up-to-date information for each command and function. This help facility is designed more for the application developer than for the end user, however. When you install your own help system, you probably want to provide application-specific information rather than FoxPro-specific help. For this reason, FoxPro allows you to integrate your own help database with the built-in online system.

To customize the FoxPro help system with your own data, you first create a .dbf that conforms to the following rules:

1. The first field must be of type character. This field is used as the Topic field.
2. The second field must be a memo field. This field contains the help text.

You can name these fields anything you like. Also, you may have additional fields in the .dbf. Any additional fields are used only for selecting and/or filtering the appropriate records. They are not displayed to users. For example, you may add a field that contains the screen variable name corresponding to the particular data item so that you can present the associated help text when the user presses the F1 key from a data entry screen.

This built-in help system may be used in several different ways. First, you can implement a help facility similar to what FoxPro provides by simply defining your own .dbf and then issuing the SET HELP TO <your-own.dbf> command. Whenever the user types HELP or presses the F1 key, your list of topics is presented. The user selects the desired topic to view the help text. Although this is very easy to implement, it does not offer any context-sensitive help processing and probably will not be satisfactory in any but the most elementary systems.

To provide context-sensitive help, use the SET TOPIC TO <topic-name> command. This predefines the topic for which the help text will be displayed. The user no longer needs to select a topic from the list. For example, an order processing system may have data entry screens for Customer information, Sales Person information, Supplier information, Order information, and Product information. Upon entry to a particular data entry module, you can issue the appropriate SET TOPIC TO command; for example, when entering the Add Products module, you can SET TOPIC TO Product. This means that you must have a record with a Topic field (the first field in the .dbf) of Product. The memo field for the Product record will probably contain information such as how to enter new Product information to the system. This method has the advantage of preselecting the relevant help text for the user.

You can provide help information that is even more specific by relating the help topic to the particular data entry field from which help is requested. To implement such a context-sensitive help system, you need a field in your help database that corresponds to the data entry field names. You also need a

Listing 4-5. A sample context-sensitive help facility using FoxPro's built-in help.

```
*  AddProd.prg code fragment
*  This example uses the FoxPro help system, called from L_Help

ON KEY = 315 DO L_Help

@2,1 SAY PADC("-- Add Product Record --",WCOLS())
@3,1 TO 12,80 DOUBLE
@5,10 SAY "Product Number: " GET mProdNum
@7,10 SAY "Product Name: " GET mPro_Name
@9,10 SAY "Product Cost: " GET mPro_Cost PICT "$9999.99"
@9,45 SAY "Supplier Number: " GET mSupplId PICT "@! ANNNN"


PROCEDURE L_HELP
********************************************************************
* Program: L_Help.prg
* Author : P.L. Olympia & Kathy Cea
* Purpose: Display context-sensitive help using the FoxPro
*        : built-in help system and the OurHelp.dbf file
*        :
* Syntax : ON KEY = 315 DO L_Help
*        :
********************************************************************

SET HELP TO OurHelp
SET TOPIC TO UPPER(ScrnFld) = SYS(18)
HELP
```

separate help procedure to determine the field from which help was called. The sample program in Listing 4-5 demonstrates how you would implement such a facility. The SYS(18) (or equivalent VARREAD( )) function is used to determine the field being entered when the help key was pressed. These functions always return the field name in uppercase. This program assumes that we have a field called ScrnFld in the OurHelp.dbf file, containing the names of the screen fields.

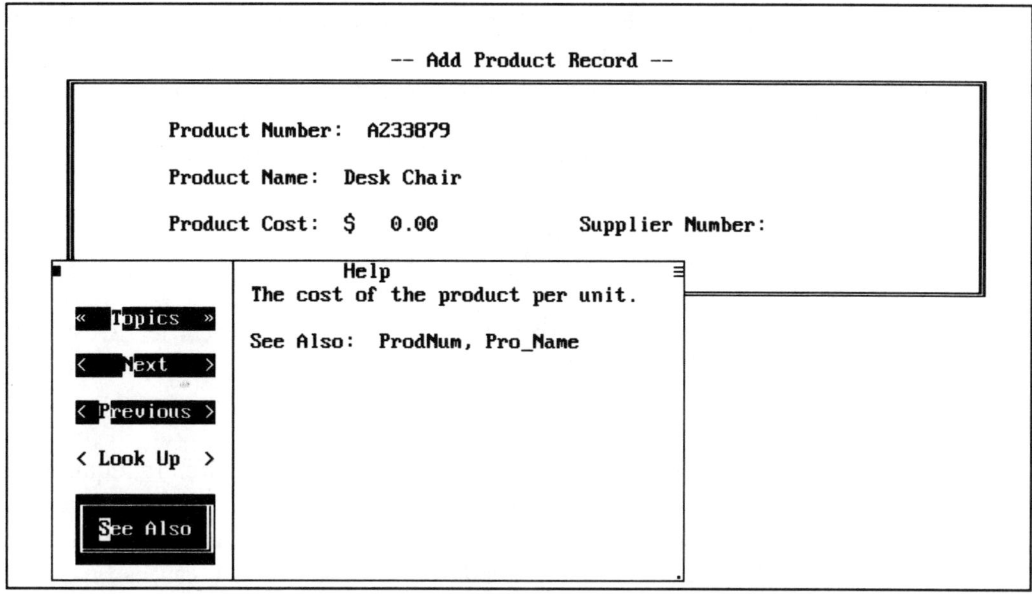

Figure 4-2. Screen display showing context-sensitive help for the Product Cost field, using the FoxPro help system.

Figure 4-2 shows the screen displayed when the F1 key is pressed over the Product Cost field. Note that if a record matching SET TOPIC TO <topic> is not found in the help database, the list of available topics is presented to the user.

FoxPro 2.0 has several new features built into the help system. These new features are a See Also popup, a Look Up button, and an ability to limit which records are available by using the new SET HELPFILTER TO command. All of these features are available to you when you implement a help system using FoxPro's help facilities.

The See Also popup presents a list of related topics from which the user may select. When a valid selection is made, that topic is displayed on the screen. FoxPro tracks which topics have been viewed and places the related topics already viewed on the top part of the See Also popup list, separating the list into two parts with a line. This allows a user to follow a logical chain of help topics, and then move back to a previously viewed topic.

Including the See Also popup in your own help system is very easy. As the last entry in the memo field that contains your help data you simply include the words "See Also" followed by a colon and one or more optional spaces. Then list each topic you want to relate to the current topic, separating each topic with a comma. For example, to relate a topic for Customer Name to topics for Customer Address (CustAddr), Customer Zip (CustZip), and Customer Phone (CustPhone), you might have a memo field as follows:

```
The customer's last name should be entered first, followed by
first name and middle initial.

See Also: CustAddr, CustZip, CustPhone
```

In this example, the See Also popup list contains three entries: CustAddr, CustZip, and CustPhone. If you do not include the See Also option in your memo field text, the See Also popup is simply unavailable for that particular topic.

FoxPro automatically implements the Look Up feature. It requires no action on your part. Whenever the user selects a word or a portion of text on the help screen for a particular topic, the Look Up button is automatically highlighted (meaning that it is available) and, if selected, causes FoxPro to look up the selected topic in the help database. If found, the topic is displayed. If the topic is not found, a list of available topics is presented.

The SET HELPFILTER command is a very important addition to the help system that allows you to limit which topics will be available for viewing at any particular time. The syntax of this command is as follows:

```
SET HELPFILTER [AUTOMATIC] TO [<expl>]
```

The AUTOMATIC option automatically removes the filter after the user exits the help system. In other words, this option makes the filter valid for just one execution of the help system. The <expl> is the filter expression that FoxPro evaluates prior to invoking the help system. Only records that meet the filter condition are available to the user. Records that do not meet the filter condition are not available on the Topics list, nor are they available through the See Also popup or the Look Up button. Normally your <expl> will include one or more fields from the help database.

For example, suppose you want to limit your user to only those help topics that are related by category. You are providing field-level context-sensitive help by including in your help .dbf a field with the screen field names. You can include another field called “Category” that identifies the record as belonging to, say, the Customer, Sales, Supplier, Order, or Product category. A subset of your database might look as follows:

```
Record#  HELPTOPIC     HELPTEXT SCRNFLD      CATEGORY
      1  ProdNum       Memo     mProdNum     Product
      2  ProdName      Memo     mProdName    Product
      3  ProdCost      Memo     mProdCost    Product
      4  SalesId       Memo     mSalesId     Sales
      5  SalesName     Memo     mSalesName   Sales
```

Upon entry to a module, you set up the appropriate filter by issuing the SET HELPFILTER TO Category = <category name> command. For example, when you enter the Sales module, you would issue the following command:

```
SET HELPFILTER TO UPPER(Category) = "SALES"
```

This limits the records that the user may view through the help system to those for which Category is "Sales." Then, as described previously, you can use the SYS(18) or VARREAD( ) function to provide field-level context-sensitive help.

As a final example, suppose that you do not want your users to be able to view any help topics other than the one you select for them. Following the example shown in Listing 4-5, at the time you issue the SET TOPIC TO command, you can also issue the SET HELPFILTER TO command, limiting the user to just that one record, as follows:

```
SET TOPIC TO UPPER(ScrnFld) = SYS(18)
SET HELPFILTER TO UPPER(ScrnFld) = SYS(18)
```

Advantages and Disadvantages to the FoxPro Help System

Using FoxPro's help system that is customized with your own database is simple and effective. Even implementing a context-sensitive help function requires very little code, as just demonstrated. In addition, it does not require you to use one of the 25 (standard FoxPro) work areas for your help database since FoxPro opens the help database in a reserved area. For a minimum of work and little overhead, you can provide a sophisticated help facility.

As has been described, the See Also option can be quite simply integrated with your own help data and FoxPro automatically provides the Look Up button. These are features that would be difficult to implement on your own. Furthermore, the new SET HELPFILTER TO command allows you to choose which records will be available to your user through the help system.

Although you may define as many extra fields as you like in the help database, you can use these fields only for selecting the appropriate record(s) to be displayed. For example, in a single record you cannot have several different memo fields that display varying levels of help that depend on a user's clearance level, department, or level of expertise. In addition, although you can use the database to store whatever related information you like, you cannot access the data directly from your application. This means that, although it may make sense to store your help text and validation criteria together in one .dbf, you cannot use the validation data if the database is already in use as the help database. To integrate help data with validation criteria, you have to write your own help system.

Writing Your Own Help System

Listing 4-6. Add Product routine modified to use our custom help facility, L_CusHlp.

```
*  AddProd.prg code fragment
*  This example uses our custom help system, called from L_CusHlp

* Open the custom help database in work area 25
SELECT 25
USE ApplHelp INDEX HelpScrn

* Define the help window
DEFINE WINDOW HelpWind ;
              FROM 18,40 TO 24,78 ;
              TITLE "Product Help"

ON KEY = 315 DO L_CusHlp

@2,1 SAY PADC("-- Add Product Record --",WCOLS())
@3,1 TO 12,80 DOUBLE
@5,10 SAY "Product Number: " GET mProdNum
@7,10 SAY "Product Name: " GET mPro_Name
@9,10 SAY "Product Cost: " GET mPro_Cost PICT "$99999.99"
@9,45 SAY "Supplier Number: " GET mSupplId PICT "@! ANNNN"
```

(continued)

Listing 4-6. Continued

```
PROCEDURE L_CusHlp
*******************************************************************
* Program: L_CusHlp.prg
* Author : P.L. Olympia & Kathy Cea
* Purpose: Custom help facility to display context-sensitive
*        : help from the ApplHelp.dbf file
*        :
* Syntax : ON KEY = 315 DO L_CusHlp
*        :
*******************************************************************

SELECT ApplHelp

* Assumes the the Custom help file, ApplHelp, is already opened
* in a work area

SEEK VARREAD()
ACTIVATE WINDOW HelpWind
IF FOUND()
        * Display help if record is found
        MODIFY MEMO HelpText NOEDIT WINDOW HelpWind
ELSE
        * Display message if there is no help
        @0,0 SAY "Sorry. There is no help available for this field."
        WAIT
ENDIF
DEACTIVATE WINDOW HelpWind
```

When you write your own help system, you can store whatever data you wish in just about any format into one .dbf. You can also control the screen presentation since you write the procedure yourself. Let us look at an example of how you might design and implement a database to both provide context-sensitive help and to store screen field validation criteria.

Listing 4-6 shows the Add Product routine, modified to work with our custom help facility. Since we are not using the FoxPro help system, we must use one work area to open our help database file, ApplHelp, indexed on the ScrnFld field in uppercase. We no longer use the SET HELP TO command, but instead we perform a SEEK to find the field being entered. We can use either the SYS(18) or VARREAD( ) function to determine the name of the field currently being entered. We also define a window in which to perform the MODIFY MEMO. This allows us to control window placement, colors, title, and so on. Our help procedure places a standard message on the screen if there is no record in the database for the field being entered. Figure 4-3 shows the screen display when the user presses the F1 key over the Product Cost field.

Once we have implemented this feature, it is easy to extend its use to automated field validation. Listing 4-7 shows the Add Product routine with field validation performed from the VALID clause on the @...SAY/GET command. Every field calls the same generic validation function, F_VALID. This function determines the field being entered with the VARREAD( ) function and then performs a seek in the Help/Validation .dbf to find the associated screen field. If the field is not found or if the validation expression is blank, .T. is returned. Otherwise, the expression is evaluated, and, if the

Listing 4-7. Add Product routine modified to perform custom help and data validation from the ApplHelp.dbf file.

```
*  AddProd.prg code fragment
*  This example uses our custom help system, called from L_CusHlp and
*  our generic data validation routine, F_Valid().

* Open the .dbf containing help and validation data
SELECT 25
USE ApplHelp INDEX HelpScrn

* Define the window for error messages
DEFINE WINDOW ErrWind ;
        FROM 20,1 TO 23,78 ;
        TITLE "Invalid Product Entry"

* Define the help window
DEFINE WINDOW HelpWind ;
              FROM 18,40 TO 24,78 ;
              TITLE "Product Help"

ON KEY = 315 DO L_CusHlp
```

(continued)

Listing 4-7. Continued

```
@2,1 SAY PADC("-- Add Product Record --",WCOLS())
@3,1 TO 12,80 DOUBLE
@5,10 SAY "Product Number: " GET mProdNum VALID F_VALID()
@7,10 SAY "Product Name: " GET mPro_Name VALID F_VALID()
@9,10 SAY "Product Cost: " GET mPro_Cost PICT "$99999.99";
       VALID F_VALID()
@9,45 SAY "Supplier Number: " GET mSupplId PICT "! ANNNN";
       VALID F_VALID()


PROCEDURE L_CusHlp
*******************************************************************
* Program: L_CusHlp.prg
* Author : P.L. Olympia & Kathy Cea
* Purpose: Custom help facility to display context-sensitive
*        : help from the ApplHelp.dbf file
*        :
* Syntax : ON KEY = 315 DO L_CusHlp
*        :
*******************************************************************

SELECT ApplHelp

* Assumes the the Custom help file, ApplHelp, is already opened
* in a work area

SEEK VARREAD()
ACTIVATE WINDOW HelpWind
IF FOUND()
        * Display help if record is found
        MODIFY MEMO HelpText NOEDIT WINDOW HelpWind
ELSE
        * Display message if there is no help
        @0,0 SAY "Sorry. There is no help available for this field."
        WAIT
ENDIF
DEACTIVATE WINDOW HelpWind
```

(continued)

Listing 4-7. Continued

```
FUNCTION F_VALID
******************************************************************
* Program: F_Valid.prg
* Author : P.L. Olympia & Kathy Cea
* Purpose: Perform screen field validation, using Valid.dbf
*        :
* Syntax : VALID F_VALID()
*        :
******************************************************************

SELECT ApplHelp
* Assumes that the .dbf containing help & validation criteria,
* ApplHelp, is already opened in a work area

* Determine screen field to be validated
SEEK VARREAD()

IF FOUND()
        Val_Expr = ApplHelp->Valid_Expr
        IF EMPTY(Val_Expr)
                * If there is no validation clause, return .T.
                RETURN .T.
        ENDIF
        IF EVALUATE(Val_Expr)
                RETURN .T.
        ELSE
                ACTIVATE WINDOW ErrWind
                @1,1 SAY ErrorMsg
                WAIT
                DEACTIVATE WINDOW ErrWind
                * Return 0 instead of .F. to suppress the
                * Standard FoxPro error message
                RETURN 0
        ENDIF
ELSE
        * If screen field is not found in .dbf, return .T.
        RETURN .T.
ENDIF
```

expression is invalid, the error message stored in the database is displayed. This function is essentially the same as the one presented in Listing 4-3, except that it now includes all our help and validation information in the same database. Figure 4-4 displays the .dbf structure we are using to store help text, data validation expressions, and error messages.

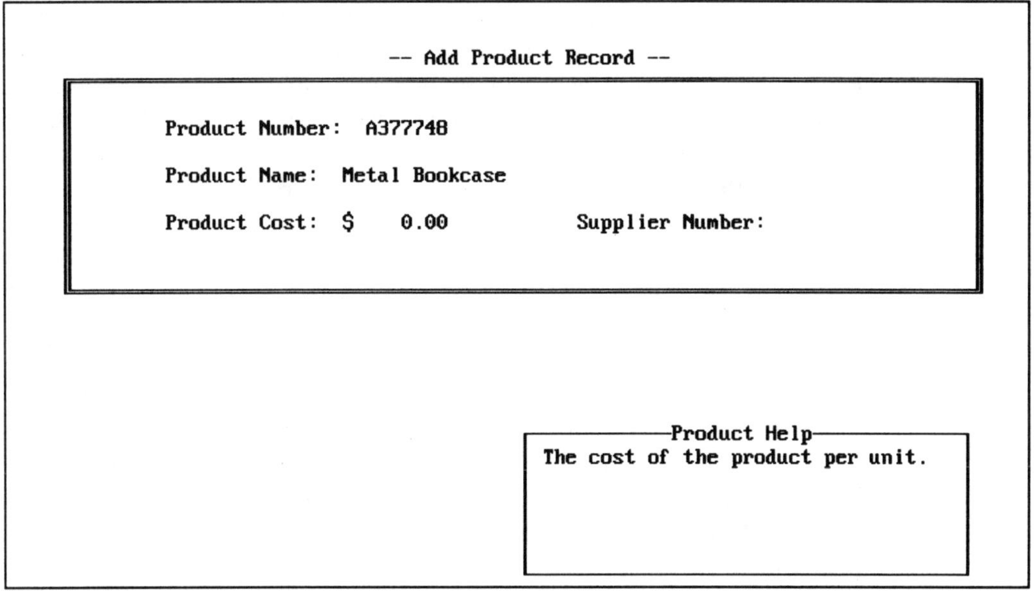

Figure 4-3. Screen display showing context-sensitive help for the Product Cost field, using our own help facility.

```
Structure for database: C:\APPLHELP.DBF
Number of data records:       12
Date of last update   : 02/28/90
Field  Field Name  Type        Width    Dec
    1  HELPTOPIC   Character      12
    2  HELPTEXT    Memo           10
    3  SCRNFLD     Character      12
    4  VALID_EXPR  Character     254
    5  ERRORMSG    Character      40
** Total **                      329
```

Figure 4-4. Sample .dbf structure to store help text, validation expressions, and error messages.

Error Handling

No matter how carefully you test and debug your code, at some time a user is going to try something with your application that you never thought of and an error is going to be generated. The best you can do is to be prepared with a comprehensive error processing routine and error report. A good error routine should provide most or all of the information you need to re-create the error and diagnose it. With such a routine, a user need not remember and describe the specific circumstances under which the error occurred.

FoxPro's ON ERROR command allows you to pass control to a specific error handling routine whenever a system error is encountered. If you do not implement the ON ERROR process in your application, your users are presented a FoxPro error message that is likely to be meaningless to them. By trapping the error and redirecting control, you can determine what the users see when an error occurs. Then you can take an appropriate course of action based on the error number and, if appropriate, generate a report that you can review later.

Table 4-1 lists useful commands and functions for an error processing routine. You may include any or all of these commands in your error trapping program. Listing 4-8 provides an example of an error processing routine that uses many of these commands and functions by writing the results to an error report. Note that it is important to turn off the error trapping facility from within your ON ERROR process to prevent an endless loop in the event that your ON ERROR process generates its own error.

Debugging Facilities

FoxPro provides a complete set of tools for debugging a program. Its Trace and Debug windows allow you to observe program execution line by line, to monitor specific program values, and to set program breakpoints. You can monitor or set a breakpoint for any expression that can be evaluated. You can also set breakpoints for specific lines of source code. Based on the nature of the error, you can decide which debugging tools to use.

Tracing Program Execution

If you wish to view your source code as it executes line by line, issue a SET ECHO ON or SET STEP ON command. Your source code appears in the Trace window for each program as it executes. You can slow program

Table 4-1. Useful Functions and Commands for an ON ERROR Process

Function	**Return Value**
DATE( )	Current system date.
TIME( )	Current system time.
ERROR( )	The number of the error causing the ON ERROR routine to be called.
LINENO( )	The number of the line being executed, relative to the top of the main program.
LINENO(1)	The number of the line being executed, relative to the top of the current program or procedure.
MESSAGE( )	The error message string corresponding to the error causing the ON ERROR routine to be called.
MESSAGE(1)	The source code line causing the error condition. Note that this function is not available in the FoxPro Runtime version. If you execute it from within the Runtime environment, it returns the value of MESSAGE( ).
PROGRAM([*n*])	The name of the program executing when the error occurred. The optional *n* parameter indicates how many levels of nesting to go back. The *n* parameter can take a value from 1 through *N*, where *N* is the level of nesting to get to the currently executing program. A parameter of 0 or 1 returns the name of the master program, and *N* (or no parameter) returns the name of the current program. PROGRAM( ) returns only the program name, without a path specification.
SYS(16[,*n*])	The name of the program being executed. As with the PROGRAM( ) function, the optional *n* parameter indicates how many levels of nesting to go back. SYS(16) returns the full path specification and program name, and also returns the name of the procedure file, if applicable. This function is most useful in a loop, as shown in Listing 4-8.
SYS(18) and VARREAD( )	The name of the field being entered.
VERSION( )	The FoxPro version number.

(continued)

Table 4-1. Continued

Command	Description
LIST STATUS	Describes the status of the FoxPro environment.
LIST MEMORY	Lists the currently active memory variables and arrays with their values.
RETRY	Returns control to the calling program and reexecutes the last line.
RETURN	Returns control to the calling program and executes the line following the last line.
RETURN TO MASTER	Returns control to the highest level calling program (normally the main routine).
RETURN TO <procedure name>	Returns control to procedure specified by <procedure name>.

Listing 4-8. L_Error.prg, sample ON ERROR procedure.

```
PROCEDURE L_Error
*********************************************************************
* Program: L_Error
* Author : P.L. Olympia & Kathy Cea
* Purpose: Error Processing routine
*        :
* Syntax : ON ERROR DO L_Error
*        :
*********************************************************************

PRIVATE mErrorNum,mFile,mCnt
SET TALK OFF

* Disable the ON ERROR routine to prevent recursive calls
ON ERROR

mErrorNum = ERROR()
mFile      = SPACE(1)
mCnt       = 0
```

(continued)

Listing 4-8. Continued

```
* Define system error window
DEFINE WINDOW SysErr ;
        FROM 10,15 TO 18,65 ;
        TITLE "System Error"

ACTIVATE WINDOW SysErr

DO CASE

*Check for recoverable errors

CASE mErrorNum = 108  && File is in use
        * For Multi-user system only
        * Ask user whether he/she wants to retry locking file
CASE mErrorNum = 109  &&Record is locked by another
        * For Multi-user system only
        * Ask user whether he/she wants to retry locking record
CASE mErrorNum = 125    && Printer not ready
        *Ask user to check printer status

* ...(Other application-specific error checks)

OTHERWISE    && Display message, print error report, return to main

   * Display error message to user
   @1,1 SAY PADC("A System Error has occurred.",50)
   @2,1 SAY PADC("Please contact your System Administrator.",50)
   @3,1 SAY PADC("Press any key to return to the Main Menu.",50)
   WAIT ""
   DEACTIVATE WINDOW SysErr

   * Determine output file name, write error report
   mFile = space(1)
   DO WHILE LEN(SYS( 2000, mFile )) > 0 .or. mCnt = 0
      mCnt  = mCnt + 1
      mFile = "ERRORS." + tran( mCnt,"9" )
      IF mCnt = 9
         EXIT
```

(continued)

Listing 4-8. Continued

```
   ENDIF
ENDDO
SET CONSOLE OFF
SET PRINTER ON
SET PRINTER TO (mFile)

* Display header
? PADC('Order Processing System Error Report',78,'*')
? 'Date: ' + DTOC(DATE())
? 'Time: ' + TIME()
?

* Loop through the FoxBASE SYS(16) function values.
* displaying all of the procedures that were called when the
* error occurred
mCnt = 1
DO WHILE LEN( SYS( 16,mCnt ) ) <> 0
    IF mCnt = 1
        ? 'Master Prg: ' + SYS( 16,mCnt )
    ELSE
        ? SPACE( mCnt - 1 ) + 'Called to: ' + SYS( 16,mCnt )
    ENDIF
    mCnt = mCnt + 1
ENDDO

* Display error message, memory, etc.
?
? 'Line causing error: '
? MESSAGE(1)
?
? 'Error code is: ' + LTRIM(STR(mErrorNum))
? MESSAGE()
?
? 'FoxPro Version: '
? VERSION()
?
? 'Display of Status:'
LIST STAT
```

(continued)

Listing 4-8. Continued

```
    ?
    ? 'Display of Memory:'
    LIST MEMO
    ?


    * Close output file
    SET PRINTER TO
    SET PRINTER OFF
    SET CONSOLE ON

    * Reset error trapping routine
    ON ERROR DO L_Error

    * Return to the main procedure
    RETURN TO MASTER

ENDCASE
RETURN
```

execution to no more than four command statements per second by pressing the Ctrl key, the Shift key, or the mouse button. Pressing any two of these together slows execution to no more than two statements per second. (Program execution is slowed only while you have these keys pressed.) If you want only one statement to execute at a time, suspend program execution and select the Step option for each line to be stepped through.

To cancel or suspend the program at any time, press the Esc key. This temporarily halts execution (unless SET ESCAPE is OFF) and makes a number of options available on the Trace window. New to FoxPro 2.0, you can now display line numbers on your traced program, indicate whether or not FoxPro should trace between breakpoints, specify the number of seconds each line of program code should be delayed when it executes, step "out of" the currently executing program and suspend execution on the first line following the command that called the current program, or skip "over" a called program that you do not want to appear in the Trace window. Note that when you select the Out or Over options, program execution continues normally, but the program is simply not displayed in the Trace window. You can also cancel program execution, execute just one line (step), clear all breakpoints, open another program in the Trace window, or resume program execution. These options are all available from the Trace window's menu bar, and you should experiment with them to determine the optimal settings for your individual needs.

Monitoring Program Values

You can specify expressions to be monitored as your program executes. You do this in the Debug window, typing your variable names or expressions in the left side of the window. When your program executes, the value of each expression is displayed on the right side of the window. The Debug window can be accessed from the Window menu. Figure 4-5 displays the Debug window with several values set for monitoring.

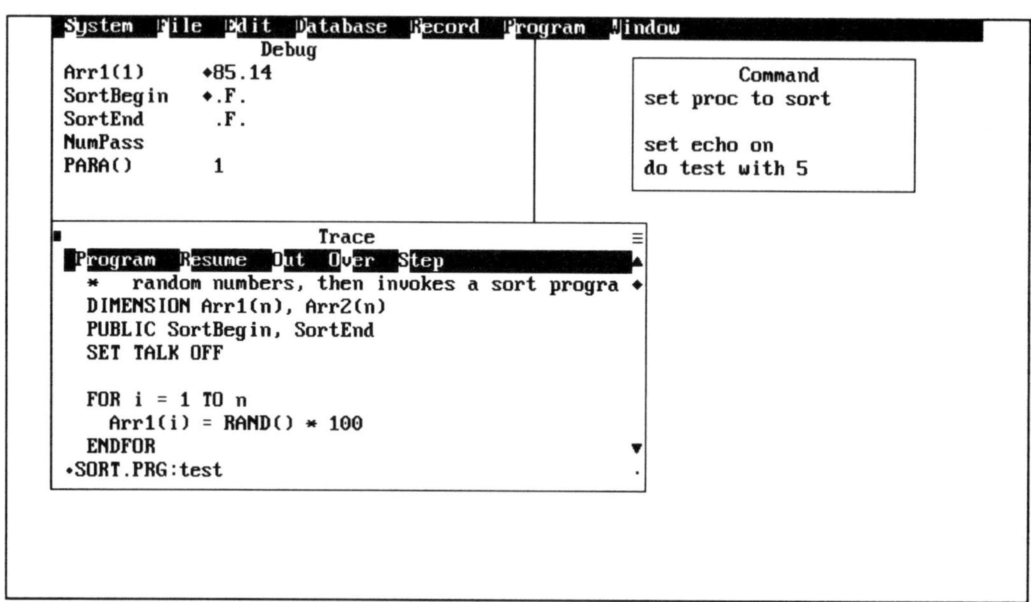

Figure 4-5. Sample screen showing the Debug and Trace windows.

Setting Breakpoints

A breakpoint can be a line of code, a memory variable, a database field, or any valid expression. Program execution is suspended whenever the line of code is reached or the value of the variable or expression changes. There are two ways to set breakpoints:

1. To designate a source line of code as a breakpoint, press the Spacebar, press Enter, or click the mouse on the desired line of code while in the Trace window.
2. To identify a variable or expression as a breakpoint, list it in the Debug window and then press the Spacebar or click the mouse in the column separating the left side of the window from the right side.

The SET DOHISTORY Option

When SET DOHISTORY is ON, program statements that have been executed are placed in the Command window. This allows you to review the program flow and, if desired, reexecute one or more of the commands from the Command window. Although this tool can be valuable during the debugging process, it slows program execution considerably. It can also temporarily consume a large amount of disk space since it builds a temporary document that contains the executed source lines. Therefore, if you SET DOHISTORY ON while in the test and debugging stage, be certain to SET it OFF before going to production. Note that if you compile a program with the NODEBUG option, DOHISTORY is not available.

The LOGERRORS Setting

If you SET LOGERRORS ON (the default setting), an error log file will be written whenever you compile a program that contains errors. This file will have the same name as the program being compiled, but with an extension of .ERR. The error log file is a useful debugging tool because it identifies each source line in error and provides a diagnostic error message. If you SET LOGERRORS OFF, however, the error log file is not written.

Custom Configuration

Many FoxPro features can be customized for each user or application. This can be done by making entries in the Config.fp file or by issuing the appropriate SET commands in a program. A variety of SET commands are provided to control such configuration options as screen display, debugging facilities, memory allocation, date and time presentation, and output destination. Appendix B lists the SET commands with descriptions, ranges of acceptable values, and default values. In this section, we address some of the more critical SET options such as the multiuser configuration options and settings that can affect system performance. We also demonstrate a technique for changing a setting in a program and introduce the FoxUser resource file.

The Config.fp file specifies the configuration options at startup. Most of these options can be changed from within FoxPro with the appropriate SET command. For example, if you wish to define default color settings for your application, you can set any of the various SET COLOR options in the Config.fp file. Any of the program modules can change the color settings by executing a SET COLOR command, thereby overriding the defaults specified in the Config.fp file. Config.fp statements that have no equivalent SET statements include COMMAND, EMS, INDEX, LABEL, MVARSIZ, MVCOUNT, REPORT, TEDIT, TIME, TMPFILES, and WP.

Multiuser Configuration Settings

In a multiuser environment (FoxPro/LAN), users can have their own Config.fp files. When FoxPro starts up, it searches the DOS path until it finds a Config.fp. To specify the location of the Config.fp to be used, a DOS environment variable may be set from the DOS command level as follows:

```
SET FOXPROCFG=<location of Config.fp>
```

For example, if user Molly stores her Config.fp in her network home directory, F:\USERS\MOLLY, the following statement may be added to her Autoexec.bat file:

```
SET FOXPROCFG=F:\USERS\MOLLY\CONFIG.FP
```

Alternatively, FoxPro can be started with the following syntax to specify the location of the Config.fp file:

```
FoxPro -C<location of Config.fp>
```

Some of the configuration settings can affect performance on a network. These are OVERLAY, EDITWORK, SORTWORK, PROGWORK, and TMPFILES. These options specify alternate locations for the FoxPro overlay files and temporary files as follows:

Option	**Description**
OVERLAY	Specifies where FoxPro should place its overlay files. (Standard FoxPro only.)
EDITWORK	Specifies where FoxPro should place its text editor work files.
SORTWORK	Specifies where FoxPro should place its temporary work files for sorting and indexing.
PROGWORK	Specifies where the FoxPro cache file will be placed.
TMPFILES	Specifies a drive for EDITWORK, SORTWORK, and PROGWORK files if not otherwise specified.

Refer to Appendix B for more details. The usual advice is for you to consider assigning an alternate location for temporary files. For instance,

1. If you have more than one disk, you can improve performance by writing the temporary files to a disk other than the default drive.
2. When running on a network, you can improve performance by assigning a local drive for the alternate location of temporary files.

In some cases, you will encounter a fatal error if you run out of disk space when writing temporary files. For this reason, it is not advisable to assign a RAM disk for the alternate drive for EDITWORK, SORTWORK, or TMPFILES since temporary editor files and sort files can become quite large. It may be desirable to assign PROGWORK to a RAM disk, however, since the program cache file is generally smaller.

The SET EXCLUSIVE command is another important multiuser setting. This specifies whether files will be opened for EXCLUSIVE use by default. Generally it is preferable to SET EXCLUSIVE OFF to permit shared access to files. Note that even if SET EXCLUSIVE is OFF, files residing on a local drive will be opened EXCLUSIVEly, unless the DOS SHARE program has been loaded. You should not load SHARE unless your network requires it because local files will be opened for shared use (nonexclusively) by default.

The SET EMS Option

By default, standard FoxPro takes advantage of all expanded memory (EMS) it finds on your computer. It uses EMS to speed up all I/O operations such as sorting, indexing and other .dbf handling tasks. Standard FoxPro also uses EMS for its overlay file.

Extended memory must be mapped to expanded memory in order for standard FoxPro to use it. Commercial products are available to convert extended memory to expanded memory. For example, QEMM and 386Max can map extended memory on 80386-based machines to expanded memory. The same software allows memory-resident programs, including network shells, to be loaded in High RAM (memory area between 640 KB and 1 MB), freeing up more general purpose memory for use by FoxPro.

You can limit the amount of expanded memory that standard FoxPro uses by placing the following statement in your Config.fp file:

```
EMS = <n>
```

where *n* is the number of kilobytes of expanded memory you are allowing FoxPro to use. To prevent FoxPro from using any expanded memory, include the line

```
EMS = OFF
```

in the Config.fp file. Alternatively, you can turn EMS usage off by invoking FoxPro with the command line parameter of -e.

The Extended Version of FoxPro can take advantage of all available extended memory.

Changing a Configuration Setting in a Program

As we mentioned earlier, many of the FoxPro configuration settings can be changed from within a procedure. When you change a setting, though, you must consider the impact this change will have on the other procedures in your application. Often you need to establish a setting for a particular procedure, then return the setting to what it was when your procedure was called. Since you do not necessarily know what the configuration settings are at the time a procedure is called, you need a technique for saving the old setting, assigning the setting you require, then returning the setting to its original state.

The following code fragment demonstrates how to do this with SET EXACT as an example:

```
OldExact = SET("Exact")
SET EXACT ON
* Do some processing
SET EXACT &OldExact
```

Note that in this example it is possible that SET EXACT is already ON when your procedure is called. If this is the case, it would appear that the preceeding code fragment is unnecessary. It is necessary, however, because you cannot be certain that a setting will be what you expect at all times. The code shown here ensures that you will return a setting to its original state before exiting your procedure.

The FoxUser Resource File

The FoxUser resource file stores specific resource information such as the position of various windows, color settings, diary data, and Browse window settings. Each time a user changes a resource setting (such as changing the position of the Command window or adding a diary entry), FoxPro updates the FoxUser file with the information required to restore the environment the next time the user runs FoxPro. Figure 4-6 displays the FoxUser.dbf structure.

The Type, Id, and Name fields are used to categorize the entries. ReadOnly is used to identify an entry as permanent (if its value is set to .T., as described later). FoxPro computes CkVal by calculating the CRC-16 value of the Data field to ensure that the record is not corrupted. If the CkVal contained in the record does not match the current value FoxPro computes, the record is ignored. The Data field contains the actual data for the record—depending upon the type of record, this may contain binary values. The Updated field is the date the record was last updated.

FoxPro 2.0 internally indexes the FoxUser.Dbf file by Type, Id, and Name. The internally maintained index is not available to you or your end users.

Two SET commands affect the resource file: SET RESOURCE ON/OFF and SET RESOURCE TO <alternate file>. SET RESOURCE OFF (it is ON by default) disables the resource file and displays the environment with its default settings. SET RESOURCE TO allows you to specify an alternate .dbf containing resource information.

You can make several types of modifications to the FoxUser file. You can establish a permanent setting by changing the ReadOnly field in the record to

```
Structure for database: D:\FOXLAN\FOXUSER.DBF
Number of data records:       22
Date of last update    : 05/03/90
Field  Field Name  Type        Width    Dec
    1  TYPE        Character      12
    2  ID          Character      12
    3  NAME        Character      24
    4  READONLY    Logical         1
    5  CKVAL       Numeric         6
    6  DATA        Memo           10
    7  UPDATED     Date            8
** Total **                       74
```

Figure 4-6. The FoxUser.dbf structure.

.T., you can delete any setting by deleting the corresponding record, and you can add application-specific records. To make any modifications, you must first disable the resource file with SET RESOURCE OFF. Then you USE FOXUSER to access the data stored in the file.

Using any of the FoxPro commands to edit a .dbf (such as BROWSE), you can change the ReadOnly field from .F. (default) to .T. for any record you wish to make a permanent setting. For example, if you have moved your Command window and you want to make the new location permanent, find the record where ID = "WindCmd" and change the ReadOnly value to .T. Then, even if you move the Command window to another location later, FoxPro will always start out with the window in the position stored in the .dbf.

You can also delete any of the records in the FoxUser file. If you do delete one or more record, you should also PACK the file. In the absence of a record specifying a particular setting, FoxPro presents a resource in its default configuration (location, color, and so on).

In addition, an application may add its own records to the FoxUser file. This is handy whenever a user-specific piece of information is required, since the application can rely on the fact that the FoxUser.dbf file is always there for each user. A good example of a record an application could add to each user's FoxUser.dbf file is a system password. If you add records to the FoxUser file, be sure to compute the CkVal value of the Data field using the SYS(2007) function.

When you are finished modifying resource information, close the FoxUser file and SET RESOURCE ON.

In a multiuser environment, either all users must have their own resource file or the resource file must be set to read-only (by setting the DOS read-only attribute) to allow it to be shared. Prior to version 2.0, FoxPro required that each user always have his or her own resource file.

If you wish to give users their own resource files, you can either run the AddUser program for each user or place a resource file in each user's home directory on the network. You can specify the location of the resource file at startup with the following setting in the Config.fp file:

```
RESOURCE = <pathname>
```

Chapter Summary

A modular approach to system design improves your application by making it easier to understand, debug, and maintain. There are a number of ways to create and call separate program modules in FoxPro. These separate program modules can be FoxPro functions or procedures, programs written in assembly language or C and either converted to .bin files or used with the FoxPro APIs, or external programs or commands that are invoked with the RUN command. Whatever your set consists of, it is important to maintain a set of library routines for use by your entire application. In this chapter we presented a number of sample library programs that you can use in your application.

FoxPro provides a built-in help facility that can be integrated with an application. We discussed the advantages and disadvantages of using this facility, and presented an alternative for implementing a custom help system. We also introduced several options for performing data validation, including the use of a .dbf containing all screen field validation expressions, and we demonstrated the various techniques with sample programs.

Error trapping and processing is an important issue that must be addressed in order to maintain and support an application. We summarized useful commands and functions for diagnosing errors and provided a program designed to trap errors, present a consistent message to the user, and generate a comprehensive error report. We also briefly summarized the FoxPro trace and debug facilities.

Finally, we reviewed customization options available in the Config.fp file and the FoxUser resource file. We discussed the highlights of these options and emphasized their use in a multiuser environment.

Chapter 5

Template Language Processing

FoxPro 1.x, like FoxBASE+, includes a utility program called FoxView, which helps ease tedious programming chores by letting you create application screens and generating the programs that use those screens. The type of programs that FoxView produces out of the screens you design depends on the template you select. Templates are like program blueprints—they contain instructions on how a program should be written as well as "blanks" that a program generator will fill in later with data from your screen forms and databases.

If you do not like the code that FoxView generates, all you need to do is change the template. You do that by using FoxCode, which is FoxView's template language compiler. The problem with FoxCode, and products like it, is that before you can use it, you need to learn yet another language—the template language. And, as if that is not enough, no two template language products in today's Dbase market use the same language. So, unless you expect to write and use a lot of templates, it hardly seems worth the trouble to learn yet another language for generating code out of screen forms.

FoxPro 2.0 Template Language

FoxPro 2.0 has a revolutionary and elegant concept in template language processing—template (or textmerge) facility without a new language. In FoxPro, you can create entire applications without learning a new and strange language. Instead you use the same, familiar FoxPro commands and functions augmented with a handful of new commands. Table 5-1 briefly describes these commands.

Note that the output, or target, file of FoxPro's textmerge facility need not be a program—it can be a plain text file. If the target file is a program, it need not be a FoxPro program. Essentially the textmerge facility can be used to write programs in any language, including C, Pascal, or WordPerfect macros.

To write a FoxPro program that writes a text file or another program, you first need to activate the textmerge facility with the SET TEXTMERGE ON command. From that point on and until you SET TEXTMERGE OFF, all expressions embedded inside the textmerge delimiters (by default, these are the double angle brackets) are evaluated. For instance, with SET TEXTMERGE ON, the code fragment

```
TEXT
  Today is <<DATE()>>
ENDTEXT
```

will output a line such as

```
Today is 02/20/92
```

If SET TEXTMERGE is off, the output will be

```
Today is <<DATE()>>
```

Similarly, with SET TEXTMERGE ON and a memory variable WName whose value is MenuWind, the command

```
\ACTIVATE WINDOW <<wname>>
```

will write the code

```
ACTIVATE WINDOW MenuWind
```

to the currently active output device. The single backslash tells FoxPro to write the line following the backslash to the output device, after first evaluating any expression inside the textmerge delimiters (since SET TEXTMERGE is ON).

Table 5-1. FoxPro 2.0 Commands to Support Template Language Processing

`\<text line>` and `\\<text line>`

Sends the ensuing text line to the textmerge file without using the TEXT-ENDTEXT construct. The text line may include any combination of memory variables, text, commands, functions, or expressions. The single backslash causes the output line to be preceded by the linefeed and carriage return pair. The double backslash suppresses sending the usual linefeed and carriage return before the text line.

```
SET TEXTMERGE [ON | OFF] [TO <file> [ADDITIVE]]
[WINDOW <window_name>] [SHOW | NOSHOW]
```

Enables or disables the evaluation of memory variables, functions, and expressions before outputting the lines to the textmerge file. Output may be directed to <file> or <window_name>. NOSHOW suppresses output to the screen.

```
SET TEXTMERGE DELIMITERS [TO] [<expC1> [, <expC2>]]
```

Specifies the textmerge delimiters. <expC1> and <expC2> are the left and right delimiters, respectively. By default, these are the double angle brackets, << and >>. If you do not specify <expC2>, <expC1> will act as both left and right delimiters.

`TEXT` and `ENDTEXT`

Sends all text lines (consisting of text, expressions, functions, memory variables, or any combination) to the current output device. Output is usually directed to a low-level file whose handle is stored in the _TEXT system memvar.

```
_PRETEXT = <expC>
```

Specifies the character expression to be used to precede all textmerge lines. For instance, the output lines can be indented by defining <expC> as the tab character.

```
_TEXT = <expN>
```

Specifies the handle of the low-level file to which output from \ , \\ , and TEXT-ENDTEXT is directed.

Specifying the Target File

Typically the output device in textmerge processing is the program being generated, that is, the target program. How do you tell FoxPro what the target program is? You can do it in either of two ways. One way is to issue the SET TEXTMERGE TO <file> command. Another way is to open or create a low-level file with FOPEN( ) or FCREATE( ), and then to assign the resulting file handle to the _TEXT system memvar. Therefore the following two commands are functionally equivalent:

```
SET TEXTMERGE TO "Nikki.Prg"
_TEXT = FCREATE("Nikki.Prg")
```

The ADDITIVE clause of the SET TEXTMERGE TO <file> command lets you cumulate output intended for the file. The _TEXT facility lets you create programs that write code to multiple files. For instance, if you want to generate an application that writes the main program to one file and all other procedures to another file, you can control which output lines go where simply by changing the value of _TEXT to the file handle of either the main program or the procedure file.

Normally, output destined for the target file also displays on the screen. To prevent generated lines from showing on the screen, use the NOSHOW option of the SET TEXTMERGE command.

Outputting Generated Lines

As was shown in Table 5-1, the textmerge facility includes the following two command sets to send output to the target file:

- \ or \\
- TEXT and ENDTEXT

Normally you would use \ or \\ to send individual lines to the target file. You would use the TEXT-ENDTEXT construct to send entire blocks of lines to the target file. Because \\ does not prepend the linefeed and carriage return pair to the output line, you would use the double backslash if you needed to build various portions of the output line from several segments of your program.

The TEXT-ENDTEXT pair is, of course, not new to FoxPro 2.0. Indeed, it has been around since dBASE II days. What is new to FoxPro 2.0 is the ability to send all lines between TEXT and ENDTEXT to the handle assigned to the

_TEXT system memvar. In this context, the TEXT-ENDTEXT pair is equivalent to the <<#PRAGMA-#>> pair of FoxCode. The TEXT-ENDTEXT construct lets you write readable FoxPro programs that use the textmerge facility.

Steps to Template Language Processing

To summarize, building a FoxPro program that writes another program or a target text file involves just a few steps:

1. Use the SET TEXTMERGE TO <file> command to define the file where the generated code will be written. Alternatively, open the file using the FCREATE( ) or FOPEN( ) command and then assign the file handle to the _TEXT system memvar.
2. SET TEXTMERGE to ON. From this point on and until you SET TEXTMERGE OFF, any expressions, functions, and memvars enclosed in TEXTMERGE delimiters and found in lines beginning with a single or double backslash or found between TEXT and ENDTEXT are evaluated before the line is written to the output file. You write lines to the file either by beginning them with a single or double backslash or by placing them inside the TEXT-ENDTEXT construct.
3. Close the output file using the SET TEXTMERGE TO command. Alternatively, you may close the file with the FCLOSE (_TEXT) command.

Template Language Processing Applications

FoxPro's template language facility becomes an even more powerful tool because FoxPro 2.0 maintains most of its files in the familiar .dbf format. These include the screen (.scx), menu (.mnx), report (.frx), and label (.lbx) files. Indeed, some of the best examples of template language processing in FoxPro are the GENMENU and GENSCRN utility programs, which come with the software. These programs can be used to automate writing entire applications around menus and screens that you design.

The WhatsNew.prg program in Listing 5-1 shows a simple example of how you might use FoxPro's textmerge facility. The program reads the Foxhelp.dbf file and extracts summary data of everything that is new in FoxPro 2.0. Note that the USE FOXHELP AGAIN command is functionally equivalent to turning on the help facility (using SET HELP TO) and then USEing the Foxhelp file.

Listing 5-1. Whatsnew.prg uses template language commands to generate a file containing summary data extracted from Foxhelp.dbf.

```
*************************************************************
* Program ...: WhatsNew.prg
* Author ....: P. L. Olympia & Kathy Cea
* Purpose....: Reads FoxPro's FoxHelp database and writes
*            : what's new entries into a textmerged file
* Syntax ....: DO WhatsNew
* Notes .....: From the book: Developing FoxPro 2.0 Applications
*            : Shows a simple example of FoxPro 2.0's textmerge
*            : facility
*************************************************************

CLEAR
SET TALK OFF
SET SAFETY OFF
SET MEMOWIDTH TO 78

USE foxhelp AGAIN     && note the new AGAIN clause

SET TEXTMERGE TO whatsnew.mrg     && Open target file
SET TEXTMERGE ON NOSHOW           && Activate template lang facility
 TEXT
              This was created using TextMerge

     Today is:                   <<DATE()>>   <<TIME()>>
     FOXHELP Last Update:        <<LUPDATE()>>
     FOXHELP Number of Records:  <<RECC()>>

 ENDTEXT

 SCAN FOR  "wn" $ class      && Process What's New entries

    TEXT

-=-=-=-=-=-=-=-=-=-=-=-=-=-=-=-=-=-=-=-=-=-=-=-=
--> Record No. <<Recno()>>
--> Topic: <<TOPIC>>

    ENDTEXT
```

(continued)

Listing 5-1. Continued

```
    ? "Writing ... ", topic

    n = MEMLINES(details)
    _mline = 0              && must reset _mline to 0
    FOR i = 1 TO n
        \<<MLINE(details, 1, _mline)>>
    NEXT
ENDSCAN

SET TEXTMERGE TO            && close target file
USE
SET SAFETY ON
SET TALK ON
RETURN
*eof*
```

The program writes extracted data to the target file WhatsNew.mrg preceded by header information, including today's date and time and Foxhelp.dbf's last update date. The program writes the text of the desired records using the \<<MLINE( )>> command.

Recall that the new Foxhelp file has the following structure:

```
Structure for database : FOXHELP.DBF
Number of data records : 725
Date of last update    : 5/13/91
Field  Field Name  Type        Width    Dec    Index
    1  TOPIC       Character      30
    2  DETAILS     Memo           10
    3  CLASS       Character      20
** Total **                       61
```

Database records with the code "wn" in the CLASS field have the summary data of new features in FoxPro 2.0. If you want to extract the complete description of most everything that is new or enhanced in FoxPro 2.0, replace the SCAN statement in the program with the following statement:

```
SCAN FOR 'nx' $ CLASS .OR. 'ex' $ CLASS
```

Lbx2Prg—Converting a Label Form into Source Code

One extremely useful application of FoxPro's template language processing facility is a utility program that can convert a mail label form into a program. With such a utility, you need not distribute a set of two files (.lbx and .lbt) for each label form that your application needs. You can simply use the utility to convert the files to source code and include that in your procedure file. An even better reason for having the utility is to get around FoxPro's inability to skip blank lines in a mail label. You can build the converted program so that it does not print blank address lines.

Listing 5-2 shows Lbx2Prg.prg, a program that converts a FoxPro 2.0 label form into source code. To keep the program short and focused on the textmerge facility, the program is designed to handle only 1-up labels. To extend the program to a version that can handle multiple labels across a page, you would probably want to use arrays to hold the data for each line of a label page.

To understand how the program works, you need to know something about the structure of the .lbx file, which is as follows:

```
Structure for database : NAD.LBX
Date of last update    : 5/13/91  (Beta4)
Field  Field Name  Type        Width    Dec   Index
    1  OBJTYPE     Numeric         2
    2  OBJCODE     Numeric         2
    3  NAME        Memo           10
    4  EXPR        Memo           10
    5  STYLE       Memo           10
    6  HEIGHT      Numeric         3
    7  WIDTH       Numeric         3
    8  LMARGIN     Numeric         3
    9  NUMACROSS   Numeric         3
   10  SPACESBET   Numeric         3
   11  LINESBET    Numeric         3
   12  ENVIRON     Logical         1
   13  ORDER       Memo           10
   14  UNIQUE      Logical         1
   15  TAG         Memo           10
   16  TAG2        Memo           10
   17  ADDALIAS    Logical         1
** Total **                       86
```

Listing 5-2. Lbx2Prg.prg uses template language commands to convert a FoxPro label form into source code.

```
************************************************************
* Program ...: Lbx2Prg.prg
* Author ....: P. L. Olympia & Kathy Cea
* Purpose....: Converts a FoxPro 2.0 label file (.lbx) into
*             : source code using FoxPro 2.0's template
*             : language facility
* Syntax ....: DO Lbx2Prg
* Notes .....: From the book: Developing FoxPro 2.0 Applications
*             : This version handles only 1-up labels
************************************************************

CLEAR
SET TALK OFF

* Get the name of the .lbx file and filter condition (if wanted)

  lbxfile = SPACE(20)
  filtexp = SPACE(40)
  @ 10, 1 SAY "Name of .lbx file to translate:  " GET lbxfile PICT "@!"
  @ 11, 1 SAY "Condition for selecting records: " GET filtexp
  READ

  lbxfile = TRIM(lbxfile)
  filtexp = TRIM(filtexp)
  i = AT(".LBX", lbxfile)
  IF i > 1
     lbxfile = SUBSTR(lbxfile, 1, i-1)   && root name
  ENDIF

  lbx = lbxfile + ".LBX"
  lbt = lbxfile + ".LBT"
  prg = lbxfile + ".PRG"

  SET TEXTMERGE TO (prg)      && Code will be written to this file
  SET TEXTMERGE ON            && Enable template lang processing

  * Write the lines between TEXT-ENDTEXT to prg
```

(continued)

Listing 5-2. Continued

```
TEXT
  *-- Created by Platinum Software International's Lbx2Prg Template
  *-- On <<DATE()>>      <<TIME()>>
  *-- This version is only for 1-up labels

  SET TALK OFF
ENDTEXT

* Make sure lbx & lbt files are available
      IF .NOT. ( FILE ((lbx)) .AND.  FILE((lbt)) )
          ? "Problem: ", lbx, " and/or ", lbt, " not found"
          QUIT
      ENDIF
SELECT 25
USE (lbx) ALIAS lbxf
* Look for record with OBJTYPE = 2 (database info)
  LOCATE FOR lbxf.objtype = 2
  DO ChkifOK

TEXT
  dbf = [<<lbxf.name>>]
  IF .NOT. FILE((dbf))
     ? dbf, " not found"
     QUIT
  ENDIF

  SELECT <<lbxf.objcode>>
  USE (dbf)
ENDTEXT

  IF EMPTY(lbxf.order) .AND. !EMPTY(lbxf.tag2)
     \     SET ORDER TO TAG <<lbxf.tag2>>
  ENDIF
  IF !EMPTY(lbxf.order)
     \     SET INDEX TO <<lbxf.order>>
  ENDIF
```

(continued)

Listing 5-2. Continued

```
    * Get the dimensions of the label
    LOCATE FOR lbxf.objtype = 30
    DO ChkIfOK

  TEXT

    *-- Define label dimensions
      m.height = <<lbxf.height>>
      m.width  = <<lbxf.width>>
      m.lmargin = <<lbxf.lmargin>>
      m.numacross = <<lbxf.numacross>>
      m.spacesbet = <<lbxf.spacesbet>>
      m.linesbet  = <<lbxf.linesbet>>
      m.indent = IIF(m.lmargin = 0, "",SPACE(m.lmargin))

      DO PrtSetup    && Call your custom set-up routine

  ENDTEXT

      IF LEN(filtexp) = 0
         \  SCAN
      ELSE
         \  filtexp = [<<filtexp>>]
         \  SCAN FOR EVAL(filtexp)
      ENDIF

         \    numwritten = 0
    SCAN FOR  lbxf.objtype = 19      && label lines
         \
      IF !EMPTY(lbxf.expr)
         \    line = <<TRIM(lbxf.expr)>>
         \    DO PrtLine
      ENDIF
    ENDSCAN

  TEXT
     *-- Advance to next label
```

(continued)

Listing 5-2. Continued

```
          lineleft = m.height + m.linesbet - numwritten
          IF lineleft > 0
             ?? REPLICATE(CHR(13)+CHR(10), lineleft)
          ENDIF
     ENDSCAN

     *-- Cleanup
     SET TALK ON
     RETURN

        PROCEDURE PrtLine
        IF !EMPTY(line)
           ?? m.indent + line
           ?
           numwritten = numwritten + 1
        ENDIF
        RETURN

        PROCEDURE PrtSetup
        *-- Set up your output device here, e.g. SET DEVICE TO, SET PRIN
        RETURN
     ENDTEXT

    =FCLOSE(_text)    && alternatively SET TEXTMERGE TO
    SET TALK ON
    RETU

   PROCEDURE ChkifOK
      IF .NOT. FOUND()
          ? "LBX file is not a FoxPro 2.0 label file"
          QUIT
      ENDIF
   RETURN
   *eof*
```

The Objtype field determines what kind of data resides in the record. For instance, the record with Objtype = 30 contains the dimensions of the label. The record with Objtype = 2 contains database information, and records with Objtype = 19 contain the expressions for the various label lines.

The program first prompts you for the name of the .lbx file to convert and the (optional) filter expression that you would normally use with the label form. One example of a filter expression is STATE = 'MD'. The program next verifies that the .lbx file and its associated memo file exist. Then it creates a target file (which will contain the generated code) using the same primary name as the .lbx file but with a .prg extension.

The program determines the environment that the label requires by retrieving the subject .dbf and its work area from the .lbx record with Objtype = 2. The program next sets the appropriate index by looking at the Order and Tag2 fields. Note that the program then locates the .lbx record with Objtype = 30 to find the label dimensions. Because Lbx2Prg works only with 1-up labels, it does not use label properties such as width. However, it uses the value of the Lmargin field for indenting each label line. It also uses the values of the Height and Linesbet fields to determine how many lines are required to advance to the next label.

The heart of the program is the block of code that SCANs for .lbx records with Objtype = 19. Each such record represents a label line, and Lbx2Prg generates the code to print each one so long as it is not blank.

The best way to understand how Lbx2Prg works is to examine the code that it produces. Listing 5-3 shows one such generated program (Nad.prg) that uses a label with five lines. The expression contained in the first four label lines is as follows:

```
TRIM(Fname) + SPACE(1) + Lname
Company
Street
TRIM(City) + ", " + UPPER(State) + SPACE(2) + Zip
```

FoxPro's label form facility can handle envelopes and Rolodex cards in addition to the usual mail labels. Thus Lbx2Prg should be able to handle envelopes and Rolodex cards as well. If you want additional practice in template language processing, a good way to start is by modifying Lbx2Prg so that it can handle multiple labels across a page.

Listing 5-3. Nad.prg is an example of a FoxPro program generated by Lbx2Prg from a mail label form.

```
*-- Created by Platinum Software International's Lbx2Prg Template
*-- On 06/01/91      15:40:57
*-- This version is only for 1-up labels

SET TALK OFF
dbf = [NAD.DBF]
IF .NOT. FILE((dbf))
   ? dbf, " not found"
   QUIT
ENDIF

SELECT 1
USE (dbf)
SET ORDER TO TAG NAME

*-- Define label dimensions
  m.height = 5
  m.width  = 35
  m.lmargin = 0
  m.numacross = 1
  m.spacesbet = 0
  m.linesbet  = 0
  m.indent = IIF(m.lmargin = 0, "",SPACE(m.lmargin))

  DO PrtSetup    && Call your custom set-up routine

filtexp = [lname = 'A']
SCAN FOR EVAL(filtexp)
  numwritten = 0

  line = TRIM(fname)+SPACE(1)+lname
  DO PrtLine

  line = Company
  DO PrtLine
```

(continued)

Listing 5-3. Continued

```
  line = Street
  DO PrtLine

  line = TRIM(City)+", "+UPPER(state)+SPACE(2)+zip
  DO PrtLine

*-- Advance to next label
   lineleft = m.height + m.linesbet - numwritten
   IF lineleft > 0
      ?? REPLICATE(CHR(13)+CHR(10), lineleft)
   ENDIF
ENDSCAN

*-- Cleanup
SET TALK ON
RETURN

  PROCEDURE PrtLine
  IF !EMPTY(line)
     ?? m.indent + line
     ?
     numwritten = numwritten + 1
  ENDIF
  RETURN

PROCEDURE PrtSetup
*-- Set up your output device here, e.g. SET DEVICE TO, SET PRIN
RETURN
```

Chapter Summary

FoxPro's template language, or textmerge facility, lets you write programs that write programs using "blanks," which are filled in later using information from databases and screen forms. Unlike any other template language facility, FoxPro's does not require you to learn yet another obscure language because it uses familiar Dbase-style commands with just a few extensions.

In this chapter, we described the set of commands you would need to perform textmerge. We also discussed the three basic steps for generating programs using FoxPro's textmerge facility. We showed two practical examples of programs that take advantage of template language commands, including Lbx2Prg, which converts a FoxPro label form to a program that can be integrated into a procedure file and then compiled.

Chapter 6

Handling Date and Time Data

The ease of unit conversion is clearly one of the advantages of the metric system over the English system of measurement. In the metric system, just about every conversion constant, regardless of the physical property being measured, is a multiple of 10; for example, there are 10 deciliters to a liter, 100 centigrams to a gram, and 1000 millimeters to a meter. On the other hand, it is difficult to keep track of the many conversion constants in the English system; for example, there are 12 inches to a foot, 3 feet to a yard, 16 ounces to a pound, and 4 quarts to a gallon.

Unfortunately our calendar system is worse than the English system of measurement where the uninitiated almost always need to carry a quick reference card to be reminded that although there are 12 months to a year, the number of days in a month may be any number from 28 through 31, depending on the month and year. As if that were not enough, people from different parts of the world cannot even agree on a standard date format. So, although Americans consider 07/04/11 to be the 135th anniversary of the Declaration of Independence, the Japanese know that date as April 11, 1907, and the French recognize it as April 7, 1911.

Imagine how much computer code could be saved if only we had a calendar system where every month had 30 days and everyone were satisfied with a single date format like YYYY/MM/DD. As it is, a typical computer program includes so much code just to do such things as date validation. Luckily FoxPro spares us much of the drudgery by providing us with date-smart facilities. For example, the @D PICTURE format of @...SAY/GET command, as in

```
@ 10,12 SAY "Enter Date of Birth: " GET dob PICTURE '@D'
```

validates the user-supplied value for the date variable, taking into account the current SETting of the date format (American, Japanese, and so on). Thus we need not write a separate procedure to break the entered data into month, day, and year. We also need not ensure that each date component falls within proper bounds, for example, the day cannot be larger than 28 if the month is February unless the year is a leap year.

Of course, we could easily write a customized date validation routine using FoxPro's date functions such as DTOC( ). For instance, a clever technique for ensuring that a user-supplied character string represents a valid date is to convert it to a date variable using the CTOD( ) function, then convert it back to characters using DTOC( ), and finally compare the result with the original, user-supplied value. If the input variable is DOB, the following code fragment illustrates the technique:

```
dob = ALLTRIM(dob)          && trim leading & trailing blanks
IF DTOC(CTOD(dob)) = dob
   * input value is valid date
   * proceed with the rest of the program
ELSE
   * invalid date input
   * process error
ENDIF
```

The technique works because FoxPro returns a blank date when CTOD( ) is invoked with a character string that translates to an invalid date, for example, 02/29/91. In that case, converting the result back to a string by way of the DTOC( ) function results in a value that is different from the original string. On the other hand, DTOC(CTOD(expC)) returns expC again if it translates to a valid date, for instance, 02/28/91. Obviously, the IF statement in the preceding code fragment could be replaced by a statement such as

```
IF EMPTY(CTOD(dob))
```

but this works only in FoxPro, whereas the earlier code works in dBASE III PLUS, dBASE IV, FoxBASE+, and others.

Table 6-1 summarizes the FoxPro functions for handling date and time data.

Table 6-1. Summary of FoxPro Time and Date Functions

Function	**Description**
{mm/dd/yy}	Converts the literal mm/dd/yy to date. See also CTOD( ). *Example:* {02/20/92}
BETWEEN(d1,d2,d3)	Returns .T. if d1 is a date that falls between the two dates d2 and d3. This function accepts date, numeric, or character arguments so long as all three parameters are of the same type. *Example:* ? BETWEEN({01/15/92}, {12/25/89},{02/20/92}) .T.
CDOW(d)	Returns the name of the weekday corresponding to date, d. *Example:* ? CDOW({02/18/92}) Tuesday
CMONTH(d)	Returns the name of the month of date, d. *Example:* ? CMONTH({12/25/92}) December
CTOD(s)	Converts character string, s, to a date variable. The format of the string depends on the current setting of SET DATE and SET CENTURY. See also {mm/dd/yy}.
DATE( )	Returns the system date. Default format is MM/DD/YY.
DAY(d)	Returns a number corresponding to the day of date, d. *Example:* ? DAY({02/20/92}) 20
DMY(d)	Returns the date in the format DD Month YY (or DD Month YYYY if SET CENTURY is on). *Example:* ? DMY({12/25/92}) 25 December 92

(continued)

Table 6-1. Continued

Function	Description
DOW(d)	Returns a number, 1–7, corresponding to the day of the week of date, d. Sunday is 1, Saturday is 7. *Example:* isweekend = MOD(DOW(date_var)-1,6) <>0 returns .T. if a date falls on a weekend.
DTOC(d,[1])	Converts date, d, to a character string. Useful for concatenating dates with character variables and literals, and for comparing two dates. The optional second parameter, 1, returns the date string in YYYYMMDD just like the DTOS function does. *Example:* ? DTOC(DATE( )) > DTOC(Today) .F. *Example:* ? DTOC({02/20/91},1) 19910220
DTOS(d)	Converts date, d, to a character string of the form YYYYMMDD regardless of the setting of SET CENTURY and SET DATE. Useful in indexing on date expressions. *Example:* INDEX ON DTOS(hiredate) TO EmpHire
EMPTY(d)	Returns .T. if date, d, is null. This function also works with arguments of character, numeric, logical, and memo data types. *Example:* IF EMPTY(HireDate) ? 'HireDate should not be blank' ENDIF
GOMONTH(d,n)	Returns the date that is n months after or before date, d. *Example:* ? GOMONTH({02/20/92},3) 05/20/92 *Example:* ? GOMONTH({02/20/92},-3) 11/20/91

(continued)

Table 6-1. Continued

Function	Description
INLIST(d1,d2,d3...)	Returns .T. if date d1 is included in the list d2,,d3... . This can be used for validating a date. INLIST( ), like BETWEEN( ), is not specific to dates per se, but can be used also for other data types such as character; the only restriction is that all arguments must be of the same data type. *Example:* IF INLIST(DATE( ),hol1,hol2,hol3) ? 'Today is one of 3 holidays' ENDIF
MDY(d)	Returns the date in the format Month DD, YY (or Month DD, YYYY, if SET CENTURY is on). *Example:* SET CENTURY ON ? MDY({12/25/92}) December 25, 1992
MONTH(d)	Returns a number representing the month of date, d. *Example:* ? MONTH({12/25/99}) 12
SECONDS( )	Returns the number of seconds since midnight with a resolution of one millisecond. This is the same value produced by the SYS(2) function except that SECONDS( ) returns the value as a number in seconds.thousandths format, whereas SYS(2) returns the value as a whole number expressed in a character string. *Example:* ? SECONDS( ) 7345.678
SYS(1)	Returns a character string representing the Julian period number of the current system date. *Example:* ? SYS(1) 2447943

(continued)

Table 6-1. Continued

Function	Description
SYS(2)	Returns a character string representing the number of seconds since midnight. This function differs from SECONDS( ) in that it returns the number as an integer and in character form, whereas SECONDS( ) returns the same value as a numeric with millisecond level precision. *Example:* ? SYS(2) 7346
SYS(10,n)	Converts the Julian period number, n, to the equivalent Gregorian date expressed as a character string. *Example:* ? SYS(10, 2447943) 02/20/90
SYS(11,d_c)	Converts a date expression or a character string in date format to the corresponding Julian number expressed as a character string. If the date parameter is the system date, this function returns the same value as the SYS(1) function. *Example:* ? SYS(11, DATE( )) 2447943
TIME( )	Returns the system time as a character string in the 24-hour format HH:MM:SS, for example, 13:55:10. *Example:* t = IIF(VAL(t)<12,t+ 'am',IIF(VAL(t)=12,t + 'pm', STR(VAL(t)-12,2)+SUBS(t,3)+'pm')) converts time, t, to standard 12-hour format.
YEAR(d)	Returns a four-digit number representing the year of date, d. *Example:* ? YEAR({12/25/92}) 1992

Summary of Important FoxPro Date/Time Features

In FoxBASE+, as in dBASE III PLUS, a character string can be converted to a date value using the CTOD( ) function. FoxPro, like dBASE IV, has a more convenient alternative to the function—the curly brackets can be used to convert a string literal to date values. Thus the following commands give the same result:

```
? DTOC("02/20/92")
? {02/20/92}
```

FoxPro has all the new date functions of dBASE IV, including MDY( ) and DMY( ) to print date values in familiar formats as well as DTOS( ) to facilitate using dates in index expressions. FoxPro has other unique commands and functions. For instance, GOMONTH( ) returns a date that is a specified number of months from a given date. The SYS(11) function, which returns the Julian date, is a great timesaver in date arithmetic operations.

In dBASE III PLUS and FoxBASE+, subtracting the base date from a date variable yields the proper numeric value. The base date is the date the world began according to dBASE. In FoxPro, as in dBASE IV, subtracting the base date from a date variable yields only zero. The earliest date that can be displayed in FoxPro is 03/00/0000, corresponding to the Julian number 1721119. Any date earlier than this yields a blank date. On the other hand, the earliest date that can be converted with the CTOD( ) function is 01/01/0100. Any string earlier than this causes CTOD( ) to return a date in the 1900s.

Date Operations

FoxPro treats dates as special types of numbers that can be used in some arithmetic operations, for example:

```
datev1 - datev2 =  number    && gives elapsed days
datev1 + number =  datev3    && new date later than datev1
datev1 - number =  datev4    && new date earlier than datel.
```

The first expression results in a positive or negative number depending on whether Datev1 is earlier or later than Datev2.

On the other hand, subtracting a date from a number or adding two dates together would not make sense, so the two commands

```
? 12345  - datev1
? datev2 + datev3
```

produce the error message "Operator/Operand type mismatch."

In a typical business application, date arithmetic operations such as those shown here ease the computation of elapsed days or of dates for making critical business decisions. FoxPro handles the chore of figuring out how many days are in each of the months involved in the computation.

dBASE IV and FoxPro have an important incompatibility related to date values and date calculations. In FoxPro any date conversion that yields an invalid date always yields an empty date. For example,

```
? {01/32/91}          && No such date
   /  /
```

In dBASE IV, there really are no invalid dates. dBASE IV automatically performs the implied arithmetic in a date that appears invalid in order to yield a valid date. For example,

```
? {01/32/91}          && Seems invalid but dBASE IV
 02/01/91             && translates to next day
```

dBASE IV's undocumented ability to perform the date arithmetic implied in a seemingly invalid date value can be put to good use for determining past and future dates with shorthand notation. For instance, if the date format is American and today's date is 02/20/92, and we want to know what date is 214 days from today, we can always say

```
? DATE() + 214, or
? {02/20/92} + 214
```

but it is much easier to say

```
? {02/234/92}          && Just add 214 to the day
```

Date Comparisons

Relational operators may be used on dates, as well as on numeric or character variables, to yield a logical (.T. or .F.) result. For instance,

```
. ? date1 >= date2
  .T.
. ? date3 = date4
  .F.
```

Use the EMPTY( ) function to test whether or not a date variable is blank, or whether or not a date literal is invalid.

```
. ? EMPTY({})
  .T.
. ? EMPTY({12/32/92})
  .T.
```

Time data may be packed with dates, so the safest way to test whether two dates are identical is to first convert them to character strings before making the comparison, for example,

```
. ? DTOC(datev1) = DTOC(datev2)
  .F.
```

Date Formats

FoxPro has the same set of display formats for dates as dBASE IV. Changing the display format does not alter the date field or the variable itself. The default format is American, but it may be overridden either by adding a line such as

```
DATE = JAPAN
```

to the CONFIG.FP file or by issuing the command

```
SET DATE <date-format>
```

in the command window or in a program, where the permissible <date-format> keywords and their display forms are as follows:

Date Format	**Display**
AMERICAN	MM/DD/YY
ANSI	YY.MM.DD
BRITISH	DD/MM/YY
FRENCH	DD/MM/YY
GERMAN	DD.MM.YY
JAPAN	YY/MM/DD
USA	MM-DD-YY
MDY	MM/DD/YY
DMY	DD/MM/YY
YMD	YY/MM/DD

Note that the French, British and DMY formats are the same; the Japan format is the same as YMD, and the American format is the same as MDY.

In dBASE IV, but not in FoxPro, you have to be wary of changing display formats while performing date arithmetic that involves date literals. As we have seen previously, dBASE IV automatically performs the date arithmetic implied in a date value. Therefore, values of date constants expressed as literals depend on the display format that is in effect, whereas the values of date fields or memory variables do not change with a change in date formats. Thus, if the currently active format is JAPAN, dBASE translates the date {02/20/90} to October 31, 1903, whereas FoxPro translates it to an empty date (since 20 is an invalid month).

If the SET CENTURY ON command is in effect, the year displays as a four-digit number, for instance, 1990. Otherwise, FoxPro defaults to SET CENTURY OFF, which assumes that the year is in the twentieth century, and only displays the last two digits of the year.

The function MDY( ), which should not be confused with the SET DATE format MDY, prints the date in the familiar display format: Month DD, YY, which comes in handy in applications that write mailmerge letters, for example,

```
. SET CENTURY ON
. ? MDY({02/20/92})
   February 20, 1992
```

Similarly, the function DMY( ) displays the preceding date in the format 20 February 1992.

Null Date

A date field in a database record that has not been initialized (to a valid date value) is a null date field. The statement

```
nulldate = {}
```

also creates a null date, which FoxPro displays as an empty (blank) date.

In FoxPro (as in FoxBASE+ and dBASE III PLUS or IV), any arithmetic operation involving a null date and a valued date field or variable always yields zero:

```
  today = DATE()
02/20/92
  ? nulldate - today
       0
  ? today - nulldate
       0
```

Similarly, all arithmetic operations involving a null date and a number always yield a null date:

```
? nulldate + 98765
/  /
? nulldate - 98765
/  /
```

In dBASE IV, comparing a null date variable to a valued (nonblank) one for inequality erroneously returns false:

```
? today <> nulldate
.F.
```

Here the dates had to be converted first to character in order to get the correct result.

```
? DTOC(today) <> DTOC(nulldate)
.T.
```

This is not a problem in FoxPro, where all comparisons with a null date always yield the correct value.

To test whether a date variable is null, use either of the following alternative IF clauses:

```
IF {} = datevar
IF EMPTY(datevar)
```

To understand why operations with null dates behave as they do, we need to know how FoxPro stores dates.

Date Storage Format

In a .dbf file, database records are stored as text. The values of numeric fields are stored as text, complete with any decimal points. Likewise, values of date fields are stored as text in the format YYYYMMDD, for example, 19901225 for December 25, 1990. On the other hand, FoxPro, like FoxBASE+ and dBASE, stores dates in memory and in .mem files not as text data, but as 8-byte numbers in IEEE (Institute of Electrical and Electronic Engineers) format consisting of an exponent, a significand, and a sign bit.

To confirm that FoxPro treats dates as numbers and stores them as such in a .mem file, all we need to do is define one date variable, save it to a .mem file, and inspect the result with DEBUG or similar utility, for example, Microsoft's symbolic debugger, SYMDEB.

```
  today = DATE()
  02/20/90
  display memory
  TODAY       pub   D  02/20/90
  save to test
  !symdeb test.mem
  -d100 12f
7D3A:0100  54 4F 44 41 59 00 00 00-00 00 00 44 00 00 00 00  TODAY......D....
7D3A:0110  00 00 00 00 00 00 00 00-00 00 00 00 00 00 00 00  ................
7D3A:0120  00 00 00 80 23 AD 42 41-1A FF 89 F0 BA 02 00 EB  ....#-  BA...p:..k
  -d1120
7D3A:0120  00 00 00 80 23 AD 42 41   +0.2447943E+7          <---- Today
```

From the 44h byte at location 010B (corresponding to the solitary "D" on the right) we know that TODAY is a date variable—44h translates to the

ASCII character "D." We can tell also that FoxPro "knows" the date 02/20/90 as the number (Julian period) 2447943.

One way to confirm that the date 02/20/90 is the same as the number 2447943 as far as FoxPro is concerned is to change the 44h byte to 4Eh (converting "D" to "N"), then restore the .mem file in FoxPro, and see what happens to the TODAY variable.

```
  -e10b 4e                    <--- change 44 to 4E
  -d100 10f
7D3A:0100  54 4F 44 41 59 00 00 00-00 00 00 4E 00 00 00 00  TODAY......N....
  -w                          <--- write the change back to file
   Writing 0029 bytes
  -q                          <--- quit Symdeb
. restore from test
. display memory
  TODAY       pub   N     2447943  (2447943.000000000000)
```

So, FoxPro now thinks TODAY is a numeric variable with the value that we expected. That confirms the notion that dates are just special types of numbers in FoxPro.

Listing 6-1 displays the Julian period corresponding to a given date, or the date corresponding to a given Julian period. The program uses as a reference date the beginning of the Gregorian calendar, namely, October 15, 1582, although any arbitrary date can be used also. This program produces the same results as the SYS(10) and SYS(11) functions.

FoxPro Base Date

We can now answer the question, "What does FoxPro consider as its base date, that is, date zero?" Since we now know that 02/20/90 is the same as the number 2447943, subtracting the latter from the former should tell us the base date.

```
. base = today - 2447943
  /  /
```

As you can see, FoxPro does not provide the information. Instead, it displays a null date. Let's check to see if it is really null, and then determine what number corresponds to a null date according to FoxPro.

Listing 6-1. F_Jul.prg, date, and Julian period converter function.

```
FUNCTION F_Jul
**********************************************************************
* Program :  F_Jul.prg
* Author :   P. L. Olympia and Kathy Cea
* Purpose :  Returns either Julian number or Gregorian date depending
*         :  whether the passed parameter is date or numeric.
*         :
* Syntax  :  x = F_Jul(date_num)
*         :  where date_num may be date or numeric. If date, the
*         :  function returns the Julian number just like SYS(11).
*         :  If date_num is numeric, the function returns the
*         :  Gregorian date, similar to that returned by the SYS(10)
*         :  function.
**********************************************************************
PARAMETER DateOrNum
Private dateref, julref, Jul_Greg
CentSet = SET("CENTURY")
SET CENTURY ON
*  Use some reference dates, e.g., the start of
*  the Gregorian calendar
dateref = {10/15/1582}
julref  = 2299161                  && Julian period for 10/15/1582
*  Determine the result depending on type of parameter passed
IF TYPE("DateOrNum") = "D"
   Jul_Greg = (DateOrNum - dateref) + julref
ELSE
   IF TYPE("DateOrNum") = "N"
      Jul_Greg = (DateOrNum - julref) + dateref
   ELSE
      Jul_Greg = "Invalid"
   ENDIF
ENDIF
* Reset CENTURY setting
SET CENTURY &CentSet
RETURN (Jul_Greg)
```

```
  nulldate={}
  /  /
  ? base = nulldate
  .T.                        && looks like base date is null
  save to test2
  !symdeb e:test2.mem
-d100 17f
891E:0100  54 4F 44 41 59 00 00 00-00 00 00 44 00 00 00 00  TODAY......D....
891E:0110  00 00 00 00 00 00 00 00-00 00 00 00 00 00 00 00  ................
891E:0120  00 00 00 80 23 AD 42 41-42 41 53 45 00 00 00 00  ....#-BABASE....
891E:0130  00 00 00 44 00 00 00 00-00 00 00 00 00 00 00 00  ...D............
891E:0140  00 00 00 00 00 00 00 00-00 00 00 00 00 00 00 00  ................
891E:0150  4E 55 4C 4C 44 41 54 45-00 00 00 44 00 00 00 00  NULLDATE...D....
891E:0160  00 00 00 00 00 00 00 00-00 00 00 00 00 00 00 00  ................
891E:0170  00 00 00 00 00 00 00 00-1A 03 2E 04 4F 04 00 00  ............O...
-dl148
891E:0148  00 00 00 00 00 00 00 00  +0.0E+0           <---  Base
-dl170
891E:0170  00 00 00 00 00 00 00 00  +0.0E+0           <---  Nulldate
```

The results show that indeed FoxPro considers its base date as a null date, and that the null date is zero. In contrast, dBASE IV considers null date as a large number (one googol), whereas dBASE III PLUS considers null date as infinity (a number divided by zero). In PLUS, the base date can be used in date calculations. For example,

```
.jul = DATE() - base
```

gives the correct numeric value, whereas the same expression gives zero in both FoxPro and dBASE IV.

We can easily deduce what date FoxPro considers as its base date. Using the function F_Jul.Prg in Listing 6-1 or the FoxPro SYS(11) function, we know that 12/31/90 is the 2448257th day in the FoxPro calendar. Therefore,

```
2448257 days ÷ 365.2425 days/year = 6703.10 years
```

have elapsed since the base date. Thus, the number of years B.C. is

```
6703.10 - 1990 = 4713.10.
```

If we can ignore the fractional part of 4713.10, the FoxPro base date must be January 1, 4713 B.C. This is the same date that astronomers consider to be the base date in the Julian calendar as devised by Joseph Scaliger in the sixteenth century.

Note that knowing FoxPro's base date, or the base date of any software for that matter, is more of an academic, rather than practical interest. It really doesn't matter which base date one chooses—it could be someone's birthday, for instance. A base date simply serves as a reference point for performing date arithmetic.

Packing Date and Time

We just saw that FoxPro stores dates in memory and in .mem files as numbers. These numbers need not be integers—they may contain a fractional component, which in this case would be time. For example (Schulman, 1987),

```
today = DATE()
02/20/92
today_noon = today + .5
02/20/92
tomorrow = today_noon + .5
02/21/92
```

We learn two lessons from this example. First, FoxPro stores date fractions. Second, precisely because of that, date comparisons such as

```
? today = today_noon
.F.
```

would seem to be inconsistent with the displayed values of the two variables. Thus the safe way to compare the two variables is to convert them first to character values:

```
? DTOC(today) = DTOC(today_noon)
.T.
```

Being able to pack date and time into one variable saves memory variable space and ensures that the two are always together. However, note that just as the DTOC( ) function strips away the fractional component of the date, time data packed with dates are lost when the date is stored in a .dbf file since, unlike dates in a .mem file, dates in a .dbf file are stored as text in the form YYYYMMDD.

Although FoxPro can pack time data into dates just like dBASE, it does not allow you to extract the fractional part of the date (that is, time data) since it insists on converting the value to an integer regardless of how SET FIXED and SET DECIMALS are defined.

Random Numbers and the System Clock

A few of FoxPro's built-in functions depend on the time kept by the system clock. For instance, the random number generator function RAND( ), when invoked with a negative number as a parameter, uses a seed value derived from the system clock. If FoxPro did not include a RAND( ) function, we could define our own equivalent function using other FoxPro functions such as SECONDS( ), which returns the number of seconds since midnight to the thousandth digit.

FoxPro developers often use the SYS(3) function, which uses the system clock, to generate a unique DOS filename for temporary files. In FoxPro 1.x, invoking this function repeatedly in a workstation with a fast processor produced nonunique filenames, causing problems in multiuser applications. This function now works as expected in FoxPro 2.0; it does not generate duplicate filenames even if two fast workstations invoked the function at the same time.

SYS(2015), new to FoxPro 2.0, is another function that uses the system clock. It generates a unique procedure name beginning with an underscore. Like SYS(3), this function generates truly unique names even if invoked repeatedly by a workstation with a fast processor.

Appending Date Data from a Delimited File

Many applications require that databases be loaded from a text file created somewhere else, for example, a mainframe computer. The FoxPro APPEND FROM...DELIMITED command provides the facility for doing just that. The traditional problem with most Dbase products is their inability to load date data contained in a DELIMITED file. In FoxPro 1.x, for example, a date value such as 12/31/91 in a DELIMITED file is ignored, resulting in a target date field that is blank. To get around this difficulty, programmers have had to write special code just to handle the chore of loading dates from a text file.

FoxPro 2.0 incorporates new logic in its APPEND FROM command which automatically takes care of loading dates from a DELIMITED file. It respects the SET DATE format that is currently active. Thus, if SET DATE is AMERICAN, and a delimited file contains the entry:

```
"Platinum Software",12/31/91,"North Potomac, MD"
```

the APPEND FROM...DELIMITED command loads the second value correctly into a date field without additional programming.

Averaging Dates

To compute the average value of a date field in a database, we need a reference point for computing elapsed days. This reference point could be the base date or some other date. In the following example, we compute the average of a date field, HireDate, using the date 01/01/80 as a reference.

```
refdate = {01/01/80}
AVERAGE ON (hiredate - refdate) TO ave_days
ave_hire = refdate + ave_days
```

Indexing on Dates

A date field may be used directly in an index expression to index a database in chronological order. For instance,

```
INDEX ON HireDate to EmpNdx.
```

If the index expression requires the concatenation of a date field and a character expression, use the DTOS( ) function to convert the date to character data in the form YYYYMMDD, regardless of the current setting of SET DATE and SET CENTURY. Alternatively, you may use the CTOD( ) function with the second parameter of 1, for example, CTOD(Date_Fld,1).

Early versions of FoxPro do not have built-in support for indexes in descending order. To index a file in reverse chronological order in those versions, we normally use a scheme where the date field is subtracted from a reference date that is early in the FoxPro calendar. For example,

```
startdate = {10/15/1582}
INDEX ON startdate  - <date_fld> TO <idxfile>
```

This is no longer necessary in FoxPro 2.0, which has the ASCENDING and DESCENDING clauses in the INDEX command for building compound index (.cdx) files. The DESCENDING clause is not supported when creating an .idx file. However, you can specify a descending order for an .idx file using the SET ORDER command.

Is It a Leap Year?

A leap year is a year that is divisible by 400 or by 4 depending on whether it is, respectively, a centennial year or not. Thus 1992 (divisible by 4) is a leap year, but 1990 is not. Similarly, 1900 was not a leap year (not divisible by 400), although the year 2000 will be. The function IsLeap in Listing 6-2 uses that definition and returns .T. if the year passed to the function is a leap year.

However, an easier way to tell whether a year is a leap year is to take advantage of FoxPro's knowledge of dates. Recall that FoxPro returns an empty date when it is asked to perform a string-to-date conversion that leads to an invalid date, for example, {12/32/90}. So, if we ask FoxPro to convert a string such as 02/29/90 to a date, it returns an empty date if 1990 is not a leap year, and a nonblank value otherwise. Thus our ISLEAP function could be coded using just one line:

```
isleap = !EMPTY({02/29/&yy})
```

where *yy* is a character variable representing the desired year and assuming a date format of American.

Note that this function does not work in dBASE IV. As we have already seen, dBASE IV does not return an empty date when given a string that represents an obviously invalid date since it automatically performs the implied arithmetic that will result in a valid date. We can use this dBASE IV feature to arrive at an equivalent function. Clearly, if 02/29 of a given year is the same as 03/01, the year is not a leap year; otherwise, it is. The equivalent dBASE IV function is then:

```
isleap = {02/29/&yy} < {03/01/&yy}.
```

Listing 6-2. IsLeap user-defined function returns .T. if a year is a leap year.

```
FUNCTION isleap
**********************************************************************
* Program :  IsLeap.prg
* Purpose :  Returns .T. if year is a leap year
*         :
* Syntax  :  YesNo = IsLeap(yy)
**********************************************************************
PARAMETER yy
* yy may be 2-digit or 4-digit numeric. Returns .T. if leap year
yy = INT(yy)
yy = IIF(yy < 100, 1900+yy, yy)     && assume 20th century year
                                    && if only two digits
yesno = (MOD(yy,4)=0 .AND. MOD(yy,100)<>0) ;
          .OR. mod(y,400)=0
RETURN(yesno)
```

How Many Days Remain in a Month or Year?

Given a date, say, Date_Fld, how many days remain in the month? The exercise is trivial once we know the last day of the month. To compute this for any month other than December, we first determine the first day of the following month and then subtract one from it.

```
last_day = CTOD(STR(MONTH(date_fld)+1) +
"/01/"+STR(YEAR(date_fld))) - 1
```

So,

```
days_left = last_day - date_fld
```

If the month is December, Days_Left is the same as the number of days that remain in a year. This number is much easier to determine since we always know the last day of the year:

```
dl_in_yr = CTOD("12/31/"+STR(YEAR(date_fld))) - date_fld
```

Computing the Number of Workdays

Many business applications require knowing the number of workdays between two dates, for example, applications that require tickler reports or reminder letters. Other applications may require knowing a future, promised date that is some number of workdays from a given start date.

Clearly the number of workdays between two dates is simply the number of elapsed days less weekends and holidays. We can always tell the weekends using the FoxPro DOW( ) function—Sundays yield 1 and Saturdays yield 7. Thus, the expression

```
isweekend = MOD(DOW(date_fld)-1,6) <>0
```

is true whenever DATE_FLD falls on a weekend.

To account for the holidays, we have a choice of either setting up a data file of holiday dates or constructing a long string of holidays that is hardcoded in the program. In general, we should avoid hardcoding constants in a program; setting up a data file of holidays gives us much more flexibility and is the preferred method, even though it requires another work area.

The user-defined function F_WRKDAY.PRG, shown in Listing 6-3, can be invoked in either of two ways:

```
Workdays = F_WRKDAY(begdate, enddate)
Fut_Date = F_WRKDAY(begdate, num_workdays)
```

The first syntax returns the number of workdays between the two specified dates. The second syntax returns a future date that is <num_workdays> days from <begdate>.

The program borrows some clever code from the Weekday.prg program (White, 1987). In particular, the line:

```
begdate = begdate + VAL(SUBSTR("1000002",DOW(begdate),1))
```

ensures that <begdate> does not fall on a weekend by advancing the date to the next Monday whenever the date falls on a Sunday (adds 1 to <begdate>) or Saturday (adds 2 to <begdate>).

Before using the program, you should create the data file Holiday.dbf and load it with all the dates your business considers as holidays. The file may

Listing 6-3. F_Wrkday.prg, returns number of workdays or future date.

```
FUNCTION F_WrkDay
**********************************************************************
* Program :  F_WrkDay.prg
* Author  :  P. L. Olympia and Kathy Cea
* Purpose :  Compute the number of workdays between 2 dates or
*         :  a future date from a given number of workdays from
*         :  a specified start date
*         :
* Syntax  :  workdays = F_WrkDay(begdate, enddate)  -or-
*         :  fut_date = F_WrkDay(begdate, num_workdays)
*         :
*         :  The first computes the # of workdays between the 2 dates
*         :  The 2nd computes a future date <num_workdays> from
*         :  <begdate>
**********************************************************************
PARAMETERS begdate,datenum
*       datenum = either enddate or number of workdays from begdate
*       Make sure begdate falls on a weekday
begdate = begdate + VAL(SUBSTR("1000002",DOW(begdate),1))
IF TYPE("datenum")="D"
   enddate = datenum - VAL(SUBSTR("2000001",DOW(datenum),1))
   elapsed = enddate - begdate + 1
   *       Subtract weekends
   workdays = elapsed - INT(elapsed/7) * 2
ELSE         && datenum = num of workdays
   workdays = datenum
   *       Add weekends
   elapsed = workdays + INT(workdays/5) * 2
ENDIF
USE holiday
COUNT TO numholi FOR holiday >= begdate;
      .AND. holiday <= begdate + elapsed - 1;
      .AND. MOD(DOW(holiday)-1,6) <>0
IF TYPE("datenum")="D"
   workdays = workdays - numholi
   RETURN(workdays)
```

(continued)

Listing 6-3. Continued

```
ELSE
   elapsed = elapsed + numholi
   enddate = begdate + elapsed - 1
   enddate = enddate - VAL(SUBSTR("2000001",DOW(enddate),1))
   RETURN(enddate)
ENDIF
*                 -EOP, F_Wrkday.Prg-
```

span a period of any number of years. Its structure consists of the following single date field:

```
HOLIDAY, D, 8.
```

The file may contain holidays, spanning multiple years if you wish, to compute the number of workdays between those years.

Chapter Summary

FoxPro treats dates as special types of numbers that can be used in some arithmetic operations. It supports a variety of formats for displaying dates. Changing display formats changes the results of arithmetic operations involving date literals.

Any arithmetic involving a null date and a valued date field or variable always yields zero. All arithmetic operations involving a null date and a number always yield a null date. Unlike dBASE IV, FoxPro produces the expected result when a null date is compared to a valued (nonblank) one. Whereas the dBASE IV null date translates to a very large number, the FoxPro null date has a numeric equivalent of zero.

FoxPro stores date values in .dbf files as text data, but stores them in memory and in .mem files as 8-byte numbers in IEEE format. The numbers are stored with fractional components, representing time values, so the safest way to check for date equality is to first convert dates to characters, using the DTOC( ) function, for example, prior to comparing them.

The FoxPro base date appears to be January 1, 4713 B.C., the same date that astronomers consider to be the base date in Joseph Scaliger's Julian Period system. FoxPro 2.0 contains new logic in its APPEND FROM...DELIMITED command that allows date data in a text file to be loaded correctly to a date field.

The chapter presents simple commands to average dates, index on dates, identify a leap year, and compute the number of days remaining in a month or year. It also shows a program that computes the number of workdays between two dates and a future date that is a given number of workdays from a start date.

Chapter 7

Memo Field Techniques

Memo fields are blocks of data normally used to store descriptive information about a database record. Unlike other FoxPro data types such as character or numeric, memo fields do not have predefined lengths—the space they occupy varies from record to record. Memo fields allow us to store and display large amounts of free-form text about the record, for example, a student's education and aptitude history, reviews of a given videotape movie by selected critics, or the text of a piece of legislation.

Why Use Memo Fields?

Most fields in a typical database (.dbf) are of type character. The perennial problem in designing a structure for a database that consists of character fields is determining the optimal length to assign to a field, given that all Dbase products preallocate the space whether or not the field contains data. For example, many applications require a REMARKS field for recording user comments about a database record. How do you arrive at the best length to assign to this field? Often, users cannot agree on the optimal length of this field. You may eventually decide on the maximum 254-character length, or even create multiple fields such as REMARK1, REMARK2, and so on, knowing that these fields could well be only partly filled for many records, thereby wasting precious disk space.

Memo fields are the way out of this dilemma for several reasons. They have variable length, the space they occupy is a function of their length, and memo fields that have not been assigned any values do not occupy any space. In the past, application users and developers avoided memo fields because they were extremely cumbersome to use and the software offered precious few commands and functions to manipulate them. These restrictions are gone in FoxPro, which treats memo fields like ordinary character fields, meaning that the rich set of functions for handling character data can be used to manipulate memo field data as well.

FoxPro's ability to store binary data in addition to text data in a memo field opens up a host of applications that truly are limited only by our imagination. For instance, graphics files or scanned images can be stored in FoxPro memo fields. Consequently we can easily develop a database of, say, WordPerfect art (.wpg files) or scanned photographs of houses for a real estate application. Given the proper hardware and sufficient memory, we could display the appropriate graphics stored in memo fields as a user browses through the database.

Another powerful way that takes advantage of memo fields' ability to contain any type of data is to use them for storing scanned letters and other correspondence in native word processing format for a correspondence control application. In Chapter 11, we will discuss how to use memo fields for producing user-revisable mailmerge letters without the aid of word processing software.

Summary of Memo Field Enhancements in FoxPro

FoxPro offers significant enhancements over FoxBASE+, dBASE IV, dBASE III PLUS, and compatible products in the use of memo fields. Some of the most important enhancements are summarized below and discussed in detail in subsequent sections.

- FoxPro allows text and binary data in a memo field including the null (ASCII decimal 0) and Ctrl-Z (ASCII decimal 26) characters. Of course, FoxBASE+ and dBASE III PLUS only allow text data.
- FoxPro memo field blocksize can be as small as 33 bytes and as large as 16,384 bytes, with the default at 64 bytes. dBASE IV's blocksize ranges from 512 through 16,384 bytes, in increments of 512, with the default at 512 bytes. Consequently FoxPro's memo files tend to occupy less space than those of dBASE IV. Note that the blocksize of FoxBASE+ and dBASE III PLUS memo fields is fixed at 512 bytes.
- Unlike dBASE IV, FoxPro has built-in commands that support storing varied types of data in a memo field, including memory variables, macros, and windows. It also has the complement commands to restore those saved values. FoxPro's ability to store memory variables in a

memo field allows us to use it as a space-saving file cabinet to store such things as printer control codes for a variety of printers supported by an application to replace multiple .mem files normally used for that purpose.

- Memo field data can be imported from, or exported to, an external file under program control, as in dBASE IV.
- In FoxPro, memo fields can be treated like character fields. It has many more functions for string manipulation of memo fields than dBASE IV.
- Memo field data can be accessed under program control. It can be viewed and edited using a predefined window. The MODIFY MEMO and @...EDIT commands permit the display and edit of multiple memo fields from any open work area in their own editing windows.
- Entry and reporting of memo fields are simple tasks in FoxPro. They can be entered, edited, or displayed in their own windows, which can be manipulated just like all other FoxPro windows.
- The new PACK MEMO command in FoxPro 2.0 gets rid of obsolete memo file data without the bother of COPYing the database.

FoxPro can read the database and memo files of all Dbase family members without first converting them with a special utility program. dBASE IV memo files are converted to FoxPro .fpt format, but they may be rewritten in dBASE III PLUS-style .dbt format with the command

```
COPY TO <dbfname> TYPE FOXPLUS
```

Once the file is converted, FoxPro can write directly to the file without first having to convert it to .fpt format. For the files to remain completely readable by other members of the Dbase family such as FoxBASE+, the memo fields should be edited in FoxPro so they do not contain binary data, particularly the Ctrl-Z character. The TYPE FOXPLUS option of the COPY command does not convert any fields of type F to the usual numeric N type. Therefore, if the .dbf structure is modified to contain a floating-point field, only dBASE IV can read the converted file since FoxBASE+ and compatible software do not support fields of type F. To export data from such a .dbf to FoxBASE+, either change the structure so it contains only N types for numeric data, or unload the data using the SDF or DELIMITED option of the COPY command and then import it to a FoxBASE+ file with a similar .dbf structure using the APPEND FROM command.

Table 7-1 summarizes the FoxPro commands and functions that involve memo fields or memo files. Commands that are specific to memo fields and files are so indicated. If a command has several forms, only the variant syntax pertinent to memo fields is listed.

Table 7-1. Summary of FoxPro Commands and Functions Involving Memo Fields and Memo Files

FoxPro Command/Function	Syntax and Description
$	<expC1> $ <memfld> Returns .T. if <expC1> is contained in memo field <memfld>.
@...SAY/GET	@ <row>, <col> SAY <expr> [PICTURE <p1>] [FUNCTION <fcode1>] GET <var> [PICTURE <p2>] [FUNCTION <fcode2>] [RANGE <expN1>[,<expN2]] [VALID <expL1> | <expN3>] [ERROR <expC3>] [WHEN <expL2>] [DEFAULT <expr2>] [MESSAGE <expC4>] [[OPEN] WINDOW <win name>] [COLOR ...] Displays formatted output to screen, window, or printer. The WINDOW clause allows editing of a memo field in a window defined previously with the DEFINE WINDOW command. The OPEN option automatically opens the editing window.
@...EDIT	@ <row, col> EDIT <var> [FUNCTION <expC2>] [DEFAULT <expr>] [ENABLE | DISABLE] SIZE <expN1>, <expN2> [, <ExpN3>] [NOMODIFY] [MESSAGE <expC3>] [VALID <expL1> [ERROR <expC4>]] [WHEN <expL2>] [TAB | NOTAB] [SCROLL] [COLOR SCHEME <expN4> | COLOR <color pair list>] Creates a rectangular text editing region for editing <var>, which may be a memo field, memvar, array element, or database field.

(continued)

Table 7-1. Continued

<table>
<tr><th>FoxPro
Command/Function</th><th>Syntax and Description</th></tr>
<tr><td>APPEND</td><td>APPEND [BLANK]
The BLANK option leaves memo fields empty.</td></tr>
<tr><td>APPEND MEMO*</td><td>APPEND MEMO <memfld> FROM <file> [OVERWRITE]
Imports data from <file> to <memfld> memo field of the current record, optionally overwriting existing data.</td></tr>
<tr><td>AT</td><td>AT(<expC1>, <memfld> [, <expN>]
Returns an integer representing the byte position of <expC1> in <memfld>. If <expN> is specified, the <expN>th occurrence of <expC1> is searched. Returns 0 if string is not found.</td></tr>
<tr><td>ATC</td><td>ATC(<expC1>, <memfld> [, <expN>]
Same as AT( ) but without regard to upper- or lower-case.</td></tr>
<tr><td>ATCLINE</td><td>ATCLINE(<expC1>, <memfld>)
Returns an integer (or 0 if not found) representing the line number in <memfld> where <expC1> appears. The search is case insensitive. Dependent on MEMOWIDTH.</td></tr>
<tr><td>ATLINE</td><td>ATLINE(<expC1>, <memfld>)
Same as ATCLINE( ), but search is case sensitive.</td></tr>
<tr><td>BROWSE
CHANGE
EDIT</td><td>Memo fields may be displayed or edited in BROWSE, CHANGE, or EDIT.</td></tr>
<tr><td>CLEAR ALL</td><td>Closes memo files along with other files.</td></tr>
<tr><td>CLOSE MEMO*</td><td>CLOSE MEMO <memfld1> [, <memfld2> ...] | ALL
Closes any memo window(s) opened with MODIFY MEMO or BROWSE.</td></tr>
</table>

(continued)

Table 7-1. Continued

FoxPro Command/Function	Syntax and Description
COPY MEMO*	COPY MEMO <memfld> TO <file> [ADDITIVE] Copies the contents of <memfld> of the current record to the file, appending to old data if the ADDITIVE option is specified.
COPY TO	COPY TO <file> ... TYPE FOXPLUS ... Copies memo files to FoxBASE+ compatible format.
DISPLAY/LIST	DISPLAY/LIST [<field list>] ... Does not display memo field data unless the memo field name is specified in the field list. DISPLAY/LIST STATUS Shows currently active memo files, blocksize, and memowidth setting.
EMPTY	EMPTY(<memfld>) Returns .T. if <memfld> has no data.
GATHER	GATHER MEMVAR | FROM <array> [FIELDS <field list>] [MEMO] Copies memory variables or array elements to database fields, now including memo fields.
INDEX	INDEX ON <expr> TO <file> [FOR <expL> [UNIQUE] Memo fields may not be used in index expressions.
LEFT	LEFT(<memfld>, <expN>) Returns <expN> number of characters beginning with the first character of <memfld>.
LEN	LEN(<memfld>) Returns the length of <memfld>.
MEMLINES*	MEMLINES(<memfld>) Returns the number of lines in <memfld>. Dependent on MEMOWIDTH.

(continued)

Table 7-1. Continued

FoxPro Command/Function	Syntax and Description
MLINE*	MLINE(<memfld>, <expN1> [,<expN2>] Returns the <expN1>th line in <memfld>, depending on the value of MEMOWIDTH. For best performance, provide the optional <expN2> parameter, which is the offset from the beginning of the memo field line. The new system memvar, _MLINE, is often used for this purpose.
_MLINE*	_MLINE = <expN> Used by the MLINE( ) function to store the location of its memo field offset. Its startup default value is 0.
MODIFY MEMO*	MODIFY MEMO <memfld1> [, <memfld2> ...] [NOEDIT] [NOWAIT] [RANGE <expN1>, <expN2>] [WINDOW win1>] [SAVE] [IN [WINDOW] <win2>]] Opens editing windows for memo fields of databases open in any work area. NOEDIT allows only viewing of text. NOWAIT is available in a program and continues execution after opening the window. RANGE opens the window with the specified range of bytes in the memo field already selected (highlighted). SAVE keeps the window on the screen if you move to another window.
PACK MEMO	PACK [MEMO] [DBF] Removes deleted records. The MEMO clause (new to FoxPro 2.0) removes unused space in the memo file without packing the .dbf file.
RAT	RAT(<expC1>, <memfld> [, <expN>] Searches <memfld> for <expC1> starting from the right and returns the position where <expC1> was found.

(continued)

Table 7-1. Continued

FoxPro Command/Function	Syntax and Description
RATLINE	RATLINE(<expC1>, <memfld>) Searches <memfld> for the last occurrence of <expC1> and returns the line number where <expC1> was found.
REPLACE	REPLACE [<scope>] [FOR <expL1>] [WHILE <expL2>]<memfld 1> WITH <expr1> [ADDITIVE] [, <memfld2> WITH <expr2> [ADDITIVE] ...] Replaces the values of memo fields with the indicated expression values. The ADDITIVE option is for memo fields only and causes new data to be appended to data already in the memo fields.
RESTORE FROM	RESTORE FROM MEMO <memfld> [ADDITIVE] Variant of the RESTORE FROM command which restores memory variables and arrays previously SAVEd to <memfld>. ADDITIVE does not remove memvars and arrays currently defined.
RESTORE MACROS	RESTORE MACROS FROM MEMO <memfld> Variant of the RESTORE MACROS command that restores keyboard macros previously SAVEd to <memfld>, adding the macros to those already defined.
RESTORE WINDOW	RESTORE WINDOW <window list> | ALL FROM MEMO <memfld> Variant of the RESTORE WINDOW command that restores windows specified in the list (or all windows if ALL is specified instead) that were previously SAVEd to <memfld>.

(continued)

Table 7-1. Continued

<table>
<tr><th>FoxPro
Command/Function</th><th>Syntax and Description</th></tr>
<tr><td>RIGHT</td><td>RIGHT(<memfld>, <expN>)
Returns the rightmost <expN> characters of <memfld>.</td></tr>
<tr><td>SAVE MACROS</td><td>SAVE MACROS TO MEMO <memfld>
Variant of the SAVE MACROS command that stores keyboard macros to <memfld>.</td></tr>
<tr><td>SAVE TO</td><td>SAVE TO MEMO <memfld> [ALL LIKE <skel> | ALL EXCEPT <skel>]
Variant of the command that stores memory variables and arrays to <memfld>.</td></tr>
<tr><td>SAVE WINDOW</td><td>SAVE WINDOW <window list> | ALL TO MEMO <memfld>
Variant of the command that stores current window definitions to <memfld>.</td></tr>
<tr><td>SCATTER</td><td>SCATTER [FIELDS <field list>] TO <array> | TO <array> BLANK | MEMVAR | MEMVAR BLANK [MEMO]
Copies data from a database record (now including memo fields) to an array or a set of memvars.</td></tr>
<tr><td>SET BLOCKSIZE*</td><td>SET BLOCKSIZE TO <expN>
Defines the size in bytes of memo file block size. If <expN> is between 1 and 32, <expN> × 512 bytes are allocated. Default is 64.</td></tr>
<tr><td>SET MEMOWIDTH*</td><td>SET MEMOWIDTH TO <cxpN>
Specifies the width of memo field output. Default is 50.</td></tr>
<tr><td>SET WINDOW*</td><td>SET WINDOW OF MEMO TO <win>
Specifies a previously defined user-defined window for editing a memo field.</td></tr>
</table>

(continued)

Table 7-1. Continued

FoxPro Command/Function	Syntax and Description
SUBSTR	SUBSTR(<memfld>, <expN1> [, <expN2>] Returns a substring of <memfld> beginning with the <expN1>th character to the end or containing <expN2> number of characters.
SYS(2012)*	SYS(2012, [<expN> | <expC>]) Returns the memo field blocksize for a database whose alias is <expC> or is in use in work area <expN>.

* Specific to memo fields/files.

Creating and Accessing Memo Fields

We define memo fields when we CREATE a .dbf file. In principle, the maximum number of memo fields in a FoxPro file is 255, which is the maximum number of fields that FoxPro allows.

In Edit/Browse mode, a memo field normally displays as a "memo marker"—the word "memo" either in all lowercase letters or with the first letter in uppercase. If the memo field contains data, the marker displays as the word "Memo," with the first letter capitalized. In dBASE IV, the equivalent memo marker shows the word "MEMO" in all uppercase letters. In an Edit screen, a memo field may also appear in a memo window. A memo window is a predefined box that displays the contents of the memo field. Memo windows may be designed as part of a custom screen format for use in data entry, edit, or view operations.

FoxPro's SET WINDOW OF MEMO TO <window name> command allows editing of memo fields within the named window whose location and other attributes are specified with the DEFINE WINDOW command. This user-defined window may be opened with APPEND, BROWSE, CHANGE, EDIT, GET/READ, or MODIFY MEMO commands. The following code fragment shows one way to view and edit a memo field under program control using a memo window.

```
DEFINE WINDOW mwind FROM 1,4 TO 16,70 TITLE "Ctrl-W to save/exit"
SET WINDOW OF MEMO TO mwind
@ 3,0 GET memofld WINDOW mwind
READ
*--- Press <Ctrl-Home> to access the memo window
```

The TITLE option of the DEFINE WINDOW command reminds the user of the keypress required to save the data and exit the window. Since the FoxPro GET/READ command has the OPEN WINDOW option, SET WINDOW is not needed. In either case, the user needs to press <Ctrl-Home>, <Ctrl-PgDn>, or <Ctrl-PgUp> to get into the window to edit the memo field. Since these are nonintuitive keypresses for those who are not Dbase-literate, one technique we can use is to stuff the keyboard with the required keypress once the cursor moves to the memo marker. Another technique is to adopt an application-wide standard such that a given function key, for example, F9 (Zoom in dBASE IV), is always used to get at the window's data.

In dBASE IV, if we want users to have automatic access to the memo window without requiring them to press <Ctrl-Home> (incidentally, <Ctrl-PgDn> is not an alternative in dBASE IV), we would define a keyboard macro that executes a <Ctrl-Home> when the cursor moves to the memo marker. Since a keyboard macro is activated only by a program request for keyboard input, the program must have the PLAY MACRO command before a READ. Also, the memo field must have its own READ command in order for the macro to affect only the memo field, rather than all the GET fields on the screen.

This technique can be used also in FoxPro. The PLAY MACRO command can be included in the WHEN clause of the @...GET command. For example,

```
@...GET <field> WHEN temp()
```

where the temp( ) function is

```
FUNCTION temp()
PLAY MACRO CtrlHome
RETURN .t.
```

Additionally, FoxPro's KEYBOARD and MODIFY MEMO commands provide better alternatives. The MODIFY MEMO command (see Table 7-1) opens a window and automatically places the user in the window to edit the data without requiring a preliminary keypress. The command opens one edit window for each memo field listed. The CLOSE MEMO command can be used to terminate editing and close the window. The NOWAIT option is available only in a program and has the effect of continuing program execution without waiting for a CLOSE MEMO command or keypresses such as <Ctrl-W> to end the editing session. This option, like the NOEDIT option, can be used to display multiple memo fields in separate windows without allowing users to edit any of them.

Other Ways to Display Memo Fields

Memo field data may also be displayed with the DISPLAY, LIST, ?/??, REPORT FORM, and LABEL FORM commands. The output of these commands may be directed to the screen, printer, or file. Directing the results to a file facilitates further processing of the data by, say, desktop publishing software. Note that the @...SAY command does not display memo field data.

The memo field name must be specified in the DISPLAY/LIST commands, or else only the memo marker shows instead of the memo field data. The display width of the memo field is dictated by the current setting of the MEMOWIDTH parameter. FoxPro's default value for this is 50. The parameter may be changed with the SET command, for example,

```
SET MEMOWIDTH TO 72
```

or by including a line in the Config.fp file such as,

```
MEMOWIDTH = 72
```

If you intend to change the MEMOWIDTH value in an application, it is a good idea to store the current value to a memory variable before you change it, and then restore the parameter to its original value when you are done. The following code fragment shows how you would do this using the SET function:

```
old_width =  SET("MEMOWIDTH")       && Store original value
SET MEMOWIDTH TO new_width          && change to new value
... rest of code goes here ...
SET MEMOWIDTH TO old_width          && restore value
```

The MEMOWIDTH setting is important, not only because it dictates how the field will be displayed or printed, but also because it affects the values returned by the ATLINE( ), ATCLINE( ), RATLINE( ), MEMLINES( ), and MLINE( ) functions. Memo field data display correctly according to the MEMOWIDTH setting if they were entered with the FoxPro editor. If they were created elsewhere with hard carriage returns and imported into the memo field, some of the lines display short of the MEMOWIDTH margins.

Probably the most versatile way of reporting memo field data is through FoxReport, invoked with the REPORT command using report definition files created by the CREATE/MODIFY REPORT command. FoxReport paginates correctly even when printing memo fields. When designing memo fields in a report, you should check the "Stretch Vertically" and "Float as the Band Stretches" options to ensure that the report zone containing the memo field stretches vertically and horizontally to accommodate the varying length of the memo field.

Memo field data may also be included in a label designed with the CREATE/MODIFY LABEL command, but the facility has little practical value. By definition, a label has limited dimensions and a memo field is meant to contain long text. The amount of memo field data that can be printed on a label is restricted by the label's skimpy dimensions.

Memo Field Length

In dBASE III PLUS, the length of a memo field is limited only by available disk space or by the maximum size of a file imposed by the operating system. However, any memo field that is edited using the dBASE III PLUS built-in editor cannot be longer than approximately 5000 bytes because that is the maximum size that the editor can handle. In dBASE IV 1.1, the maximum length of a memo field is 64K bytes. The dBASE IV text editor can handle a maximum of 32,000 lines of up to 1024 characters each, effectively limiting the length of a memo field to 32K bytes. In FoxPro, a memo field can be any size, limited only by available disk space or by restrictions imposed by the operating system on file sizes. The FoxPro editor also does not set any bounds on the size of a file, so it does not impose any artificial constraint on the length of a memo field.

Memo fields and memory variable strings can be used interchangeably; indeed, one can be assigned the value of the other. However, note that in the standard FoxPro version a memory variable string cannot be longer than 65,504 bytes and FoxPro has the additional limitation that the total size of all strings stored in memory variables cannot exceed the size of the string pool as defined by the MVARSIZ value in Config.fp, which itself is limited to 64K bytes. There are no practical limits on MVARSIZ and variable strings in the Extended Version.

.dbf and .fpt Files

A FoxPro database without a memo field (and without a floating field) is virtually indistinguishable from a database created by FoxBASE+ and dBASE. Such a file contains the hexadecimal value of 03H in byte 0 (the "signature" byte) of the .dbf header. On the other hand, the signature byte differs among the products for a database with memo fields, as Table 7-2 shows.

A FoxPro database with memo fields really consists of two files: the usual .dbf file and a .fpt file where the actual memo field data is stored. Each memo field occupies only 10 bytes in the .dbf file; these bytes are used to store the block number in the corresponding .fpt file where the memo field value is stored.

The FoxPro .dbf File Structure

A FoxPro .dbf file consists of a header record and data records. The header record contains identifying information about the file (such as the date of last update and the number of database records) in the first 32 bytes, followed by field subrecords. Each field subrecord is 32 bytes long and contains information about database fields such as field names and field types. Clearly, there are as many field subrecords as there are database fields, so the length of the header record depends on the number of fields in the database. Table 7-3 shows the structure of a .dbf file header record, and Table 7-4 shows the structure of a field subrecord.

Each .dbf data record begins with a delete flag byte which is either a space (ASCII decimal 32) if the record is not deleted, or an asterisk (ASCII decimal 42) if the record is deleted. Following the delete flag are the field data without any separator among the fields.

The FoxPro .fpt File Structure

A FoxPro memo file consists of a header record and one or more memo blocks. The header record is 512 bytes long and contains the location of the next available block and the blocksize in the file. A block consists of a block header (containing the block signature and the length of the memo field data)

Table 7-2. Signature Byte of Dbase Family Products' .dbf with Memo Fields

Product	Signature Byte
FoxBASE+, Clipper, dBASE III PLUS, dBXL/Quicksilver	83H
dBASE IV	8BH (no SQL)
FoxPro	F5H

followed by the actual memo text. All memo blocks start at even block boundary addresses. Table 7-5 shows the structure of a FoxPro memo file.

As we have seen, memo field data in the .fpt file is stored in blocks after the header block. In FoxBASE+ and dBASE III PLUS, the blocksize is fixed at 512 bytes. dBASE IV has the same default blocksize, but its blocksize can be changed, beginning with 512, in increments of 512 bytes up to 32 x 512

Table 7-3. The Structure of a FoxPro .dbf Header Record

Byte	Description
00	Signature byte. Contains 03H if the database has no memo fields, and F5H otherwise
01–03	Date of last update (YYMMDD)
04–07	Number of records in the database
08–09	Length of the header record
10–11	Length of a data record including the delete flag
12–31	Reserved
32–*n*	Field subrecords
n + 1	Header record terminator. Contains 0DH

Table 7-4. The Structure of a Field Subrecord

Byte	Description
00–10	Field name
11	Field data type. Contains one of the following; C, D, F, L, M, N
12–15	Displacement of field in the record
16	Field length
17	Number of decimal places in the field
18–31	Reserved

(16,384 bytes). FoxPro supports a blocksize smaller than 512 bytes (in fact, as small as 33 bytes) up to a maximum of 16,384 bytes, with the default set at 64 bytes. The command to change the blocksize is

```
SET BLOCKSIZE TO <expN>
```

where <expN> is the desired number of bytes, except that if it is an integer from 1 through 32, memo field storage is allocated in blocks of <expN> x 512 bytes. Thus SET BLOCKSIZE TO 64 defines a blocksize of 64 bytes, but SET BLOCKSIZE TO 32 defines a blocksize of 32 x 512, or 16,384, bytes. The COPY TO command must be issued thereafter in order for the software to re-create the .fpt file with the new blocksize. Of course, the COPY TO command also packs the .fpt file by recycling the space used by obsolete data. The current setting of BLOCKSIZE may be obtained either by using the DISPLAY/LIST STATUS command or the SET("BLOCKSIZE") function. The new SYS(2012) function can be used to determine the blocksize of a database in use in any work area.

Choosing the Optimum Blocksize

What is the optimum blocksize to use? It depends on the anticipated average length of memo field data. To understand this, let's look at how FoxPro stores information in both .dbf and .fpt files. For our purposes, assume that the blocksize is set at 64 bytes.

Table 7-5. The Structure of a FoxPro .fpt File

Byte	Description
A. Memo Header Block	
00–03	Location of next available block
04–05	Reserved
06–07	Blocksize (bytes per block)
08–511	Reserved
B. Memo Block	
00–03	Block signature. Contains 0 for picture, and 1 for text.
04–07	Length of memo (in bytes)
08–*n*	Memo text (*n* = length). Data spills over consecutive blocks.

FoxPro, like FoxBASE+ and dBASE, does not preallocate any space in the .fpt (.dbt) file for memo fields in each .dbf record. Rather, only those memo fields with actual data occupy space in the .fpt file. Like dBASE, FoxPro stores memo field data in the .fpt file in the order they are entered, not in the order of record number in the .dbf file. When a database with a memo field is CREATEd, the .fpt file consists of only the header block. The header block is 512 bytes long, independent of the setting of the blocksize, and it contains the address of the first empty block (the next available block for storing memo field data) which, in this case, would be 1.

Assume we have a .dbf file with one record and one memo field containing, say, 32 bytes of data. Disregarding any constraints on minimum file sizes that may be imposed by the operating system, the .fpt file should contain only one 64-byte data block, sufficient to contain the 32 bytes of actual data. Clearly, except for a few bytes of pointer information, the remainder of the 64-byte block is empty. If we now edit this field to add more information such that the length of the field is now 65 bytes, FoxPro allocates a second data block to contain data that exceeds the blocksize. This second data block will be mostly empty because not much data spilled over from the first block. The location of the first block containing the memo field data for a given .dbf record is stored in the 10 bytes allocated in the .dbf file for each memo field. To retrieve the value for a given memo field in a specified record, FoxPro reads these 10 bytes, which direct it to the appropriate block in the .fpt file. FoxPro then continues to read data for the same memo field that goes on for two or more blocks.

From this example it is easy to see that choosing the right blocksize often requires a tradeoff between speed of I/O processing and conservation of disk space. Small blocksizes are best for relatively short memo field data. Choose larger blocksizes for storing large amounts of memo field information.

Managing Memo Field Space

One of the deficiencies of dBASE III PLUS pertains to the way it manages memo field space. It rewrites an entire block of memo field data to the next available block at the end of the .dbt file even if a user changed only a single byte in the data. This causes the file to grow rapidly and be filled with obsolete data that simply wastes disk space. FoxPro, like dBASE IV, is more intelligent in managing .fpt (.dbt) file space. When SET EXCLUSIVE is ON, it does not rewrite a block after an edit as long as the edit does not result in the addition of text that exceeds the length of the block. This approach has the additional advantage of minimizing I/O activity because the memo field pointer in the .dbf file need not be updated.

However, dBASE IV is better than FoxPro in recycling space containing obsolete memo field data. When dBASE IV rewrites a block to the end of the .dbt file because new edits have caused an overflow in the current block space, the block number occupied by the original data is pointed to in the header record as the next available block. Thus it first tries to recycle newly vacated space to keep the .dbt file size from growing unnecessarily. FoxPro does not appear to recycle unused space as dBASE IV does.

Importing and Exporting Memo Field Data

In FoxBASE+ and dBASE III PLUS, data for memo fields may only be entered, exported, or imported in interactive mode while we are in the memo field editor. Were we to import data to, or export data from, a large number of database records, this procedure would quickly become cumbersome. FoxPro, like dBASE IV, permits importing and exporting memo field data both interactively under the memo field editor, and in unattended mode, with a command, under program control. Selected portions of the data, rather than the entire contents of the memo field, can be exported consistent with the block operations (marking, moving, and copying) of the editor.

Exporting Memo Field Data with a Command

Memo fields may be written to an external file from the command windows or under control of a program with the COPY MEMO command. The following command writes the contents of the Notes memo field in the current record to the Notes.out file on the A: drive.

```
COPY MEMO Notes TO a:Notes.out ADDITIVE
```

The optional ADDITIVE clause appends the memo field contents to the data already in the file; otherwise, information already in the file is overwritten without further warning unless SET SAFETY is ON. The clause implies that the target file already exists; otherwise, FoxPro generates an error message. Note that if you do not specify the target file's extension, FoxPro assumes a file extension of .txt. Data written to the file is in the same raw format with which it was created, independent of the current setting of MEMOWIDTH. The COPY MEMO command may be used to export text as well as binary data. Along with the APPEND MEMO command, it is very useful in applications such as a program version control system that maintains and tracks application programs and executables.

Suppose we have a customized help file similar to Foxhelp.dbf that contains the Details memo field. We want to copy the contents of Details for selected database records, where the field has values, into one text file for use in preparing the application's documentation. The DumpMemo procedure, which exports the data using the COPY MEMO command, can be used to do this. The program is shown in Listing 7-1. The procedure uses several commands new to FoxBASE+ users. For example, SCAN/ENDSCAN is a looping construct that is easier and more efficient than DO WHILE/ENDDO with a SKIP. The program also uses filename substitution, for example,

```
USE (DbfName)
SET ALTERNATE TO (outfile)
```

instead of using macros, as in USE &dbf.

Listing 7-1. DumpMemo.prg, a procedure to export memo field contents of selected records to a target file.

```
PROCEDURE DumpMemo
******************************************************************
* Program :  DumpMemo.Prg
* Author  :  P. L. Olympia & Kathy Cea
* Purpose :  Copies contents of selected records of a specified
*         :  memo field to a target file.
* Syntax  :  DO DumpMemo WITH DbfName, MemFld, RecBeg, RecEnd,
*         :     OutFile
*         :   RecBeg and RecEnd define the beginning and ending
*         :   record numbers to copy. Outfile is the target
*         :   file.  DbfName is the .dbf file. MemFld is the
*         :   memo field.
* Note    :  Error trapping excluded from code.
******************************************************************
PARAMETER DbfName, MemFld, RecBeg, RecEnd, Outfile
*-- Store, then change,  environment
 SafeSW = SET("SAFETY")
 SET SAFETY OFF

 rec_str   = STR(RecBeg,4)       && for use as macro

 USE (DbfName)
 &rec_str                        &&  move pointer to start

 SCAN  WHILE (recno() >= RecBeg .AND. recno() <= RecEnd ;
         .AND. !(EMPTY(MemFld)))
    COPY MEMO (MemFld) TO (OutFile) ADDITIVE  && Exports memo
 ENDSCAN
 SET SAFETY &SafeSW
 RETURN
**================================================================
```

Importing Memo Field Data with a Command

Text or binary data from an external file may be loaded into a memo field from the command window or under control of a program with the APPEND MEMO command. For instance, the command

```
APPEND MEMO Notes FROM Notes.txt OVERWRITE
```

imports all data from the Notes.txt file to the Notes memo field of the current database record. The OVERWRITE option erases the contents of the memo field before the data transfer is performed. If the option is omitted, information from the external file is appended to the current memo field data.

Note that APPEND MEMO is intended for data transfer between one memo field and one external file at a time. Nonetheless, this command has a host of uses, especially when coupled with FoxPro's facility for treating memo fields just as though they were character fields. For example, the FindStr.prg procedure in Listing 7-2 uses properties of a FoxPro memo field to search a text file for the desired *N*th occurrence of a specified string. It uses APPEND MEMO to load the file to a memo field, and then uses the ATC( ) function to perform a case-insensitive search of the string. To highlight the string just located, it uses the RANGE option of the MODIFY MEMO command. You can easily modify this program to find all occurrences of the specified string by invoking ATC( ) in a loop where the Noccur parameter changes each time. If you need to extract every line containing the string for printing or for appending to an open .dbf file, set MEMOWIDTH to 80 or a large enough number, and then use MLINE( ) to return the desired line.

The same memo field handling facility used in FindStr.prg can be used to determine if two DOS files are identical. Here all we need to do is use APPEND MEMO to import one file to one memo field and import the other file to a second field, and then compare the two. Also, with just a little bit more work, we can expand upon FindStr.prg and exploit FoxPro's versatile memo field handling facility to write a program that builds an Index of terms and phrases for a given manuscript or document. If the electronic form of the document contains the page number in the header or footer, we can easily determine the page number(s) in the document where the desired word or phrase can be found.

Listing 7-2. The FindStr.prg procedure finds and highlights the *n*th occurrence of a specified string in a given text file using memo field commands and functions.

```
PROCEDURE FindStr.prg
**********************************************************
* Program ...: FindStr.prg
* Author     :  P. L. Olympia & Kathy Cea
* Purpose....: Searches a text file for the Nth occurrence of
*            : a specified string using FoxPro memo field
*            : commands/functions
* Syntax ....: DO FindStr WITH <string>, <txtfile>, <Noccur>
* Notes .....: Assumes .dbf in current area has memo field
*            :  called MemFld
**********************************************************
PARAMETERS string, txtfile, Noccur

*-- Make sure file exists

IF !FILE((txtfile))
   ? "Can't seem to find " + txtfile
   RETURN
ENDIF

Noccur = IIF(Noccur < 1, 1, Noccur)    && Can't be less than 1

*-- Load the file to the memo field
APPEND MEMO memfld FROM (txtfile) OVERWRITE

*-- Search the memo field for the string
start = ATC(string, memfld, Noccur)
IF start = 0
   ? string + 'not found'
ELSE
   *  Display string highlighted in window
   long = start + LEN(string)
   MODIFY MEMO memfld NOEDIT RANGE start, long
ENDIF
RETURN
```

Importing/Exporting Memo Field Data From and To Character Fields

Like other Dbase family products, FoxPro does not allow indexing on a memo field (although a memo field may appear in the FOR clause). However, with some advanced planning we can get around this limitation. If we are careful to reserve the first line of a memo field's value so it contains identifying information suitable for indexing (for example, Social Security number, date of birth, and part number), we can equate a character field in the file to the contents of the memo field's first line and sort the records based on the value of the character field. The following code copies the first line of the ClientHist memo field to a character field called ClientName and then indexes the database based on ClientName:

```
REPLACE ALL ClientName WITH MLINE(ClientHist,1)
INDEX ON ClientName TO <newindex>
```

To load a memo field with data from a character field, memory variable, or string, use the REPLACE command. Although REPLACE requires that the field to be replaced and its replacement have the same data type, memo fields may be replaced by any character expression. FoxPro's REPLACE command, like that of dBASE IV, includes the ADDITIVE option to enable memo fields to be loaded incrementally from various character expressions. This option is valid only for memo fields. We can take advantage of the ADDITIVE option by using a memo field to hold historical information of various character fields in the record. For instance, we can easily build a program library system for a complete application that, like a simple program version control system, tracks the modification history for any program in the application, and also uses a memo field to store the most current version of the program. Assume that the database has the following fields:

Field Name	**Field Type**	**Width**	**Description**
PgmName	C	12	Program name
PgmRevNo	C	5	Revision number
PgmRevDate	D	8	Revision date
PgmRevNote	C	254	What's new in this version
PgmRevHist	M	10	Revision history
PgmSrc	M	10	Current program copy

Every time we generate a new version of the program, we need to move the data from the other fields to the PgmRevHist memo field, which maintains the modifications history, before the other fields are overwritten with new data. We use the REPLACE command with the ADDITIVE option to accumulate historical data, and APPEND MEMO to replace the copy of the program in the second memo field:

```
REPLACE PgmHist WITH PgmRevNo + ", " + DTOC(PgmRevDate) + ;
   CHR(13) + CHR(10) + PgmRevNote  ADDITIVE
APPEND MEMO PgmSrc FROM <new pgm version>
```

Note that this technique offers the facility for moving data from a hierarchical database system to a relational type of system such as FoxPro. Entire nodes or repeating groups can be stored and manipulated as memo fields.

APPEND MEMO and the Phantom Record

You should be wary of some interesting behavior (if not anomalies) exhibited by FoxPro 1.x and early versions of 2.0 related to memo field commands such as APPEND MEMO. Briefly, if you have an empty database or if you are at the end of file in a populated database, you may be surprised to note that the APPEND MEMO command creates a new record that is entirely blank except for the memo field. Additionally, if you save memory variables to a memo field with SAVE ALL LIKE <skeleton> TO MEMO <memoname>, the command adds a record to the file whether or not the variable mask defined in <skeleton> produces a match.

This unusual property is apparently due to the "infamous" phantom record—that blank record that sits just past the bottom of the file. Your database pointer is always on this record in an empty .dbf. In a populated file, you will find yourself on this record after a command such as LIST ALL.

Because of the phantom record, an empty .dbf would show a RECCOUNT( ) value of 0 but a RECNO( ) value of 1. Similarly, when you are on this record in a populated database, the value returned by RECNO( ) is always one greater than the record count. In this situation, it appears that commands such as APPEND MEMO and SAVE TO MEMO cause FoxPro to store data into the current record, which in this case is the phantom record.

Of course, once FoxPro adds memo field data to the record, it ceases to be a phantom record; the record count goes up by 1, and for all intents and purposes, FoxPro unexpectedly has appended a record. If you routinely use SAVE TO MEMO, you should check for the EOF( ) condition to ensure that the data goes to the intended record, and not to the newly populated phantom record. Note also that SAVE ALL LIKE <skeleton> TO MEMO writes three characters (M, Ctrl-O, and Ctrl-Z) in the memo field even if the <skeleton> mask fails to produce a match. The net effect of this is the addition of a record if the database pointer is positioned in the phantom record.

Memo Fields as Filing Cabinets

One of the most outstanding enhancements in FoxPro, and surely one of the least documented, pertains to the use of memo fields as repositories of information, much like an application's massive file cabinet. As Table 7-1 shows, FoxPro's enhancements to the various "flavors" of the SAVE and RESTORE commands enable us to store memory variables, memory variable arrays, window definitions, and keyboard macros to memo fields. Immediately this saves us from having to create a multitude of DOS files with the attendant problems not only of maintaining them, but even of just coming up with unique filenames in a multiuser environment. In essence, this facility lets us capture the entire environment of an application, including its keyboard macros, windows, and memory variables, and lets us restore that environment simply with a RESTORE from a given memo field.

All we need for each application is one data file containing at least three memo fields, one for storing values of memory variables and arrays, a second for keyboard macros, and a third for windows. With the SAVE ... MEMO <memfld> command, one .dbf/.fpt file set stores the same information that would require separate .mem, .win, and .fky files. Users may still define their keyboard macros or windows and have them available alongside the application's standard values as long as the organization adopts a naming convention that eliminates the possibility that a user-defined keyboard macro or window name will conflict with those used by the standard application.

The ability of FoxPro to save and restore memory variables and arrays from a memo field takes on special significance. This facility can be put to good use in the following applications.

Saving and Restoring Screens

Suppose we want to maintain a copy of an application screen or output window image so it can be reused in other modules of the application without us having to redraw the screen each time. We can do this by saving the screen to a memory buffer, or better yet, to a memory variable. Storing the screen to a memory variable and then saving that variable to permanent storage means that the screen never has to be redrawn again. Normally you would save memory variables to .mem files, but saving them to a memo field has the advantage that you won't need to create and track many small files. The sequence of commands for saving and restoring screens to a memo field is as follows:

```
SAVE SCREEN TO scr1              && scr1 is a memvar
SAVE TO MEMO Memfld              && scr1 and other memvars saved
RESTORE FROM MEMO Memfld         && Later restores scr1 and others
RESTORE SCREEN FROM scr1         && restores screen scr1
```

Tracking Changes to a Record

A popular way to copy a record of one database to another uses FoxPro's versatile SCATTER and GATHER commands. SCATTER copies a record to an array, creating the array as needed, with each array element containing the value of the corresponding field in the record, including memo fields. This procedure is useful in multiuser applications where we may want to maintain snapshots of the record at various times to determine whether or not the record has changed between the time we started editing it and the time we finished. We can save the array to a memo field to guard against system failure before we can use it. With the MEMO clause of the SAVE and RESTORE commands, we can store multiple records of one or more databases and use only those that we need at one time to conserve string or memory variable space.

Accommodating Different Printers

In the Dbase world, a widely accepted tenet is never to hardcode any output with printer-specific codes, for example,

```
@ 1, 0 SAY CHR(15) + title + CHR(18).
```

This is good advice because a program containing such code quickly becomes obsolete with a change of printers. Before the advent of printer drivers, application developers like to define a set of memory variables such as BoldOn or BoldOff so that output destined for a printer can have some semblance of printer independence. For instance, the statement

```
@ 1, 0 SAY BoldOn + title + BoldOff
```

should work for any printer as long as the memory variables have been assigned the proper control sequence.

The usual way to implement this approach is to define a set of identically named memory variables for each printer and store those to separate memory variable files, for example, Epson.mem, Hp.mem, and Okidata.mem. Then, depending on the printer currently in use, the appropriate .mem file can be used to restore the correct set of printer control codes. This procedure works well except that the proliferation of small .mem files, one for each supported printer, eventually presents a maintenance nightmare.

Again, this is not a problem with memo fields. All we need to do is define a simple .dbf consisting of as many records as there are printers to support. With SAVE TO MEMO, we can save to each one a set of memory variables for a given printer. This solution requires one .dbf/.fpt file set compared to a large number of .mem files.

Of course, with the new printer driver facility in FoxPro 2.0, you may not need this technique anymore.

Getting Around Missing Memo Files

Sooner or later, Dbase users will misplace or inadvertently delete a memo file corresponding to a .dbf. Normally Dbase does not allow the file to be USEd if the corresponding memo file in missing. In dBASE III PLUS/FoxBASE+ and clones, the trick around this is simply to rename any file, including a completely irrelevant file such as Config.sys or Autoexec.bat, as the missing .dbt file. As long as you do not attempt to add or edit memo fields, the software allows full access to the rest of the data.

FoxPro, on the other hand, refuses to be fooled by such trickery because it checks the header record of the .fpt file. To force FoxPro to USE the file with the missing .fpt anyway, all you have to do is copy (or rename) any existing .fpt to the missing memo file. This permits you to access the database file so you can at least copy all nonmemo data to another file.

Memo File Corruption

When you try to USE a FoxPro database but instead get a "MEMO file is Invalid or missing" message, the .fpt file could well be damaged. Memo file corruption has long been a problem in all Dbase products and generally results from abnormal exits from applications, including sudden hardware failure caused by such things as someone inadvertently disconnecting a network cable.

Why is a memo file so prone to corruption? It is partly because of the way in which the .dbf and .fpt (.dbt) files are linked. As we indicated earlier, each memo field occupies only 10 bytes in the .dbf file; these bytes are used to store the block number in the corresponding .fpt file where the memo field data resides. Thus the only link between the database record and its memo field data is this 10-byte pointer to the .fpt file. One form of memo file corruption results when this pointer becomes so damaged that it is pointing to a nonexistent .fpt block, pointing to a completely different block, or pointing to the middle of the correct .fpt block.

Clearly, correcting the problem requires resynchronizing the block pointers in the .dbf file (called the memo marker block) with the actual memo data in the .fpt file. One way to do this is to unload the .fpt file data and then edit it by placing tags to identify which blocks belong to which .dbf record. The edited file can then be reloaded and, guided by the edit tags, should produce a completely resynchronized data file. Platinum Software's MemoPlus product can be used to correct a corrupted memo file with this technique.

Damaged memo files would be much easier to repair if Dbase producers would only modify the memo file structure enough to add a back pointer to the .dbf memo marker block. To date, this much needed facility is still missing from FoxPro and other Dbase products.

Data belonging to a specific memo field of a given record is stored in the .fpt file in contiguous blocks. FoxPro knows how far down in the contiguous blocks to read because it stores the length of the memo field data for each field. Another form of memo file corruption results when this stored length value becomes damaged or overwritten by garbage. To correct this type of damage simply requires that you replace the stored value with the correct length or something fairly close to the correct length.

To help you determine if a memo file contains corrupted data, you can use the ChkFptPO utility, which is one of many programs included in this book's program disk. The program examines all FoxPro database records, tells you if the file appears truncated, and alerts you if one or more memo file blocks appear damaged.

Chapter Summary

Memo fields are useful for storing and displaying varied and vast amounts of information associated with a database record. Unlike other data types, memo fields have lengths that may vary from record to record. This makes memo fields very useful along with the desirable attribute that unlike other data types, memo fields do not occupy disk space unless they have assigned values. Memo fields can be used to hold historical information for one or more fields in the data file and, more importantly, can be used as an infinitely expanding file cabinet for storing memory variables, arrays, printer definitions, screens, keyboard macros, and windows for an entire application.

The length of FoxPro's memo fields is limited only by available disk space. Memo fields may contain any type of data, text as well as binary, including pictures, sound, graphics, and executable programs. In FoxPro, anything you can do with a string you should also be able to do with memo fields. FoxPro provides a host of commands and functions, discussed in this chapter, to permit manipulating memo fields as though they were character fields.

Memo field data can be imported and exported interactively under the memo field editor or in unattended (batch) mode under program control. Thus data created from other software can be loaded easily into memo fields. Conversely, memo field data can be exported easily to another environment.

In this chapter, we discussed the structure of a FoxPro .fpt file. We discussed how FoxPro manages memo field space and how the BLOCKSIZE setting affects disk space and data retrieval speed. We also discussed techniques that take advantage of the facilities offered by memo fields, including the use of memo fields to accumulate historical data about the record, to locate strings in a DOS text file, or to determine if two files are the same.

Memo files can be easily corrupted (for example, by sudden hardware failure) primarily because of the simplistic way in which .dbf and .fpt files are related. In this chapter, we discussed a technique for forcing FoxPro to USE a database whose .fpt file is missing. We also discussed common forms of memo file corruption, their causes, and techniques for dealing with them.

Chapter 8

Handling String and Character Data

In FoxPro, as in most other database management systems, character data is the data type processed by most applications. Given that memo fields and character strings also consist of character data, it is easy to see why the FoxPro language has an extensive set of commands and functions to manipulate, format, and transform character data. Most Dbase language novices make the mistake of defining fields such as employee number or social security number as numeric rather than character fields. In general, even fields that are expected to contain numbers should be defined as character fields, unless they are to be used in computations. For example, fields such as document number that may consist partly of characters and partly of numbers that are intended to be incremented serially can be safely defined as character fields.

This chapter examines the various FoxPro facilities for manipulating character data, beyond those already discussed in Chapter 7. It discusses practical applications of commands and functions that support character data and describes generically useful string-handling UDFs.

Data Type Conversion

Table 8-1 summarizes the FoxPro commands and functions to convert numeric, date, logical and memo data types to and from character type.

Note that the numeric values returned by the VAL( ) function are dependent on the current setting of SET DECIMALS. A few nonnumeric characters

Table 8-1. FoxPro Functions and Commands To Convert Various Data Types To and From Character.

Conversion	Function/Command
Numeric to Character	STR(<expN1> [,<expN2>] [,<expN3>]]) ? STR(576) 576 ? STR(576.12, 8, 3) 576.120 && 8 chars long, 3 dec.
Character to Numeric	VAL(<expC>) ? SET("DECIMALS") 2 ? VAL("-254.1") -254.10 ? VAL("3.75E4") 37500.00 ? VAL("X123") 0.00
Character to Date	CTOD(<expC>), or {<expC>} ? CTOD("10/03/91") 10/03/91
Date to Character	DTOC(<expD> [,1]) DTOS(<expD>) ? DTOC({10/03/91} + 2, 1) 19911005
Logical to Character	IIF(<expL>, <expr1>, <expr2>) ? IIF(isopen, "Open", "Closed") Open
Character to/from Memo	REPLACE <field1> WITH <expr1> [<scope>] [ADDITIVE] [, <field2> WITH <expr2> ...] [FOR <expL1>] [WHILE <expL2>]

such as E, used in exponential notation, and the minus sign are valid characters in the VAL( ) argument field. If the argument begins with a character that is not a digit, the VAL( ) function returns zero; in that sense, it serves as an alternative to the ISDIGIT( ) function.

To copy memo field data to a character field, use the REPLACE command. The same command, of course, can be used to copy the value of a character field to a memo field. In this case, the ADDITIVE option of the command does not overwrite any previous data in the memo field.

The IIF( ) function's facility to convert logicals to character values is useful in creating an index with a compound key expression. The function allows a logical field to be concatenated with a character field, for example,

```
INDEX ON IIF(IsMember, "Y", "N") + Name TO MemName
```

Some applications, for example, a correspondence control system, use a system-generated record id number as a key. Often this number is a composite that includes such things as document type in combination with today's date and a serial number maintained by the system. The DTOC( ) and DTOS( ) functions, which we have already seen to be useful in index key expressions involving dates, can be used for the date-dependent portion of the record id number.

At the beginning of this chapter, we mentioned that unless a field is to be used in computations, the field is best defined as character rather than numeric. Any requirement to increment a portion of the field serially, for example, to produce the next record id in the series, is easily satisfied. For instance, suppose that the record id has a format of IDnnnn, where *nnnn* is to be incremented from one record to the next. The following command generates the next ID in the series:

```
next_id = LEFT(rec_id,2) +  STR(VAL(RIGHT(rec_id,4)) + 1, 4, 0)
```

Searching Character Strings

FoxPro has a number of functions designed to help search a string for a character or another string. These are shown in Table 8-2.

With one or more of these functions, it is relatively easy to write a FoxPro program similar to the UNIX utility Fgrep to search all the text files in a subdirectory for a desired string. Such a program would use FoxPro's low-level file I/O functions as well. Alternatively we can read the file's data into a memo field and search the memo field for the desired string. The following code fragment shows how this is done:

```
* Assume a .dbf with memo field Notes in the active select area
* "Substring" is the string to find
```

Table 8-2. FoxPro Functions to Search Characters or Strings

Function	Summary
$	Returns .T. if a substring is contained in a string or memo field.
AT( )	Returns an integer representing the position of the first occurrence of a substring in a string or memo field.
ATC( )	Like AT( ) but is *not* case sensitive.
ATCLINE( )	Returns an integer representing the line number where a substring first occurs within a string or memo field. Matching proceeds without regard to case.
ATLINE( )	Same as ATCLINE( ) but matching is case sensitive.
BETWEEN( )	Returns .T. if an expression lies between two other expressions.
DIFFERENCE( )	Returns a number from 0 through 4 representing the relative phonetic difference between two strings.
INLIST( )	Returns .T. if a character expression is contained in a series (list) of expressions.
LIKE( )	Returns .T. if a character expression, which may include wildcard characters, is contained in another character expression.
OCCURS( )	Returns the number of times that a substring appears in a string or memo field. This is a case-sensitive function.
RAT( )	Returns an integer representing the position where a substring last appears in a string or memo field. This is a case-sensitive function.
RATLINE( )	Returns an integer representing the line where a substring last appears in a string or memo field.

(continued)

Table 8-2. Continued

Function	Summary
SOUNDEX( )	Returns the phonetic code of a character expression, useful in comparing two or more strings.

```
APPEND MEMO Notes FROM <filename> OVERWRITE
SET MEMOWIDTH TO 80
FOR i = 1 TO MEMLINES(Notes)
  line = MLINE(Notes, i)
  IF ATC(substring, line) > 0
     ? line
  ENDIF
ENDFOR
```

With very little effort, we can make the program even more versatile by allowing wildcards in the target substring. In this case, all we need to do is replace ATC( ) with the LIKE( ) function. So the IF statement now reads

```
IF LIKE("*" + substring + "*", line)
```

Unlike ATC( ), LIKE( ) performs a case-sensitive match except that both wildcard characters (* and ?) will match both lowercase and uppercase letters. If it is important to have the search remain case-insensitive, apply the UPPER( ) function to both arguments of LIKE( ).

A similar technique can be used to quickly count the number of times a given word or string appears in a document or text file. In this case, use APPEND MEMO to load the file to a memo field, and then use the OCCURS( ) function to report the desired count. For example,

```
? 'The word ' + word + ' appears ', OCCURS(word, Notes), ' times.'
```

Remember that OCCURS( ) is a case-sensitive function.

The RAT( ) function is particularly useful for tasks such as word wrapping, which is described in the next section. It is also handy for such things as removing path and subdirectory prefixes from a fully qualified filename. For instance, if the filename is something like C:\DOS\UTILITY\-WP\LJ\WHATSUP.DOC, stripping the prefix usually entails going through a loop to look for the \ character and stripping the appropriate substring. With RAT( ), the filename can be extracted with one command:

```
FileName = SUBSTR(FileName, RAT("\", FileName) + 1).
```

Word Wrapping in a Character Field During Data Entry

Due to serious limitations in memo field handling in most Dbase family products prior to FoxPro, many developers have resorted to holding text information in multiple character fields rather than in a single memo field. For instance, a travel tracking system might include four long character fields, say, Justif1 through Justif4, to record the travel justification narrative. One disadvantage of such a structure, of course, is that most records probably will not have data in all four of these fields, so the structure unnecessarily wastes disk space. Another disadvantage is that although the user has the benefit of word wrap during memo field entry, such a facility is never built into data entry involving character fields.

On the other hand, we can use one of FoxPro's many character handling functions to provide the necessary word wrap capability as users enter narrative text into contiguous character fields or memory variables. The technique consists of extracting the spillover (last) word on a line, using RAT( ), and then stacking the keyboard buffer with the word using the KEYBOARD command. That way, the spillover word wraps to the next character field. Listing 8-1 shows how this is done in the Wrapit user-defined function. As usual, we take advantage of the VALID clause of the @...GET command to force the Wrapit UDF to be invoked. The function uses VARREAD( ) to identify the currently active GET field or memvar. Note that the VALID clause is omitted in the GET statement for the last character field because word wrapping ceases on that field.

Comparing Strings

FoxPro's equal sign operator is commonly used to test if two values of the same type (character, numeric, date, or logical) are the same. When used to test the equality of two character expressions, this operator begins by comparing the strings character for character from left to right until it encounters the

Listing 8-1. Wrapit user-defined function and driver program. The function shows a technique for enforcing word wrap during data entry on contiguous character fields or memory variables.

```
*-- This is a sample driver program for the Wrapit UDF
*-- to show word wrap during data entry on contiguous
*-- character fields or memvars

SET TALK OFF
STORE SPACE(50) TO note1, note2, note3, note4

@ 10,10 GET note1 VALID wrapit()
@ 11,10 GET note2 VALID wrapit()
@ 12,10 GET note3 VALID wrapit()
@ 13,10 GET note4       && No VALID here since there
                        && is no place to word wrap
READ

SET TALK ON
RETURN

FUNCTION Wrapit
**************************************************************
* Program ...: Wrapit.prg
* Author ....: P. L. Olympia & Kathy Cea
* Purpose....: Performs word wrap during data entry on
*            : contiguous character fields. Uses RAT() to
*            : find the last (spillover) word.
* Syntax ....: @ row, col GET <charfield> VALID Wrapit()
* Notes .....: Adapted from a public domain program by G. Neill
**************************************************************

*-- Use VARREAD() to save field or memvar name
fld = VARREAD()
long = LEN (EVALUATE (fld))

*-- Don't need word wrap if trimmed(fld) < long
IF LEN(TRIM(EVALUATE (fld)) < long
   RETURN (.T.)              && just return true
```

(continued)

Listing 8-1. Continued

```
ELSE
*-- Save spillover word and strip it from current field
   LastWord = SUBSTR(EVALUATE (fld), RAT(' ', EVALUATE (fld) + 1)
   &fld = STUFF(&fld,RAT(' ',&fld)+1,LEN(LastWord), ;
          SPACE(LEN(LastWord)))
ENDIF

*-- Stuff the keyboard with the last word
KEYBOARD LastWord
RETURN(.T.)
```

---

first inequality between the two strings. The result of the operation also depends on the value of SET EXACT.

With SET EXACT OFF, the operation ceases as soon as the characters of the string to the right of the equal sign are exhausted. Thus, the command

```
? "123.4" = "123"
```

yields .T., but the command

```
? "123" = "123.4"
```

yields .F.

Clearly any string comparison involving a null string to the right of the equal sign, for example,

```
? "123" = ""
```

always yields .T. with SET EXACT OFF.

With SET EXACT ON, the comparison operation continues through to the end of the two strings. The operation ignores trailing blanks, so the following commands both yield .T.

```
? "123" = "123 "
? "123 " = "123"
```

Table 8-3. FoxPro Functions for Replacing Characters and Strings

Function	Summary
CHRTRAN( )	Translates the characters of a string using translation tables defined by two other strings.
STRTRAN( )	Searches a string for a specified substring, and then replaces it with another substring.
STUFF( )	Returns a string resulting from the insertion, deletion, or replacement of a component substring.
SYS(15)	Translates the characters of a string using a character expression as a translation table.

From this example it is clear that SET EXACT ON does not guarantee complete equality between the two strings before the operation yields .T. If you need to compare two strings for exact equality, use the double sign operator. This operator yields .T. if, and only if, the two strings contain exactly the same sequence of characters including the same number of trailing blanks. Regardless of the setting of SET EXACT, the following commands all yield .F.

```
? "123" == "123 " && Trailing blanks not ignored
? "123" == ""
? "123" == "123.4"
```

String Comparisons in SQL

SET EXACT has no effect on SQL commands (for example, WHERE clause of SELECT) involving string comparisons. Switching strings to the left or right side of the = or = = comparison operator does not affect the result of the comparison.

In SQL, comparing strings of different lengths may produce different results depending on the setting of SET ANSI. With SET ANSI ON, the shorter string is padded with blanks to the length of the longer string before comparing the two. With ANSI SET OFF, the shorter string is not padded;

rather, the two strings are compared character for character until the shorter string is exhausted. Thus, with SET ANSI ON

```
"123" = "1234"
```

yields .F. since FoxPro will pad the left string with a blank (resulting in "123 ", which is not equal to "1234." With SET ANSI OFF, the comparison yields .T. because the two strings are equal up to the length of the shorter string, and FoxPro stops comparing the two after the third character.

Replacing Characters and Strings

FoxPro also has powerful functions designed to search and replace a character or a string with another character or string. These are summarized in Table 8-3.

Traditionally Dbase developers employ two general procedures for replacing one character with another in a string:

1. Using AT( ) and SUBSTR( ) (or its variant LEFT( ) and RIGHT( )).
2. Using AT( ) and STUFF( ).

For example, if Memvar = "Radar" and we want to replace the first "a" with "i", the following statements demonstrate the two methods:

1. Using SUBSTR( ) and AT( ).

```
Memvar = IIF("a" $ Memvar, SUBSTR(Memvar, 1, AT("a", Memvar) ;
 - 1) + "i" + SUBSTR(Memvar, AT("a", Memvar) + 1), Memvar)
```

2. Using STUFF( ) and AT( ).

```
Memvar = IIF("a" $ Memvar, STUFF(Memvar, AT("a", Memvar), 1, ;
"i"), Memvar)
```

To replace both occurrences of "a" in the string, we need a loop. Ordinarily we have no choice but to write a program. However, FoxPro's CHRTRAN( ) can make the global replacement with one statement:

```
? CHRTRAN(Memvar, "a","i")
```

Both CHRTRAN( ) and STRTRAN( ) are extremely useful for replacing substrings in database fields. Suppose we want to replace all occurrences of "%" with "#" in a database field called CharFld for all records in the database. In dBASE III Plus, we would need a program with a clever twist, for example,

```
*-- dBASE III Plus program to replace all occurrences of one
*-- character with another. Adapted from a program by H. Vega.
DO WHILE .NOT. EOF()
   REPLACE CharFld WITH IIF("%" $ CharFld, STUFF(CharFld, ;
     AT("%", CharFld), 1, "#"), CharFld)
*-- Note the following technique to decide what to do next
   next_cmd = IIF("%" $ CharFld, "LOOP", "SKIP")
   &next_cmd
ENDDO
```

With CHRTRAN( ) the entire preceding program is reduced to one command:

```
REPLACE ALL CharFld WITH CHRTRAN(CharFld, "%", "#")
```

Now, suppose we need to update a mailing list database because the zip code 12345 is no longer valid, having been replaced by the code 34567. This still remains a trivial exercise in FoxPro:

```
REPLACE ALL zipcode WITH STRTRAN(zipcode, "12345", "34567")
```

Both STRTRAN( ) and CHRTRAN( ) are useful for removing unwanted characters from a file, for instance, null characters sent out by a mainframe during a communication session that had been captured to a file. User manuals that describe the use of the PC function keys often have a problem printing on devices such as the Hewlett-Packard LaserJet printers because the ASCII character representing the keyboard's right arrow key is really ASCII decimal 26, the end of-file character. Consequently the printer stops printing as soon as it encounters the right arrow key character. To counter this, use CHRTRAN( ) to replace the character with a printable one, and then restore it after the file is printed.

dBASE III Plus had a little-known bug where the APPEND FROM SDF or APPEND FROM DELIMITED command caused database corruption if the SDF or delimited file contained ASCII decimals 138 and 141 (soft linefeed and carriage return). Such a file could originate as a WordStar document. Because the dBASE III APPEND command strips the high bit off the ASCII character, CHR(138) becomes CHR(10), the linefeed character, and CHR(141) becomes CHR(13), the carriage return character. It appears that dBASE III was treating these characters as record terminators, causing it to truncate the data. One fix, of course, is to use CHRTRAN( ) to substitute another character before the APPEND and restore the characters later.

Soft spaces, soft hyphens, and soft carriage returns that have the high bit set may present problems in searching for substrings. For instance, if we were looking for the substring "Hot Dog", we may not find the string if CHR(141) is between the two words. In this case, we can just substitute a space for every occurrence of CHR(141) between the two words. The FoxPro SYS(15) function is designed primarily for European users whose character sets have the high bit set. With the European memory variable as a translation table (the variable is supplied in the European.mem distribution file), characters with diacritical marks are translated into corresponding characters with the high bit set off. In essence, SYS(15) in conjunction with the European memvar performs the same function as utility programs that convert a WordStar document to non-document mode. However, SYS(15) is slightly more versatile than most WordStar conversion programs because with it we can define the translation table in such a way that the conversion preserves the IBM box drawing symbols.

Encrypting and Decrypting Strings

Many applications institute a password system to control access to various system functions. Usually the security system is set up for multilevel access so that some users can perform only certain select functions, but the application administrator or "super-user" has access to all facilities, including maintenance functions such as deleting records and rebuilding indexes.

Password systems generally rely on the encryption of character strings. FoxPro's character functions make elaborate string encryption a simple task. Although most people have their own favorite encoding scheme, the scheme shown in Encrypt.prg (Listing 8-2) provides enough security to make the enrypted string difficult to decode. The encryption algorithm is in just one line. In essence, each character of the string is first converted to its ASCII decimal equivalent with the ASC( ) function. The program then adds to that value the character's position in the string and also the length of the string. This helps ensure that the same letter or number in the string or a similar string is encrypted differently. Finally, the resulting ASCII code is converted back to character using the CHR( ) function.

Listing 8-2. UDFs to encrypt and decrypt a string.

```
FUNCTION Encrypt
************************************************************
* Program ...: Encrypt.prg
* Author ....: P. L. Olympia & Kathy Cea
* Purpose....: Encrypt a string (for example a password)
* Syntax ....: Encoded = Encrypt(string)
*            :   String is the string to be encrypted
*            :   Returns the encoded string
************************************************************
PARAMETERS string
estring = ""
long = LEN(string)
FOR i = 1 TO long
 estring = estring + CHR(ASC(SUBSTR(string,i,1)) + i + long)
ENDFOR
RETURN estring


FUNCTION Decrypt
************************************************************
* Program ...: Decrypt.prg
* Author ....: P. L. Olympia & Kathy Cea
* Purpose....: Decrypt a string (for example a password)
* Syntax ....: Decoded = Decrypt(string)
*            :   String is the string to be decrypted
*            :   Returns the decoded string
************************************************************
PARAMETERS string
estring = ""
long = LEN(string)
FOR i = 1 TO long
 estring = estring + CHR(ASC(SUBSTR(string,i,1)) - i - long)
ENDFOR
RETURN estring
```

To use the function to encrypt a user-supplied password, you should take steps to keep the password from being echoed as it is being typed. You don't need an elaborate routine to accomplish this. The following code fragment shows how this can be done easily with FoxPro:

```
oldcolor = SET ("COLOR")        && save color setting
SET COLOR TO ,X                 && make GET data entry invisible
@...GET <password>              && get password
READ
SET COLOR TO (oldcolor)         && restore old color
```

Note that the SET COLOR TO ,X command makes the password invisible during data entry.

Listing 8-2 also shows Decrypt.prg, a function that decodes the string encrypted by Encrypt.prg. Clearly the decoding scheme uses the same functions used to encode the string.

String Animation

One way to attract a user's attention in an application and focus it on an important screen message is to use string animation. For instance, we can have an application welcome message move slowly across the screen, perhaps inside a graphics box such as a drawing of a computer monitor.

The user-defined function, Animate1.prg, shown in Listing 8-3 is one of the shortest animation programs you can write to move a specified string from right to left across the screen. For instance, the command:

```
= Animate1("Welcome to the LRAP System", 11, 16, 15)
```

moves the quoted string from right to left at screen row 12 (remember that the screen home position is 0, 0). The string begins to fade at column 17. The string moves in an area that is 15 characters wide.

FoxPro is so fast at running this function that in order to see the animation, you'll need to put in a delay loop just before the ENDFOR statement. A delay loop could be something as simple as

```
FOR j = 1 TO 200
ENDFOR
```

You may wish to add more pizzazz to the animation by changing the text color of the string using commands such as @...FILL.

Listing 8-3. Animate1.prg, a simple string animation function.

```
FUNCTION Animate1
*********************************************************
* Program ...: Animate1.prg
* Author ....: P. L. Olympia & Kathy Cea
* Purpose....: Animate a string by moving it from right to left
*            : at screen row Nrow, fading at column Ncol.
*            : Animation area is Nwide characters long.
* Syntax ....: = Animate1(string, Nrow, Ncol, Nwide)
*********************************************************
PARAMETERS message, nrow, ncol, nwide
FOR i = 1 TO LEN(message) - nwide + 1
   @ nrow, ncol SAY SUBSTR(message , i, nwide)
ENDFOR
RETURN ""
```

Listing 8-4 is a slightly more elaborate animation program. It moves two strings—first vertically on each side of the screen and then horizontally toward each other at a specified row—until they come together at the center.

The REPLICATE( ) Function

After converting a number to character using STR( ), you may want to replace the leading blanks in the resulting string with zeros. One way to accomplish this is to use STUFF( ) along with REPLICATE( ). Assuming that the string is *s*, the desired statement becomes simply

```
s = STUFF(s, 1, LEN(s) - LEN(LTRIM(s)), REPLICATE("0", ;
    LEN(s) - LEN(LTRIM(s))))
```

One of the most popular uses of REPLICATE( ) is in drawing extended IBM graphic character symbols as in a bar chart. Figure 8-1 shows a chart with four vertical bars drawn by the Vbar.prg program. The program is shown in Listing 8-5. The graph is drawn by calling two procedures. The first procedure, DrawAxis, draws the graph axis, prints a graph title, labels the vertical axis, and prints the axis tick marks. Note that this procedure uses the FoxPro PADC( ) function to print a centered string.

Listing 8-4. Animate2.prg, an animation function that moves two strings on either side of the screen and then joins them at the center of a specified row.

```
FUNCTION Animate2
************************************************************
* Program ...: Animate2.prg
* Author ....: P. L. Olympia & Kathy Cea
* Purpose....: Animate two strings (Lstring and Rstring) by
*            : moving them vertically (ending at row Erow)
*            : on either side of the screen then joining them at
*            : the center.
* Syntax ....: = Animate2(Lstring, Rstring, Erow, Width
*            :  Width = screen area where animation occurs, usually
*            :  80.
************************************************************
PARAMETERS Lstring, Rstring, Erow, Width

LenLeft=LEN(lstring)
LenRight=LEN(rstring)

FOR i = 1 TO Erow - 1
   @ i,1 SAY SPACE(LenLeft)
   @ i,width-LenRight SAY SPACE(LenRight)
   @ i+1,1 SAY lstring
   @ i+1,width-LenRight SAY rstring
   * Delay to slowdown FoxPro a bit
     FOR j = 1 to 200
     ENDFOR
ENDFOR

lstop=(width-LenLeft+LenRight+1)/2
lstop=lstop-10
rstop=lstop+LenLeft

moveit = IIF(lstop > (width - rstop), lstop, width - rstop)

FOR i = 1 TO moveit
   IF i <= lstop
      @ Erow, i SAY lstring
   ENDIF
```

(continued)

Listing 8-4. Continued

```
      IF width-(LenRight-1+i) >= rstop
         @ Erow, width-(LenRight-1+i) SAY rstring
      ENDIF
    ENDFOR

   FOR i = 1 TO moveit
      IF i <= lstop-1
         @ Erow, i SAY " "
      ENDIF

      IF width-i >= rstop+LenRight
         @ Erow, width-i SAY " "
      ENDIF
   ENDFOR
   RETURN ""
```

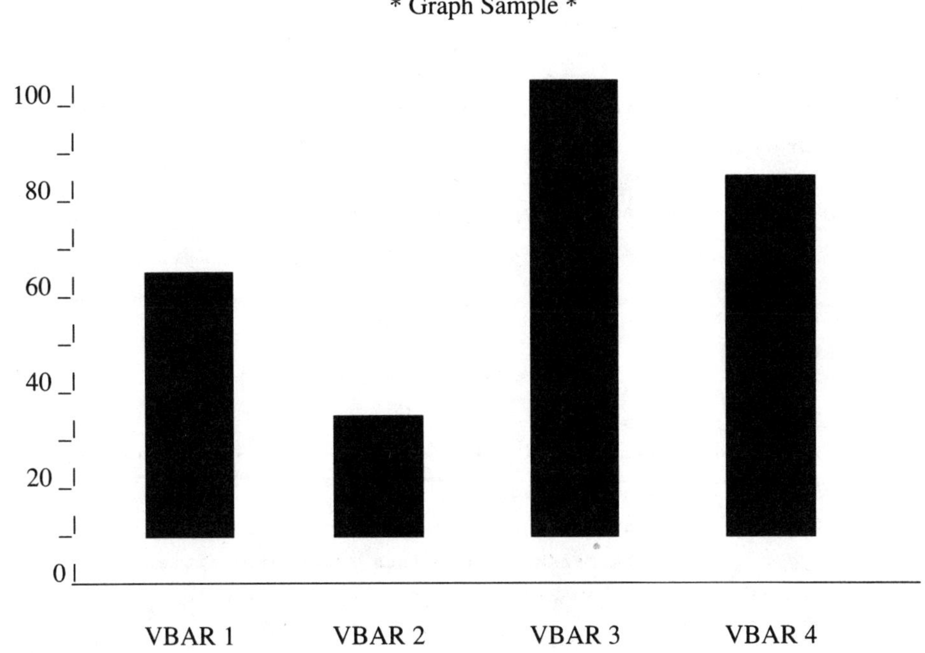

Figure 8-1. Vertical bar chart drawn by Vbar.prg using REPLICATE( ).

Listing 8-5. Driver program and procedures for drawing bar charts using the REPLICATE() function.

```
*************************************************************
* Program ...: Vbar.prg
* Purpose....: Draws vertical bar chart using REPLICATE()
*            : This driver program first calls DrawAxis to draw
*            : the graph axis, then calls DrawBar to draw a
*            : vertical bar
* Notes .....: Set to draw a bar with maximum value of 100,
*            : Resolution set at 5.
*************************************************************

*-- This is the driver program that calls the two graph programs

SET TALK OFF
CLEAR

PUBLIC ymax, ymin, yincr, row0
*-- Define bounds
ymax = 100
ymin = 0
yincr = 20

DO DrawAxis WITH 16, 4, "g+", "w+", "* Graph Sample *"
DO DrawBar WITH 60, 6, 17, 16, "VBAR 1", "r"
DO DrawBar WITH 32, 6, 17, 30, "VBAR 2", "g"
DO DrawBar WITH 100, 6, 17, 44, "VBAR 3", "g+"
DO DrawBar WITH 82,  6, 17, 58, "VBAR 4", "r+"

SET TALK ON
RETURN

PROCEDURE DrawAxis
*************************************************************
* Program ...: DrawAxis.prg
* Purpose....: Draws the graph axes including labels and
*            : tick marks. Also prints a centered title.
* Syntax ....: DO DrawAxis with x_row, t_row, ax_color,
```

(continued)

Listing 8-5. Continued

```
*             :    ti_color, title
*             : x_row = row where the x-axis is drawn
*             : t_row = row where the title is drawn
*             : ax_color = color of axis
*             : ti_color = color of title
*             : title = graph title
* Notes .....: Adapted from a program by Jon Wind.
************************************************************
PARAMETERS  x_row, t_row, ax_color, ti_color, title

SET COLOR TO (ti_color)
@ t_row, 0 SAY PADC(title, 80)          && Note PADC to center
SET COLOR TO (ax_color)

@ x_row-10,10 TO x_row,10               && draw y axis
@ x_row,10 SAY CHR(192)                 && draw corner
@ x_row,11 TO x_row,70                  && draw x axis

row0 =x_row - 1
FOR i = ymin TO ymax+1 STEP yincr
  @ x_row,5    SAY STR(i,3)+IIF(i > ymin," _","")  && Label
  @ x_row-1,9 SAY IIF(i < ymax,"_","")             && tick marks
  x_row=x_row-2
ENDFOR
RETURN


PROCEDURE DrawBar
************************************************************
* Program ...: DrawBar.prg
* Purpose....: Draws a vertical bar given a value
* Syntax ....: DO DrawBar with value, barwidth, g_row, g_col
*             :  g_label, bar_color
*             : Value = numeric value to graph
*             : barwidth = width of bar (in chars) to draw
*             : g_row = start row where bar is drawn
*             : g_col = column where bar is drawn
*             : g_label = bar label (limit to barwidth)
```

(continued)

Listing 8-5. Continued

```
*             : bar_color = color of bar
* Notes .....: Based on a program by Jon Wind
**************************************************************
PARAMETERS value, barwidth, g_row, g_col, g_label, bar_color

row = row0
gyval = 2.5
resol = 5
ntick = 10

SET COLOR TO (bar_color)
@ g_row,g_col + barwidth/2)-(LEN(g_label)/2) SAY g_label

DO WHILE gyval <= ymax  .AND. gyval <= value
  IF value >= gyval + resol
    @ row, g_col SAY REPLICATE(CHR(219),barwidth)  && long vert bar
ELSE

    IF value >= gyval
      @row, g_col SAY REPLICATE(CHR(220),barwidth)  && short Vbar
    ENDIF
  ENDIF
  gyval = gyval + ntick
  row = row-1
ENDDO
SET COLOR TO
RETURN
```

The second procedure, DrawBar, draws the actual bar chart in the specified screen column position. As implemented, the program is set to chart data values less than or equal to 100, with a resolution of about 5. A desirable enhancement you may pursue is to make the programs generic so they can handle any data values with appropriate scaling.

Chapter Summary

Character data is the predominant data type in typical database applications. FoxPro has an extensive set of commands and functions for manipulating character string data. In this chapter, we discussed how to convert various data types to character and some of the practical advantages of defining database fields as character.

We discussed the FoxPro functions for searching strings and memo fields for a character or substring with or without regard to case. We showed a code fragment to search a text file for a desired substring, with or without wildcard characters, by first loading it into a memo field and performing the search there with one FoxPro function. The chapter describes how to use the RAT( ) function, along with the KEYBOARD command, to allow word wrapping during data entry on character fields or memory variables.

We also discussed functions such as CHRTRAN( ) and STRTRAN( ), which are designed to replace characters and strings, including removing unwanted characters from DOS files. Both functions solve the problem of removing or replacing characters with the high bit set so that string matches can proceed as expected.

The results of string comparisons in non-SQL FoxPro commands depend on SET EXACT and the position (left or right) of the string relative to the = operator. Results of string comparisons in SQL depend on SET ANSI and not on SET EXACT. Results of string comparisons in SQL also do not depend on whether the string is to left or right of the comparison operator.

The chapter provided examples of procedures and user-defined functions that demonstrate character data handling. These include functions to encrypt and decrypt a user-supplied password, functions to animate a string to focus users' attention to the message, and functions to draw a vertical bar chart based on user-supplied values.

Chapter 9

Array Techniques

Arrays in FoxPro

Arrays have varied uses in a typical application. For example, they provide the facility for building and displaying menus, implementing table lookups, and allowing direct edits on database records without necessarily compromising the integrity of the data. FoxPro memory variable arrays may be either one- or two-dimensional. Arrays may be defined with the DECLARE, DIMENSION, REGIONAL, or PUBLIC commands. The following statements all create a one-dimensional array of ten elements and a two-dimensional array with two rows and three columns:

```
DIMENSION ArrayA(10), ArrayB[2,3]
DECLARE   ArrayA[10], ArrayB(2,3)
PUBLIC ARRAY ArrayA(10), ArrayB(2,3)
PUBLIC ArrayA[10], ArrayB[2,3]
```

Note that FoxPro recognizes both the parentheses (used by FoxBASE+) and the square brackets (used by Clipper and dBASE IV) to reference array elements. The size of an array may be declared using a numeric expression. For instance, the statement

```
DIMENSION B[FCOUNT()]
```

defines a one-dimensional array with as many elements as there are fields in the currently active .dbf file. An array may also be redimensioned at will. In

FoxPro 2.0, array elements are not reinitialized to the default logical .F. values when the array is redimensioned. Thus array elements retain their original values.

Arrays created by a program are normally private or local—available only to the program that created them and its subprograms. However, arrays defined with the PUBLIC command are available throughout the application just like regular memory variables.

A FoxPro array uses only one memory variable from the memory variable pool, MVCOUNT, regardless of the size of the array. Recall that MVCOUNT can be set to a maximum of 3600 in Config.fp in the standard version. The maximum number of elements in an array is 3600, and the maximum number of arrays active at one time is also 3600 in the standard version. The Extended Version allows up to 65,000 elements in an array.

Array Element Addressing

Unlike arrays in C, which are zero-based, FoxPro arrays are one-based—array subscripts begin with 1. A two-dimensional array may be accessed with a single subscript, because, in fact, declaring a two-dimensional array of *r* rows and *c* columns simply allocates storage for a one-dimensional array of *r* ∗ *c* elements. FoxPro and languages like Basic that support two-dimensional arrays really just provide the facility for referencing a desired element using a row-column index address. This built-in facility is missing in the Summer '87 version of Clipper, so it does not appear to support two-dimensional arrays explictly. However, it is easy enough to write UDFs to translate two-dimensional index addresses to one-dimensional addresses. FoxPro's built-in AELEMENT( ) function does just that.

FoxPro arrays are stored in row-major order and single subscript addressing is based on this storage order. For example, Figure 9-1 shows the single subscript address of an array with two rows and three columns.

Note that the array element B(2,1) may also be referenced with B(4). The single subscript address of an element in a two-dimensional array located at row *r* and column *c* is defined by the formula

```
Index1 = (r - 1) * numcols + c
```

where numcols is the number of columns in the array. FoxPro's AELEMENT( ) and ASUBSCRIPT( ) functions facilitate the conversion of element addresses in one- and two-dimensional arrays.

	Column		
Row	**1**	**2**	**3**
1	1	2	3
2	4	5	6

Figure 9-1. Single subscript address of a 2 x 3 array.

Initializing Arrays

Elements of the same array need not be of the same data type. One element may contain character data and another may contain numeric or date data.

When an array is first defined, all its elements are initialized as logical data types with values of .F. They retain those values until they are changed with the assignment statement or with commands such as COPY TO ARRAY. Figure 9-2 shows a series of commands that first defines an array of three elements and then stores a date value to the second element and a character value to the third element. The DISPLAY MEMORY command shows the result.

```
DIMENSION ArrayA(3)
ArrayA(2) = DATE()
ArrayA(3) = "Sneakers"
DISPLAY MEMORY LIKE ARRA*

  ARRAYA       Pub    A
       (   1)      L  .F.
       (   2)      D  02/20/90
       (   3)      C  "Sneakers"
    1 variables defined,       15 bytes used
  255 variables available,   5985 bytes available
```

Figure 9-2. Defining and initializing an array. Note that the array elements may be of different data types.

The effect of an assignment statement in initializing an array depends on the setting of the COMPATIBLE switch. With the default setting of SET COMPATIBLE FOXPLUS, the assignment statement

```
ArrayB = SPACE(1)
```

changes all elements of ArrayB to type character and each element of the array is initialized to one space. If the same command had been issued with SET COMPATIBLE DB4, the memory variable array would be replaced by a scalar variable of the same name initialized to a single space. In effect, the array is erased.

FoxPro Arrays versus Clipper Arrays

As we mentioned before, the Summer '87 release of Clipper supports only one-dimensional arrays. However, it is possible, via a scheme similar to the single subscript formula described earlier, to refer to a specific element as though it were part of a two-dimensional array.

FoxPro, like Clipper, allocates array memory dynamically. A pointer is set from the memory variable area to a chunk of memory where reference to array elements is kept. This array area is 18 bytes wide (Clipper's is 22 bytes wide) and its length is equal to the dimension of the array. Numeric values of array elements are stored in the 18-byte area for the element. If the element is of type character, the 18-byte area contains a pointer to a contiguous area of memory where the actual value for the element is stored.

In Clipper, the TYPE( ) function returns "A" for an array. FoxPro's TYPE( ) function does not return the same result. Instead, it returns the type of the first element of the array. For instance,

```
DECLARE ArrayA[3]
? TYPE("ArrayA")
   L                    && Array type is Logical, initial
                        && default

ArrayA[1] = "Molly"
? TYPE("ArrayA")
   C                    && Array type is now Character.
```

FoxPro's TYPE( ) function correctly returns the data type of a specified array element. For example,

```
ArrayA[5] = 12
ArrayA[6] = "Donnie"
? TYPE("ArrayA[5]")
  N                   && Type is Numeric
? TYPE("ArrayA[6]")
  C                   && Type is Character
```

In Clipper, the TYPE( ) function returns "U" (for undefined) if provided a specific array element such as ArrayA[6]. For it to behave like FoxPro's function, we must first assign a memory variable to the array element and then use that memory variable name as the argument to the function.

Clipper has one other deficiency concerning arrays—it returns a runtime error message when an attempt is made to perform a GET directly into an array element. To work around this problem, Clipper developers have had to first assign the array element to a memory variable and then perform a GET on that variable. FoxPro does not have this problem, so the following commands work as expected in FoxPro:

```
@ 7, 11 GET ArrayA[12]
READ
```

FoxPro 2.0 has all of Clipper's built-in array functions, except ACHOICE( ), and then it adds a few more of its own (see Table 9-1). The FoxPro equivalent of ACHOICE( ) can be coded easily with a few lines because its MENU command is functionally equivalent to Clipper's ACHOICE( ).

Passing Arrays to Procedures

In most Dbase dialects, including FoxPro 1.x, array names are passed to functions and procedures either as a literal enclosed in quotes or square brackets, or as the name of a memory variable containing the array name, for example,

```
arg1 = "Array1"      && Array1 and Array2 are arrays
DO MyProc WITH arg1, "Array2"
```

The invoked procedure, in turn, had to have code that is replete with macros, such as

```
&Array1[j] = &Array1[j - 1]
```

In FoxPro 2.0, an entire array can be passed to a procedure or function by just passing its name. So, in 2.0, the preceding code fragment becomes simply

```
DO MyProc WITH Array1, Array2
```

and the arrays can be addressed in the invoked procedure without using macros.

Built-in Array Functions

Table 9-1 shows the syntax for FoxPro's built-in array functions and briefly describes each one. You can use ALEN( ) to determine if an array has been dimensioned with one or two subscripts. For a two-dimensional array, ALEN(array, 2) yields the number of columns. For a one-dimensional array, this number is 0, and both ALEN(array) and ALEN(array, 1) return the same number—the array's dimension.

Before FoxPro 2.0, you were forced to either resort to the RUN command or to create .bin routines to bring disk directory information to your application. For instance, if you wanted to write a disk catalog program in FoxPro 1.x, you probably would issue the RUN DIR command and then load the result to a scratch .dbf for further processing. The new ADIR( ) function has immensely simplified the task of writing a disk catalog program or bringing disk directory data to an application. The function automatically creates an *N* x 5 array where *N* is the number of files that satisfies the desired file mask. Columns 1 through 5 contain, respectively, the filename, filetype, creation date, creation time, and file attributes. File attributes may be

- R—Read-Only
- A—Archive
- S—System
- H—Hidden
- D—Directory

or any combination.

Since ADIR( ) can return the names of subdirectories (by specifying "D" as the third argument to the function), your disk catalog program can easily traverse through all subdirectories on the disk. To get the disk's volume name, use "V" as the third argument to the function. Doing that creates a one-element array containing the name of the volume. You can also use ADIR( ) to report on all hidden files on disk.

Table 9-1. FoxPro Built-in Array Functions

ACOPY(<array1>, <array2> [,<expN1> [,<expN2> [,<expN3>]]])	Copies elements from <array1> to <array2>, optionally beginning with the <expN1>th element of <array1> for <expN2> elements. <expN3> specifies the element number of <array2> where copying begins.
ADEL(<array>, <expN> [,2])	Deletes an element, row, or column from <array>. The optional ,2 argument specifies that <expN> is a column.
ADIR(<array> [,<expC1> [,<expC2>]])	Places in <array> the name, size, and date/time of creation and DOS attributes of all files matching a file mask specified by <expC1> and returns the number of files that match the file mask. <expC2> can have the values D, H, S, or V, depending on whether additional information on subdirectories, hidden files, system files, or volume name, respectively, is desired.
AELEMENT(<array>, <expN1> [,<expN2>])	Returns the element number of an array where <expN1> is its row subscript and <expN2> is its column subscript.
AFIELDS(<array>)	Places database structure information (field name, field type, field length and number of decimal places) in an array and returns the number of fields in the database.
AINS(<array>, <expN> [,2])	Inserts an element into a one-dimensional array or a row or column into a two-dimensional array. The optional ,2 argument specifies that <expN> is a column number.
ALEN(<array> [,<expN>])	Returns the number of elements, rows, or columns in an array, depending on whether <expN> is 0, 1, or 2, respectively.
ASCAN(<array>, <expr> [,<expN1> [,<expN2>]])	Returns the number of the array element that matches the <expr> expression, optionally beginning the search at the <expN1>th element and continuing for <expN2> elements.

(continued)

Table 9-1. Continued

ASORT<array> [,<expN1> [,<expN2> [,<expN3>]]])	Sorts <array> in ascending or descending order, depending on whether <expN3> is 0 or 1, respectively. Sorting can be specified to begin at the <expN1> element/row and <expN2> column.
ASUBSCRIPT(<array>, <expN1>, <expN2>)	Returns an array row or column subscript given its element number in <expN1>. If <expN2> = 1, the row subscript is returned. If <expN2> = 2, the column subscript is returned.

One practical use of ADIR( ) is to copy all data files of an application to a backup medium as part of the system maintenance function. Formulating the proper file mask for ADIR( ) becomes greatly simplified if you are consistent in the way you name the application's data files, for example, beginning all filenames with the same two letters. The Ok2Back.Prg program in Listing 9-1 shows how you would use ADIR( ) to determine if there is enough room on the backup drive or medium for all the files that you want copied. The program simply adds up column 2 of the array that ADIR( ) creates to obtain the total size of the desired files. It then compares that size to the space remaining on the backup medium as reported by DISKSPACE( ). Note the last statement in the program. Instead of using the verbose set of statements

```
IF TotBytes <= DriveBytes
   RETURN .T.
ELSE
   RETURN .F.
END
```

you can get the same result with the single command:

```
RETURN (TotBytes <= DriveBytes)
```

Another useful built-in array function is AFIELDS( ), which creates an array containing structure information for the currently active database. It can

Listing 9-1. The Ok2Back.Prg function uses ADIR( ) to determine if there is sufficient space on a target disk to copy all the files that need to be backed up.

```
FUNCTION Ok2Back
************************************************************
* Program ...: Ok2Back.prg
* Author ....: P. L. Olympia and Kathy Cea
* Purpose....: Demonstrates one use of FoxPro 2.0's ADIR()
*            : function. Returns .T. if a specified target drive
*            : has enough room to copy a set of desired files
* Syntax ....: IF Ok2Back(TgtDrive, FileMask)
*            :    .. go ahead and back up
*            : ENDIF
*            :  TgtDrive = Drive letter of the target drive
*            :  FileMask = file skeleton for the desired set of
*            :             files, e. g., APP*.*
************************************************************
PARAMETERS TgtDrive, FileMask
PRIVATE TmpArry, NumFiles, i, TotBytes, DriveBytes

*-- Use ADIR to create an array of desired files
NumFiles = ADIR(TmpArry, FileMask)

IF numfiles = 0
   RETURN .T.
ENDIF

TotBytes = 0
FOR i = 1 TO NumFiles
    TotBytes = TotBytes + TmpArry(i, 2)   && filesize in 2nd column
ENDFOR

*-- Get the space remaining on target drive
old_defa = SET("DEFAULT")
SET DEFAULT TO (TgtDrive)
DriveBytes = DISKSPACE()
SET DEFAULT TO (old_defa)

*-- Comment out the next 2 lines if you don't want the output
```

(continued)

Listing 9-1. Continued

```
? "Total Bytes of files with mask ", FileMask, " are ", TotBytes
? "Bytes remaining in target drive ", TgtDrive, " are ", DriveBytes

*-- Look at this technique for generating logicals
RETURN (TotBytes <= DriveBytes)
```

be used as an alternative to COPY STRUCTURE EXTENDED. With this function, you can allow users to modify the length of database fields (or even field names, assuming that doing so will not wreak havoc on the application code as well as screen layouts). In this scenario, you would use AFIELDS( ) to create an array of .dbf structure data, let users modify the data contained in the array (perhaps using MENU and MENU BAR), and then re-create the modified .dbf using the CREATE TABLE FROM <array> command.

The IsDbfSame.Prg function in Listing 9-2 shows another example of how you might use AFIELDS( ) in an application. This function determines if two .dbfs have the same structure simply by loading their structures to separate arrays and then comparing the arrays.

FoxPro Commands Involving Arrays

As we have seen, FoxPro arrays are usually created using the DIMENSION, DECLARE, or PUBLIC commands, although a few commands such as SCATTER will also create arrays as required. The memory space occupied by arrays is released with the RELEASE, CLEAR MEMORY, or CLEAR ALL commands. Since RELEASE supports an optional clause such as LIKE <skel> or EXCEPT <skel>, it can be used to release a given set of arrays whose names match or do not match the specified name skeleton.

Arrays, like ordinary memory variables, may be saved to a .mem file or memo field with the SAVE TO command and restored with the RESTORE FROM command. If you issue the RESTORE FROM command in the command window, the arrays are restored as public variables. Issuing the command from a program restores the arrays as private variables.

Listing 9-2. The IsDbfSame.Prg function uses AFIELDS( ) to determine if two .dbfs have the same structure.

```
FUNCTION IsDbfSame
************************************************************
* Program ...: IsDbfSame.prg
* Author ....: P. L. Olympia and Kathy Cea
* Purpose....: Demonstrates one use of FoxPro 2.0's AFIELDS()
*            : function. Quickly compares the structure of two
*            : .dbf files and returns .T. if they are identical
* Syntax ....: IF IsDbfSame(dbf1, dbf2)
*            :    ... the two .dbfs are identical
*            : ENDIF
*            :  Dbf1 and Dbf2 are the two database files whose
*            :  structures are to be compared.
************************************************************
PARAMETERS Dbf1, Dbf2
PRIVATE Dbf1Arry, Dbf2Arry, n1, n2
  SELECT (Dbf1)
  n1 = AFIELDS(Dbf1Arry)
  SELECT (Dbf2)
  n2 = AFIELDS(Dbf2Arry)

  IF n1 <> n2
     RETURN .F.
  ENDIF
  *-- Compare the two arrays
  FOR i = 1 TO n1
      FOR j = 1 TO 4
         IF Dbf1Arry[i, j] <> Dbf2Arry[i, j]
            RETURN .F.
         ENDIF
      ENDFOR
  ENDFOR
RETURN .T.
```

FoxPro's command system uses arrays in various ways, for example,

- To move database fields to arrays.
- To move array data to database fields.
- To store results of computations.
- To store screens or window images.
- To use as an integral part of the FoxPro menu facility.

Table 9-2 summarizes the FoxPro commands that support these functions. For the sake of completeness, the table also includes the commands to define, initialize, save, release, and restore arrays.

Moving Data to/from Arrays and Database Fields

FoxPro's set of commands that include SCATTER, GATHER, COPY TO ARRAY and APPEND FROM ARRAY facilitate a number of database operations by reducing entire subroutines into a few lines of code. We discuss the use of these commands in greater detail in Chapters 14 and 15.

One of the most popular uses of the SCATTER and GATHER commands is to allow application users to edit a database record directly, instead of having to first copy the field values to corresponding memory variables. In this technique, SCATTER is used to store the contents of the current record to an array. The user is then free to edit the current record directly. If the user decides later to discard the edits, the record is restored to its original state with the GATHER command. The same set of commands is useful also in copying the contents of one record to another or in blanking a record. Blanking a record is another popular technique for recycling a record instead of deleting it and later getting rid of it permanently by packing the database. Packing a database not only requires exclusive use of the file, thereby making it temporarily unavailable to others, but also entails extensive and unnecessary disk I/O activity.

An important database operation that benefits from the use of arrays is table lookup, which searches a sorted array for a key, returning one or more column values from the table or array. This operation executes faster when implemented using arrays rather than related data files because all searches use only random access memory. It has the added advantage of saving a file handle and a work area in which to open another database, an important consideration in applications that require a large number of databases to be open at one time.

Table 9-2. Summary of FoxPro Commands That Use Arrays

Commands to Move Database Fields to Arrays

Command	Description
`COPY TO ARRAY <array> [FIELDS <field list>] [<scope>] [FOR <expL>] [WHILE <expL2>] [NOOPTIMIZE]`	Copies data from one or more records of the currently selected database to an array. Each record becomes a row in the array. The command ignores memo fields.
`SCATTER [FIELDS <field list>] TO <array> | TO <array> BLANK | MEMVAR | MEMVAR BLANK [MEMO]`	Moves data from the current record of the selected database to an array or a set of memory variables (with the same name as database fields). The BLANK option leaves the array or memory variables empty. The command can handle memo fields.

Commands to Move Array Data to Database Fields

Command	Description
`APPEND FROM ARRAY <array> [FOR <expL>] [FIELDS <field list>]`	Adds one or more records to the currently selected database from data stored in an array. Each row of the array becomes a record in the database. The command ignores memo fields.
`GATHER MEMVAR | FROM <array> [FIELDS <field list>] [MEMO]`	Transfers data from an array or a set of memory variables (with the same names as database fields) into the current record of the selected database. The command can handle memo fields.

Commands to Store Computation Results to Arrays

Command	Description
`AVERAGE [<expr list>] [<scope>] [FOR <expL1>] [WHILE <expL2>] [TO <memvar list> | TO ARRAY <array>] [NOOPTIMIZE]`	Computes the arithmetic mean of numeric fields in the database and optionally stores the results to a one-dimensional array or a set of memory variables.

(continued)

Table 9-2. Continued

Command	Description
CALCULATE <expr list> [<scope>] [FOR <expL1>] [WHILE <expL2>] [TO <memvar list> | ARRAY <array>] [NOOPTIMIZE]	Computes various statistical and financial measures involving database fields and stores the results to a one-dimensional array or a set of memory variables. The quantities computed include average, count, maximum value, minimum value, net present value, standard deviation, sum, and variance.
SUM [<expr list>] [<scope>] [FOR <expL1>] [WHILE <expL2>] [TO <memvar list> | TO ARRAY <array>] [NOOPTIMIZE]	Computes the totals of one or more numeric fields in the database and stores the results to a one-dimensional array or a set of memory variables.

Commands to Store Screens or Window Images

Command	Description
SAVE SCREEN [TO <memvar>]	Saves the current screen or output window image to a buffer, memory variable, or array element. The memory variable or array element has a data type of "S."
RESTORE SCREEN [FROM <memvar>]	Restores a screen or window image, previously stored by the SAVE SCREEN command, from a buffer, memory variable, or array element.

Commands to Use Arrays in FoxPro Menus

Command	Description
@ <row, col> MENU <array>, <expN1> [, <expN2>] [TITLE <expC>] [SHADOW]	Creates a menu popup, activated by the READ MENU command. Options that appear on the menu popup are stored previously in a one-dimensional character array with elements no longer than 76 characters.

(continued)

Table 9-2. Continued

`MENU BAR <array1>, <expN1>` `MENU <expN2>, <array2>, <expN3> [, <expN4>]`	Along with the READ MENUBAR TO command that activates them, these two commands constitute FoxPro's menu creation facility. MENU BAR installs <array1> into the menu bar. The array is a two-dimensional character array, the first column of which constitutes the menu pads. If defined, elements in the second column of the array appear in the SET MESSAGE location as additional message. MENU installs a menu popup into a menu bar. The menu options are stored in the one-dimensional character array <array2>.

Commands to Define and Initialize Arrays

`DIMENSION <array1> (<expN1> [, <expN2>]) [<array2> ...]`
`DECLARE <array1> (<expN1> [, <expN2>]) [<array2> ...]`
`PUBLIC [ARRAY] <array1> (<expN1> [, <expN2>]) [<array2> ...]`
`REGIONAL<array1> (<expN1>[,<expN2>]) [<array2>...]`
	Create one or more memory variable arrays of one or two dimensions.

`STORE <expr> TO <memvar list> | TO <array>`	Like the assignment statement (for example, A = 1), stores data to a memory variable, array, or array element. The SET COMPATIBLE switch determines whether the entire array can be initialized by a single STORE command.

(continued)

Table 9-2. Continued

Commands to Release Memory Space Occupied by Arrays

`CLEAR MEMORY`
`CLEAR ALL`
`RELEASE ALL [LIKE <skel> | EXCEPT <skel>]`
	Frees up memory occupied by arrays or memory variables with names that match the pattern defined by <skel>.

Commands to Save/Restore Arrays

`SAVE TO <file> | TO MEMO <memfield> [ALL LIKE <skel> | ALL EXCEPT <skel>`	Saves arrays and memory variables to a .mem file or memo field.
`RESTORE FROM <file> | FROM MEMO <memfield> [ADDITIVE]`	Restores arrays and memory variables previously saved in a .mem file or memo field.

In implementing table lookup using arrays, we normally have the data stored permanently in a .dbf file. The application opens this file, copies its contents to an array, and then closes the file. The amount of coding, along with the usual overhead associated with copying the .dbf records to the array, is reduced drastically because it takes just one COPY TO ARRAY command to load the array. The only serious limitation to this approach is the finite size of the array, which in standard FoxPro cannot exceed 3600 elements (65,000 elements in the Extended Version).

In moving database field values to and from arrays, remember that the operation can now include memo fields, and that the data transfer occurs in one-to-one correspondence between fields and array elements. Thus, if there are more array elements than there are fields in the database, the values of the extra elements remain unchanged by the SCATTER or COPY TO ARRAY command. Conversely, if there are more fields than there are array elements, the values of the extra fields are not copied.

We have repeatedly made the point that in most languages the only real distinction between one- and two-dimensional arrays is the manner in which the index address is referenced. This is not exactly correct in FoxPro because the results of the COPY TO ARRAY and APPEND FROM ARRAY commands depend on the dimension of the specified array. Recall that these commands can copy data to and from multiple records. The command

```
COPY TO ARRAY x
```

where *x* is a one-dimensional array copies only the values of the fields in the current record even though *x* has a size that can accommodate field values from several records. On the other hand, if *x* is a two-dimensional array, this command copies the field values from the current record to as many records as there are rows in the array. Naturally we can limit the range of records that the command transfers by using a scope specification such as NEXT 3.

Note that COPY TO ARRAY creates the array if it does not exist. In that case, it creates as many rows as there are records (subject to FoxPro array limits) if a scope is not specified.

SCATTER/GATHER versus COPY/APPEND Commands

SCATTER and COPY TO ARRAY both copy database fields to arrays, but they differ in that SCATTER copies database field values from the current record to a one-dimensional array. On the other hand, COPY TO ARRAY can copy field values from one or more database records, depending on the dimension of the array and the scope specified in the command. Also, SCATTER copies memo fields while COPY TO ARRAY does not.

GATHER and APPEND FROM ARRAY are the complement commands of SCATTER and COPY TO ARRAY, respectively. They differ in the same ways that their complement commands differ. Thus, APPEND FROM ARRAY can create multiple records, but GATHER is confined to only one record.

Sorting Data

Sorting data is one of the most commonly used operations in computer applications. FoxPro, like other members of the Dbase family, provides a convenient way of sorting data. For instance, assume that we want to sort a table of survey results in ASCII that may have been downloaded from a mainframe or produced by an optical scanner. We can simply create a database structure that matches the table and then write a sorted file back to disk with the following commands:

```
USE <dbfname>
APPEND FROM <tablefile> SDF
INDEX ON <sortfield>
COPY TO <sortedfile> SDF
```

One of the most useful array functions in FoxPro is ASORT( ), which can sort both one- and two-dimensional arrays in ascending or descending order. This function is also much faster than any program you can devise using the FoxPro language. In the next section we explore various array sorting techniques, partly to acquaint you with the various algorithms and their relative strengths and weaknesses, and partly so you would know how to code the best sort procedure for a given set of data in the event that you port your applications to another Dbase dialect that does not have an ASORT( ) function.

Array Sorting Techniques

Lookup procedures that are implemented using arrays clearly require the arrays to be sorted. There are a number of sorting algorithms we can use. Our choice is usually governed by efficiency considerations: the time required to code the program, the machine time required to execute the sort, and the amount of memory or disk space that the program needs.

The optimal sort algorithm is one in which the sort time is always of the order of the item count, that is, $O(n)$, independent of whether the input data is already almost sorted or not. Unfortunately such an algorithm does not exist. Sort time is most commonly a function of the original sequence of data. For most algorithms, sort time is $O(n)$ if the items are almost sorted, and $O(n*n)$ if the items are in completely reversed order. If we have no advanced knowledge of the original sequence of data, we may want to select the sort strategy that can handle the average case in $O(n \log n)$. Such an algorithm increases sort time by less than 3000 for every 1000-fold increase in the number of items to sort compared to a million-fold increase in a method where the sort time is $O(n*n)$.

However, note that when n is small, an $O(n*n)$ sort may still be preferable to an $O(n \log n)$ sort because the former is usually much easier to program and has little overhead since most of the operations are comparisons and replacements during each pass through the data.

Let's look at some common sort methods—their strengths and weaknesses and how we would code them as FoxPro procedures.

Bubble Sort

The Bubble sort, so called because each item slowly "bubbles" to its proper position, is the easiest sort technique to code but is probably the most inefficient. Thus it is most suited for sorting a short list of items or records in a small file. Its efficiency is usually $O(n*n)$, but this improves considerably up to $O(n)$ for a list that is almost sorted.

This method requires passing through the array items several times. Each pass consists of comparing each element to its successor and exchanging the two if they are not in proper order. Since each iteration places a new element in its proper position, the procedure requires no more than $n - 1$ iterations to sort an array of n items. After k iterations, elements in positons $(n - k + 1)$ and greater will be in their proper order and need not be compared in succeeding iterations. We can speed up the procedure by recognizing if the array is already sorted after less than $n - 1$ iterations. Clearly the array is completely sorted as soon as no element interchange occurs in any one pass.

Listing 9-3 is a FoxPro procedure that sorts an array using the Bubble technique. A sample invocation syntax is shown in the code.

Shell Sort

The Shell (or Diminishing Increment) sort orders separate subarrays of the original array. The subarrays contain every mth element (the increment) of the original. For instance, if m is 7, the elements A[1], A[8], A[15], ... are sorted first. Seven subarrays, each containing one-seventh of the original array elements, are sorted this way. After the first m subarrays are sorted, a new smaller value of m is chosen and the array is partitioned into a new set of subarrays. Eventually m is set to 1 and the entire array is sorted.

The Shell method is ideal for moderately sized arrays of a few hundred elements. Its efficiency is influenced by the value of the increment and approaches $O(n (\log n)(\log n))$ when an appropriate set of increments is used. In the Shell sort, partial sorts on a subarray do not disturb subarrays that have already been sorted earlier using a larger increment value.

Listing 9-4 shows a FoxPro procedure that implements the technique.

Listing 9-3. A FoxPro program that sorts an array using the Bubble sort technique.

```
PROCEDURE Bubble.prg
************************************************************
* Program ...: Bubble.prg
* Copyright..: (c) 1990, P. L. Olympia & Kathy Cea
* Purpose....: Sorts an array using the Bubble technique
* Syntax ....: DO Bubble WITH "Arr", n
*            :  Arr = Array, n = elements
************************************************************
PARAMETERS Arr, n

   IntChange = .T.
   NumPass = 1
   DO WHILE NumPass <= n-1 .AND. IntChange
      IntChange = .F.
      FOR j = 1 TO n - NumPass
          IF Arr(j + 1) < Arr(j)  && Out of order, so interchange
             Temp = Arr(j)
             Arr(j) = Arr(j+1)
             Arr(j+1) = Temp
             IntChange = .T.
          ENDIF
      ENDFOR    && j
      NumPass = NumPass + 1
   ENDDO
RETURN
```

Quicksort

Quicksort (or Partition Exchange sort) is a recursive procedure. It rearranges the keys and partitions the array into two subsections such that all keys in the first subsection are smaller than all keys in the second subsection. The two subsections are then sorted recursively, after which the array is completely sorted.

Quicksort's efficiency is of the range $O(n \log n)$ through $O(n*n)$, depending on the input data and the size of the array. The unmodified Quicksort

Listing 9-4. A FoxPro program that sorts an array using the Shell sort technique.

```
PROCEDURE Shelsort.prg
************************************************************
* Program ...: Shelsort.prg
* Copyright..: (c) 1990, P. L. Olympia & Kathy Cea
* Purpose....: Sorts an array using the Shell sort technique
* Syntax ....: DO ShelSort WITH "Arr", n
*             : Arr = Array, n = elements
************************************************************
PARAMETERS Arr, n

midl = INT(n/2)
DO WHILE midl > 0
      i =  midl + 1
      DO WHILE i <= n
            j = i - midl
            DO WHILE ((j >= 1) .AND. (Arr[j] > Arr[j+midl]))
                  hold = Arr[j]
                  Arr[j] = Arr[j+midl]
                  Arr[j+midl] = hold
                  j = j - midl
            ENDDO
            i = i + 1
      ENDDO
      midl = INT(midl / 2)
ENDDO
RETURN
```

algorithm ironically works best for items that are completely unsorted and worst for those that are already almost sorted. Quicksort is also much better for medium to large arrays than for very small ones.

Listing 9-5 shows a FoxPro procedure that implements the Quicksort technique.

Note that the procedure uses recursive function calls to QSortSub. Without the ability to make recursive calls, this procedure would be difficult to code. The following code fragment demonstrates a very simple use of recursive function calls—it computes the factorial of the parameter *x*. Bear in mind that

Listing 9-5. A FoxPro program that sorts an array using the Quicksort sort technique.

```
PROCEDURE QSort.prg
**********************************************************
* Program ...: Qsort.prg
* Copyright..: (c) 1990, P. L. Olympia & Kathy Cea
* Purpose....: Sorts an array using the Quicksort technique
* Syntax ....: DO Qsort WITH "Arr", n
*            :  Arr = Array, n = elements
* Calls .....: QSortSub which calls PART and recursively calls
*            : itself.
**********************************************************
PARAMETERS Arr, n

PUBLIC pivot
=QSortSub(arr,1,n)
RETURN

FUNCTION QSortSub
PARAMETERS arr,low,high
IF low < high
        DO PART WITH arr,low,high
        =QSortSub(arr,low,pivot-1)
        =QSortSub(arr,pivot+1, high)
ENDIF
RETURN .T.

PROCEDURE Part
PARAMETERS arr, startlow, starthigh
pos = arr(startlow)
high = starthigh
low = startlow
DO WHILE low < high
        DO WHILE (arr(low) <= pos) .AND. (low < starthigh)
                low = low + 1
        ENDDO
        DO WHILE (arr(high) > pos)
                high = high - 1
        ENDDO
```

(continued)

Listing 9-5. Continued

```
        IF low < high
                temp = arr(low)
                arr(low) = arr(high)
                arr(high) = temp
        ENDIF
ENDDO
arr(startlow) = arr(high)
arr(high) = pos
pivot = high

RETURN
```

the use of a recursive procedure in this example is very inefficient; it is shown merely to demonstrate the capability.

```
PROCEDURE recurse
PARAMETERS x
* Demonstrate recursive capability by
* computing x! (factorial)
Factrl = 1
=factor(x)
? Factrl
FUNCTION factor
PARAMETERS x
IF x > 2
     =factor(x-1)
ENDIF
Factrl = Factrl * x
RETURN .T.
```

The recursive capability works regardless of whether the parameters are passed by value or by reference. Generally it is advisable to use recursion only when absolutely necessary (such as in our Quicksort example). This is because the recursive function must place a copy of all parameters on a stack for each separate call, usually slowing execution and consuming additional system resources. Note also that recursion in FoxPro has one major limitation:

recursion that results in a <program> nesting which is more than 32 levels deep produces a runtime error.

The Quicksort procedure in Listing 9-5 sets element partitioning such that all elements below a given pivot point are less than or equal to the value of the pivot, and all elements above are greater than or equal to the pivot point value. The pivot point is simply an arbitrary element of the array. In our example, we select the first element of each partition to act as the pivot point. Once we have separated our initial array into two partitions, we treat each partition separately, again selecting a pivot element and rearranging elements so that they meet the preceding criteria. We continue partitioning and rearranging elements until the entire array is sorted. Again, this technique cannot be used if the recursion results in program nesting that is more than 32 levels deep.

Heapsort

The Heapsort technique uses a data structure that is essentially a binary tree with some of its rightmost leaf nodes removed. The structure may be defined as a descending heap or an ascending heap. A descending heap with n elements is an almost complete binary tree with n nodes; the content of each node is less than or equal to the content of its father node. Conversely, an ascending heap is an almost complete binary tree with the contents of each node greater than or equal to the contents of its father node. In this example we will be using a descending heap.

Heapsort processing consists of two parts. In the first part, we build the heap from the unordered array. We do this by traversing the tree from the bottom up for each element of the array, seeking the first element greater than or equal to the element we wish to insert. When an element is inserted, the nodes it has passed are shifted down. This is called a shiftup operation.

The second part of the process uses a shiftdown operation to delete nodes from the heap in descending order and place them in their proper position in the array. The result is a sorted array.

In a heap, both insertion and deletion can be done in $O(\log n)$ operations, and the sorting can be done in place with no additional space requirements except for program variables. Thus the Heapsort algorithm is an in-place sort with an efficiency of $O(n \log n)$, even in the worst case. It is not very efficient for small n because of the overhead associated with constructing the heap.

Listing 9-6 shows a FoxPro procedure that implements the Heapsort technique.

Listing 9-6. A FoxPro program that sorts an array using the Heapsort technique.

```
PROCEDURE HeapSort.prg
*************************************************************
* Program ...: HeapSort.prg
* Copyright..: (c) 1990, P. L. Olympia & Kathy Cea
* Purpose....: Sorts an array using the Heapsort technique
* Syntax ....: DO HeapSort WITH "Arr", n
*            :  Arr = Array, n = elements
*************************************************************
PARAMETERS Arr, n

* Build the heap
FOR i = 2 TO n
        element = arr(i)
        son = i
        father = INT(son/2)
        DO WHILE (son > 1) .AND. (arr(father) < element)
                arr(son) = arr(father)
                son = father
                father = IIF((son > 1), INT(son/2),1)
        ENDDO
        arr(son) = element
ENDFOR

maxint = 9999999   && assign to # larger than any element
* Sort the Heap
FOR i = n TO 2 STEP -1
        lastval = arr(i)
        arr(i) = arr(1)
        father = 1
        son = IIF((i = 2),0,2)
        FOR j = 3 TO (n - 1)
                IF ( i > j) .AND. (arr(j) > arr(j-1))
                        son = j
                ELSE
                        EXIT
                ENDIF
        ENDFOR
```

(continued)

Listing 9-6. Continued

```
          newval = IIF ((son > 0), arr(son),0)
          DO WHILE (son > 0) .AND. (lastval < newval)
                    arr(father) = arr(son)
                    father = son
                    son = 2 * father
                    IF ((son + 1) <= (i - 1)) .AND. ;
                        (arr(son) < arr(son + 1))
                              son = son + 1
                    ENDIF
                    IF son < i
                              newval = arr(son)
                    ELSE
                              son = 0
                              newval = maxint
                    ENDIF
          ENDDO
          arr(father) = lastval
ENDFOR

RETURN
```

Chapter Summary

Standard FoxPro supports one- or two-dimensional arrays of up to 3600 elements while the Extended Version allows arrays of up to 65,000 elements. FoxPro's array subscript notation is compatible with those of FoxBASE+, Clipper, and dBASE IV. An array can contain elements of varying data types. When provided a literal with the name of an array, FoxPro's TYPE( ) function returns the data type of the first array element.

FoxPro uses arrays extensively in its own command language. Array usage in FoxPro falls into the following categories:

- To move database fields to arrays.
- To move array data to database fields.
- To store computation results to arrays.
- To store screens or window images.
- To use as an integral part of the FoxPro menu facility.

We discussed how some of the array-related commands can be used to allow direct edits on database records without compromising the integrity of the data, and how they can be used for table lookups. We also discussed the primary differences between SCATTER and COPY TO ARRAY, and between GATHER and APPEND FROM ARRAY.

In this chapter we discussed the differences in FoxPro and Clipper arrays. We described FoxPro's built-in array functions and showed two programs that take advantage of ADIR( ) and AFIELDS( ).

The chapter concluded with an extensive discussion of array sorting algorithms including Bubble sort, Quicksort, Shell sort, and Heapsort. We discussed the general principle involved in each technique, along with its efficiency and the circumstances under which each one is suited. We also presented FoxPro programs to show how each sort algorithm is implemented.

Chapter 10

Indexing and Sorting

Database management systems allow us to store and quickly retrieve data items. Indexing and sorting are the two methods for manipulating a database file to facilitate searches and to report in a prescribed order. In this chapter we examine both methods, including their strengths and weaknesses, and the circumstances under which each is more appropriate.

Sorting

A database may be physically reordered with the SORT command. This command creates a new .dbf in the order specified by the SORT statement. The SORT command's options allow you to sort on any number of database fields, in ascending or descending order. Additionally the FIELDS option allows you to include in the sorted file any or all of the fields in the original database file. You can use a FOR or WHILE clause to limit the records included in the sorted file.

You can SORT only on database fields. FoxPro does not allow sorting on expressions of any type, memory variables, or calculated values. Thus you cannot include an expression such as TRIM(UPPER(LName)) in the ON clause.

A sorted database is most often created for temporary purposes such as to output a report in a given order. It is a temporary solution since the sorted file is out of date as soon as the original file is modified. The SORT command also consumes a great deal of disk space, sometimes as much as three to four times as much space as the original .dbf occupies. Before performing a SORT, you should verify that you have sufficient disk space. You can use the FoxPro functions DISKSPACE( ), HEADER( ), RECCOUNT( ), and RECSIZE( ) to compute the available or required disk space.

You can also produce a sorted file by opening a database file with an index, or creating an index (where the index expression matches the expression you wish to sort on), and then COPYing the file. This results in a new .dbf file in sorted order. Although this approach requires less available disk space, we found it to be slower during our testing. In tests involving a sample database with 10,000 records of randomly generated numbers, a SORT took an average of 22 seconds, whereas an INDEX ON and COPY sequence required a total of 44 seconds (20 and 24 seconds, respectively). This means that even if the index had already existed, the SORT was faster than the COPY.

Searches are not usually performed on a sorted database because FoxPro offers a rich and powerful set of searching commands for indexed databases. However, as discussed later in this chapter, you can design your own algorithm to speed up searches in a sorted database, if necessary.

Sorting is also slow, especially when a large file is involved. Often it is too slow to be acceptable in an interactive environment and is reserved only for overnight batch report runs.

Indexing

The alternative to sorting a database is to create index files. An index file has one record for each corresponding database record. This record consists of the value of the key expression and a pointer to the record in the .dbf. An index logically reorders the database without affecting the physical order of the records. It is useful for reporting data in a given order, for quickly searching for a key expression, and for relating databases with primary and secondary keys using the SET RELATION command.

FoxPro 2.0 supports the following three types of index files:

1. Traditional index (.idx) files—Traditional index files are the same as those supported by FoxPro versions 1.x and FoxBASE+.
2. Compact index (.idx) files—Compact index files use data compression to produce a file as small as one sixth the size of the comparable traditional index file, and may be accessed faster.

3. Compound index (.cdx) files—Compound index files contain multiple index entries called tags. A structural compound index file is a special type of .cdx file that is automatically opened whenever the associated database file is opened.

Applications that must maintain compatibility with FoxPro 1.x or FoxBASE+ can use the traditional .idx files under FoxPro 2.0. However, if compatibility is not an issue, you should use compound and/or compact index files for efficiency. A compact index is not only smaller, requiring less storage space, but it can also be accessed by FoxPro faster. A compound index file is always compressed, like a compact index, and has several important advantages. First, a number of indexes (tags) can be opened and maintained by opening just one file, the .cdx file. Second, a .cdx file can be indexed in ascending or descending order. Finally, and most importantly, a structural .cdx is always opened automatically whenever the associated .dbf is opened. This eliminates the old problem of index files being out of sync with their .dbfs. The number of tags you can include in a .cdx file is limited only by memory and disk space, so you will normally want to include all of your required permanent indexes in a structural .cdx.

Under FoxPro 1.x, a maximum of 25 index files could be open at one time in an application. Once you reached the limit of 25 open index files, you were unable to open additional index files, meaning that you could be left with out-of-date indexes. Under FoxPro 2.0, the number of open index files you can have is limited by memory and by FoxPro's maximum of 99 total open files. (With the FoxPro 2.0 Extended Version, the number is limited only by memory.) You can limit the number of files the application needs to open by creating index tags in a compound index, and you can eliminate the problem of outdated indexes by placing the permanently needed tags in a structural .cdx.

Open indexes add processing overhead when database records are being added, deleted, or modified because each index must be examined to determine the impact of the changes. The processing overhead is particularly noticeable with large files. For this reason, you should create and maintain an index only if the key is frequently searched, if the resulting order is commonly used for reporting purposes, and/or if the file will be related to other database files with the SET RELATION command. You can create temporary index files or sorted files for reports that require infrequently used sort orders.

Table 10-1 displays useful commands and functions for working with index files.

Table 10-1. Commands and Functions for Working with Index Files

<table>
<tr><td>CDX(<expN> [, <alias>])</td><td>Returns the names of open .cdx files. The CDX( ) function is identical to the MDX( ) function.</td></tr>
<tr><td>CLOSE INDEX</td><td>Closes all open index files open within the current work area.</td></tr>
<tr><td>COPY INDEXES <index file list>
| ALL [TO <.cdx file>]</td><td>Copies single entry index files to a .cdx file.</td></tr>
<tr><td>COPY TAG <tag name>
[OF <.cdx file>] TO <index file></td><td>Creates a single entry index file from a tag in a .cdx file</td></tr>
<tr><td>DELETE TAG <tag name1>
[OF <.cdx file1>] [, <tag name2>
[OF <.cdxfile2>]] ... |
ALL [OF <.cdx file>]</td><td>Removes a tag or tags from a .cdx file.</td></tr>
<tr><td>FIND <char str> | <n></td><td>Finds a database record whose index key matches the character string <char str> or the number <n>.</td></tr>
<tr><td>INDEX ON <expr> TO <.idx file>
| TAG <tag name> [OF <.cdx file>]
[FOR <expL>] [COMPACT]
[ASCENDING | DESCENDING] [UNIQUE]
[ADDITIVE]</td><td>Creates an index file or tag to order a database in the currently selected work area.</td></tr>
<tr><td>KEY([<.cdx file>,] <expN>
[, <alias>])</td><td>Returns the index expression of an open index file. KEY( ) is similar to the SYS(14) function.</td></tr>
<tr><td>MDX(<expN> [, <alias>])</td><td>Returns the names of open .cdx files. MDX( ) is identical to the CDX( ) function.</td></tr>
<tr><td>NDX(<expN> [, <alias>])</td><td>Returns the name of an open .idx file.</td></tr>
<tr><td>ORDER([<expN1> | <expC>
[, <expN2>]])</td><td>Returns the name of the master index file or master tag.</td></tr>
<tr><td>REINDEX [COMPACT]</td><td>Rebuilds open index files and tags in .cdx files in the currently selected work area.</td></tr>
<tr><td>SEEK <expr></td><td>Searches an indexed database for the first occurrence of a record whose index key expression matches the specified <expr>.</td></tr>
</table>

(continued)

Table 10-1. Continued

`SEEK(<expr> [, <alias>])`	Searches an indexed database for the first occurrence of a record whose index key expression matches <expr> and returns true (.T.) if a SEEK was successful.

`SET INDEX TO`
`[<index file list> | ?`
`[ORDER <expN>`
`| <.idx index file>`
`| [TAG] <tag name>`
`[OF <.cdx file>]]`
`[ASCENDING | DESCENDING]`
`[ADDITIVE]`
	Opens index files for the currently selected database file.

`SET ORDER TO`
`[<expN> | <.idx index file>`
`| [TAG] <tag name>`
`[OF <.cdx file>]`
`[IN <work area | alias>]`
`[ASCENDING | DESCENDING]]`
`[ADDITIVE]`
	Designates the controlling (master) index file or tag.

`SET RELATION TO [<expr1> INTO`
`<alias> [ADDITIVE]]`
`[, <expr2> INTO <alias>`
`[ADDITIVE]] ...`
	Links two open databases by evaluating <expr> to either an index key or a record number.

`SET UNIQUE ON | OFF`	Specifies if records with duplicate index keys will appear in an index file.
`SYS(14, <expN1> [, <expN2>])`	Returns the index expression for an index file.
`SYS(21)`	Returns the number of the controlling index in the currently selected work area.
`SYS(22 [, <expN>])`	Returns the name of the controlling tag or index for a database.
`TAG([<.cdx file>, ] <expN>` `[, <alias>])`	Returns tag names from .cdx files or the names of .idx index files.

Rushmore

FoxPro 2.0 includes a highly efficient data access technique called Rushmore. Rushmore works with any FoxPro index, including the traditional .idx file. It speeds up searches for data with a command that uses a FOR clause matching the expression of any open index. It also works with a SET FILTER command that specifies a condition that matches the expression of an open index, and with FoxPro's SQL facility. Table 10-2 lists the commands that can utilize Rushmore to optimize a search.

Rushmore cannot use a filtered or unique index (that is, indexes created with the FOR and/or UNIQUE clause). Also, Rushmore performs better without a controlling index. As discussed later, SET ORDER TO 0 leaves your indexes open without a designated controlling or master index.

The result of Rushmore is that a data search is optimized if you are accessing a data set using an expression that matches any index that exists and is open. Unlike FIND and SEEK, to be used for optimizing a search, the index does not need to be the controlling index.

Rushmore builds a temporary set of records that meet the FOR criteria whenever a Rushmore-optimizable command is issued. The records in the set are then available to the command for processing. If there is a chance that the record set could change while the command is active, Rushmore should be disabled by including the NOOPTIMIZE clause in the command. For example, a SCAN FOR...ENDSCAN sequence that modifies key expressions of records could potentially change which records should be included in the set for processing. To ensure correct processing, include the NOOPTIMIZE clause on the SCAN command. Note that when Rushmore is disabled in these cases, processing will be accurate but slower.

Table 10-2. FoxPro Commands That Are Potentially Optimizable by Rushmore

AVERAGE	DISPLAY	RECALL
BROWSE	EDIT	REPLACE
CALCULATE	EXPORT	REPORT
CHANGE	INDEX	SCAN
COPY TO	JOIN	SORT
COPY TO ARRAY	LABEL	SUM
COUNT	LIST	TOTAL
DELETE	LOCATE	

Indexing Options

The INDEX command has been enhanced in FoxPro 2.0 to include several new options. The format of the command is as follows:

```
INDEX ON <expr> TO <.idx file> | TAG <tag name> [OF <.cdx file>]
      [FOR <expL>]
      [COMPACT]
      [ASCENDING | DESCENDING]
      [UNIQUE]
      [ADDITIVE]
```

New to FoxPro 2.0, you can include a user-defined function (UDF) in the index expression <expr>. If you use a UDF in the index expression, be certain that the keys generated will be of constant length. As discussed later, variable length keys can produce unpredictable results. Also, the UDF must be available to FoxPro whenever the index is accessed. Using a UDF in the index expression may increase the time required to build the index.

A traditional .idx file is created if you include the TO <.idx> file clause. If you also include the new COMPACT option, a compact .idx file is created.

If you include the TAG <tag name> clause in lieu of the TO <.idx> clause, a new index tag is created. If the compound index (.cdx) file already exists, the tag is added to the .cdx file. Otherwise, a new .cdx file is built. If you omit the [OF <.cdx file>] clause, the .cdx file becomes a structural compound index. Since compound indexes are always compact (compressed), there is no need to include the COMPACT clause.

The [ASCENDING | DESCENDING] clause specifies the order of the index tag. Indexes are created in ascending order by default. If you include the DESCENDING option, the records will be indexed in descending order. This clause is available only in connection with the TAG <tag name> clause; single-file indexes cannot be created in descending order. However, as described later in this chapter, data in a single-file .idx can be accessed in descending order by means of a DESCENDING option on the USE or SET ORDER TO command.

The FOR and UNIQUE clauses are retained from FoxPro 1.x. The FOR option allows you to specify a condition for including records in the index; any record not meeting the <expL> condition is excluded from the index file (although not from the .dbf). The UNIQUE clause specifies that only the first record containing any particular key value will be included in the index file. If SET UNIQUE is ON, an index is created with the UNIQUE option even if it is not specified in the command. SET UNIQUE's default setting is OFF.

Note that an index that is created using the FOR and/or UNIQUE clause cannot be used by Rushmore to optimize searches.

If you include the ADDITIVE clause, you can create an index without closing previously opened index files.

Index File Format

Traditional (.idx) index files consist of one header record and one or more node records in a tree structure. The header record contains information pertaining to the entire file such as the file size and index key expression. Appendix E displays the index file header format and additional format information.

Nodes are categorized as index, root, or leaf. The root node is the top node in the tree, where a search always begins. Leaf nodes are the bottom nodes of the tree and point to database records. Index nodes are indexes into other nodes; they narrow down the set of nodes to be searched as they are traversed. Figure 10-1 shows the structure of the index tree.

The key value in the search expression is compared to the values stored in the root node to determine the direction to search in the tree. A path is

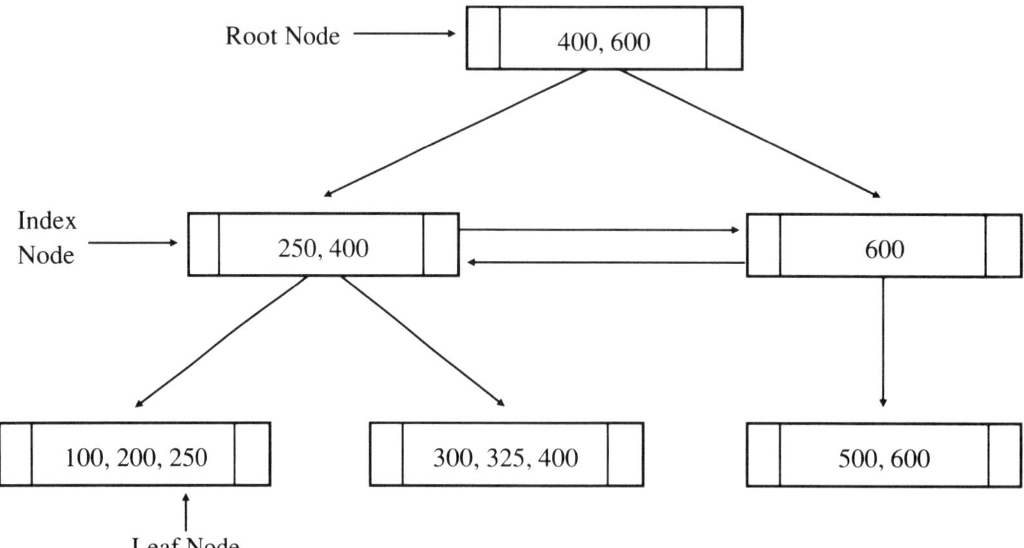

Figure 10-1. An index tree structure.

determined from root node to leaf node, based on the comparisons of the search value against the key values stored in each node traversed. Nodes are traversed until the leaf node is reached; the leaf node points to the desired database record. This structure is a very fast, efficient search mechanism.

Database Searches

As stated earlier, one of the primary goals of a database application is to be able to locate specific data items quickly. Depending on whether your database is sorted, indexed, or unordered, there are several ways to search for a particular record. In this section, we look at options for searching an indexed database, a sorted database, and an unordered database.

Indexed Databases

If your database is indexed on the key value you wish to search for, you can use the FIND or SEEK commands, or the SEEK( ) function. The command syntax for each of these is as follows:

```
FIND <char string>|<n>
SEEK <expr>
SEEK(<expr>[,<alias>])
```

The FIND command accepts only a character string or number and moves the record pointer to the first record whose key matches the specified value. Note that numbers are treated as character strings when used with the FIND command. The value must be passed as a literal; if you wish to FIND a memory variable that contains a character expression, precede the variable with the & function. A literal may be passed with or without quotes. The following examples are valid statements:

1. FIND “Abc”
2. FIND Abc
3. mString = “Abc”
   FIND &mString
4. mExpr = TRIM(UPPER(“xxx”))
   FIND &mExpr
5. FIND 123

However, the following examples are invalid. Even though they do not generate a syntax error, they will not produce the desired results.

6. mString = "Abc"
   FIND mString

   * A search will be performed for a character string of "mString",
   * not "Abc".
7. mNum = 123
   FIND &mNum

   * A search will be performed for a right-justified, 10-byte character string.
8. FIND TRIM(UPPER("xxx"))

   * Searches for a character string containing the expression
   * TRIM(UPPER("xxx")).

Since macro substitution slows program execution and since you are limited to a data type of character (or numeric treated as character), the SEEK command is preferred to FIND. SEEK can be used with any valid expression, and it works with memory variables without requiring macro substitution. As with the FIND command, SEEK moves the record pointer to the first record whose key matches <expr>. The equivalent commands that use SEEK for the preceding examples are as follows:

1. SEEK "Abc"
2. SEEK "Abc"
3. mString = "Abc"
   SEEK mString
4. mExpr = TRIM(UPPER("xxx"))
   SEEK mExpr
5. SEEK 123
6. mString = "Abc"
   SEEK mString
7. mNum = 123
   SEEK mNum
8. SEEK TRIM(UPPER("xxx"))

The SEEK( ) function is more powerful than even the SEEK command. This function combines the SEEK command with the FOUND( ) function, returning .T. if a match is found, and .F. if not. In addition to eliminating one line of program code for each SEEK( ), an optional parameter may be passed to indicate the work area (alias) in which the search is to be performed. FIND and SEEK both work only in the current work area. Unless compatibility with an existing system is an issue, you should use SEEK( ) in place of SEEK or FIND. If you must maintain compatibility with a system that does not support the SEEK( ) function, you are better off using the SEEK command than FIND, for the reasons discussed earlier.

The Effect of SET NEAR and SET EXACT With FIND or SEEK, the record pointer moves to the bottom of the file if a matching record is not found in the database, unless SET NEAR is ON. If SET NEAR is ON, the pointer is moved to the record whose key value immediately follows the value sought.

Both FIND and SEEK return a value of true (.T.) for FOUND( ) if a matching record is found, and a value of false (.F.) otherwise. However, the return value for EOF( ) varies depending on the SET NEAR setting. If SET NEAR is OFF (the default), a value of .F. is returned for EOF( ) if the record is found, a value of .T. is returned otherwise. If SET NEAR is ON, a value of .F. is always returned for EOF( ) unless the search fails and the closest matching record happens to be the last record in the file. Since .F. is usually returned for EOF( ) with SET NEAR ON even if the match fails, it is better to check the value of FOUND( ) when determining whether a match was found.

If SET EXACT is ON, FIND and SEEK will match two character strings only if they are of equal length. If SET EXACT is OFF, a match will be found if the leftmost part of the record key matches the string being searched for. This is described in greater detail later in this chapter.

Searching for Multiple Records If you are going to search for multiple occurrences of a specified key, you should perform a SEEK( ) (or SEEK or FIND) to position the record pointer to the first matching record. The most efficient means of processing at that point is to use the SCAN...ENDSCAN structure. For example, to find all Customer records with a Last Name of "Smith" on a database file indexed on Last Name, your program code might look as follows:

```
mLName = UPPER(TRIM("Smith"))
IF SEEK(mLName)
  SCAN WHILE UPPER(TRIM(Cust->LName)) = mLName
    * process record
  ENDSCAN
ELSE
    * No matching records found
ENDIF
```

Remember that, with the Rushmore technology, you can perform an efficient search on an index expression even if that index is not the controlling index. For example, if in the last example the index on Last Name is open but not the master, you could perform an efficient search with the following code:

```
mLName = UPPER(TRIM("Smith"))
LOCATE FOR UPPER(TRIM(Cust->LName)) = mLName
DO WHILE FOUND()
     * process record
     CONTINUE
ENDDO
```

Searching a Sorted Database

As we previously discussed, a database is normally sorted only for temporary reporting purposes. However, if you happen to have a sorted database from which you need to extract a particular data item, how do you search it? You can't use the SEEK, FIND, or SEEK( ) commands designed for indexed databases because your database is not indexed, and you surely do not want to use LOCATE to perform a record-by-record search when you know that the records are in order. What you need is a search algorithm designed specifically for a set of sorted records.

The binary search is one such algorithm. It starts its search in the middle of the set (in our case, at the record in the middle of the .dbf) and determines whether the value in that record is equal to, greater than, or less than the search key. If they are equal, we've found the record and processing is complete. Otherwise, if the record value is less than the search key, the algorithm finds the record halfway between the current record and the end of the file; if the record is greater than the search value, it finds the record halfway between the top of the file and the current record. This logic continues until either the desired item is found or there are no additional records to search. If there is more than one record matching the search key, this algorithm does not necessarily find the first—it simply finds one of the matching records.

Listing 10-1 demonstrates a program, BinSrch, to perform a binary search on a sorted database. It requires two parameters: the name of the field to be searched and the field value to be found. The .dbf to be searched must already be open in the current work area. The program verifies that the field exists in

Listing 10-1. BinSrch.prg, a binary search program.

```
*******************************************************************
* Program: BinSrch.prg
* Author : P.L. Olympia & Kathy Cea
* Purpose: Performs a binary search on the open sorted .dbf
*        :  in order to locate a value of FldVal for field
*        :  FldName.
*        :
* Syntax : BinSrch(<FldName>,<FldVal>)
*        : where <FldName> is the field to be searched and
*        : <FldVal> is the value to be searched for
******************************************************************

FUNCTION BinSrch
PARAMETERS FldName, FldVal

* Make sure there is a field FldName
mNumFlds = FCOUNT()
i = 0
FoundFld = .F.
DO WHILE (i <= mNumFlds) .AND. (!FoundFld)
     i = i + 1
    IF TRIM(UPPER(FldName)) = FIELD(i)
       FoundFld = .T.
    ENDIF
ENDDO

IF !FoundFld
* If there is no FldName Field in the database, Return .F.
   RETURN .F.
ENDIF

* Make sure the FldName TYPE matches the Field TYPE
IF TYPE("FldVal") <> TYPE(FIELD(i))
     RETURN .F.
ENDIF
```

(continued)

Listing 10-1. Continued

```
SET TALK OFF
FoundRec = .F.
Low = 1
High = RECCOUNT()

DO WHILE ( Low <= High) .AND. (.NOT. FoundRec)
        Mid = INT((Low + High) / 2)
        GOTO RECORD Mid
        IF (EVALUATE(FldName) = FldVal)
                FoundRec = .T.
        ELSE
                IF FldVal < EVALUATE(FldName)
                        High = Mid - 1
                ELSE
                        Low = Mid + 1
                ENDIF
        ENDIF
ENDDO

RETURN FoundRec
* If found, returns .T. and the .dbf pointer is set to matching record
*  Otherwise, returns .F. and the .dbf pointer location is random
```

the database and that the data type of the field matches the data type of the key value. Then it performs the search algorithm.

Since each pass reduces the number of records to be compared by a factor of 2, the maximum number of comparisons required is log *n*. Compare this to a sequential search, where the maximum number of comparisons is *n*. Although not usually as fast as a SEEK on an indexed database, the BinSrch program does perform reasonably well. In tests run on a sample database of 10,000 records, a SEEK typically required less than 1 second, and the binary search required about 1 second.

Note that the BinSrch program could be modified slightly to perform a binary search on a sorted array. (We discuss array sort techniques in Chapter 9.)

Searching an Unordered File

If you need to find a record in a database that is not indexed on the expression you want to search for and the database is not sorted on your expression, you have several options. You can create a temporary index, with or without the FOR and UNIQUE clauses. You can also sort the file to a temporary file, which you delete upon completion of your processing. Or you can leave the file unordered and perform a sequential search.

An indexed file can be searched very quickly. Using the FOR clause with the INDEX command creates a smaller index to be searched, speeding things up even more. Although the search is very fast, you must consider the time required to create the index and the extra disk space required.

Similarly, a database may be SORTed to a temporary file. Again, extra time and much more additional disk space are required to perform the sort. Then, once your file is in sorted order, the efficiency of the search depends on your search algorithm. Since an indexed file can be searched faster than a sorted file, this option is not practical unless you also need the sorted file for reporting purposes.

If you opt not to temporarily index or sort your file, you still have several ways to find a record. The SET FILTER command is available, although it is not usually recommended. This command limits all access to the .dbf to those records that meet your specified condition. The operation of the filter is very slow because each record is read to determine whether or not it will be included in the accessible set. Unless most of your records meet the filter condition, you should not use the SET FILTER command.

The LOCATE command is similar to the FIND and SEEK commands in that it searches for a record matching the expression you supply. However, it is considerably slower because it operates on an unindexed database file and therefore must read the database file sequentially. It is best used for an occasional search of a nonkey value. The CONTINUE command may be used in conjunction with the LOCATE command to continue searching for records that satisfy the LOCATE criteria.

The SCAN...ENDSCAN command, described earlier, can also be used to search an unordered database. The FOR clause is particularly useful when searching for multiple records that meet a particular condition.

If you use the SET FILTER, LOCATE, or SCAN commands, be sure to turn off any active index. An active (but unrelated) index serves only to slow processing when performing sequential searches, for example, with the SET FILTER and LOCATE commands. To ensure that your indexes are kept updated but inactive, you may issue the SET ORDER TO 0 command.

Formulating Index Expressions

Creating indexes is critical to the efficiency of your entire application. To build efficient and useful indexes, you need to understand how to formulate the index expression.

Indexes may be created on any combination of numeric, character, logical, or date fields, although the entire expression must evaluate to just one data type. Special consideration must be given to character type indexes and to indexes made up of multiple data types.

Indexing on a Character Expression

A character field type can contain values in a number of different ways. Consider, for example, a code field containing two character positions. If left unedited during data entry, a user can elect to enter a code of 2 as " 2", "2 ", or "02". A search for " 2" will not find "2 " or "02". In addition, consider the following set of codes: 2, 4, 5, 6, 9, 12, 14, 21, 23, 26, 30, 35. If you index on this field, the result is as follows:

```
12
14
2
21
23
26
30
35
4
5
6
9
```

This is probably not the result you want. There are several ways to get around this problem. One way is to format the character field during the data entry process so that the string is right justified and padded with zeros. In this case, your values would look like: 02, 04, 05, 06, 09, 12, 14, 21, 23, 26, 30, 35. Thus they would sort in the order you expect.

If this requirement is too burdensome, you also have the option of converting the character string to a numeric value with the VAL( ) function. You can index on the numeric value and achieve the correct result, for example, INDEX ON VAL(Code) TO <IdxName>.

Indexing on Mixed Data Types

Although you can include different data types in your index expression, the entire expression must evaluate to just one data type. FoxPro offers a number of data conversion functions that make this task easier (see Chapter 8).

Example 1: Indexing on Date and Character Fields Consider an order database that should be indexed on Date of Order + Customer number. Date of Order is a date field type, and Customer number is a character field. The DTOS function (or equivalent DTOC(<expD>,1)) returns the date as an eight-digit character field, in the format YYYYMMDD, which is useful for indexing. Thus the index expression for the order database might be

```
DTOS(Order_Dt) + Cus_Id
```

Example 2: Indexing on Date and Numeric Fields Let's look at another date example where, instead of combining the date with a character expression, we want to combine it with a numeric expression. For example, an Accounts Overdue file might need to be ordered on Date_Billed + Days_Overdue, where Date_Billed is a date field and Days_Overdue is a numeric calculated field. Assume we have the following values in one of our records:

```
Date_Billed:    01/01/91
Days_OverDue:   95
```

If we index on Date_Billed + Days_Overdue, our key value for the preceding record would evaluate to 04/06/91. FoxPro actually adds the number of days to the date, and the result is a new, valid date. Although this can be a useful feature at times, it is hardly what we want when we index this file. Therefore, the correct expression would be

```
DTOS(Date_Billed) + STR(Days_Overdue,4)
```

This converts each value to a character string and concatenates them. Note that we included the ",4" in our STR function. Although any number can be used, this option should be specified whenever converting a numeric field to character for indexing purposes. This is because a variable-length index can yield unpredictable results.

Example 3: Indexing on Logical and Character Fields Suppose we have a database in which we wish to index a logical field and a character field. For example, a department store's customer file includes a logical field for credit customers (Credit_Cus) and a Customer id character field. If we want to index on Credit_Cus and Customer id, we can write the following expression:

```
INDEX ON IIF(Credit_Cus,"1","0") + TRIM(Cus_Id)
```

This places the Credit_Cus = .F. records before the Credit_Cus = .T. records, the same order FoxPro uses if we index on just a logical field. Of course, you can always reverse this to suit your needs by simply modifying the IIF to

```
IIF(Credit_Cus,"0","1").
```

Conditional Indexes

The IIF( ) function is also useful for indexing on a field conditionally. For example, if you want to index on the first five digits of a company's phone number if it exists or on the first five digits of their zip code if the phone number does not exist, you could issue the command

```
INDEX ON IIF(EMPTY(Co_Phone),SUBSTR(Co_Zip,1,5),
  SUBSTR(Co_Phone,1,5))
```

Descending Indexes

FoxPro 2.0 offers a number of ways to access data in descending order. The INDEX command includes a DESCENDING clause that can be used to build an index tag in reverse order. This clause cannot be used when creating a traditional or compact (.idx) index. However, any index—traditional (.idx), compact (.idx), or compound (.cdx)—can be opened in descending order by including the DESCENDING clause on either the USE command or the SET ORDER TO command. Additionally an index tag that was created in descending order may be opened in ascending order by including the

ASCENDING clause in the USE or SET ORDER TO command. Note that including an ASCENDING or DESCENDING clause on the USE or SET ORDER TO command does not modify the index in any way; it simply specifies how the data is to be accessed.

Index Expression Length

The maximum allowable length for an index expression and an optional FOR expression in an .idx file is 220 characters each. In a .cdx index, the maximum combined length of both expressions is 512 characters. Also, as indicated earlier, when converting a numeric expression to a character expression for indexing, you should always include the optional parameter to specify the length of the field. This ensures a fixed-length index expression. A variable-length index expression can lead to unpredictable results.

It is also a good idea, when indexing on a long character string, to use the SUBSTR function to limit the size of the index expression, if possible. This conserves disk space and also speeds up the search.

Opening Indexes and Index Order

When you open a database file, you should open all of its associated index files at the same time. Although opening all the files could require additional time and it does slow the processing of new records, we recommend this approach to ensure that all your indexes are kept up to date. Some applications open only the index needed to establish record order (the master index) and those that will be affected by data modifications. This approach has two problems. First, future program modifications that change the open index requirements could easily be missed. Second, as you move from program module to program module, you may have to open and close different sets of index files. This could increase delays in your system because opening and closing files (especially large ones) can be very time consuming. Of course, if you include all of your indexes in structural .cdx files, the opening of indexes with associated database files is automatic.

As indicated earlier, commands that process records sequentially and commands that use the Rushmore technology are actually hindered by the presence of an active index. In these situations, issue a SET ORDER TO 0 command. This leaves all your indexes open for updating without activating any index for the purpose of determining record order.

The SET ORDER TO command is very useful in other situations as well. This command specifies the index or tag in a list of indexes to be the master (controlling) index. The following code fragment demonstrates the use of this command:

```
USE Customer INDEX Cus_Id, Cus_Zip, Cus_Bal
SET ORDER TO 2
```

In this case, the Cus_Zip index is designated as the master index because it is the second index in the list. When you need to temporarily change your index order and then restore it to the original, you can include the following lines:

```
OldOrder = SYS(21)              && Store value of current index order
SET ORDER TO 4                  && Set new order to 4 (or whatever)
* Do some processing
SET ORDER TO EVALUATE(OldOrder) && Restore original index order
```

As demonstrated in this code fragment, SYS(21) returns the currently active index order number. SYS(21) returns a null string if no indexes are open.

The USE command now has an ORDER clause that can be used to designate a master index or master tag at the time the database file is opened. When you specify an index order with either the USE...ORDER <expN> command or the SET ORDER TO <expN> command, you specify a numeric expression representing the index file or tag's position in the list of open indexes and tags. In determining the numeric sequence of index files and tags, FoxPro first numbers .idx files in the order they appear in the index file list when they are opened. Next, tags in the structural .cdx are numbered in the order they were created. Then, tags in non-structural .cdx files are numbered in the order they were created.

Other useful functions in determining current index status are the SYS(14) and equivalent KEY( ) functions. These functions return the index expression for the index or tag in the position specified. Combining the SYS(21) and SYS(14) functions, you can obtain the index expression of the currently active (master) index as follows:

```
mOrder = SYS(21)              &&Store current index order in mOrder
mCurrExpr =
  SYS(14,EVALUATE(mOrder))    &&Ask for expression of current index
?mCurrExpr                    &&Display expression
```

The NDX( ) function returns the name of the single-file index file opened in order <expN>. It ignores any open .cdx files. CDX( ) and MDX( ) are identical functions that return the name of the compound (.cdx) index file opened in order <expN>. The CDX( ) and MDX( ) functions ignore any open .idx files in the index file list. Finally, TAG( ) returns tag names from .cdx files or names of .idx files, depending on the parameters it is passed.

The SET INDEX command closes all active index files (unless the ADDITIVE clause is used) and opens those listed in the file list, opening the first index file in the list as the master index file. SET INDEX is not an efficient means of changing the master index file. The SET ORDER command is a better choice to designate a new master index. However, if additional or different index files need to be opened with the currently open database file, SET INDEX is preferred to reissuing the USE <dbfname> INDEX <index file list> command.

Reindexing

It is not difficult for an index file, other than a structural .cdx, to become outdated. If a record is added, deleted, or modified in such a way that the key field is changed and the index file is not open at the time, the database file and the index file will no longer be synchronized. When this happens, the index file must be rebuilt.

FoxPro's two facilities for rebuilding a corrupted index are REINDEX and INDEX ON. The REINDEX command updates each index (.idx or .cdx) in the currently selected work area, using the index expression that was defined when the index was first created. The REINDEX command also recognizes the FOR criteria, if any, and the UNIQUE option. Although this command is useful if the file is simply out of date, it cannot restore the index if the file has become physically damaged (for example, if the header was corrupted). Therefore, we recommend that whenever you need to reindex in your application, you rebuild your indexes with the INDEX ON command rather than the REINDEX command. This way, a new file is built, and you will have recovered from both a synchronization problem and any physical file damage.

Indexing in a Multiuser Environment

In a multiuser environment, when you create (or rebuild) an index, or when you sort a database file, you must consider the implications of file availability. FoxPro does not require any lock when creating an index with the INDEX ON command or when creating a sorted file with the SORT command. However, if users are modifying the database file while an index or sorted file is being built, an invalid or inconsistent file could result. Thus, although not required by FoxPro, you should lock the .dbf with the FLOCK( ) function prior to issuing an INDEX ON or SORT command.

Searching for Close Matches

When we discussed the FIND and SEEK commands earlier in this chapter, we mentioned the effect of SET NEAR and SET EXACT on the placement of the record pointer and the result of comparing strings of different lengths. In this section, we look at how to use these settings as well as some additional functions for locating records that are close but not identical to the key being searched. Table 10-3 summarizes the commands and functions that assist you in finding close matches.

When SET EXACT is OFF (the default), the FIND and SEEK commands may find a match even if the key value is of different length than the string being searched for. For example, SEEK "ABC" can find any of the following strings: ABC, ABCDE, or ABCDEFGHIJ. This can be useful when searching for a string whose exact contents are not known. For instance, if a user is trying to locate a manufacturer in a specific city and remembers only that the city begins with "Fa," a SEEK "Fa" could be issued to find any of the following: Fairbanks, Fairfax, Fall River, or Fayette. If SET EXACT is ON, however, only strings that match exactly will qualify for the SEEK and FIND commands.

The SET NEAR command is also useful when looking for close matches. If SET NEAR is ON and a FIND or SEEK fails to find a matching record, the record pointer is moved to the record immediately following the location where a matching record would have been. This lets you show the user the value that comes closest to matching the requested key value.

Another means of looking up a key value when you are not sure of the exact spelling is to use the SOUNDEX( ) function. This function returns a four-character string that contains the first letter of the string and a three-number substring that represents the phonetic sound of the string. This is particularly useful in locating strings that sound the same but may be spelled differently. For example "HEAL" and "HEEL" both return a value of H400. However, this does not work in all cases; for example, "RAIN" returns a value of R500 and "REIGN" returns R250.

The DIFFERENCE( ) function is useful in determining how similar two character strings are. DIFFERENCE( ) returns a value from 0 through 4, with 4 meaning identical or very similar and 0 meaning very little is in common.

Table 10-3. Commands and Functions for Finding Close Matches

Command/Function	Description
SET EXACT	Specifies whether an exact match in the length of two strings is required.
SET NEAR	Specifies the location of the record pointer after an unsuccessful search.
SOUNDEX( )	Returns a four-character string containing the phonetic representation of the string supplied.
DIFFERENCE( )	Returns a value from 0 through 4 representing the relative phonetic difference between two character expressions.
LIKE( )	Returns a logical value indicating whether a character string matches a given pattern.

For example, DIFFERENCE("HEAL","HEEL") returns 4, DIFFERENCE("RAIN","REIGN") returns 3, and DIFFERENCE("DAY","EVENING") returns 0.

Finally, the LIKE( ) function returns a logical value indicating whether a string matches a given character pattern. The format of this command is:

```
LIKE(<expC1>,<expC2>)
```

and the * and ? wildcard characters may be used in <expC1>. A value of .T. is returned if <expC1> is contained in <expC2>. The * wildcard character replaces any number of characters, and the ? character substitutes for exactly one character. The following examples demonstrate the use of LIKE( ):

```
?LIKE("TIG??","TIGER")
.T.
?LIKE("T*","TIGER")
.T.
?LIKE("T*","CAT")
.F.
```

This, too, can be useful when searching for strings whose exact content is unknown.

Chapter Summary

Indexing and sorting are two alternative means of establishing a particular record order. Sorting physically rearranges the file to a new file and is most useful for reporting output in a given order. A sorted file becomes outdated as soon as the original database is modified. Sorting can be slow and can consume a large amount of disk space.

Indexes are files containing pointers into a database file. They are used to logically reorder a database, to facilitate fast searching, and for relating databases with the SET RELATION TO command. FoxPro keeps indexes up to date provided that they are opened with the associated .dbf. Structural compound (.cdx) indexes, described in this chapter, are automatically opened with their associated .dbf files.

Rushmore is a highly efficient data access technology that can use existing indexes to speed certain database operations. We presented a list of commands that can potentially be optimized by Rushmore, and briefly discussed when Rushmore is used and when it should be disabled.

Indexed databases can be searched very quickly with the FIND, SEEK, and SEEK( ) commands. Although databases are not usually sorted to perform a search, you can develop your own search algorithm for a sorted database. We presented a binary search program in this chapter.

Unordered database files can also be searched, although the search time is typically longer. The SET FILTER, SCAN, and LOCATE commands can be used with unordered files.

The formulation of an index expression can be tricky, especially if mixing data types. We presented techniques for handling these situations. We also discussed some important considerations when indexing on character fields.

A variety of FoxPro commands and functions are available for opening indexes, changing index order, and querying index order and index filenames. There are also two methods of rebuilding an out-of-date index file: the REINDEX command and the INDEX ON command. We reviewed the use of these commands and discussed the impact of indexing and reindexing in the multiuser environment.

Finally, we examined several approaches to searching for database records that are similar to but not exactly matching a given key value. We looked at options for finding related records and determining how similar two values really are.

Chapter 11

Report and Printing Techniques

In FoxBASE+ you've always been able to create reports with or without writing a program. For instance, its built-in report writer, activated by way of the CREATE/MODIFY REPORT command, lets you create simple reports interactively without requiring you to know any additional FoxBASE+ commands. On the other hand, if you want to create more complex reports that require more precise control of where on the page data should print, you had to write a program using the ?/ ?? and @...SAY commands to control the output.

FoxPro's Report Writing Facilities

FoxPro's report writing facilities are similar to those of dBASE IV's and are a vast improvement over those of FoxBASE+. The following list summarizes FoxPro's report and print capabilities:

- To help you create intricate reports, FoxReport, the built-in report writer, provides a work surface with report bands that can be "painted" with database fields, text, lines, boxes, and user-defined functions. FoxReport stores the report specifications in a .frx file (equivalent to FoxBASE+'s .frm) which is a regular .dbf file. Unlike dBASE IV, FoxPro does not translate the .frx file into a user-modifiable program (.prg). FoxReport can read and use FoxBASE+'s .frm file.
- To manage the printed page, FoxPro has system memory variables similar to those of dBASE IV. System memory variables define such

things as page margins, page indents, text alignment, number of copies, and whether automatic word-wrapping of text is in effect.

- To control text alignment, the @...SAY command has picture functions such as I and J.
- To define the start of the output column, the ?/ ?? command has the AT clause. The command also supports PICTURE, FUNCTION, and STYLE clauses.
- To print data in a column using a fixed number of (horizontal) character positions, the ?/ ?? command has a vertical stretch function.
- To write directly to the printer, FoxPro, like dBASE IV, has the ??? command. You can use this command to send any control character, including the null byte, to the printer.
- To initialize the printer and define system memory variables (for example, the number of copies) that affect printed output, FoxPro has the PRINTJOB-ENDPRINTJOB command similar to dBASE IV's.
- To facilitate the handling of page breaks, footers, and headers, FoxPro has the ON PAGE command. The command is used to specify what action to take when a given line number is reached during report generation or when an EJECT PAGE command is issued. The page handler is also available in dBASE IV.
- To control the print destination including a file, local printer, or network printer, FoxPro has the SET PRINTER TO command. Additionally, the SET DEVICE TO command redirects @...SAY output to a file.
- To take maximum advantage of your printer's capabilities, FoxPro 2.0 supports printer drivers, including Postscript printers.

Summary of FoxReport Features

FoxReport uses a what-you-see-is-what-you-get work surface (report layout window) on which you can place any report object virtually anywhere. Report objects include database fields, calculated fields, text, and boxes. The layout window is divided into report bands, which include the Title, Page Header, Group Header, Detail (Report Body), Group Footer, Page Footer, and Summary bands. A band may consist of any number of lines subject to the constraint that the maximum number of lines in the report definition is 255. The maximum width of a report is 255 columns, but FoxReport allows the fields in the Detail band to be stretched vertically so that the field data can be printed within a fixed number of columns.

To speed up the process of designing reports, FoxReport includes a Quick Report facility when nothing has yet been defined in the Detail band. The two report layouts supported are Column and Form (dBASE IV has a third layout, MailMerge, that is not supported by FoxPro). Column layout is similar to the result of FoxBASE's REPORT FORM command, where fields are arranged in tabular form. Here, the field names act as column headings and are placed in the Page Header band. Fields that overflow the dimensions of the report are not included. Form Layout resembles the format of the FoxPro Edit screen, where each field is in a row preceded by the field name.

The Report Expression Dialog (shown in Figure 11-1) can be used to help define how you want a report field to display on the report. For instance, you can define the field's format or total option (such as count, sum, average, lowest, or highest). Choosing the <Expr...> button brings up the Expression Builder (Figure 11-2) to help you formulate the desired field expression. The expression can consist of one or more database fields; the appropriate math, string, logical, or date functions; as well as user-defined functions. By checking the Verify box, you can ask FoxReport to confirm that the report expression you just built is correct.

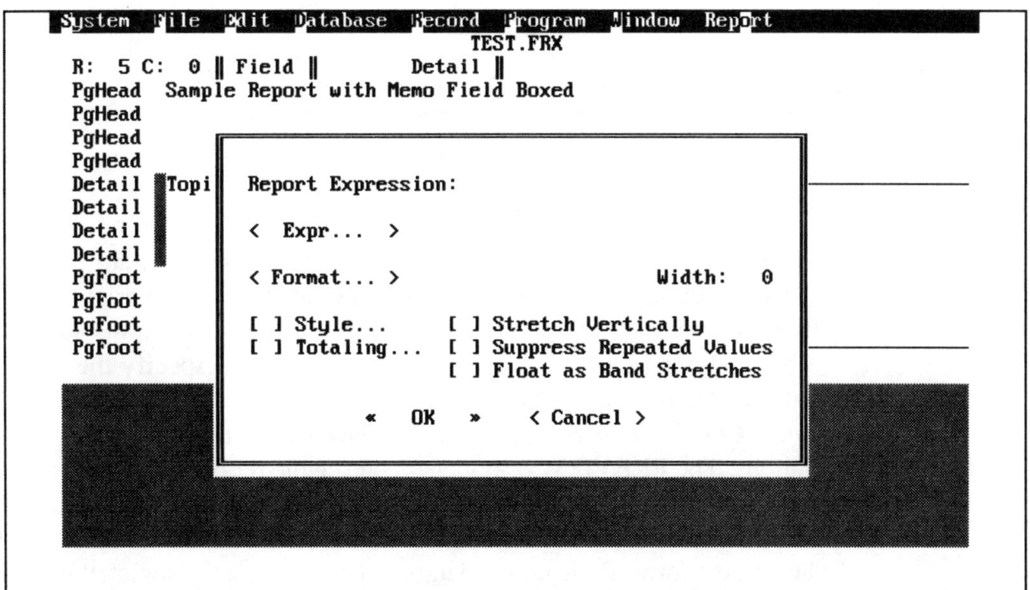

Figure 11-1. The FoxReport Expression Dialog screen.

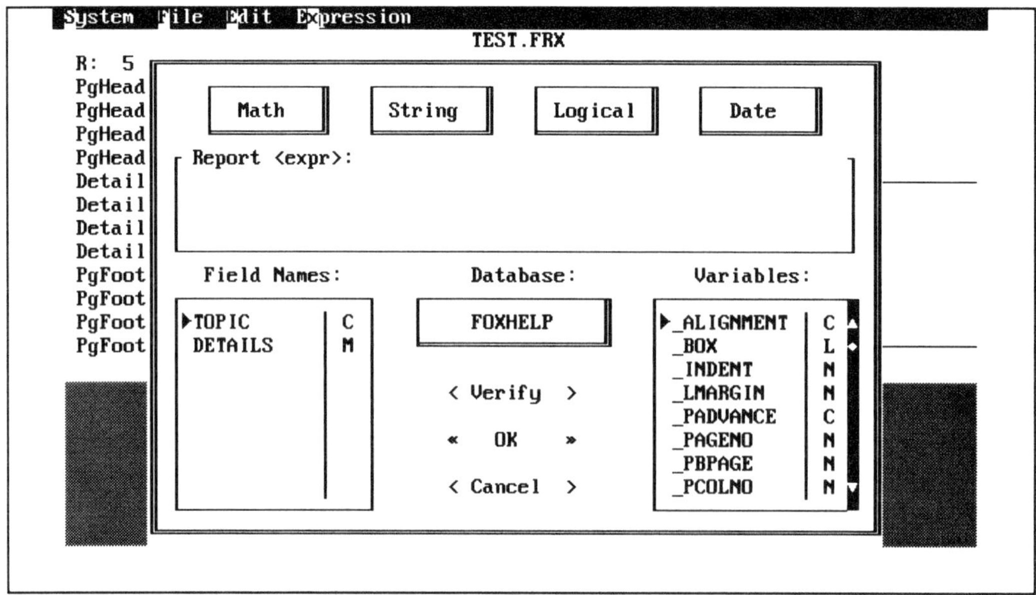

Figure 11-2. The FoxReport Expression Builder.

Report Enhancements in FoxPro 2.0

The following list summarizes the important enhancements in the report writing capabilities of FoxPro 2.0 over version 1.x.

1. The CREATE REPORT command has a second syntax that lets you create quick reports (either Form or Column) from a program, rather than from the report writer layout window. In this syntax, the subject .dbf need not be open in a work area, and you can specify the set of database fields you want included.
2. The REPORT FORM command has PREVIEW and NOCONSOLE options. The PREVIEW option lets you see the report before you print it. The NOCONSOLE option disables displaying the report on the screen as it is being output to another device.
3. The report form file is now a database (.frx) with an associated memo (.frt) file. This lets you modify the database without going back to FoxReport.

4. In FoxReport, you can open as many layout windows as memory allows. You can then open multiple reports and cut and paste objects between them.
5. You can stretch and shrink a band by dragging the mouse. You can also stretch an object, which causes the screen to scroll automatically to accommodate the action.
6. You can select multiple objects with the selection marquee. You can also group and ungroup objects.
7. You can assign a comment to every object in the report to record reminders about the object. The comment itself may contain code snippets and binary data.
8. You can select standard deviation and variance options in both the Total dialog and the Calculate Field dialog.
9. You can create memory variables in reports to store the results of calculations as the report prints.
10. In the Group Info dialog, you can specify whether or not you want to reprint the group header if the group appears on more than one page and reset the page number to 1 every time a group break occurs.

Including Percentages in a Report

Suppose your report includes a column for a numeric field, say, Salary, and you want to print alongside it another column that shows each record's salary value as a percentage of the total. You can easily do this in FoxReport. First, you'll need to compute the total value for the field and then store it in some memory variable, say, TotSalary. The SUM command that does that for you is as follows:

```
SUM salary TO TotSalary.
```

Next, include in the detail band of the report, a calculated field with the expression (Salary / TotSalary) * 100. The report column with the desired percentages now prints every time you invoke the report with the REPORT FORM command.

So that you don't forget to issue the SUM command before calling up the report form, you might want to write a two-line program that includes the SUM and REPORT FORM commands one after the other.

The FoxPro Report Form File

When you compose a report using the CREATE REPORT <RptName> command, FoxPro creates a report form file with the name <RptName>.frx, which contains the report layout and data that you defined. FoxPro uses the information stored in this file to produce the report when you issue the REPORT FORM <RptName> command. Unlike dBASE IV, FoxPro does not translate the file into a program that it can then execute. Thus, although dBASE IV lets you further customize the translated program according to your needs (just like any other program) or even use it as a learning tool, FoxPro does not provide you with the same facility.

To convert a FoxPro .frx file into modifiable source code, you can either obtain a third-party utility such as Platinum Software's Frx2Prg program or create a utility of your own, perhaps by using FoxPro's textmerge facility. Creating your own version of Frx2Prg requires that you fully understand the structure of the .frx database. The format of this file is documented in the FoxPro manuals. Like the label form file (see the section on Lbx2Prg in Chapter 5), the .frx database stores different types of data, depending on the value of the Objtype field. For instance, records with Objtype = 5 contain data about text objects, whereas records with Objtype = 7 contain data about box objects.

Printing Memo Fields

Memo fields included in a REPORT FORM print as expected, wrapping within the print columns assigned to them and printing correctly during page breaks. If you want a report where a memo field prints inside a box, you should define the box, place the memo field at the appropriate column inside the box, and check the options Stretch Vertically and Float as Band Stretches in the Report Expression Dialog screen.

On a custom report, you can still display a memo field inside a box by setting the dimensions of the box slightly larger than the MEMOWIDTH setting and the number of lines in the memo field. The PrtMemo.prg procedure, shown in Listing 11-1, prints a memo field beginning at a specified column inside a box. The procedure uses MEMLINES( ) to determine the number of lines in the memo field and assigns the height of the box to be 2 larger than MEMLINES( ) to account for the box characters. Similarly the procedure assigns the box width to be 2 larger than the MEMOWIDTH setting. Note that the system memvar _box must be .T. in order for the box to

Listing 11-1. PrtMemo.prg prints a memo field inside a box.

```
PROCEDURE PrtMemo
************************************************************
* Program ...: PrtMemo.prg
* Author ....: P. L. Olympia and Kathy Cea
* Purpose....: Prints specified memo field inside a box of
*            : given width beginning at specified column
* Syntax ....: DO PrtMemo WITH <memofld>, <col>, <width>
* Notes .....: Actual print width is either the specified
*            : width or number of print positions in the line
*            : whichever is less
************************************************************
PARAMETERS memofld, col, width

OldWidth = SET("MEMO")
Memwidth = MIN(_rmargin - _lmargin,  width)
SET MEMOWIDTH TO Memwidth
DEFINE BOX FROM col-1 TO (col+Memwidth+1);
    HEIGHT MEMLINES((memofld)) + 2
_box = .T.         && Must be True for box to print
?
?? (memofld) AT col
?
?
_box  = .F.
SET MEMOWIDTH TO Oldwidth
RETURN
```

print. The procedure determines the number of print positions in the line using the two system memvars _rmargin and _lmargin. The procedure defines the number of print positions to be the MEMOWIDTH setting if it is less than the specified print width.

A memo field may also be printed at precise locations on a page without regard to the MEMOWIDTH setting. For instance, the command

```
?? memofld FUNCTION "I;V45" AT 10
```

prints the field centered between columns 10 and 55, wrapping the field in a column width of 45.

System Memory Variables

FoxPro automatically maintains a set of system memory variables to control the nature and appearance of printer and screen output. These memory variables are initialized with default values on startup. They are unaffected by the RELEASE or CLEAR MEMORY commands, although their values may be changed at any time.

System memvars such as _wrap that control the appearance of a paragraph have rendered FoxBASE+ or dBASE III programs that allow wordwrapping of long text obsolete. Thus, to print a mailmerge letter, all you need to do is set the memvar _wrap to .T.; define the application's alignment, indent, and margins; and then print the text using the ?/ ?? command. For instance,

```
_wrap = .T.
_indent = 5             && indentation of paragraph's 1st line
_lmargin = 10           && left margin
_rmargin = 70           && right margin
_alignment = [LEFT]     && left justify
? details               && print the text
```

Note that paragraph-specific memvars such as alignment and margins have no effect on the output unless _wrap is set to TRUE. If the text to be printed is a memo field, the resulting output is affected by the values of the system memvars as well as by the current setting of MEMOWIDTH.

With some system memvars you do not have to remember and issue control characters to the printer to achieve a desired result. For example, if you want to change the form (page) size, you can simply assign the appropriate value to the memvar _plength. Also, FoxPro keeps track of where you are on the page through the _plineno variable.

Page Handler

Remember the old days when you had to keep track of the number of lines that had been printed on a report so you would know when to write the report footer, issue a page break, and call the report's page header routine? With

FoxPro, you won't have to work so hard to handle page breaks and the like. First, the system memvar _plineno automatically keeps track of the number of lines that have been printed on the page. Second, FoxPro's ON PAGE command provides a convenient way of handling end-of-page processing. With it you define what action to take during report generation when the output line reaches a specified line on the current page, for example,

```
ON PAGE [AT LINE <expN> <command>]
```

where <command> is usually a page break procedure.

The ON PAGE command is activated by EJECT PAGE or when the current line number reaches the number specified in the AT LINE clause. It is also activated automatically by the REPORT FORM command for reports that contain headers and footers. Invoking ON PAGE without the AT LINE clause disables the page handler.

Listing 11-2 shows a sample program that uses the page handler. It defines the trigger line number (AT LINE number) differently, depending on whether or not the report is single spaced. The page header routine writes the report title centered on the page. Above that, the routine writes the page number beginning with page 2. The page footer routine merely writes the revision date.

Mailmerge Reports

Mailmerge reporting produces what may look like a custom letter by inserting information from a database record into a form letter template. In the past, this activity was handled by exporting the necessary data file from database management systems to full-featured word processing packages. For instance, we can use WordPerfect to produce mailmerge letters to a set of addressees from a FoxPro database. To do this, we would generate the required WordPerfect secondary merge files using the FoxPro COPY TO <txtfile> DELIMITED command. Much of the reluctance on the part of many to use Dbase or compatible software for mailmerge reports stems from the difficulty or tedium of exercising precise control over the printed page, including wordwrap. As we shall see, all that has changed with FoxPro. Indeed, a FoxPro mailmerge program, which has access to all of FoxPro's commands and functions, has numerous advantages over word processing software.

Listing 11-2. OnPage.prg, sample page handler.

```
PROCEDURE OnPage
*************************************************************
* Program ...: OnPage.prg
* Author ....: P. L. Olympia and Kathy Cea
* Purpose....: Sample procedure to demonstrate FoxPro's
*            : ON PAGE command
* Syntax ....: DO OnPage
* Notes .....: Calls Pg_Brk, Pg_foot and Pg_Head
*************************************************************
SET PRINT ON
Title = "My Report Title"

* Define OnPage AT Line depending on report spacing
OnPageLine = IIF(_pspacing > 1, _plength - (2 * _pspacing +1), ;
                                _plength - 6)

ON PAGE AT LINE OnPageLine DO Pg_Brk

DO Pg_head                          && Print page 1 header
SCAN ALL
   ? Field_1, Field_2               && Print fields
ENDSCAN
ON PAGE                             && disable PAGE handler
FOR i = _plineno TO OnPageLine STEP _pspacing
  ?
ENDFOR
DO Pg_foot
SET PRINT OFF
RETURN

PROCEDURE Pg_Brk
  DO Pg_foot
  DO Pg_head
RETURN

PROCEDURE Pg_foot
  ? 'Revised on ', DATE()
```

(continued)

Listing 11-2. Continued

```
  EJECT PAGE
RETURN

PROCEDURE Pg_head
  ?
  IF _pageno <> 1
     ? 'Page ' AT 65, LTRIM(STR(_pageno,4))
  ENDIF
  ?
  ? PADC(Title, _rmargin - _lmargin)
  ?
RETURN
```

Simple mailmerge letters that do not require the insertion of database fields or functions in the body of the letter can be composed easily in any of the Dbase-compatible products. Here, we could just embed the letter inside a TEXT-ENDTEXT block and use the ?/ ?? commands to print the rest of the letter, including addressee information. Alternatively, we could store the letter as a memo field and print it with the ?/ ?? command.

Mailmerge letters that do require inserting database fields or functions in the body of the letter traditionally have been cumbersome to produce because of the excessive processing overhead associated with handling wordwrap correctly. In FoxPro, the system memvar _wrap and functions like RAT( ) greatly simplify coding a wordwrap routine. Additionally, mailmerge letters can be generated using FoxPro's template language processing facility.

Designing a Generalized FoxPro Mailmerge System

A generalized mailmerge system should be able to handle variable formatting requirements such as margin changes, hanging indents, and text alignment. It should also be able to use information from multiple data files and suppress segments of the letter for which the current database record has no information. For instance, it would be inappropriate to include in a letter to pet owners a paragraph expounding on the wonders of the company's new dog food product when the addressee is a cat owner.

A generalized mailmerge reporting system consists of three parts:

1. Letter template
2. Generic mailmerge routine
3. Mailmerge driver program that manages the first two.

To understand how the components fit together, consider a sample letter (Figure 11-3) produced by such a system.

The Letter Template

The letter template that produced the letter in Figure 11-3 is shown in Figure 11-4. Note that the template consists of fixed text and variable data. Variable data are bounded by delimiters. You are free to use any set of delimiters you want as long as they are consistent and will not appear in the letter in another context, for example, as a literal string. The sample presented in Figure 11-4 uses the following four types of delimiters:

1. The /* */ delimiter pair is used for comments. The generic mailmerge routine ignores comments.
2. The << >> delimiter pair is used for page format directives or processing directives. Examples of format directives include:

`<<LM 5>>`	Sets left margin to 5.
`<<TS 5, 10>>`	Sets tab stops to 5 and 10.
`<<TAB>>`	Executes a TAB command.
`<<CR>>`	Forces a hard carriage return.
`<<IB>>`	Begins indent.
`<<RJ>>`	Begins right justify.
`<<WB>>`	Begins wordwrap.
`<<WE>>`	Ends wordwrap.

   Processing directives include looping constructs such as <<WHILE-ENDWHILE>> designed to retrieve database records that meet specific criteria.
3. The {{ }} delimiter pair is used for FoxPro functions, variable names, field names, and expressions. For example, {{DATE( )}} prints today's date in the currently active date format.
4. The [[ ]] delimiter pair is used for FoxPro commands. For example, [[SET DATE MDY]] simply defines the date format to be MDY.

```
May 28, 1990

Mr. J. K. Jones
123 Main Street
Buffalo, NY 14022

Dear Mr. Jones:

     Thank you for your recent inquiry about our new product,
Forever, the indestructible roofing material, Part Number TK3457.
Enclosed is the complete literature on this exciting product.

     The following are homeowners in your neighborhood who will be
able to provide you with testimonials about Forever's staying
power.

Emily Leak     555-3456
Earl Spout     555-4257

     If we can be of further assistance, please call our tollfree
number at 800-555-5432.

Sincerely,


Jim Roof
Accounts Manager
```

Figure 11-3. Sample letter produced by a mailmerge reporting system.

For maximum flexibility, you should store letter templates in a memo field of a letters database rather than storing them individually in small text files or hardcoding them in any program. Letter templates that are stored as memo fields can be easily retrieved and manipulated in FoxPro. If users need additional letters, you can simply provide them with another template in a different record rather than provide them with a completely different program. Users who are familiar with the database fields often become adept at creating additional letter templates of their own by copying and modifying those that they already use.

```
/* Define page settings */
<<LM 5>>
<<RM 65>>
<<TS 5, 10, 15, 20>>

/* Define date format */
[[SET DATE MDY]]
{{DATE}}

{{TRIM(Customer->Cus_Title)}} {{TRIM(Customer->Cus_Fname)}}
  {{TRIM(Customer->Cus_Lname)}}
{{TRIM(Customer->Cus_Street)}}
{{TRIM(Customer->Cus_City)}} {{Customer->Cus_State}}
  {{Customer->Cus_Zip}}

Dear {{TRIM(Customer->Cus_Title)}} {{TRIM(Customer->Cus_Lname)}}

<<TAB>>Thank you for your recent inquiry about our new product,
{{TRIM(Product->Pro_Name)}}, {{TRIM(Product->Pro_Slogan)}},
{{TRIM(Product->Pro_PartN)}}. Enclosed is the complete literature
on this exciting product.

/* Include the next paragraph if there are testimonials */
<<IF SEEK(Customer->Cus_Zip, "Testimon")>>
The following are homeowners in your neighborhood who will be able
to provide you with testimonials about Forever's staying power.
<<WHILE Testimon->Tes_Zip = Customer->Cus_Zip>>
 {{TRIM(Testimon->Tes_Name)}} <<TAB>> {{Testimon->Tes_Phone}}
 [[SKIP IN Testimon]]
<<ENDWHILE>>
<<ENDIF>>

<<TAB>>If we can be of further assistance, please call our
tollfree number at 800-555-5432.

Sincerely, <<CR>><<CR>><<CR>>
Jim Roof
Accounts Manager
```

Figure 11-4. Sample letter template.

The Generic Mailmerge Routine

The generic mailmerge routine processes the letter template stored in a memo field by scanning the template for the four delimiter pairs and taking the appropriate action. For instance, it sets the relevant system memory variable when it encounters a format directive. Thus it issues the command

```
_rmargin = 65
```

when it encounters the directive <<RM 65>>, and it issues the command

```
_wrap = .T.
```

when it encounters the directive <<WB>>.

If the delimited string is a FoxPro command or function, the generic routine simply casts the string as a macro and then executes it. The routine also ensures that the letter template uses the delimiters correctly; for example, the delimiters should always appear in matching pairs.

The Mailmerge Driver Program

The driver program is responsible for setting the environment for the generic mailmerge routine. It opens the appropriate databases with their required indexes, sets any required database relations, or, using the SEEK( ) function, positions the pointers of all databases to related records.

The program can include a user dialog to prompt the user for the desired letter template. The program then retrieves the appropriate template from the letters database and executes the generic mailmerge routine.

Snaked Column Reports

A snaked column report is a multicolumn report that resembles the format of a newspaper or telephone directory page. Entries on a page are arranged such that the item at the bottom of a given column is followed by the item at the top of the next column, rather than by the item to the right of it in the next column. Basically, in a snaked column report, order exists within a column, but not across columns. The schematic in Figure 11-5 shows a snaked column sequence typical of a telephone directory.

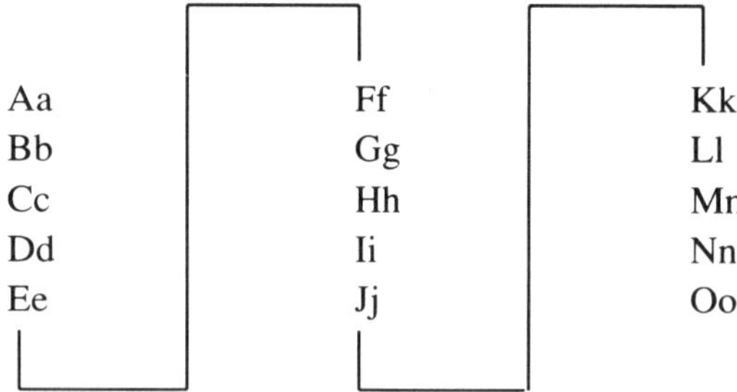

Figure 11-5. Snaked column schematic.

If the items to be included in a snaked column report will fit on a single line, for instance,

```
Name ........... Phone
```

the simplest way to handle the report is to use arrays. In the preceding example, you would loop through the indexed database, concatenating Name, the series of dots, and the phone number, and then assigning the whole string to an array element. Of course, the array solution assumes that no more than 3600 array elements are needed at one time if you are using standard FoxPro. Assuming that the report only needs two columns and that the maximum number of items in a column is MaxPerCol, the code fragment that prints the report is simply

```
FOR i = 1 TO MaxPerCol
  ? item(i) AT 1, item(i+MaxPerCol) AT 41
ENDFOR
```

What happens if the items to be reported consist of multiple lines, for instance, a set of names and addresses similar to those in a mailing label? As you may suspect, the FoxPro mail label generator is a natural for the job because it allows multiple labels across a row. The trick is to index the database in such a way that the records appear in the order of the snaked column. Consider a report that requires 4 rows and 3 columns. The required index is one such that record 1, then record 5, and then record 9 are printed in the first row as shown here:

```
1    5    9
2    6   10
3    7   11
4    8   12
```

The following expression (Russell, 1989) gives the desired index.

```
INT(( RECNO() - 1)/Recs_on_Page) * 1000 + ;  && accounts for page
  INT( MOD( RECNO() - 1, Recs_on_Page) / Num_rows) + ; && rows
  MOD( RECNO() - 1, Num_Rows) * Num_Cols.              && cols
```

The snaked column report is then produced with the single command

```
LABEL FORM <LblName> NEXT Recs_on_Page TO PRINT.
```

Note that to maintain the proper snaked column format in the report's last page, there should be enough database records to produce Recs_on_Page number of entries. If there are not, you should append enough blank records to the database to fill the last page of the report.

Sending Commands Directly to the Printer

A control code sequence to take advantage of a specific printer capability (for example, go into landscape mode) may be issued directly to the printer using FoxPro's ??? command. The command leaves the printer row and column position unchanged. Thus it has the advantage over the usual FoxBASE+ (or dBASE III) command sequence such as

```
@ 2, 0 SAY CHR(27)+"G"    && Epson double strike mode
@ 2,20 SAY "Title"        && this prints beginning at 18, not 20
```

where the two control codes to put the printer in double strike mode count as characters even though they do not print and thus do not move the printhead. The result is that the word "Title" begins printing at column 18, not 20. To get around this problem, the usual technique is to pad the first command with as many spaces as there are control codes in the command stream, for instance,

```
@ 2, 0 SAY CHR(15)+"G"+SPACE(2)
```

Both printable and nonprintable ASCII characters may be sent directly to the printer. Nonprintable characters may be referred to in a variety of ways, including the CHR( ) function, the ASCII digit enclosed in curly braces, and control character specifiers. Thus, noting that {ESC} is the control specifier for the <Escape> character (which also has the ASCII decimal code of 27), the following commands are all equivalent:

```
??? CHR(27)+"G"
??? "{ESC}G"
??? "{27}G"
??? "{27}{71}"          && "G" is ASCII decimal 71
```

The control character specifiers for ASCII code 1 through 26 are simply {CTRL-A} through {CTRL-Z}. FoxPro also recognizes the usual "names" for the common control codes, for example, {RETURN} for {CTRL-M} and {TAB} for {CTRL-I}.

In FoxPro, the control character specifier is not case sensitive as it is in dBASE IV. For instance, the following commands are all equivalent in FoxPro and will ring the printer bell.

```
??? "{CTRL-G}"
??? "{ctrl-G}"
??? "{ctrl-g}"
```

In dBASE IV, the last command has no effect on the printer because all it does is send the small letter "g" to the printer.

Sending Nulls to a Printer

Some printers require the null character (ASCII decimal 0, or CHR(0)) to be part of a command. For instance, the command to change the form length to 3 inches in an Epson LQ printer is

```
CHR(27) + "C" +  CHR(0) + CHR(3)
```

This has been a constant source of frustration to dBASE III PLUS and FoxBASE+ users. Neither program is able to send the null byte because they use CHR(0) internally to mark the end of strings. Thus, if you want to print the letter "P" and you give the command:

```
?? CHR(80)
```

what you are really printing are two bytes, namely, the letter "P" followed by the null byte, which terminates the string. Similarly, the command

```
?? CHR(0)
```

should print two null bytes. However, the first null byte effectively terminates the string and the printer "sees" nothing.

Fortunately there are workarounds to the problem. First, you can write a .bin routine to send a null byte to a printer (see Listing 11-3 and the following discussion). The .bin routine can then be LOADed and later CALLed in any Dbase program. Second, some printers have alternative commands to those that involve the null byte, so those should be used instead. Third, printers such as those from the Okidata line ignore the eighth bit of the ASCII code, so the character CHR(128) may be used in place of CHR(0). Fourth, printers such as those from the Epson line have a command to turn off the eighth bit, so to send a null byte to a printer you would turn off the eighth bit, send CHR(128), and then turn on the eighth bit again.

For instance, suppose that you want to print addresses on 3-inch mailing labels using an Epson LQ printer. The FoxBASE+ code to change the form length to 3 inches is

```
SET PRINT ON
?? CHR(27) + "="                        && turn off eighth bit
?? CHR(27) + "C" + CHR(128) + CHR(4) && form length to 3"
?? CHR(27) + ">"                      && turn on eighth bit
```

With FoxPro you no longer have to go through this roundabout procedure because the software can send the null byte to a printer without any problems. Thus the FoxPro equivalent to the preceding code is simply

```
??? "{ESC}C{NULL}{CTRL-C}"
```

where, again, codes such as {ESC} and {CTRL-C} are FoxPro control character specifiers. It appears that such codes are really one-byte characters and not null-terminated strings.

Listing 11-3. PrtNull.asm can be turned into a .bin file to allow Dbase programs to send nulls to a printer.

```
; PrtNull.asm
;

CODESEG SEGMENT PARA 'CODE'
        ASSUME CS:CODESEG

PRTNULL  PROC  FAR
         PUSH  AX
         PUSH  DX
         XOR   DX, DX
         MOV   AX, 0500H
         INT   21H
         POP   DX
         POP   AX
EXIT:
         RET
PRTNULL  ENDP
CODESEG  ENDS
         END   PRTNULL
```

The ability of FoxPro to avoid the use of the null byte to terminate a string and determine its length has important ramifications. For instance, Russ Freeland (Freeland, 1989) has shown that the ??? command, with output redirected to a file, can be used to create small .bin, .com, or .exe files. Consider the assembly language program, PrtNull.asm, in Listing 11-3.

It is a utility that allows nulls to be sent to a printer from dBASE III or FoxBASE programs that cannot do it otherwise. Before you can use the utility, you must first assemble it, link it, and then use EXE2BIN to convert it to a .bin file. Alternatively, you can just write a three-line FoxPro program that does the same thing. The program is as follows:

```
SET PRINTER TO FILE prtnull.bin
???"PR1{210}{184}{0}{5}{205}!ZX{203}"
SET PRINTER TO
```

Redirecting Printer Output to a File

One of the most vexing deficiencies of dBASE III PLUS is its inability to redirect printer output produced by the @...SAY command to a file. This limitation is gone in FoxPro, which has a built-in facility to capture @...SAY command output to a file by way of the command

```
SET DEVICE TO FILE <filename>
```

Additionally, FoxPro streaming output, including that produced by the ??? command, can be directed to a file using the command

```
SET PRINTER TO FILE <filename>
```

followed by

```
SET PRINTER ON
```

Redirecting printer output to a file has several uses. First, it is useful for trapping an application system's reports for inclusion in the system documentation. Second, it is an indispensable tool for diagnosing program or printer problems. When a printer does not appear to respond correctly to commands being issued to it by a program, redirecting the output to a file permits closer examination of exactly what codes, if any, the printer is receiving from the program. Having seen too many networked printers, under the misguided direction of a run-away Dbase program, spew forth mountains of paper containing nothing but garbage, we can attest to the utility of redirecting printer output to a file if nothing else but to save the nation's trees.

Finally, redirecting printer output to a file permits testing of a program even when a printer is unavailable. The FoxPro PRINTSTATUS( ) or SYS(13) function may be used to determine if the printer is ready to accept output. However, if a print spooler is active, the PRINTSTATUS( ) function returns a logical true (.T.), and SYS(13) returns "ONLINE" regardless of the printer's actual status. Therefore, the presence of a print spooler also permits testing of a report-producing program even when a printer is unavailable.

Printing on a Network

Surely one of the rewards of networking is the facility for sharing expensive print devices such as laser printers. The traditional problem with printing on a network is that between the time an application system generates its report and the time the report actually prints, someone else on the network may have changed fonts or paper orientation. Sooner or later, you could wind up with a report printed sideways even if you had not intended it to be.

FoxPro/LAN has facilities that help manage printing on a network. For instance, the SET PRINTER TO command allows redirection of printer output to a local printer, a network printer, or a file. The network SET PRINTER TO command has two alternative forms. One form is

```
SET PRINTER TO [\\<machinename> \<printername> = <dest>]
```

which spools printer output to the network printer assigned the name <printername>. <machinename> is a unique name assigned to your workstation and <dest> may be LPT1, LPT2, or LPT3.

On a Novell network, the command can take the form

```
SET PRINTER TO [\\SPOOLER [\NB] [\F = <expN>] [\B = <expC>]
  [\C = <expN>] [\P = <expN>] [\S = <server>] [\Q = <queue>]
```

which has parameters similar to Novell's SPOOL or CAPTURE command. For instance, NB means no banner page, F refers to a form number, B specifies a banner name, C specifies the number of copies, and P identifies the network printer number.

In FoxPro/LAN 2.0, the SET PRINTER command has two new clauses to direct the printer output to named queues and fileservers. Thus, the clauses \S=Arc01 \Q=Donnie_Laser send printer output to the printer queue named Donnie_Laser attached to the network server named Arc01.

The _pscode and _pecode system memvars, which define a printer initialization and deinitialization string, respectively, can be used to ensure that the printer is in the desired state for a given report. These memvars are particularly useful with the PRINTJOB/ENDPRINTJOB programming construct, which defines the environment for a print task. Unfortunately, since a typical network printer supports a multitude of applications including spreadsheet and word processing, users must agree on a standard printer deinitialization protocol so that users who either forget, or do not bother, to initialize the printer can expect to find the printer in a reasonably standard state.

Of course, this is easier said than done, and there is a better way. You could, for example, code a utility program that combines the functions provided by the Novell SPOOL or CAPTURE facility with your own printer configuration functions. Such a program would use a printer definition file that includes the escape sequences of all supported devices. The heart of the system is its ability to precede output from any workstation with user-specified printer control commands. Thus it does not matter in what state a previous network job leaves a printer—any report should print just the way you expect it to.

How is it done? Quite simply, by using two little-known DOS INT 21H extended functions. Function 5EH, Code 02H, is the Printer Setup function that takes a string of desired control characters and puts them at the beginning of every print job. Function 5FH, Code 02H, is the complement function that allows you to obtain the printer's "list entry index," from which you can identify the printer to which the control string will be sent. A printer with an entry index of 0 is the first printer on the list. Before invoking the Printer Setup function, you load the BX register with the entry index and the CX register with the length of the string.

Printjob and Endprintjob

Some system memvars (for example, _pcopies, _pecode, _peject, and _pscode) can be assigned values from the command window, but they can only be used in a program because they become active only with the PRINTJOB and ENDPRINTJOB commands. The PRINTJOB/ENDPRINTJOB commands are structured programming constructs that define the environment for a print task. The system memvars should be defined before the PRINTJOB statement. Output commands, including invocations of print procedures, should appear inside the PRINTJOB/ENDPRINTJOB construct. For example,

```
_pcopies = 2
_pscode = "<printer initialization string>"
_pecode = "<printer deinitialization string>"
_peject = "AFTER"
PRINTJOB
     ?/?? or DO <proc>
     .. other FoxPro commands including loops ..
ENDPRINTJOB
```

The PRINTJOB statement causes _pcolno (print column number) to be initialized to 0, the string assigned to _pscode to be sent to the printer, and the paper to be ejected if _peject has the value "BEFORE" or "BOTH." The ENDPRINTJOB statement causes the string assigned to _pecode to be sent to the printer, a page to be ejected if _peject has the value "AFTER" or "BOTH," and the statements within the PRINTJOB loop to be executed the number of times defined by _pcopies. Only the pages that are within the range specified by the _pbpage (begin page number) and _pepage (end page number) system memvars are output by the print job.

Printer Drivers

FoxPro 2.0 supports printer drivers enabling you to fully exploit the capabilities of your printers, including Postscript printers. Briefly, a printer driver is a piece of software that mediates between your program and the printer so you do not have to worry about what commands to give the printer to change attributes such as pitch, underline, or bold. With a printer driver, all your program has to do is issue a command such as

```
?? RepTitle AT 35 STYLE "BI"
```

and the translation of the style code "BI" (for Bold and Italics) becomes the responsibility of the driver. To do its job, the printer driver has to know that BI means Bold and Italics, and it also has to know what specific codes the printer needs to print with those attributes.

In most software products, including dBASE IV and WordPerfect, the printer drivers are binary files containing the control codes for each supported printer. In most cases, you would need a vendor-supplied utility to modify the driver for your supported printer, or you could build one of your own if you happen to have an unsupported printer. FoxPro takes a completely different approach that gives you enormous flexibility in how you implement printer drivers in applications.

In FoxPro 2.0, a printer driver is nothing more than a FoxPro program (.prg) or an Application Program Interface (API) routine. Typically this driver .prg file contains specially named procedures, for example, PDDOCST and PDDOCEND. In the PDDOCST procedure, you define what you want to do before each document is printed. For instance, this procedure could return to your application the appropriate printer codes to change the print quality (draft or letter quality) and page orientation (portrait or landscape). Similarly, your PDDOCEND procedure could return to the application the set of control codes you want sent to the printer after a document is printed. These codes can include those to restore the page orientation or print quality.

FoxPro automatically invokes the appropriate printer driver procedure whenever it is needed. Thus, when a report form signals for printing on a new page, FoxPro automatically executes the driver procedure called PDPAGEST. Similarly, FoxPro executes the PDONUNLOAD and PDONLOAD procedures whenever you change printer drivers.

In the simplest case, assume that the appropriate codes to change print quality and orientation are stored in array elements _pdparms[2] and _pdparms[3]. Then, your PDDOCST procedure may look something like this:

```
PROCEDURE PDDOCST
PARAMETERS height, width  && this procedure expects doc dimensions
 ctrlchars = _pdparms[2] + _pdparms[3]
RETURN ctrlchars
```

Printer Driver Procedures

Table 11-1 lists the specially named procedures that you would normally include in a printer driver program. Note that your driver program does not have to contain all, or even any, of these special procedures. Some of the procedures, for example, PDDOCST, expect input parameters to be passed from FoxPro. Similarly, some of the procedures, for example, PDLINEEND, are expected to return control characters to FoxPro. No error message is generated if the procedures that are expected to return codes to FoxPro in fact do not. In that case, FoxPro does not send any codes to the printer. Table 11-1 shows which procedures can obtain input parameters from FoxPro and also those that are expected to return a control string to FoxPro.

All of the procedures except PDONLOAD and PDONUNLOAD (which are general, configuration-type routines) can be used by reports and labels. However, note that FoxPro does not invoke PDPAGEST and PDPAGEEND for printing labels. Four of the procedures, namely, PDOBJST, PDOBJECT, PDOBJEND, and PDADVPRT, can be used by the ?/?? commands as well.

Implementing FoxPro Printer Drivers

Assume that you have written two printer driver programs called Driver1.prg and Driver2.prg. If you want FoxPro to use Driver1 on startup, define a printer driver setup (say, MySetup) containing Driver1.prg, and include the following line in your Config.fp file:

```
PDSETUP = <MySetup> [WITH <parm list>]
```

Table 11-1. Summary of Special Printer Driver Procedures

Procedure	Used By[1]	Input Parms[2]	Description
PDONLOAD	—	None	Executed immediately when a printer driver is specified with SET PDRIVER, _PDRIVER, or Config.fp entry.
PDONUNLOAD	—	None	Executed when driver is changed or unloaded.
PDDOCST	R, L	Form height, Form width	Document start procedure. Returns value which is sent to the printer before report/label set is printed.
PDDOCEND	R, L	None	Document end procedure. Returns value which is sent to the printer after report/label set is printed.
PDPAGEST	R	None	Page start procedure. Returns value which is sent to the printer before each report page is printed.
PDPAGEEND	R	None	Page end procedure. Returns value which is sent to the printer after printing a report page.
PDLINEST	R, L	None	Line start procedure. Returns value which is sent to the printer before each report/label line is printed.
PDLINEEND	R, L	None	Line end procedure. Returns value which is sent to the printer after each report/label line is printed.
PDOBJST	R, L, ?	Style	Object start procedure. Returns value which is sent to the printer before each object is printed.

(continued)

Table 11-1. Continued

Procedure	Used By[1]	Input Parms[2]	Description
PDOBJECT	R, L, ?	Obj, Style	Object procedure. Returns value (including modified object) which is sent to the printer to print the object.
PDOBJEND	R, L, ?	Style	Object end procedure. Returns value which is sent to the printer after each object is printed.
PDADVPRT	R, L, ?	OldEndCol, NewBegCol	Object advance printer procedure. Returns value which is sent to the printer to advance the printer from one object to the next.

[1] R = Report, L = Label, ? = ?/?? commands

[2] Style = Style code string, for example, "BI"
OldEndCol = Ending column of the previous object
NewBegCol = Beginning column of the next object

With this command, FoxPro executes the PDONLOAD procedure before you see the command prompt, or before executing the program you include in the FoxPro command line.

You can install a new or different printer driver any time by assigning the name of the new driver program to the system memvar called _PDRIVER, for example,

```
_PDRIVER = driver2
```

You can also define a new printer driver and printer driver setup with the SET PDSETUP command. The command syntax is as follows:

```
SET PDSETUP TO <setup prg> [WITH <exp1>, <exp2>, ..., <expN>]
```

If you include the optional WITH clause, FoxPro creates a memory variable array called _PDPARMS and assigns <exp1>, <exp2>, ..., <expN> to the first, second, and Nth element of the array. The WITH parameters typically are character strings containing printer control codes, but they can be any data type. If _PDPARMS have been defined previously, the WITH clause causes the array to be redimensioned if necessary. To unload the current driver without defining a new one, use the SET PDSETUP TO command without any additional parameters.

The easier way to store values to _PDPARMS is not through the SET PDSETUP command but through the PDONLOAD procedure. Indeed, the sample driver program that is shipped with FoxPro 2.0 takes this approach. In the sample driver, PDONLOAD lets you choose a printer from a database of printers, and then it loads the _PDPARMS array from values stored in the selected record. We, the authors of this book, are pleased to note that the initial database of printers that comes with FoxPro 2.0 originated with us.

Chapter Summary

FoxPro has a powerful set of report writing and printing facilities to handle even the most intricate reports. Its built-in report writer, FoxReport, provides a WYSIWYG work surface with report bands that can be painted with database fields, text, lines, and boxes. The report writer's expression dialog facilitates the formulation and verification of report field expressions. Vertical stretch and floating band options permit maximum utilization of the 255 columns allowed in a report. With FoxReport, printing memo fields in a box and printing a column showing a numeric field's value as a percentage of the total are almost trivial exercises.

FoxPro's page handler, activated by the ON PAGE command, eases end-of-page processing such as the handling of page headers and footers. It specifies the action to take when an EJECT PAGE command is issued or when a specified line number is reached during report generation.

In this chapter, we also discussed mailmerge reporting and the design of a generalized mailmerge system. We described a generic mailmerge routine that uses a set of delimiter pairs in a letter template to handle page format directives, processing directives, FoxPro commands and functions, field names, and expressions. We also discussed two strategies for snaked column reporting, including a technique that uses the facilities offered by the mail label generator.

Commands can be issued directly to the printer using the ??? command, which also leaves the printer row and column unchanged. Unlike FoxBASE+ and dBASE III Plus, FoxPro can send the null character to a printer. Thus, with FoxPro, we can create .bin files on the fly using only the ??? command with the output redirected to a file instead of a printer.

The SET PRINTER TO command allows output to be directed to a local device, network printer, or a file. The SET DEVICE TO command can redirect @...SAY output to a file. FoxPro's ability to redirect printer output to a file, including those generated by the @...SAY command, can be used to test programs even when a printer is unavailable. The presence of an unfilled print spool causes the PRINTSTATUS( ) function to always yield .T. and therefore can be used also to test a program in the absence of a printer.

FoxPro automatically maintains system memvars to control the appearance of printed output, including page margins and alignment. System memvars cannot be released by the RELEASE or CLEAR MEMORY commands, but they are initialized with default values on startup.

A FoxPro 2.0 printer driver is just a regular, user-defined program (or API routine) containing specially named procedures that FoxPro automatically executes, depending on its current print tasks. Some of the procedures obtain parameters from FoxPro. Most of the procedures return control codes to FoxPro, which FoxPro then sends to the printer. Typically you store printer control codes in a printer database, and then populate the _PDPARMS memory variable array with values for the active printer. Printer drivers can be activated with the SET PDSETUP command by assigning the driver program to the _PDRIVER system memvar or by an entry such as PDSETUP = <setup> in the Config.fp file.

Chapter 12

Relationality with SQL

Introduction to SQL

In October 1986, the American National Standards Institute (ANSI) adopted Structured Query Language (SQL) as the standard language for relational database management systems. SQL is a nonprocedural language used for data definition, queries, access control, and data manipulation. SQL processes sets of records rather than just one record at a time.

SQL commands fall into the following four categories:

1. Query
2. Data Manipulation
3. Data Definition
4. Data Control

FoxPro 2.0 has three SQL commands: SELECT, CREATE TABLE, and INSERT. SELECT falls into the Query category, CREATE TABLE is a Data Definition command, and INSERT falls into the Data Manipulation category. Although not a full ANSI SQL implementation, FoxPro's SQL is significant.

SELECT is a powerful command that can perform complex queries with minimal coding. In addition, FoxPro automatically optimizes the execution of SELECT, relieving you of the burden of determining the most efficient means of accessing data. The CREATE TABLE command allows you to create a .dbf from a program, without requiring that any other .dbf be present. INSERT appends a new record to a database and assigns field values for the record.

SQL commands are normally described in terms of tables, rows, and columns. In FoxPro, a table is equivalent to a .dbf, a row is a record, and a column is a field.

The SELECT Command

The SELECT command is a very powerful FoxPro query tool. Its syntax is as follows:

```
SELECT [ALL | DISTINCT]
     [<alias>.]<select_item>
          [AS <column_name>]
          [, [<alias>.]<select_item>
          [AS <column_name>]...]
     FROM <database> [<local_alias>]
     [,<database>[<local_alias>]...]
[[INTO <destination>]
     | [TO FILE <file> [ADDITIVE]
     | TO PRINTER]]
[NOCONSOLE]
[PLAIN]
[NOWAIT]
[WHERE <joincondition>
     [AND <joincondition> ...]
     [AND | OR <filtercondition>
     [AND | OR <filtercondition>...]]]
[GROUP BY <groupcolumn>
     [, <groupcolumn> ...]]
[HAVING <filtercondition>]
[UNION [ALL] <SELECT command>]
[ORDER BY <order_item>
     [ASC | DESC][, <order_item>
     [ASC | DESC]...]]
```

We are going to examine the SELECT statement by starting with its simplest form and then incrementally adding complexity in order to understand the numerous options available. A one-line SQL statement can often produce results that would otherwise require a difficult, complex FoxPro program. There are several important facts to note about SELECT. First, it does not require the tables (.dbf files) to be open prior to executing a query.

Employee.dbf

Record#	EMP_NAME	EMP_ID	EMP_SAL	EMP_HIRED	EMP_TITLE	EMP_MGR	DEPTNO
1	Lewis	1000	2000.00	04/01/89	Analyst	1002	1
2	Clark	1001	3000.00	01/01/87	Programmer	1002	2
3	Sandler	1002	5000.00	09/01/90	Manager	1010	2
4	Arnold	1003	3500.00	02/01/87	Analyst	1009	3
5	Johnson	1004	2500.00	01/01/91	Analyst	1002	2
6	Morton	1005	2000.00	03/01/89	Programmer	1009	3
7	Smith	1006	3750.00	09/01/90	Writer	1002	4
8	Sterling	1007	5000.00	09/01/90	Manager	1009	2
9	Allen	1008	4000.00	04/17/88	Consultant	1002	2
10	Williams	1009	3600.00	03/02/91	Sr. VP	1010	1
11	Jackson	1010	7500.00	06/29/85	President		2

Dept.dbf

Record#	DEPTNO	DEP_NAME
1	1	Accounting
2	2	Marketing
3	3	Sales
4	4	Human Res.

Figure 12-1. Our sample Employee and Dept database files.

FoxPro opens any .dbf it needs to execute the query. Any file that FoxPro opens remains open after the query has completed. Second, FoxPro optimizes the query execution, determining the optimal data access path. Finally, after a query completes, the _Tally system memory variable contains the number of records selected.

All of the examples shown in this section use two databases: Employee and Dept. These databases are shown in Figure 12-1.

Example 1: The Basic SELECT Statement

The basic SELECT command specifies the columns that will be included in the query results. Usually these are field names, but they can also include constants, calculated fields, and expressions. Note that an expression can include a UDF, with some restrictions. Briefly these restrictions are:

- The speed of the SELECT execution may be limited if a UDF is used.
- UDFs cannot make assumptions about the FoxPro environment, for example, work areas in use.
- Changes to FoxPro's environment from a UDF may lead to unpredictable results.
- Values passed to UDFs should be passed in an argument list.

In SQL, an asterisk (*) may be used to indicate all fields in the database. For example, the following SQL query includes all fields in our Employee database:

```
SELECT * FROM Employee
```

The results are as follows:

```
EMP_NAME EMP_ID  EMP_SAL EMP_HIRED EMP_TITLE  EMP_MGR DEPTNO
Lewis    1000    2000.00 04/01/89  Analyst    1002    1
Clark    1001    3000.00 01/01/87  Programmer 1002    2
Sandler  1002    5000.00 09/01/90  Manager    1010    2
Arnold   1003    3500.00 02/01/87  Analyst    1009    3
Johnson  1004    2500.00 01/01/91  Analyst    1002    2
Morton   1005    2000.00 03/01/89  Programmer 1009    3
Smith    1006    3750.00 09/01/90  Writer     1002    4
Sterling 1007    5000.00 09/01/90  Manager    1009    2
Allen    1008    4000.00 04/17/88  Consultant 1002    2
Williams 1009    3600.00 03/02/91  Sr. VP     1010    1
Jackson  1010    7500.00 06/29/85  President          2
```

Example 2: Specifying Output Columns

To specify columns on the output, name the fields, constants, and/or calculated values. For example,

```
SELECT Emp_Name, Emp_ID, Emp_Title, Emp_Sal * 12 FROM Employee
```

This query displays columns for name (Emp_Name), employee ID (Emp_ID), Title (Emp_Title), and annual salary (Emp_Sal * 12) as follows:

```
EMP_NAME EMP_ID EMP_TITLE     EXP_4
Lewis    1000   Analyst       24000.00
Clark    1001   Programmer    36000.00
Sandler  1002   Manager       60000.00
Arnold   1003   Analyst       42000.00
Johnson  1004   Analyst       30000.00
Morton   1005   Programmer    24000.00
Smith    1006   Writer        45000.00
Sterling 1007   Manager       60000.00
Allen    1008   Consultant    48000.00
Williams 1009   Sr. VP        43200.00
Jackson  1010   President     90000.00
```

Example 3: Obtaining Unique Values

The optional DISTINCT clause excludes duplicates of any row in the query results. For example, to display a list of employee titles, you would issue the following command:

```
SELECT Emp_Title DISTINCT FROM Employee
```

The results are as follows:

```
EMP_TITLE
Analyst
Consultant
Manager
President
Programmer
Sr. VP
Writer
```

Note that you can use only one DISTINCT clause per SELECT statement.

Example 4: Selecting Specific Rows

You can specify that only certain rows (records) be included in the output by using the WHERE clause with a filter condition. Only records meeting the filter condition will appear in the results. You can precede any filter condition with the NOT operator to reverse the outcome of the query.

For example, to select only employees that work for Williams (ID 1009), you would issue the following statement:

```
SELECT Emp_Name, Emp_ID FROM Employee WHERE ;
          Emp_Mgr = "1009"
```

The query results are as follows:

```
EMP_NAME EMP_ID
Arnold   1003
Morton   1005
Sterling 1007
```

Example 5: Selecting Rows That Satisfy One of Several Conditions

As shown in Example 4, the WHERE clause filter condition is used to specify the rows to be included in the query result. The WHERE clause can contain multiple filter conditions that are combined with ANDs and ORs. For example, to select all employees who either have a monthly salary greater than $3000 or were hired prior to 1988, you would issue the following statement:

```
SELECT Emp_Name, Emp_ID, Emp_Sal, Emp_Hired FROM Employee WHERE ;
          Emp_Sal > 3000 OR Emp_Hired < {01/01/88}
```

The results are as follows:

```
EMP_NAME EMP_ID  EMP_SAL EMP_HIRED
Clark    1001    3000.00 01/01/87
Sandler  1002    5000.00 09/01/90
Arnold   1003    3500.00 02/01/87
Smith    1006    3750.00 09/01/90
Sterling 1007    5000.00 09/01/90
Allen    1008    4000.00 04/17/88
Williams 1009    3600.00 03/02/91
Jackson  1010    7500.00 06/29/85
```

Example 6: Selecting Rows That Satisfy Multiple Conditions

To select all employees who are managers and work for the Marketing department, you would issue the following command:

```
SELECT Emp_Name FROM Employee WHERE Emp_Title = "Manager" ;
         AND DeptNo = "2"
```

The results are as follows:

```
EMP_NAME
Sandler
Sterling
```

Note that, although we show the AND and OR conjunctions without surrounding periods, FoxPro accepts a WHERE clause that uses ".AND." and ".OR.".

Example 7: Ordering the Results and Specifying Column Headings

So far, all of our examples have produced output in an unspecified order. Actually, rows are listed in the order in which they appear in the database unless you include the ORDER clause. For example, to produce a list in employee name sequence of those who are programmers or managers, you would issue the following command:

```
SELECT Emp_Name, Emp_Title FROM Employee WHERE ;
         Emp_Title = "Programmer" OR Emp_Title = "Manager" ;
         ORDER BY Emp_Name
```

The results of this query are as follows:

```
EMP_NAME EMP_TITLE
Clark    Programmer
Morton   Programmer
Sandler  Manager
Sterling Manager
```

To assign your own column headings, use the AS clause as shown in the following command:

```
SELECT Emp_Name AS "Employee", Emp_Title AS "Position" ;
     FROM Employee WHERE ;
     Emp_Title = "Programmer"  OR Emp_Title = "Manager" ;
     ORDER BY Emp_Name
```

Your results will then look as follows:

```
EMPLOYEE POSITION
Clark    Programmer
Morton   Programmer
Sandler  Manager
Sterling Manager
```

Example 8: Performing a Join

One of SQL's powerful capabilities is the joining of two or more tables. You specify the key field on which to link the tables (called the join condition), and SQL performs the join transparently. For example, to join the Employee table with the Dept table to display data from both, you would issue the following command:

```
SELECT Emp_Name, Dep_Name FROM Employee, Dept WHERE ;
          Employee.DeptNo = Dept.DeptNo ;
          ORDER BY Dep_Name, Emp_Name
```

The results of this command are as follows:

```
EMP_NAME DEP_NAME
Lewis    Accounting
Williams Accounting
Smith    Human Res.
Allen    Marketing
Clark    Marketing
Jackson  Marketing
Johnson  Marketing
```

```
Sandler  Marketing
Sterling Marketing
Arnold   Sales
Morton   Sales
```

In this example, we produced the results in department name order, rather than in employee name order, by including the ORDER clause. Note that when you specify a table name, you must separate the table name from the field name with a period.

A join condition specifies the relationship between two or more tables. If you include more than one table in your query and do not specify the join condition, your query will include every record in the first database joined with every record in every other database as long as any filter condition is met. This can produce an unwieldy result that may not be what you had intended. Under most circumstances, you will want to establish a join condition for each table after the first.

Example 9: Joining a Table with Itself

One of the most powerful but most confusing features in SQL is its ability to join a table with itself. To do this, you must specify local aliases for the table, one alias for each separate join. This example joins the employee table with itself by searching for all employees who earn more than their managers. To do this, we set up two local aliases: Staff and Manager. Staff is joined with Manager (both are actually the Employee table) in order to compare an employee's salary with his or her manager's salary. You would issue the following SQL statement:

```
SELECT Staff.Emp_Name, Staff.Emp_Sal, Manager.Emp_Name,
Manager.Emp_Sal ;
     FROM Employee Staff, Employee Manager ;
     WHERE Staff.Emp_Mgr = Manager.Emp_Id ;
          AND Staff.Emp_Sal > Manager.Emp_Sal
```

The results are as follows:

```
EMP_NAME_A EMP_SAL_A EMP_NAME_B EMP_SAL_B
Sterling     5000.00 Williams     3600.00
```

Example 10: Grouping Results

You can group your query results using the GROUP BY clause. If you group your data and want to select only those records that meet a certain filter condition, use the HAVING clause with the GROUP BY clause. The HAVING clause works like a WHERE clause for groups.

For example, to display the number of employees that work for each department, you would issue the following command:

```
SELECT Dept.Dep_Name, COUNT(Emp_Name) FROM Dept, Employee WHERE ;
     Dept.Deptno = Employee.Deptno GROUP BY Dept.DeptNo
```

The results of the query are as follows:

```
DEP_NAME          CNT
Accounting          2
Marketing           6
Sales               2
Human Res.          1
```

If you want to display a count of employees who work for departments that do not start with the letter "S," you can issue the following command:

```
SELECT Dept.Dep_Name, COUNT(Emp_Name) FROM Dept, Employee WHERE ;
     Dept.Deptno = Employee.Deptno GROUP BY Dept.DeptNo HAVING ;
     Dept.Dep_Name NOT LIKE "S%"
```

The results are as follows:

```
DEP_NAME          CNT
Accounting          2
Marketing           6
Human Res.          1
```

Example 11: Executing a Subquery

An SQL SELECT statement can contain within it another SELECT statement. This is known as a subquery. The current release of FoxPro limits the number of subqueries that can be included in a SELECT statement to one. However, this subquery can be a compound statement as shown in

Example 12. To show a simple example, you can list all employees whose job title is the same as Lewis's (employee ID 1000) job title by issuing the following command:

```
SELECT Emp_Name, Emp_Title FROM Employee WHERE ;
     Emp_Title = (SELECT Emp_Title FROM Employee WHERE Emp_ID = "1000")
```

The results are as follows:

```
EMP_NAME EMP_TITLE
Lewis    Analyst
Arnold   Analyst
Johnson  Analyst
```

FoxPro first performs the subquery, producing a query result, and then it evaluates the main SELECT statement using the results from the subquery. In this case, FoxPro first found the Emp_Title for employee 1000, Analyst, and then it selected all employees whose job title is "Analyst."

Note that a subquery must always be enclosed in parentheses.

Example 12: Compound Subqueries

Although you are limited to just one level of subquery, you can include a WHERE clause with multiple subqueries at the same level. To show this technique, you can select all employees who have the same title as Johnson (1004) or whose salary is greater than or equal to Smith's (1006) salary by issuing the following SQL statement:

```
SELECT Emp_Name, Emp_Title, Deptno, Emp_Sal from Employee ;
    WHERE Emp_Title = ;
        (SELECT Emp_Title FROM Employee WHERE Emp_ID = '1004') ;
    OR Emp_Sal >= ;
        (SELECT Emp_Sal from Employee WHERE Emp_ID = '1006')
```

The query results are as follows:

```
EMP_NAME EMP_TITLE  DEPTNO  EMP_SAL
Allen    Consultant 2       4000.00
Arnold   Analyst    3       3500.00
Jackson  President  2       7500.00
```

```
Johnson  Analyst   2       2500.00
Lewis    Analyst   1       2000.00
Sandler  Manager   2       5000.00
Smith    Writer    4       3750.00
Sterling Manager   2       5000.00
```

Example 13: Repeating Subqueries

A repeating subquery is one that is executed once for each row considered by the main SELECT statement. For example, you can select all employees whose salary is higher than the average salary of the department they work in. In this case, you would include the AVG( ) function in the subquery. The query evaluates AVG( ) for each row in the table in order to determine the records that satisfy your criteria. You can issue the following SQL statement:

```
SELECT Deptno, Emp_Name, Emp_Sal FROM Employee Emp WHERE Emp_Sal > ;
   (SELECT AVG(Emp_Sal) FROM Employee;
   WHERE Emp.Deptno = Employee.Deptno);
   ORDER BY DEPTNO
```

The results of the query are as follows:

```
DEPTNO EMP_NAME  EMP_SAL
1      Williams  3600.00
2      Jackson   7500.00
2      Sandler   5000.00
2      Sterling  5000.00
3      Arnold    3500.00
```

Note that we used a local alias, Emp, in order to join the table to itself. We did this so that SQL could calculate the average salary for those employees whose department matches the department of the particular row being evaluated. The average salary was calculated for each row in the table. This is why the query is called a repeating subquery.

SQL Functions

Table 12-1 lists the functions that can be included in a SQL SELECT statement. Using these functions within a SELECT statement often reduces an otherwise complex process to just one command.

Table 12-1. Functions Available in a SQL SELECT Statement

Function	Value Returned
AVG( )	The average of a column of numeric data.
COUNT( )	The number of items in a column. The DISTINCT clause can be used to eliminate duplicate rows from the count.
MIN( )	The smallest value in a column.
MAX( )	The largest value in a column.
SUM( )	The total of a column of numeric data.

Additional WHERE Clause Filter Condition Keywords

In addition to the standard comparison operators (= , <> , != , # , == , > , >= , < , <=), several keywords can be included in a WHERE clause's filter condition. These keywords, shown in Table 12-2, give you additional processing options for query formulation. Remember that you can precede any condition with the NOT operator to reverse the condition.

Table 12-2. Additional SQL Keywords for WHERE Clause Filter Conditions

Keyword	Description
ALL	Used when comparing a field to a set of values returned from a subquery. The row is included if the field meets the condition for all the values in the set. *Usage:* `<field> <comparison> ALL (<subquery>)`
ANY	Used when comparing a field to a set of values returned from a subquery. The row is included if the field meets the condition for at least one of the values in the set. *Usage:* `<field> <comparison> ANY (<subquery>)`
BETWEEN	The row is included if the <field> value falls within the specified range. *Usage:* `<field> BETWEEN <start range> AND <end range>`

(continued)

Table 12-2. Continued

Keyword	Description
EXISTS	The filter condition evaluates to true unless the subquery returns an empty set. *Usage:* EXISTS (<subquery>)
IN	The <field> must be part of a given set in order for the row to be included in the results. *Usage:* <field> IN <value set> <field> IN (<subquery>)
LIKE	Permits the use of the wildcard characters % and _ for evaluating a character string <expC>. *Usage:* <field> LIKE <expC>
SOME	Used when comparing a field to a set of values returned from a subquery. The row is included if the field meets the condition for at least one of the values in the set. (Same as ANY.) *Usage:* <field> <comparison> SOME (<subquery>)

Examples of SELECT statements that take advantage of the keywords shown in Table 12-2 are as follows:

ALL Show all employees who earn more money than the highest paid managers:

```
SELECT Emp_Name, Emp_Sal FROM Employee WHERE Emp_Sal > ALL ;
        (SELECT Emp_Sal FROM Employee WHERE Emp_Title = "Manager")
```

ANY/SOME Show all employees who earn less money than at least one of the programmers:

```
SELECT Emp_Name, Emp_Sal FROM Employee WHERE Emp_Sal < ANY ;
        (SELECT Emp_Sal FROM Employee WHERE Emp_Title = "Programmer")
```

BETWEEN Show all employees who earn between $2000 and $3000 per month, inclusive:

```
SELECT Emp_Name, Emp_Sal FROM Employee WHERE ;
          Emp_Sal BETWEEN 2000 AND 3000
```

EXISTS Show all the managers' names and salaries if any manager's salary is greater than $5000 per month:

```
SELECT Emp_Name, Emp_Sal FROM Employee WHERE Emp_Title = "Manager" ;
          AND EXISTS (SELECT Emp_Name FROM Employee WHERE ;
          Emp_Title = "Manager" AND Emp_Sal > 5000)
```

IN Show all the managers and presidents:

```
SELECT Emp_Name, Emp_Title FROM Employee WHERE Emp_Title IN ;
          ("Manager", "President")
```

LIKE List all employees whose name starts with "S":

```
SELECT Emp_Name FROM Employee WHERE Emp_Name LIKE "S%"
```

Writing Query Results to an Alternate Destination

By default, SELECT results are displayed on the screen. If you include the optional INTO clause, your results are directed to an alternate destination. The three options for alternate output are as follows:

ARRAY <array>	Stores the query results to a memory variable array named <array>.
CURSOR <database>	Stores the query results to a temporary database file named <database>. The temporary database remains open after the query is complete and is automatically deleted whenever it is closed.
DBF <database> | TABLE <database>	Stores the query results to a permanent database file named <database>.

A cursor database is particularly useful if you need to perform a series of iterative queries against a database; for example, if you need to perform a SELECT with multiple levels of nested subqueries. Since FoxPro limits you to just one level of subqueries, you can store your results to a cursor database, and then execute the next level of subquery against the cursor database to achieve the desired results. For example, consider a rather complicated request for all employees in the Marketing department whose job title is the same as any employee in the Sales department. Assume that you do not know the Department number of Sales. If FoxPro allowed multiple levels of nested subqueries, you could write the following statement:

```
SELECT Emp_Name, Emp_Title FROM Employee WHERE ;
   DeptNo = "2" AND Emp_Title IN ;
        (SELECT Emp_Title FROM Employee WHERE DeptNo = ;
             (SELECT DeptNo FROM Dept WHERE Dep_Name = "Sales"))
```

You could also achieve the same results by executing a series of two SQL SELECT statements that use a cursor database as follows:

```
SELECT Emp_Title FROM Employee WHERE DeptNo = ;
   (SELECT DeptNo FROM Dept WHERE Dep_Name = "Sales") INTO Cursor First

SELECT Emp_Name, Emp_Title FROM Employee WHERE Deptno = '2' AND ;
   Emp_Title IN (SELECT Emp_Title FROM First)
```

The first of these two SQL SELECT statements finds the job titles of employees in the "Sales" department and stores them in a cursor (temporary) database file called First. The second query then selects the names and job titles of employees in department "2" (Marketing) whose titles match one of the titles included in the First database file.

FoxPro actually assigns the cursor databases a unique name (with a .TMP extension), with the name you specified in <database> assigned as an alias.

If you wish to write your query results to a file or printer, you can use the TO FILE or TO PRINTER option in lieu of the INTO option.

RQBE

FoxPro's RQBE (Relational Query-By-Example) window allows you to build a SQL query interactively using the familiar FoxPro interface. Using FoxPro objects such as check boxes, radio buttons, and push buttons, you can identify the .dbf file(s) to be queried, specify the relationship between files (join conditions), select fields for output, specify the selection criteria (WHERE clause filter conditions), order the output, identify output destination, and more. This facility is particularly useful if you are just learning SQL, as it builds the SELECT statement needed to execute your query. By examining the resulting SELECT statement, you can learn how to construct a query in SQL. By default, the query is stored in a file with a .QPR extension. Compiled queries have an extension of .QPX.

You can open the RQBE window in one of two ways:

1. Type CREATE QUERY [<query name>] in the Command window.
2. Choose New from the File menu popup and select the Query radio button.

CREATE TABLE

The CREATE TABLE command allows you to create a new .dbf without using the interactive facility (CREATE) or requiring the presence of another .dbf. The command syntax is as follows:

```
CREATE TABLE | DBF <dbf_name>
      (<fname1> <type>
      [(<precision> [, <scale>])
      [, <fname2> ... ]])
      | FROM ARRAY <array>
```

The first form of the command requires that you specify the name, type, precision (width), and scale (number of decimals) for each field to be included in the .dbf. Precision and scale are only used for certain field types; Table 12-3 displays the valid types and whether or not precision and scale are used.

For example, to create a .dbf named Sample, you could issue the following command:

```
CREATE TABLE Sample ;
    (Sam_Char C(10), Sam_Num N(10,2), Sam_Date D, Sam_Log L, Sam_Memo M)
```

The structure of the Sample.dbf that is created is as follows:

```
Structure for database: F:\USERS\KATHY\SQL\SAMPLE.DBF
Number of data records:        0
Date of last update   : 05/17/91
Memo file block size  :       64
```

```
Field  Field Name   Type        Width    Dec    Index
    1  SAM_CHAR     Character      10
    2  SAM_NUM      Numeric        10      2
    3  SAM_DATE     Date            8
    4  SAM_LOG      Logical         1
    5  SAM_MEMO     Memo           10
** Total **                        40
```

The second form of the CREATE TABLE command creates a .dbf from an array. The array must contain the field name, field type, precision, and scale for each field.

For example, to create a database called Sample2.dbf with the same structure as Sample.dbf, you could issue the following commands:

```
USE Sample
=AFIELDS(SampArray)     && Store the Sample field info in SampArray
CREATE TABLE Sample2 FROM ARRAY SampArray
```

Of course, you could modify any of the array elements prior to issuing the CREATE TABLE command if you wanted to change the .dbf structure definition.

Table 12-3. The Valid Field Types, Precision, and Scale Used with the CREATE TABLE Command

Type	Precision	Scale	Description
C	n	–	Character string of width *n*
D	–	–	Date
F	n	d	Float of width *n* with *d* decimal places
L	–	–	Logical
M	–	–	Memo
N	n	d	Numeric of width *n* with *d* decimal places
P	–	–	Picture (not currently available)

INSERT INTO

The INSERT INTO command appends a new record, with data, to the end of a .dbf file. Essentially it works like an APPEND BLANK followed by a REPLACE. It does not require the .dbf to be open—FoxPro itself opens the .dbf, if necessary.

The INSERT INTO command takes two forms:

```
INSERT INTO <dbf_name>
     [(<fname1> [, <fname2> [, ...]])]
     VALUES (<expr1>
     [, <expr2> [, ...]])
```

or

```
INSERT INTO <dbf_name>
     FROM ARRAY <array> |
     FROM MEMVAR
```

With the first form of the command, you specify the field values in the VALUES clause. The field name list is optional; you need to use it only if the values you are providing are not in the .dbf field sequence. An example of this form of the command is as follows:

```
INSERT INTO Sample ;
     (Sam_Char, Sam_Num, Sam_Date, Sam_Log, Sam_Memo) ;
     VALUES ("Sneakers", 14711, {06/29/91}, .T., "Molly and Frankie")
```

This command inserts a record at the end of the Sample .dbf file (shown earlier), with the field values assigned as specified in the VALUES clause. Note that you can assign a value to a memo field this way. This command is equivalent to the following series of commands:

```
USE Sample
APPEND BLANK
REPLACE ;
     Sam_Char WITH "Sneakers" ;
     Sam_Num WITH 14711 ;
     Sam_Date WITH {06/29/91} ;
     Sam_Log WITH .T. ;
     Sam_Memo WITH "Molly and Frankie"
```

The second form of the INSERT INTO command assigns field values that are stored in either an array or memory variables. The following sample code fragment defines an array, stores data in the array, and then adds a record to the end of the .dbf using the data found in the SampData array:

```
DECLARE SampData[5]
SampData(1) = "Tiger"
SampData(2) = 460
SampData(3) = {12/25/91}
SampData(4) = .F.
SampData(5) = "Nikita and Jack"
INSERT INTO Sample FROM ARRAY SampData
```

The FROM MEMVAR option copies data from memory variables into the new record. Note that memory variables must have the same names as their corresponding fields in order to be copied. If you issue an INSERT INTO <dbf_name> FROM MEMVAR command and no corresponding memory variables are found, FoxPro appends a blank record.

Any .dbf that is opened by FoxPro during an INSERT INTO command is left open after the command has completed.

Chapter Summary

FoxPro 2.0 introduces several Structured Query Language (SQL) commands that can be used interactively or in FoxPro programs. These commands are: SELECT, CREATE TABLE, and INSERT. SELECT is an extremely powerful query tool that can often execute in one statement a complex query that would otherwise require a complicated program. The SELECT statement includes a number of optional clauses that can be used alone or together to provide sophisticated report capabilities. We showed some uses of the basic SELECT statement and covered a number of the optional clauses to give you an idea how you can build on the basic command to produce various results. You can send query output to one of several alternate locations, for example, an array, a temporary .dbf (called a cursor database), a permanent .dbf, a file, or a printer. FoxPro's Relational Query-By-Example facility, RQBE, is an interactive window for designing a query. It is a useful learning tool because it composes the SELECT statement for you, which you can then study and learn from.

The CREATE TABLE command allows you to build a new .dbf from a program. It does not require the presence of another .dbf or the use of an interactive facility. You can create a .dbf with this command by either defining the structure in a list, or from an array that contains the structure information. We showed examples of both methods.

The INSERT INTO command appends a new record to the end of a .dbf file and assigns values to the fields all in one command. It is similar to performing an APPEND BLANK followed by a REPLACE. As with the CREATE TABLE command, INSERT INTO can accept field names and associated values in a list, or from an array. Again, we showed an example of each form.

Chapter 13

Low-Level File I/O

FoxPro provides a set of low-level input/output (I/O) functions that offer the ability to manipulate files of any format. They are particularly valuable in accessing non-FoxPro formatted files. The functions are comparable to I/O functions available with the C programming language and, like C, can be used for buffered or unbuffered I/O. Although the set FoxPro provides is actually a subset of the functions typically found in a C compiler, the FoxPro functions offer a great deal of programming power and flexibility. The FoxPro low-level file I/O functions are summarized in Table 13-1.

Note that files opened with FoxPro's FOPEN (when opened for writing) and FCREATE functions open the file for exclusive use. If FOPEN is used to open a file with read-only privileges (<expN> is 0 or 10), the file is opened for shared use.

How does buffered file I/O compare to unbuffered I/O? Buffered I/O systems use a temporary storage area in memory called a buffer to store data being read from or written to a disk file. The program actually reads from and writes to the buffer. When data is read from disk, a fixed number of bytes are read and stored in the buffer. Thus a request for additional data does not require an additional disk read if the requested data is already contained in the buffer.

This method provides more efficient file I/O since it requires fewer disk accesses. However, since updates are written to the buffer and not immediately back to disk, the buffer must be "flushed" (written back to disk) before any updates will appear in the disk file. As Table 13-1 shows, the FCLOSE function, which should be called to close a file, flushes the associated buffer. Therefore, a program that terminates normally flushes all file

Table 13-1. FoxPro Low-Level File I/O Functions

Function	Description
FCHSIZE	Changes the size of the file and returns the final size in bytes. (The file must be opened with read/write privileges in order for its size to be changed.)
FCLOSE	Writes file buffers to disk and closes the file.
FCREATE	Creates a file for input and/or output and returns a numeric file handle.
FEOF	Returns .T. or .F., indicating whether the file pointer is at the end of the file (EOF).
FERROR	Returns a nonzero value if the last file function caused an error; otherwise, returns zero.
FFLUSH	Writes file buffers to disk.
FGETS	Returns a string of characters from the file. If a number is provided, returns the specified number of bytes (or fewer, if a carriage return is encountered); otherwise, returns all characters from the current pointer position until the next carriage return.
FOPEN	Opens a previously created file for input and/or output and returns a numeric file handle.
FPUTS	Writes the specified character string to a file, adding a carriage return and line feed, and returns the number of bytes that were written.
FREAD	Returns a specified number of bytes from a file.
FSEEK	Moves the file pointer in a file and returns the current pointer position.
FWRITE	Writes characters to a file, returning the number of bytes that were written to the file.

buffers before exiting. Updates that have not yet been flushed to disk are lost if a program terminates abnormally.

Unbuffered file I/O systems, on the other hand, do not use a buffer in memory, but perform all file I/O directly on the disk file. These functions are inherently less efficient than their buffered counterparts, but they have the advantage that the disk file will contain current updates even if the program terminates abnormally. By default, FoxPro opens files for buffered I/O, unless the file being opened is a communications port (COM1 or COM2). By passing the appropriate parameter to FOPEN( ), you can specify whether a file is to be opened for buffered or unbuffered I/O.

Comparison with the C File I/O Functions

FoxPro's file I/O functions perform essentially the same processing as their C counterparts. However, experienced C programmers should note the minor discrepancies between the two. One difference is that FoxPro uses a numeric file handle, whereas the C buffered file I/O system uses a FILE pointer for a file handle. This should be transparent to the FoxPro programmer.

The file I/O functions in C and FoxPro have subtle differences. The return values differ for many of these functions. In many cases, FoxPro returns .T. or .F. to indicate the function's success or failure, whereas the C functions typically return a zero or nonzero value. C does not have a function equivalent to FCREATE. To create a new file in C, the FOPEN function is called with a specific file access mode parameter indicating that a new file is to be created.

C functions that return a string (for example, FREAD and FGETS) typically require a pointer to a buffer for storage of the string; the equivalent FoxPro functions simply return the string to the calling procedure. Also, some parameters that are required in C (such as the origin for the FSEEK function and the maximum number of characters for the FGETS function) are optional in FoxPro.

Formats for the functions differ significantly for the FGETS, FPUTS, FREAD, and FWRITE functions. Also, there is no FCHSIZE function in C.

These comparisons between FoxPro and C functions are based on the C functions found in the Microsoft C and Borland Turbo C compilers.

Uses of the Low-Level File I/O

So far we have just discussed the low-level file I/O functions and compared them to equivalent C functions. But how are they used normally? Primarily, these functions are used to read from and/or write to any non-FoxPro formatted file. They allow you to manipulate any file directly, regardless of its format.

The advantages to using these functions should become clearer after a few examples. You can manipulate text files as well as binary files directly. Although there are alternatives to working with text and binary files from within FoxPro, the low-level functions are simpler and more efficient.

Manipulating Text Files

Sometimes an application system needs to read from or write to a file that was not created by FoxPro. For example, an application may need to report from an existing free-formatted text file. There are several ways to accomplish this in FoxPro.

One option is to create a "scratch" or temporary file and append data from the alien data file to the temporary .dbf. Since there is no means for selectively appending data records from a free-formatted text file, the entire data file would be appended to the .dbf. This could result in a very large temporary file. The use of the low-level file I/O functions saves both disk space and processing time. No temporary storage is required, and the record-by-record overhead is minimized by sequentially reading each line and determining whether further processing is required on a line-by-line basis.

For example, consider a 20,000-line text file in which you want to locate and process only 10 lines. Using the scratch .dbf method, you must create a temporary .dbf containing one character field of the maximum width of 254. You must allocate the maximum number of characters because you do not know the size of the longest line in your text file. Next, you must append the entire text file into the scratch .dbf because you have no way to selectively append data. This means that you will have 20,000 records in your scratch .dbf. Now, to locate the desired 10 lines, you search record by record through your .dbf.

To perform this same process using low-level functions, you simply open your text file directly and read each line until you locate the ones you want. No temporary storage is required, and the overhead of a record-by-record search through a database is eliminated. Once you locate the lines you want, you can process them further by perhaps importing only these lines into a .dbf file.

Another option for reading the text file uses a shareware program called MAKEMEM, written by Andrew Schulman. This utility accepts a text file as input and writes a series of memory variables to a .mem file. Each line in the file is written to a different memory variable. A FoxPro program can process each memory variable in turn in order to process the entire report file one line at a time. This alternative also has limitations. First, the maximum number of variables that can be created by MAKEMEM is 235, thus limiting the size of the text file to 235 nonblank lines. Second, temporary storage (memory) is required for each line of the file.

The following example shows how you might use MAKEMEM to import text data into a FoxPro application. Assume that you are writing a floppy disk catalog program and need to import the disk's filenames into your database. As long as you have no more than 235 files in any one disk, one way to do that is to run the DOS DIR command and pipe the output to MAKEMEM. When you issue the command

```
!DIR | MAKEMEM -x disk
```

MAKEMEM creates a memory file, Disk.mem, containing one memory variable (named Var_1, Var_2, and so on) for each line of output from the DIR command, along with the memory variable MemNum which tells you how many memory variables the program created. For instance, the following lines from the DISPLAY MEMORY command show the values of Var_3 and Var_4:

```
VAR_3       pub  C    "FILES     LST     43092    1-01-90   12:42p"
VAR_4       pub  C    "CALCULON TXT      4992    1-01-90   11:42a"
```

Clearly the filenames that your disk catalog program needs can be extracted as substrings from the values of the memory variables. (You can also write a disk catalog program using the ADIR( ) function, as described in Chapter 9.)

The low-level file I/O functions eliminate some of the limitations imposed by these alternate methods by permitting direct access to the text file. With these functions, the FoxPro program may open the text file, read from and/or write to the file, and close the file without requiring additional temporary storage or the use of a utility program.

Let's consider the use of the low-level functions for reading a network system error file. A good example of this is the Net$Log.Msg file used on a Novell LAN (described in Chapter 15). The Net$Log.Msg file is available to programmers for recording system errors or for recording user access to particular applications. Assume that an application has written a series of messages to this file as errors occurred, as shown in Figure 13-1. A FoxPro program can be written to provide summary reporting of the error messages reported by a given application. The sample program shown in Listing 13-1 performs this function by reading the Net$Log.Msg file and determining for each record whether it was written by the application identified in the

```
06/26/90 15:39 STN  8:   Inventory  Mod1 Error opening Stock.Dbf file
06/26/90 15:42 STN  8:   Inventory  Mod3 Error printing report
06/27/90 09:22 STN  2:   Financial  Mod2 Unable to obtain record lock
06/27/90 12:00 STN 12:   Sales  Mod1 Error writing to Comm.Dbf
06/27/90 12:54 STN 10:   Sales  Mod4 Error printing report
06/27/90 15:42 STN  8:   Inventory  Mod3 Missing Parts.Dbf file
06/28/90 09:22 STN  2:   Financial  Mod2 User abort
06/29/90 12:00 STN 12:   Sales  Mod2 Error writing to Customers.Dbf
06/29/90 12:54 STN  5:   Sales  Mod4 User Abort
06/29/90 13:00 STN  7:   Sales  Mod1 Unable to obtain file lock
06/29/90 14:54 STN 14:   Sales  Mod4 User Abort
06/29/90 15:00 STN 12:   Sales  Mod2 Corrupted Index
06/29/90 16:54 STN 10:   Sales  Mod4 Missing Comm.Dbf
```

Figure 13-1. Sample Net$Log.Msg file.

Appl-Name parameter. For each record found, the appropriate counter is incremented.

This simple example returns only a count of errors found and assumes that the application has exactly four modules. Of course, it could be enhanced to allow for a variable number of modules and to provide additional summary reporting. To do this, we could use an array to keep track of errors by module.

In addition to providing a count of errors by module, the program deletes the records as they are processed. Actually, to delete records, the program rewrites the Net$Log.Msg file to a temporary file, writing only those records not processed, and finally overwrites Net$Log.Msg with the new file. Note that in order to run this program, the user (presumably the network SUPERVISOR) must have full rights to the Novell NetWare SYS:SYSTEM directory, the directory where the Net$Log.Msg file resides.

A sample report from this program (using a parameter of Sales) is shown in Figure 13-2.

Another good use of the FoxPro low-level file I/O functions is for extracting data from a large text file. Data can be read from a non-FoxPro formatted file in order to respond to a user query or to be included in a .dbf file. For example, consider a system designed to report budget figures for a selected department. This application reads a large budget file (stored as a text file) containing figures for all departments within a company, and it returns only those numbers pertaining to the specified department. Figure 13-3 shows a sample portion of a company budget report stored as a text file used for this example.

Listing 13-1. RdNetErr.prg, procedure to read the NetWare Net$Log.Msg file.

```
PROCEDURE RdNetErr
*****************************************************************
* Program: RdNetErr.prg
* Author : P. L. Olympia and Kathy Cea
* Purpose: Reads the Net$Log.Msg file on a Novell NetWare LAN and
*        : tallies the count of errors reported for the application
*        : identified by the ApplName parameter.  Also deletes the
*        : records it processes by rewriting the Net$Log.Msg file.
*        :
* Syntax : Do RdNetErr WITH <applname>
*        : where <applname> is the name of the application to be
*        : reported against.
*        :
*****************************************************************
PARAMETERS ApplName

* Set up environment
SET TALK OFF
SET SAFETY OFF

*Open Network message file for reading and
* temporary file to rewrite messages not
* processed
handle = FOPEN("SYS:SYSTEM\NET$LOG.MSG")
IF handle < 0
     ?"Can't open message file"
     RETURN
ENDIF
newhand = FCREATE("TEMP.MSG")
IF newhand < 0
     ?"Can't create temporary file"
     =FCLOSE(handle)
     RETURN
ENDIF

* Process Application identified by ApplName, assuming
* exactly 4 modules
```

(continued)

Listing 13-1. Continued

```
Repl_Msg = .T.
Mod1Cnt = 0
Mod2Cnt = 0
Mod3Cnt = 0
Mod4Cnt = 0
DO WHILE !FEOF(handle)
        rec = FGETS(handle)
        IF UPPER(ApplName) $ UPPER(rec)
                DO CASE
                CASE "Mod1"$rec
                        Mod1Cnt = Mod1Cnt + 1
                CASE "Mod2"$rec
                        Mod2Cnt = Mod2Cnt + 1
                CASE "Mod3"$rec
                        Mod3Cnt = Mod3Cnt + 1
                CASE "Mod4"$rec
                        Mod4Cnt = Mod4Cnt + 1
                ENDCASE
        ELSE
                write_out = FPUTS (newhand, rec)
                IF write_out = 0
                        ?"Error writing to NET$LOG.MSG file."
                        ?"File not modified"
                        Repl_Msg = .F.
                ENDIF
        ENDIF
ENDDO

*Close the network message file and the temporary file
* The = allows you to call a function without assigning the
*  return value to a memory variable or field
= FCLOSE(handle)
= FCLOSE (newhand)

*If no errors occurred writing the temporary file
* make a backup copy of the network message file then
* overwrite it with the temporary file
```

(continued)

Listing 13-1. Continued

```
IF Repl_Msg
        COPY FILE SYS:SYSTEM\Net$Log.Msg TO SYS:SYSTEM\Net$Log.Sav
        COPY FILE Temp.Msg TO SYS:SYSTEM\Net$Log.Msg
        DELETE FILE Temp.Msg
ENDIF
SET CONSOLE OFF
SET PRINTER ON
SET PRINTER TO ErrSumm.Rpt
?
?"SUMMARY OF ERRORS REPORTED TO SYSTEM ERROR FILE" AT 1
?
?"Date:" AT 1,DATE() AT 8,"Application: " AT 24,UPPER(ApplName) AT 38
?
?"Module Number           Count of Errors" AT 1
?
?"1" AT 6,LTRIM(STR(Mod1Cnt)) AT 32
?"2" AT 6,LTRIM(STR(Mod2Cnt)) AT 32
?"3" AT 6,LTRIM(STR(Mod3Cnt)) AT 32
?"4" AT 6,LTRIM(STR(Mod4Cnt)) AT 32
?
SET PRINTER TO
SET PRINTER OFF
SET CONSOLE ON
```

```
  SUMMARY OF ERRORS REPORTED TO SYSTEM ERROR FILE

Date:  07/02/90         Application: Sales

  Module Number           Count of Errors
      1                         2
      2                         2
      3                         0
      4                         4
```

Figure 13-2. Sample RdNetErr output.

```
ABC Corporation
Budget for FY 1990

Department:      Sales

Staff                                    $ 200,000
Commissions                                220,000
Office Furniture                            50,000
Supplies                                    10,000


Department:      Accounting

Staff                                    $ 500,000
Temporary Staff                            100,000
Equipment                                  250,000
Office Furniture                            70,000
Supplies                                    40,000

Department:      Data Processing

Staff                                    $ 300,000
Office Furniture                            12,000
Supplies                                    20,000
Equipment                                  200,000

Department:      Support

Staff                                    $ 150,000
Office Furniture                            50,000
Supplies                                    15,000
```

Figure 13-3. Portion of a sample company budget file.

To extract data from the budget report using the scratch .dbf method, the FoxPro program would have to append a potentially large company report to a temporary, or "scratch" .dbf, and then process record by record to find the desired department and associated budget figures. Listing 13-2 demonstrates a process to read a text file containing budget data into a scratch .dbf,

Listing 13-2. RdTxtScr.prg, procedure to process a text budget file by reading it into a scratch .dbf.

```
PROCEDURE RdTxtScr
*******************************************************************
* Program: RdTxtScr.prg
* Author : P. L. Olympia and Kathy Cea
* Purpose: Reads a budget report in text format into a "scratch"
*        : .dbf file.
*        :
* Syntax : Do RdTxtScr WITH <budgfile>,<dept>
*        : where <budgfile> is the name of the file containing the
*        : budget report, and <dept> is the name of the department
*        : to be reported.
*******************************************************************
PARAMETERS BudgFile, Dept

* Set up environment
SET TALK OFF
SET SAFETY OFF

*Use temporary dbf to store contents of budget file
USE SCRATCH EXCLUSIVE
APPEND FROM (BudgFile) TYPE SDF
GO TOP

*Search Scratch.Dbf record-by-record until find Dept or
* End-of-File
Found = .F.
SCAN WHILE (.NOT. Found)
        IF (UPPER(Dept) $ UPPER(Line_Item))
                Found = .T.
        ENDIF
ENDSCAN

*Check whether Dept was found
IF .NOT. Found
```

(continued)

Listing 13-2. Continued

```
        ?"Department " AT 1, UPPER(Dept) AT 12
        ??" Budget not available"
        ZAP
        RETURN
ENDIF

*Send report to file
SET CONSOLE OFF
SET PRINTER ON
SET PRINTER TO Dept + ".Rpt"

EndDept = .F.
*Write report header
?"Budget for Department: " AT 1, UPPER(Dept) AT 25
?
?"Date:  " AT 1, DATE() AT 9
?
*Print each line item until find next Department or end-of-file
DO WHILE .NOT. EndDept
        SKIP
        IF ("DEPARTMENT" $ UPPER(Line_Item) .OR. EOF())
               EndDept = .T.
        ELSE
                ?SUBSTR(Line_Item,1,20)
                ??SUBSTR(Line_Item,40,12)
        ENDIF
ENDDO

*Close report file
SET CONSOLE ON
SET PRINTER OFF
SET PRINTER TO

*Zap temporary Scratch.Dbf
ZAP
```

```
Structure for database: D:\FOXCODE\SCRATCH.DBF
Number of data records:        0
Date of last update   : 12/06/89
Field  Field Name  Type        Width    Dec
    1  LINE_ITEM   Character     254
** Total **                      255
```

Figure 13-4. Structure of a scratch .dbf file.

determine if the department specified in the Dept parameter is listed on the report, and print a small report containing the figures for that department. Although this method works, it can potentially consume a large amount of disk space to temporarily store the budget file into a scratch .dbf, and it incurs extra overhead by processing database records sequentially. Note that the scratch .dbf (shown in Figure 13-4) structure simply contains one character field with a width of 254 (the maximum). Since we do not know how long the longest line will be in the budget file, we must allocate the maximum amount of space. Although most of the space goes unused, it still requires disk storage.

Listing 13-3 demonstrates the same process using low-level file I/O functions. A scratch .dbf is no longer needed because we can open and read the report file directly. We simply search each line in the budget file for the desired department. If found, we produce the same report provided by the last program. This method saves us disk space by not requiring temporary storage for the scratch file, and eliminates the database processing overhead by reading the file directly.

These sample programs simply write the desired budget information to a text file that uses the Department as the filename and .Rpt as the extension. Alternatively they could write the extracted budget information to a separate .dbf file for processing at a later date.

Working with Binary Files

In addition to providing an easier way to read from and write to text files, the low-level file I/O functions allow us to work with binary files. Without these functions, it is very difficult to read or write to a binary file from within the FoxPro language.

Listing 13-3. RdTxtLow.prg, procedure to process a text budget file using low-level file functions.

```
PROCEDURE RdTxtLow
********************************************************************
* Program: RdTxtLow.prg
* Author : P. L. Olympia and Kathy Cea
* Purpose: Reads a budget report in text format using low-level
*        : file I/O functions.
*        :
* Syntax : Do RdTxtLow WITH <budgfile>,<dept>
*        : where <budgfile> is the name of the file containing the
*        : budget report, and <dept> is the name of the department
*        : to be reported.
********************************************************************
PARAMETERS BudgFile, Dept

* Set up environment
SET TALK OFF
SET SAFETY OFF

*Open File containing the Budget
handle = FOPEN(BudgFile)
IF (handle < 0)
        ?"Can't open budget file"
        RETURN
ENDIF

*Read each record until find Dept or End-of-File
Found = .F.
rec = FGETS(handle)
DO WHILE (.NOT. Found) .AND. (!FEOF(handle))
        IF UPPER(Dept) $ UPPER(rec)
                Found = .T.
        ELSE
                rec = FGETS(handle)
        ENDIF
ENDDO
```

(continued)

Listing 13-3. Continued

```
*If End-of-File, Dept was not found
IF FEOF(handle)
        ?"Department " AT 1, UPPER(Dept) AT 12
        ??" Budget not available"
        = FCLOSE(handle)
        RETURN
ENDIF

*Send report to file
SET CONSOLE OFF
SET PRINTER ON
SET PRINTER TO Dept + ".Rpt"

EndDept = .F.
* Write report header
?"Budget for Department: " AT 1, UPPER(Dept) AT 25
?
?"Date:  " AT 1, DATE() AT 9
?

* Print each line item until find next Department or end-of-file
DO WHILE .NOT. EndDept
        rec = FGETS(handle)
        IF ("DEPARTMENT" $ UPPER(rec) .OR. FEOF(handle))
               EndDept = .T.
        ELSE
                ?SUBSTR(rec,1,20)
                ??SUBSTR(rec,40,12)
        ENDIF
ENDDO

*Close report file
SET CONSOLE ON
SET PRINTER OFF
SET PRINTER TO

*Close the budget file
= FCLOSE(handle)
```

For example, a useful utility for any FoxPro application would be one that identifies for each .idx file the index expression and the .dbf to which it belongs. Since FoxPro does not maintain in the index file any information regarding the associated .dbf file, this is a two-part process. The first part requires a program to write the .dbf name somewhere in the index header area. Of course, the user (or more likely, the program developer) must supply the .dbf name. The second part, executed after all the index files have the .dbf identified, is to read each index file, obtain the .dbf name and the index expression, and store the information in another .dbf.

As described in Appendix E, the standard .idx file's header record is a 512-byte block, with most of the bytes currently unused. The TagIdx program shown in Listing 13-4 writes the .dbf name provided on the command line starting at byte offset 496. This program, designed to work with standard .idx files, accepts the index filename (wildcards allowed) and the .dbf name as command line parameters as follows:

```
DO TagIdx WITH <Idx-Name>, <Dbf-Name>
```

The string identified in <Dbf-Name> is written to each .idx file named by <Idx-Name>. Note that the program does not verify the <Dbf-Name> —it is up to the user to provide a valid .dbf name. The string provided in <Dbf-Name> is written into the header record of each index file identified by <Idx-Name>, starting at offset 496. This string can be a maximum of 12 characters. This area in the header record is currently unused. If Fox Software changes the format of the standard .idx file in a future FoxPro release, you may have to adjust the starting offset.

Once the index files have been updated to contain the .dbf name in the header, you can read that information together with the index expression stored by FoxPro. In the ReadIdx program shown in Listing 13-5, each index file identified by <Idx-Name> is processed by reading the index expression (starting at byte offset 16, where FoxPro puts it) and the .dbf name (starting at byte offset 496, where we wrote it). Note that we remove the trailing NULLs (CHR(0)) on the index expression; FoxPro pads this area with NULLs, not spaces. The NULLs must be removed before the string is written into a database file because the TRIM function removes only trailing spaces. If the string were left containing NULL values, it might be impossible to use as part of another command. For example, if you wish to re-create your index with the INDEX ON <expr> TO <file> command, the string containing <expr> cannot contain NULL values.

The information obtained by this program is stored in the DbfIdx.dbf database (displayed in Figure 13-5) for later use. This database can prove very

Listing 13-4. TagIdx.prg, procedure to write a .dbf name into an index file header record.

```
PROCEDURE TagIdx
*******************************************************************
* Program: TagIdx.prg
* Author : P. L. Olympia and Kathy Cea
* Purpose: Writes the associated .dbf name into header record of
*        : index file.
*        :
* Syntax : Do TagIdx WITH <idx-name>,<dbf-name>
*        : where <idx-name> is the name of the index file(s) to be
*        : written to, and <dbf-name> is the .dbf filename to be
*        : stored in the index header.
*******************************************************************
PARAMETERS Index, DbfName

* Set up environment
SET TALK OFF
SET SAFETY OFF

* Define the byte offset and maximum string length
byte_off = 496
max_len = 12

init_val = SPACE(max_len)

* Check for wildcards in filename.
* The SYS(2000) function returns the name of the first
* file that matches the character expression.  This
* allows the use of wildcards in filenames.

IF ("*" $ Index) .OR. ("?" $ Index)
        IdxFile = SYS(2000,Index)
        IF IdxFile == ""
                ?"No matching index files found"
                RETURN
        ENDIF
ELSE
        IdxFile = IIF(".IDX" $ UPPER(Index), Index, Index + ".Idx")
ENDIF
```

(continued)

Listing 13-4. Continued

```
DO WHILE .NOT. (IdxFile  == "")
        * Open .idx file named in IdxFile
        handle = FOPEN(IdxFile,2)
        IF (handle < 0)
                ?"Can't open Index file " + LTRIM(IdxFile)
                RETURN
        ENDIF

        * Position file at byte offset
        = FSEEK(handle,byte_off)

        * Append the .dbf extension if necessary
        DbfFile = IIF( ".DBF" $ UPPER(DbfName), ;
                        UPPER(DbfName),UPPER(DbfName) + ".DBF")

        *Initialize the area with spaces
        write_out = FWRITE (handle, init_val)
        IF write_out < max_len
                ?"Unable to write to index header record"
        ELSE
                * Write the .dbf name into the index file
                = FSEEK(handle,-max_len,1)
                write_out = FWRITE (handle, DbfFile, max_len)
                IF write_out < LEN(DbfName)
                        ?"Error - DbfName truncated"
                ENDIF
        ENDIF

        * Close the index file
        = FCLOSE(handle)

        * Allow for wildcards in index name
        IdxFile = IIF (("*" $ Index) .OR. ("?" $ Index), ;
                        SYS(2000,Index,1),"")
ENDDO
```

Listing 13-5. ReadIdx.prg, procedure to extract index expression and .dbf name from index file and store to a .dbf file.

```
PROCEDURE ReadIdx
*******************************************************************
* Program: ReadIdx.prg
* Author : P. L. Olympia and Kathy Cea
* Purpose: Reads the index expression and associated .dbf name from
*        : the header record of the index file(s).
*        :
* Syntax : Do ReadIdx WITH <idx-name>
*        : where <idx-name> is the name of the index file(s) to be
*        : read.  Filename wildcards are accepted.
*******************************************************************
PARAMETERS Index

* Set up environment
SET TALK OFF
SET SAFETY OFF

* Define the byte offsets
expr_off = 16
dbf_off = 496

* Define the maximum length of the index expression and .dbf name
max_expr = 220
max_dbf = 12

* Check for wildcards in file name
IF ("*" $ Index) .OR. ("?" $ Index)
        IdxFile = SYS(2000,Index)
        IF IdxFile == ""
                ?"No matching index files found"
                RETURN
        ENDIF
ELSE
        IdxFile = IIF(".IDX" $ UPPER(Index), UPPER(Index), ;
                        UPPER(Index) + ".IDX")
ENDIF
```

(continued)

Listing 13-5. Continued

```
* Open the .dbf containing index information
USE dbfidx INDEX dbfidx

DO WHILE .NOT. (IdxFile == "")
        * Open .idx file named in IdxName
        handle = FOPEN(IdxFile)
        IF (handle < 0)
                ?"Can't open Index file " + LTRIM(IdxFile)
                USE
                RETURN
        ENDIF

        * Position file at byte offset
        = FSEEK(handle,expr_off)
        expr = TRIM(FREAD(handle, max_expr))

        * Remove trailing NULL values
        nullpos = AT(CHR(0), expr)
        IF nullpos > 0
                expr = SUBSTR(expr,1,nullpos - 1)
        ENDIF

        = FSEEK(handle,dbf_off)
        dbfname = TRIM(FREAD(handle, max_dbf))

        * Close the index file
        = FCLOSE(handle)

        * Update the dbfidx.dbf file
        IF SEEK (UPPER(IdxFile))
                REPLACE Dbf WITH dbfname, ;
                        IndexExpr WITH expr
        ELSE
                APPEND BLANK
                REPLACE DBFIDX->IdxName WITH IdxFile, ;
                        Dbf WITH dbfname, ;
                        IndexExpr WITH expr
        ENDIF
```

(continued)

Listing 13-5. Continued

```
            * Allow for wildcards in index name
            IdxFile = IIF(("*" $ Index) .OR. ("?" $ Index), ;
                           SYS(2000,Index,1), "")
ENDDO
USE
```

useful for system maintenance and even for use in conjunction with a library routine designed to open all associated index files with any .dbf file that is opened. Note that the programs shown in Listing 13-4 and 13-5 are designed to work only for standard .idx files—they do not work with compact .idx or compound (.cdx) files.

Although you can obtain the expression of any index by executing the SYS(14) or KEY( ) function, the TagIdx and ReadIdx programs also allow you to store the .dbf name in a standard .idx file and to retrieve both the .dbf name and the index expression for permanent storage in the DbfIdx.dbf file. This can be done without using any .dbf or .idx file in any SELECT area.

Accessing Communications Ports

The file I/O functions may be used to write to or read from your computer's communications ports (COM1 and COM2). Communications ports are always opened for unbuffered I/O. It is important to note that prior to accessing a COM port, you must initialize it external to FoxPro. The easiest way to do

```
Structure for database: D:\FOXCODE\DBFIDX.DBF
Number of data records:       3
Date of last update    : 01/02/90
Field  Field Name  Type        Width    Dec
    1  IDXNAME     Character      12
    2  DBF         Character      12
    3  INDEXEXPR   Character     220
** Total **                      245
```

Figure 13-5. Structure of the Dbfldx.dbf file.

this is to execute the DOS MODE command prior to entering FoxPro. For example, the following command will initialize the COM1 port for 2400 baud communications, no parity, 8 data bits, 1 stop bit, and continuous retries:

```
MODE COM1 2400,N,8,1,P
```

Once your port has been initialized, you can open it with the FOPEN function.

The following code fragment demonstrates a capability to dial a number from your modem. It assumes that the port has already been initialized.

```
PARAMETERS phonenum

handle = FOPEN("COM1",12)
IF handle < 0
     ?"Can't open COM1"
     RETURN
ENDIF
dialphone = "ATDT " + TRIM(phonenum)

=FPUTS(handle, dialphone)
WAIT
=FCLOSE(handle)
```

This code sample opens the COM1 port, dials a phone number that is passed to the program in the PhoneNum parameter, waits for a keystroke, and closes the COM1 port. It could be integrated into a more sophisticated facility, for example, one that allows a user to select a person to call from a list, and dials the phone for them.

Chapter Summary

The FoxPro low-level file I/O functions provide an efficient means for reading any non-FoxPro formatted file. They let you directly manipulate text files without using temporary .dbf files or third-party utilities. In addition, they let you work directly with binary files. In short, they allow you to perform certain types of processing previously available only through C and assembly language programs.

The sample programs in this chapter demonstrate the power and flexibility available with these functions. The examples should give you some ideas for additional uses of the FoxPro low-level functions in your own application programs.

Chapter 14

Multiuser Procedures and Techniques

Local Area Network (LAN) installations are rapidly increasing—Novell alone estimates that five million workstations are installed currently, and this number is growing. As the opportunities for data sharing increase, so does the need for multiuser application development. FoxPro/LAN, the multiuser version of FoxPro, enables us to share data on a network. The multiuser version offers all the features of single-user FoxPro and also provides mechanisms for controlling shared data access.

This chapter introduces some of the unique issues that must be considered for multiuser applications and explores procedures and techniques for database design and programming with FoxPro/LAN.

Shared Files

In a single-user application, there is no contention for files or records; in effect, all files are opened for exclusive use. In a multiuser application, you have a choice of opening a file for exclusive or shared use. However, opening a file for exclusive use eliminates the ability to share data since no other user can open the file even for reading. For this reason, exclusive use of a file in a multiuser system should be used only when absolutely necessary.

Exclusive control of shared data results from, in order of progressively reduced concurrency, locking a record (RLOCK or LOCK), locking a file (FLOCK), or using a file in exclusive mode. Opening a file for shared use (through the SET EXCLUSIVE OFF command) requires that you control concurrent reads and updates through file and record locks. A user who has locked a record or file is permitted to write to the resource, and any attempt by anyone else to write to, or obtain a lock on, the record or file will fail. When a file is locked, other users can open the file for reading but not for update. When a record is locked, other users can view the locked record but not update it; however, other records in the file can be locked by other users.

Some operations such as PACK or REINDEX require that the data files be opened for exclusive use. Files that are so opened cannot be accessed by other users even for read-only operations.

Note that if you open a file that resides on a local drive, it is opened for EXCLUSIVE use even if SET EXCLUSIVE is off, unless you have loaded the DOS SHARE module at your workstation. If SHARE has been loaded, files residing on your local drive are opened for shared use by default. If you must load the SHARE module, the FoxPro/LAN documentation recommends that you open local files for EXCLUSIVE use.

To maintain data integrity in a multiuser system, locks are required for the duration of an update operation. This ensures that only one user updates any given data item at one time. Of course, these file and record locks reduce concurrency by denying other users access to the data. One of the primary goals in multiuser programming is to ensure data integrity (through file and record locks) while maintaining maximum concurrency. This requires determining the minimum amount of time during which files and records must be locked for update operations.

FoxPro Implicit Locking

In many cases, FoxPro/LAN automatically imposes a file or record lock when required for an update. This facility is particularly useful when converting a single-user system to a multiuser system. Whenever a file or record is locked implicitly by FoxPro, it is also automatically unlocked at the completion of the update.

There are times when you will want or need to specify the points at which a record or file is locked and unlocked. In these cases, the RLOCK( ) and FLOCK( ) functions are used to lock records and files, respectively. The UNLOCK command releases the record or file lock in the currently selected work area; the optional [IN <alias>] clause allows you to release a file or record lock in another work area. The UNLOCK ALL command releases all locks in all work areas.

Locks are also released when the locked file is closed with the USE command and when a program terminates normally. Unlike many of the other

Dbase products, issuing another lock command for a different record of the same file does not necessarily release the lock on a previous record. If SET MULTILOCKS is ON, FoxPro, like dBASE IV, allows multiple records of the same file to be locked simultaneously.

With SET MULTILOCKS ON, a set of records in the same work area may be locked by either issuing a series of RLOCKs or by passing a set of record numbers to the RLOCK( ) function. An UNLOCK command will still release all record locks in the specified work area, even if SET MULTILOCKS is ON. If SET MULTILOCKS is OFF, locking a record will automatically release a previous record lock in the same work area. If MULTILOCKS is OFF and LOCK( ) is called with a string of several records, FoxPro successively locks and unlocks each record in the string until it reaches the last record, which it locks and leaves locked. Note that toggling the MULTILOCKS setting performs an implicit UNLOCK ALL.

Table 14-1 displays the minimum lock requirements for FoxPro and other Dbase family products for selected operations. This table shows only the minimum required locks without indicating whether the user must impose them or the software automatically imposes them.

As you can see from the table, FoxPro's general approach to shared use is not to lock files or records for operations that read, but do not modify, the data. This approach gives you more precise control of your applications. Thus commands such as REPORT FORM do not require a lock but you may impose one anyway if there is a chance that the data will change while the report is in progress.

Although Table 14-1 shows that BROWSE requires a record lock, FoxPro does not require one if the command is invoked with the NOMODIFY option. Like FoxBASE+ and dBASE IV, FoxPro performs automatic locks on commands that require them if you do not explicitly obtain the required locks yourself.

Note that the INDEX and JOIN commands do not require a lock. You should lock the file yourself before executing either one of these commands to ensure the integrity of the newly created file.

FoxPro 2.0 contains the new SYS(2011) function, which returns a character string indicating the current lock status of a work area. It can be used to determine whether a file is used EXCLUSIVEly, a file is locked, a record is locked, or nothing is locked.

Also new to FoxPro 2.0, is that you can specify whether records used in @...GETs are automatically locked during a READ by including the [LOCK|NOLOCK] clause in the READ command.

Table 14-1. Minimum Locks Required by FoxPro and Other Dbase Family Products

Command	FoxPro	FoxBASE+	dBASE IV	dBASE III Plus	Clipper	dBXL/ Quicksilver[8]
APPEND	Entire DBF[1]	Entire DBF	Current record	Entire DBF	N/A	Entire DBF
APPEND BLANK	DBF header	DBF header	DBF header	Entire DBF	Record[7]	Entire DBF
APPEND FROM	DBF header	Entire DBF	Entire DBF	Entire DBF	Record[7]	Entire DBF
AVERAGE	none[5]	none	none[5]	Entire DBF	none	Entire DBF
BROWSE	Current record[2]	Entire DBF	Current record[6]	Entire DBF	N/A	Entire DBF
CHANGE	Current record[2]	Entire DBF	Current record	Entire DBF	N/A	Current record
CHANGE NEXT 1	Current record[2]	Current record	Current record	Current record	N/A	Current record
CHANGE <scope>	Current record[2]	Entire DBF	Current record[6]	Entire DBF	N/A	Current record
CHANGE RECORD <n>	record <n>[2]	record <n>	record <n>	record <n>	N/A	record <n>
COPY	none[5]	none	none[5]	Entire DBF	none	Entire DBF
COPY STRUCTURE	none	none	none[5]	Entire DBF	none	Entire DBF
COUNT	none[5]	none	none[5]	Entire DBF	none	Entire DBF
DELETE	Current record	Current record	Current record	Current record	Current record	Current record
DELETE <scope>	Entire DBF	Entire DBF	Entire DBF	Entire DBF	Entire DBF	Entire DBF
DELETE RECORD <n>	record <n>	record <n>	record <n>	record <n>	record <n>	record <n>
EDIT	Current record[2]	Entire DBF	Current record	Entire DBF	N/A	Current record
EDIT NEXT 1	Current record[2]	Current record	Current record	Current record	N/A	Current record
EDIT <scope>	Current record[2]	Entire DBF	Current record[6]	Entire DBF	N/A	Current record
EDIT RECORD <n>	record <n>[2]	record <n>	record <n>	record <n>	N/A	record <n>
INDEX	none[3,5]	Entire DBF	Entire DBF	Entire DBF	none	Entire DBF
INSERT [BLANK]	Exclusive use	Exclusive use	Exclusive use	Exclusive use	N/A	Exclusive use
JOIN	none[5]	Entire DBF	Entire DBF	Entire DBF	none	Entire DBF
MODIFY STRUCTURE	Exclusive use	Exclusive use	Exclusive use	Exclusive use	N/A	Exclusive use
PACK	Exclusive use	Exclusive use	Exclusive use	Exclusive use	Exclusive use	Exclusive use
RECALL	Current record	Current record	Current record	Current record	Current record	Current record

Command	FoxPro	FoxBASE+	dBASE IV	dBASE III Plus	Clipper	dBXL/ Quicksilver[8]
RECALL <scope>	Entire DBF	Entire DBF	Entire DBF	Entire DBF	Entire DBF	Entire DBF
RECALL RECORD <n>	record <n>	record <n>	record <n>	record <n>	record <n>	record <n>
REINDEX	Exclusive use	Exclusive use	Exclusive use	Exclusive use	Exclusive use	Exclusive use
REPLACE	Current record	Current record[4]	Current record	Current record	Current record	Current record
REPLACE <scope>	Entire DBF	Entire DBF	Entire DBF	Entire DBF	Entire DBF	Entire DBF
REPLACE RECORD <n>	record <n>	record <n>[4]	record <n>	record <n>	record <n>	record <n>
SORT	none[5]	none	none[5]	Entire DBF	none	Entire DBF
SUM	none[5]	none	none[5]	Entire DBF	none	Entire DBF
TOTAL	none[5]	none	none[5]	Entire DBF	none	Entire DBF
UPDATE	Entire DBF	Entire DBF	Entire DBF	Entire DBF	Entire DBF	Entire DBF
ZAP	Exclusive use	Exclusive use	Exclusive use	Exclusive use	Exclusive use	Exclusive use

[1]During an APPEND, FoxPro actually locks just the DBF header and serially locks the records as they are APPENDed.

[2]During a Browse, Change, or Edit, FoxPro locks the current record once editing begins.

[3]FoxPro does not require a lock to INDEX but will not index correctly if another user is updating the primary key field.

[4]FoxBASE+ automatically places a record lock during REPLACE RECORD <n>, but it requires a user to place a record lock manually for a REPLACE command.

[5]FoxPro and dBASE IV perform automatic locks with commands that only read data (e.g., SUM, COUNT, LABEL) if SET LOCK is on.

[6]dBASE IV BROWSE requires only a record lock even when adding new records. Records are locked one a time as they are edited or added. CHANGE/EDIT <scope> require a series of record locks.

[7]Clipper does not really require locks on APPEND BLANK/FROM.

[8]Quicksilver version 1.3, like Clipper Summer '87 version, does not support interactive commands. dBXL/LAN behaves like dBASE III PLUS except that it performs automatic locks on most commands. In Browse, for example, it locks a record or the entire file depending on what is being changed.

Deleting Records on a Network

Typically, when you delete records in a single-user FoxPro system, you plan to PACK the database at a later time in order to permanently remove the deleted records and recapture the space they occupy. In a multiuser system, the PACK command requires EXCLUSIVE use of the .dbf file, which presents a concurrency problem because all other users are locked out of the file for the duration of the PACK operation.

An alternative approach to the DELETE command can be used in a multiuser system to avoid locking everyone out of the files being PACKed. One such alternative is to recycle the record by first blanking it and then marking it as deleted. Later, when the application requires a record to be APPENDed, it may simply RECALL (undelete) the deleted record and return it to the requesting application as a new record. Of course, if you run out of blank, deleted records, you still need to APPEND new ones. When this time comes, the recommended technique is to APPEND a batch of blank records and then mark all of them as deleted except the one you are going to return to the application. This approach reduces the amount of time that the file is inaccessible to others because APPEND and APPEND BLANK require a lock on the header data.

Note that if you choose to implement this method for deleting and appending records, you should SET DELETED ON to ensure that your blank, deleted records are "invisible" during normal application processing.

To find an already blank record to use in an indexed database, make sure that you have SET DELETED OFF and then look at the top of the file. If there are any blank records, they will be at the top of the .dbf because these records have a blank key. When you find a blank record, mark it undeleted and return it to the calling procedure.

How do you blank a record that is about to be deleted? In FoxBASE+, the easiest way to do this is to use an undocumented feature known as the "phantom" record. This phantom record is a blank record found just past the end of the file (EOF). It is ideal for use in blanking another record. To get to the record, go to the bottom of the file and then perform a SKIP. The database pointer is now at the phantom (blank) record. Figure 14-1 shows a sequence of commands demonstrating the existence of the phantom record just past the end of the file.

Note that the record number is actually one greater than the count of records in the file. Also, notice that a display command shows a series of blank fields. Since FoxBASE+ supports arrays, the phantom record serves conveniently as a blank record that can be SCATTERed to an array.

```
. use employee
. ?reccount()
       45
. go bottom
. ?recno()
       45
. skip
. ?recno()
       46
.display
Record#  EMP_ID EMP_NAME HIRE_DT EMP_DEPT
```

Figure 14-1. Series of commands demonstrating the existence of the FoxBASE+ phantom record.

Since dBASE IV's "phantom" record cannot be used to blank a record, a different approach is required. The recommended solution in dBASE IV is to retain a small set of blank records and then copy one of the already blank records to the record originally targeted for deletion. To do this, the already blank record is copied to an array using the COPY TO ARRAY NEXT 1 command, and the array is copied to the record earmarked for deletion using the REPLACE FROM ARRAY NEXT 1 command. You need the NEXT 1 clause because, without it, COPY TO ARRAY attempts to copy all records in the file beginning with the first record and continues until all array elements are exhausted, rather than copying just the blank record where the database pointer rests.

Although FoxPro also has the phantom record, you don't need it if you only want to blank a record. FoxPro has new options in both the SCATTER and GATHER commands that make blanking a record a breeze. For instance,

```
Alternative 1
   SCATTER TO x BLANK     && x will be an array with empty elements
   GATHER FROM x          && blanks the current record

Alternative 2
   SCATTER MEMVAR BLANK   && Creates set of empty memory variables
   GATHER MEMVAR          && blanks the current record
```

SCATTER MEMVAR creates a set of memory variables with the same name and type as the database fields, just like the useful AUTOMEM facility of dBXL and Quicksilver. As expected, this set of memory variables is empty if the BLANK option is used.

If your database contains memo fields, you will need to include the MEMO keyword on the SCATTER and GATHER commands to blank the memo fields.

Controlling Concurrent Updates

As discussed previously, a multiuser system must impose locks on files and records in order to prevent two or more users from updating the same data at the same time. On a typical network, user requests for data involve copying the file from disk into the user's workstation memory. This can result in erroneous updates even if the records or files are locked. Several users can have copies of the same data in workstation memory. If one user modifies the data, writes it back to disk, and then unlocks the record or file, another user may now try to update the old copy of the data still residing on his or her workstation. This user's update will now be written to disk, overwriting the previous update. Thus a "lost update" is possible unless some measures are taken to control concurrent updates.

Some of the methods and techniques that deal with this issue of concurrent updates are as follows:

1. Open files exclusively.
2. Flag records in use.
3. Use NetWare semaphores.
4. Simulate the dBASE IV Convert utility.
5. Compare before/after values in arrays.

Open Files Exclusively

The simplest approach is to EXCLUSIVEly open the file(s) involved in an update action for the duration of the read/update cycle. This precludes any other users from even obtaining a read-only copy of the file while any update takes place within the file. Although this provides an effective means of controlling concurrent updates, it denies other users access to entire files for unnecessarily extended periods. For that reason, it is an extremely inefficient solution and would be difficult to justify or recommend.

Flag Records in Use

As part of an application, you can create a "master" .dbf that stores in each record the primary key and a flag indicating whether the record is in use. Any request for access (read or update) to a record must first check this .dbf to determine whether the record is in use. If so, the user is denied access to the record. This is more efficient than exclusively locking the file(s) because it effectively locks only the records in use and leaves the remaining records in the files available to other users. Its drawback is in programming overhead, particularly if the application already exists, because each request for record access must first call a routine to check the record's availability. If the record is available, the flag must be updated to indicate that it is in use; upon release of the record, the flag must again be updated.

A sample master .dbf file structure is presented in Figure 14-2. As you can see, this file contains fields for the primary key and a flag as well as fields for date and userid. The primary key is stored in this .dbf as a character string of up to 64 bytes. Although not required, the date and userid fields are useful for reporting back to the user if a record is not available.

```
Structure for database: D:\FOXCODE\RECLOCK.DBF
Number of data records:       24
Date of last update    : 01/07/90
Field  Field Name  Type        Width    Dec
    1  REC_ID      Character      64
    2  IN_USE      Logical         1
    3  DATE_USED   Date            8
    4  USERID      Character       8
** Total **                       82
```

Figure 14-2. Sample "master" .dbf file structure.

Listing 14-1 demonstrates two simple functions: LockRec and RelRec. LockRec is called with the following syntax:

```
LockRec (<record-id>,<user-id>)
```

where <record-id> is a character string containing the primary key for the record to be checked, and <user-id> is a unique id for the user, probably the

Listing 14-1. LockRec and RelRec functions.

```
FUNCTION LockRec
******************************************************************
* Program: LockRec.prg
* Author : P. L. Olympia and Kathy Cea
* Purpose: Determines whether the requested record is available.
*        : If the record is not already in the database, adds the
*        : record, marks it In-Use, and returns .T.  If the record is
*        : in the database and not already In-Use, marks it In-Use
*        :  and returns .T. Otherwise returns .F.
*        :
* Syntax : LockRec (<rec-id>, <user-id>)
*        : where <rec-id> is the primary key of the record to be locked
*        : <user-id> is the name of the user requesting the record.
*        :
* Notes  : The RecLock .dbf file with RecId .idx must be open in
*        : the current work area.
******************************************************************

PARAMETERS mRec_id, mUserid

SEEK (ALLTRIM(mRec_id))
IF FOUND()
        IF RecLock->In_Use
                RETURN .F.
        ELSE
                REPLACE RecLock->In_Use WITH .T., ;
                        RecLock->Date_Used WITH DATE(), ;
                        RecLock->UserId WITH mUserId

        ENDIF
ELSE
        APPEND BLANK
        REPLACE RecLock->Rec_Id WITH mRec_id, ;
                RecLock->In_Use WITH .T., ;
                RecLock->Date_Used WITH DATE(), ;
                RecLock->UserId WITH mUserid
ENDIF
RETURN .T.
```

(continued)

Listing 14-1. Continued

```
FUNCTION RelRec
******************************************************************
* Program: RelRec.prg
* Author : P. L. Olympia and Kathy Cea
* Purpose: If the record is currently In-Use, marks it available
*        : (sets In-Use to .F.) and returns .T.  Otherwise
*        : returns .F.
*        :
* Syntax : RelRec (<rec-id>)
*        : where <rec-id> is the primary key of the record to be
*        : released.
*        :
* Notes  : The RecLock .dbf file with RecId .idx must be open in
*        : the current work area.
******************************************************************

PARAMETERS mRec_id

SEEK (ALLTRIM(mRec_id))
IF FOUND()
        REPLACE RecLock->In_Use WITH .F.
                RETURN .T.
        ELSE
                RETURN .F.
ENDIF
```

network userid. If the record is not already contained in the file, it is added and marked In-Use. If it is available, the In-Use flag is changed to .T. and the date and userid are written. If the record is not available (In-Use is .T.), the function returns .F.

The RelRec function marks a record available. This function is called as follows:

```
RelRec (<record-id>)
```

where <record-id> is the primary key of the record to be released. If the record identified by <record-id> is found, it is marked available (In_Use is set to .F.), and the function returns .T. Otherwise, the function returns .F. Note that both the LockRec and RelRec functions require that the RecLock .dbf be opened with the RecId index (indexed on the Rec_Id field) in the current work area prior to calling the function.

The following code fragment demonstrates the use of the LockRec and RelRec functions:

```
mRecId = "123-45-6789"
mUser = "J_SMITH"
SELECT 9
USE RecLock INDE RecId
IF LockRec(mRecId, mUser)
        * Process the record
        SELECT RecLock
        = RelRec (mRecId)
ELSE
        ?"Record is currently unavailable"
        ??" - please try again later"
ENDIF
```

Use NetWare Semaphores

For FoxPro/LAN applications running on a Novell NetWare LAN, the NetWare semaphore function may be implemented to control access to the records based on their primary key. A NetWare semaphore is a mechanism that associates a user-defined label (representing some resource) with a counter that may take a value from 0 through 127. It is used to control access to a resource. Table 14-2 lists the NetWare semaphore functions.

Each semaphore has an open count and a value associated with it. The open count is simply the number of processes that have the semaphore open, which means that it is the number of applications that have called OpenSemaphore and have not yet issued a call to CloseSemaphore. The open count information has very little use—it simply indicates the number of processes that may request access to the resource. The value is the number of resources still available; this number is set initially by the first process that calls OpenSemaphore for a particular resource. The semaphore value is maintained by the system, and it is the crucial element in controlling access to a resource. When the value becomes negative, a process must wait for the resource to become available—it must wait for one or more processes to release the resource with a call to SignalSemaphore.

Table 14-2. Netware Semaphore Functions

Function Name	Description
OpenSemaphore	Opens a semaphore; creates it if it does not already exist. A semaphore must be opened before any other call can be made to it.
ExamineSemaphore	Returns the current value and open count for a semaphore.
WaitOnSemaphore	Decrements the value of a semaphore. This function is called when an application requests access to the resource represented by the semaphore. A timeout is specified, which defines the maximum time that a process will wait for the resource to become available.
SignalSemaphore	Increments the value of a semaphore. This function is called when an application releases the resource.
CloseSemaphore	Closes a semaphore. This function is normally invoked when the application terminates.

An application using semaphores to control concurrent access to a record would call OpenSemaphore with the primary key as the label and an initial count of 1. It would then call WaitOnSemaphore when it is ready to access a record; if the record is unavailable, the WaitOnSemaphore function would place the requesting program in a queue until either the record becomes available or the timeout limit (specified by the application) expires. When an application is finished using a record, it must call SignalSemaphore to increment the count and permit another user to access the record. Finally, the application must call CloseSemaphore before terminating. Of course, for this method to effectively control access to a record, all programs must recognize the same naming convention (assignment of semaphore labels) for the database records.

This solution is similar to the Flag Records in Use option described earlier in that it locks only the record(s) in use and leaves the rest of the file available to other users. It is an effective solution but may require significant program modifications in an existing system because a call to an external routine (either a .bin file or a C or Assembly program integrated via the FoxPro APIs) would be required for each request to access a record (read, lock, or unlock).

Simulate the dBASE IV Convert Utility

CONVERT is a new dBASE IV command that, together with related functions called LKSYS( ) and CHANGE( ), provides multiuser lock detection features. CONVERT adds a field (named _DBASELOCK) to a .dbf, which is used to store resource locking information. The contents of the _DBASELOCK field are shown in Table 14-3.

Once a .dbf has been CONVERTed, you can run the CHANGE( ) and LKSYS( ) functions against it. The CHANGE( ) function returns .T. or .F. to indicate whether or not the record has been updated since it was read into workstation memory. It does this by comparing the Count values in the _DBASELOCK field on disk and in memory. This function can be used within an application to determine whether someone else has updated a record since it was read from the file. The record need not be locked until it is about to be updated; just prior to updating the record, the application should invoke the CHANGE( ) function to ensure that the record has not been altered by another user. If CHANGE( ) returns .T., the copy of the record in memory at

Table 14-3. Data Contained in the _DBASELOCK Field

_DBASELOCK Contents	Description
COUNT	A 2-byte hexadecimal value containing the number of times the field has been updated.
TIME	A 3-byte hexadecimal value containing the time the field was last locked. The time is stored in the format HHMMSS.
DATE	A 3-byte hexadecimal value containing the date the field was last locked. The date is stored in the format YYMMDD.
NAME	An 8-byte field containing the id of the user who locked the field.

the workstation is no longer current and must be reread from disk before the lock is applied and the record is updated. This requires special processing to notify the user that the record has been modified since it was last read, and that the user's changes are now outdated.

The LKSYS( ) function returns date, time, or user information based on the parameter passed to it. If a parameter of 0, 1, or 2 is passed, the time, date, or userid (respectively) associated with the current lock is returned. Note that a value is returned only if the record or file is currently locked. If a parameter of 3, 4, or 5 is passed, the time, date, or userid associated with the last lock placed is returned. If a record is locked, the lock information is stored in the _DBASELOCK field in that record. If the file is locked, the lock information is stored in the _DBASELOCK field in record 1.

CONVERT, CHANGE( ), and LKSYS( ) features are not currently available in FoxPro. However, it is possible to write your own functions to simulate the processing. The CONVERT function is relatively straightforward; it simply adds a field called FoxLock (the equivalent of dBASE's _DBASELOCK) to the .dbf. A FoxPro CONVERT function is shown in Listing 14-2. This function is called as follows:

```
= Convert (<dbfname>)
```

where dbfname is the name of the .dbf file to be CONVERTed. The function first verifies that the file has not already been CONVERTed. If the FoxLock field is found in the file, the function returns .F. because it assumes that CONVERT has already been run. Of course, this means that you cannot have a field named FoxLock in any of the .dbf files you want to CONVERT.

If the CONVERT function does not find the FoxLock field, it adds the field and initializes the count field to zero.

Once a .dbf file has been CONVERTed, dBASE IV takes care of updating the _DBASELOCK field values. Of course, if you implement this feature in FoxPro, you have to handle the update of the FoxLock field values yourself. In dBASE IV, the Count value is incremented each time the record is updated. You must write a COUNT function equivalent to the dBASE COUNT function and ensure that it is called each time a record is updated. For example, you should call this function each time a REPLACE command is executed for any given record.

In addition, dBASE IV writes current date, time, and user information into the _DBASELOCK field each time a record is locked. You must write a function to update these values, and you must ensure that the function is called whenever a lock (implicit or explicit) is placed on a record.

Listing 14-2. FoxPro CONVERT function.

```
FUNCTION CONVERT
*****************************************************************
* Program: Convert.prg
* Author : P. L. Olympia and Kathy Cea
* Purpose: Simulate the dBASE IV Convert utility by adding the
*        : FoxLock field to the database file.  Returns .F. if
*        : the FoxLock field already exists in the .dbf, otherwise
*        : adds the field and returns .T.
*        :
* Syntax : Convert (<dbfname>)
*        : where <dbfname> is the .dbf to be CONVERTed. The .dbf
*        : extension must be included.
*****************************************************************
PARAMETERS dbfname

USE (dbfname)
Found = .F.
* Check whether the FOXLOCK field already exists
FOR I = 1 to FCOUNT()
        IF FIELD(I) = "FOXLOCK"
                Found = .T.
                EXIT
        ENDIF
ENDFOR
USE

IF Found
* The FoxLock field already exists in the database
        ?"File already CONVERTed"
        RETURN .F.
ENDIF

SET SAFETY OFF
* Copy .dbf to a backup file
COPY FILE (dbfname) TO Save.dbf

* Use dbfname exclusively since you are modifying the structure
USE (dbfname) EXCLUSIVE
```

(continued)

Listing 14-2. Continued

```
* Save data to a temporary file in text delimited format
COPY TO convtemp.txt DELIMITED

* Copy structure extended
COPY STRUCTURE EXTENDED TO convtemp

* Use the file containing the structure extended to
* add the new FoxLock field
USE convtemp
APPEND BLANK
REPLACE field_name WITH "FoxLock"
REPLACE field_type WITH 'C'
REPLACE field_len WITH 16
* Overwrite existing .dbf with new structure
DELETE FILE (dbfname)
CREATE (dbfname) FROM convtemp
USE (dbfname)

* Load data into .dbf from temporary file
APPEND FROM convtemp.txt DELIMITED

* Initialize Count to zero for all records
lockstr = CHR(0) + CHR(0)
REPLACE ALL FoxLock WITH lockstr
USE

* Delete temporary files
DELETE FILE convtemp.txt
DELETE FILE convtemp.dbf
RETURN .T.
```

Once this processing is implemented in your system, you can write the CHANGE( ) and LKSYS( ) functions. CHANGE( ) requires that the count in FoxLock stored in workstation memory be compared to the count stored on disk. You can implement the LKSYS( ) function by passing a parameter into the function as described earlier. When the function is passed a parameter of 0, 1, or 2, it must ensure that a lock attempt has failed before it returns the requested data. When the LKSYS( ) function is passed a parameter of 3, 4, or 5, it simply returns the requested data from the FoxLock field in the appropriate record.

Although the CONVERT option and associated CHANGE( ) and LKSYS( ) functions can be implemented to some degree in FoxPro, it may not be worth your time given the limited benefit it offers. First, unlike dBASE IV, you cannot protect the FoxLock field containing the lock information from accidental or intentional updates. This is because the FoxLock field name does not begin with an underscore (to indicate that it is a system variable), as the dBASE IV _DBASELOCK field does. Second, to effectively implement these features, your application must ensure that the function to update the count is called anytime a record is updated, and that the function to update date, time, and userid is called anytime a lock is placed either implicitly or explicitly. This burden alone may be enough to dissuade you.

Finally, even if you are able to overcome all of these obstacles, the best you can do with the CHANGE( ) function is determine that an interim update has been made and disallow a user's update. This may be an unsatisfactory solution to end users, who will probably not be too happy to find that after entering several screens full of updates, their changes are invalid and they must now either start over or abandon the operation.

Compare Before/After Values in Arrays

You may implement your own procedure to verify that a record has not been modified by another user between the time the record is read into workstation memory and the time the record is updated. At the time you read a record, copy its contents into an array (using the SCATTER command). Then copy the record to a temporary file where a user may modify the data. Just prior to updating the record, copy the record into another array. Now, compare the first array with the new array; if there are any differences, you know that the record has been changed. This should be communicated to the user, who will have to reenter the edits. If the arrays match, write the updates contained in the temporary file to the permanent .dbf.

The following code fragment demonstrates this technique:

```
numfield = FCOUNT()
DIMENSION bef_changes(numfield), aft_changes(numfield)
SCATTER TO bef_changes
```

```
COPY TO tempfile NEXT 1
* Select available work area
USE tempfile
* Process user updates in tempfile
* SELECT your permanent .dbf
* GOTO record to be modified
IF RLOCK()      && Lock record while comparison is made
     SCATTER TO aft_changes
     Changed = .F.
     fld = 1
     DO WHILE ((fld <= numfield) .AND. (.NOT. Changed))
          IF bef_changes(fld) <> aft_changes(fld)
               Changed = .T.
          ENDIF
          fld = fld + 1
     ENDDO
     IF Changed
          * Inform the user that data has changed
     ELSE
           SELECT tempfile
           SCATTER TO moverec
           * SELECT your permanent .dbf
           GATHER FROM moverec
     ENDIF
     UNLOCK
ELSE
     * Unable to lock record, perform alternate processing
ENDIF
RELEASE bef_changes, aft_changes, moverec
```

Note that if your database file contains memo fields, you must include the MEMO keyword on the SCATTER and GATHER commands so that the memo fields are copied.

Deadlock

Once you introduce file and record locking into your multiuser application, you also introduce the possibility of a resource contention problem called deadlock. Deadlock occurs when two or more processes are in a wait state, each waiting to lock a resource (file or record) currently locked by one of the other processes.

Figure 14-3 demonstrates an example of deadlock resulting from file locking. Process 1 locks Customer.dbf, whereas Process 2 locks Sales.dbf. Process 1 requires a lock on Sales.dbf to proceed; Process 2 requires a lock on Customer.dbf before it can continue. When this happens, Process 1 and Process 2 will wait indefinitely unless the system detects and resolves the deadlock.

Figure 14-4 demonstrates an example of deadlock based on record locking. In this case, Process 1 locks record 1 in Customer.dbf, and Process 2 locks record 1 in Employee.dbf at the same time. Process 1 requires a lock on record 1 in Employee.dbf before it can continue; Process 2 requires a lock on record 1 in Customer.dbf in order to proceed. Again, both processes will wait indefinitely unless one of the processes is aborted.

The following alternatives can prevent deadlock situations:

1. Open files in a prescribed order.
2. Preassign files to specific work areas.
3. Lock all files and records needed at program initiation.
4. Use the FoxPro SET REPROCESS option.
5. Implement NetWare synchronization services.

Process 1

```
SELECT 1
USE Customer
DO WHILE .NOT. FLOCK()
ENDDO
SELECT 2
USE Sales
DO WHILE .NOT. FLOCK()
ENDDO
* Process
UNLOCK ALL
```

Process 2

```
SELECT 1
Use Sales
DO WHILE .NOT. FLOCK()
ENDDO
SELECT 2
USE Customer
DO WHILE .NOT. FLOCK()
ENDDO
* Process files
UNLOCK ALL
```

Figure 14-3. Two processes contending for file locks that result in a deadlock.

Process 1

```
SELECT 1
USE Customer
GOTO Record 1
DO WHILE .NOT. RLOCK()
ENDDO
SELECT 2
USE Employee
GOTO Record 1
DO WHILE .NOT. RLOCK()
ENDDO
*Process records
UNLOCK
```

Process 2

```
SELECT 1
USE Employee
GOTO Record 1
DO WHILE .NOT. RLOCK()
ENDDO
SELECT 2
USE Customer
GOTO Record 1
DO WHILE .NOT. RLOCK()
ENDDO
*Process records
UNLOCK
```

Figure 14-4. Two processes contending for record locks that result in a deadlock.

Open Files in a Prescribed Order

An application system can adopt a standard calling for all .dbf files to be opened and locked in a predetermined order, regardless of the order in which they will be used. For example, an application program could be required to open .dbf's in alphabetical order. In this case, the deadlock situation shown in Figure 14-3 would not occur because Process 2 would have to be rewritten to open and lock the Customer.dbf before the Sales.dbf (since the letter "C" comes before the letter "S"). This solution eliminates the possibility of deadlock when opening and locking files.

This alternative can also be modified slightly to avoid deadlock situations when locking records. In this case, the application system must require that records be locked in an order based on the .dbf file to which they belong. For example, a program could be required to lock records from files in alphabetical order. In the example shown in Figure 14-4, records from the Customer.dbf file must be locked before records are locked from the Employee.dbf file (since "C" comes before "E"). Unfortunately this solution quickly falls apart if you are processing (and locking) records from multiple files in a serial fashion, or if you are locking multiple records from the same file.

The requirement that a program lock files or records in a prescribed order can very easily lead to an impractical and inefficient design. At best, it could require files or records to be locked in a way that does not exactly match the needs of the program. At worst, it could require files or records to be locked long before they are needed, thus keeping them locked for unnecessarily long periods of time.

Preassign Files to Specific Work Areas

This solution also requires that a standard be imposed on an application system. In this case, each .dbf may be opened only in a preassigned work area. Then, the work areas must be selected in numeric sequence.

This alternative has several major drawbacks. First, FoxPro allows a maximum of 25 work areas. (Note that the maximum of 25 work areas does not apply to FoxPro's Extended Version.) Therefore, this alternative is unworkable for a large application that uses more .dbfs than the maximum number of work areas. Second, the standard may be even more difficult to enforce than the solution described earlier where .dbf's are opened in a prescribed order. Every programmer involved in the application development must have access to some list indicating the work area assigned to each .dbf in the system. Maintenance of such a system is a burden when the preassigned areas must be changed or new .dbf's are added. Finally, this method is effective for avoiding deadlock when locking files (as in Figure 14-3), but it cannot prevent deadlock situations when locking records (as in Figure 14-4).

Lock All Files and Records Needed at Program Initiation

Another alternative to avoid deadlocks is to require that each application program in a system lock either all files or all records that it will need at the beginning of the procedure. If even one lock cannot be obtained, the program should release all its locks. This avoids the deadlock resulting from locking files as well as records because a program never waits for the availability of a file or record.

This solution would eliminate the file and record deadlock situations shown in Figures 14-3 and 14-4. These programs would have to be rewritten to eliminate the endless loop while waiting for a file or record lock. As soon as one file or record was unavailable, all locks would have to be released with the UNLOCK ALL command. For example, the programs in Figure 14-3 would be rewritten as follows:

Process 1

```
SELECT 1
USE Customer
IF FLOCK()
   SELECT 2
   USE Sales
   IF FLOCK()
      * Process files
   ELSE
      UNLOCK ALL
      ?"Unable to lock files"
   ENDIF
ELSE
   ?"Unable to lock files"
ENDIF
```

Process 2

```
SELECT 1
Use Sales
IF FLOCK()
   SELECT 2
   USE Customer
   IF FLOCK()
      * Process files
   ELSE
      UNLOCK ALL
      ?"Unable to lock files"
   ENDIF
ELSE
   ?"Unable to lock files"
ENDIF
```

This solution forces an application to know up front exactly what resources it will require. This can present a problem if the processing varies depending on data provided by the user. It could also make maintenance more difficult. This solution could also monopolize resources because all the resources (files and records) that the application needs are locked for the duration. On the other hand, if many resources are required up front, the program could wait a long time for all of them to be available simultaneously.

Use the FoxPro SET REPROCESS Option

FoxPro/LAN provides an option for specifying the maximum length of time a program should wait for a record or file lock. It can be used to specify either the maximum number of retries or the maximum number of seconds during which retry attempts will be made. This feature can be used in place of the endless loop shown in Figures 14-3 and 14-4 to specify a maximum time period to wait for availability of a record or file lock.

Table 14-4 displays some average time delays associated with a number of retry attempts for record or file locks. These numbers were obtained on a Novell NetWare LAN with little or no traffic. The waits were the same regardless of whether the program was attempting to lock a record or a file. The numbers are not conclusive, but they can be used to determine relative waits experienced for different numbers of retry attempts. FoxPro executes a maximum of 18.3 retry attempts per second, so you can easily calculate the minimum wait times associated with a given number of retries.

Table 14-4. Average Time Delays for Different Numbers of Lock Retry Attempts

Number of Retries	Seconds
1	< 1
10	< 1
100	6
1000	56
10,000	550

Specifying a maximum wait for a lock eliminates deadlock possibilities by defining a finite time period during which a program will wait for a resource to be available. If the lock cannot be obtained within the defined period, the application's ON ERROR process takes over, allowing the programmer to define an alternative course of action. (Chapter 15 discusses ON ERROR processing in more detail.)

Implement NetWare Synchronization Services

Systems running on a Novell NetWare operating system have another alternative. The Novell APIs (Application Program Interfaces, available to developers) provide an option called synchronization services. The Synchronization Services offer facilities for both file and record locking used in conjunction with C and Assembly language programs. Programs written to take advantage of these services may be converted to .bin files for use in a FoxPro application or they may be integrated into the application using the FoxPro APIs.

The Novell APIs provide three types of synchronization services: File Locking, Physical Record Locking, and Logical Record Locking. The File Locking services use a log table that records all the files to be locked. Similarly, the Physical Record Locking services use a log table that stores information pertaining to each record to be locked. An application can then request that the set of files or records contained in the log table be locked. The set is either locked in its entirety or not at all. The application releases the set before it terminates. The log table concept is useful in that the set of files or records can be unlocked but kept in the table for later use. With Physical

Record Locking services, the records are actually specified with a DOS file handle, the starting offset, and the record length.

Unfortunately the File Locking services and Physical Record Locking services cannot be easily implemented in a FoxPro application. Complex code is required to determine and monitor the file handles for open files. Another problem is that an update made by the C or Assembly routine to a field that is part of the database's primary key will not be reflected in the index file, resulting in an index file that is out of sync with the corresponding .dbf file.

The NetWare Logical Record Locking services present a more reasonable solution. These facilities do not actually place any physical locks, but rather they keep track of logical locks placed on names representing records. These features coordinate multiuser access to shared data without physically locking data. A greater degree of internal control is required of an application to effectively implement logical record locking. The key to using this facility is to establish a standard for assigning names to records to be locked. A logical record name can be a maximum of 100 bytes in length, including a null terminator. Thus a reasonable naming convention might be to assign a name consisting of the .dbf name plus the value of the key field(s) for the record to be locked. The FoxPro program could formulate the string value and pass it to the .bin files, which would then take care of the appropriate locking/unlocking function.

Table 14-5. NetWare Logical Record Locking Functions

Function	Description
LogLogicalRecord	Adds a logical record to the log table and optionally locks the record.
LockLogicalRecordSet	Attempts to lock all logical records in the log table.
ReleaseLogicalRecord	Unlocks a logical record, but leaves it in the log table.
ReleaseLogicalRecordSet	Unlocks all logical records currently locked in the log table, but leaves them in the table.
ClearLogicalRecord	Unlocks a logical record and removes it from the log table.
ClearLogicalRecordSet	Unlocks all logical records in the log table and removes the records from the table.

The Logical Record Locking services are similar to the File Locking and Physical Record Locking functions in that a log table is maintained to track the records to be locked; a set is either locked in its entirety or not at all. Table 14-5 shows the Logical Record Locking functions.

Chapter Summary

Multiuser programming introduces important issues that are not concerns in a single-user environment. Users may contend for the same data in a multiuser environment, so an application must ensure data integrity through appropriate record and file locking. At the same time, we would like to maximize concurrency, that is, we want to provide as much access to shared data as possible. The tradeoff between data integrity and concurrency requires that programmers pay special attention to the locks imposed by an application.

FoxPro/LAN implicitly locks a file or record in many cases. However, a programmer can specify the points at which a record or file is to be locked or unlocked, thereby overriding the FoxPro defaults. In deciding when and how to place a lock, you should consider the problem of the "lost update" and potential deadlock situations. In this chapter, we discussed these problems and presented techniques for avoiding them.

We also presented an alternative approach to deleting records. Since a PACK requires exclusive use of a database file, a technique that eliminates the need to periodically PACK the database will increase concurrency. We discussed a method of deleting and reusing records.

The techniques presented in this chapter should help you avoid many of the potential pitfalls of multiuser programming.

Chapter 15

More Multiuser Techniques

In Chapter 14, we introduced some of the issues that must be addressed when programming in the multiuser environment. In this chapter, we will look at some additional concerns and alternative techniques.

Reporting

When a user runs a report in single-user FoxPro, data cannot possibly be updated while the report is generated. In a multiuser environment, however, there is always the possibility that another user is updating the database while the report is running. In some cases, this is not a problem. However, when you want to run a program such as an accounting summary where the figures must balance, you have to consider what will happen if a few of the numbers are changed between the time the report program begins execution and the time it completes.

If you require that the data remain static once the report run begins, you have several options:

1. Lock all .dbf files for the duration of the report run.
2. Copy .dbf files to temporary files.
3. Create temporary files by selectively copying records.

Lock All .dbf Files for the Duration of the Report Run

The obvious solution to the problem of a changing database during report execution is to lock all the files that the report program needs for the duration of the run. Then, although other users can obtain a read-only copy of these .dbf files, they cannot change the data until the report program completes and releases the file locks.

In most cases, this technique is too extreme to be considered viable. It eliminates the benefits of running in a multiuser environment because it monopolizes normally shared resources while the report runs. You should consider one of the other alternatives before looking at this option.

Copy .dbf Files to Temporary Files

Another method for ensuring that the .dbf files are not modified while a report program runs is to copy the .dbf files to another set of "temporary" files, for use only by the report program. The report program then deletes the temporary files before terminating.

Files may be copied using either the COPY or SORT command. If the report you will be running processes data in a prescribed order, SORT is preferable since it can create the temporary file in the required order.

Clearly this alternative provides greater concurrency. It ensures that data is not changed by creating temporary files for the report program's exclusive use. At the same time, it does not lock anyone out of the production .dbf files. To effectively implement this method, you must have a means of uniquely naming your temporary files. This issue is addressed later in this chapter.

This method also raises the issue of disk space usage. In addition to the disk space that the production files need, you now must have sufficient space for all the temporary files. This means that if several users run the report program concurrently, you will have several sets of temporary files.

If you consider implementing this option, you have two choices for the location of your temporary files. You may write them to a network disk or to a local hard disk. If you write to a network disk, the user contends with normal network traffic for all file I/O. You also risk monopolizing a large amount of network disk space if the files are very large or if you have a number of users running against temporary files simultaneously.

If you run the report against temporary files written to a local hard disk, you eliminate the network traffic factor. However, there is always a chance that a user will run the report from a workstation that has no hard disk. Also, unless all the workstation hard disk directories are standardized at your site, you do not have the advantage of knowing the directory structure, and thus you have to take your best guess as to where to write the temporary files. In addition, you have no way of centrally monitoring available disk space on local drives, whereas the system administrator typically has utility programs for monitoring network disk space usage. Finally, you must consider the average access speeds on the network drive versus the local drive. Often, network disk drives are faster than local disk drives.

Create Temporary Files by Selectively Copying Records

Rather than copying the contents of every .dbf needed for a report, you can use one of several different FoxPro options to selectively copy only those records you will be using. This reduces the size of your temporary files and may speed up the report process because many or all of the unneeded records have already been filtered out.

One option for selectively copying records is to use the SET FILTER TO option for your database files. You then use the COPY TO command to copy the records that meet your filter criteria to a temporary file. However, unless FoxPro's Rushmore technology can be used, SET FILTER TO is normally very slow. If you must use it, you should release your indexes with the SET ORDER TO 0 command.

A better alternative could be to create a filtered index using the FOR clause of the INDEX command. This creates an index that acts as a filter by including only those records that meet the FOR criteria. You then use the FoxPro COPY TO command to copy the records that meet your selection criteria to a temporary file. Only those records that met the FOR condition when the index was created will be present in the temporary database file. This option has the added advantage of producing a temporary file in sorted sequence.

Finally, you can use FoxPro's COPY TO or SORT command options to limit the fields or records to be copied to the temporary file. This includes the FIELDS, FOR, and WHILE options. The SORT command has the advantage in that it can create a file in the order required by the report.

The disadvantage to using one of the alternatives described in this section is the time FoxPro requires to select the records that meet your specified criteria. If you expect to be using a lot of temporary files for application reporting, you may want to set up your own tests to determine which method is most efficient in your environment.

Network Conventions for Assigning Unique Filenames

If you choose to create temporary files for any of your application programs, and these files are written to the network disk, it is critical that you implement a procedure that ensures unique temporary filenames. Otherwise, you will have users overwriting each other's temporary files and running against each other's database files.

FoxPro provides the SYS(3) function to help you create unique filenames. It is based on the system clock and returns a unique 8-digit character string that you can use to compose a filename. For example, if you are creating a temporary .dbf file, you can build a filename as follows:

```
ToFile = SYS(3) + '.DBF'
```

Alternatively, you can use a unique network identifier to build your filenames. For example, on a Novell NetWare LAN, you can use the STATION parameter. This parameter is unique for every separate user login, regardless of which physical workstation the user is logged in to or what the userid is. To obtain the STATION id, you can set an environment variable in the System Login Script using a statement such as:

```
SET STA = "%STATION"
```

Or, you can write a C or assembly program that picks up the user's STATION id dynamically, and then you can either convert the program to a .bin file or call it as a function using the FoxPro APIs.

The following code fragment assumes that the environment variable STA has been set in the System Login Script to the STATION id, and it generates a unique filename by appending the STATION id to the name of the file being copied, that is, Sales.

```
FromFile = "SALES.DBF"     && You can use any filename here
ToFile = TempName(FromFile)

FUNCTION TempName
PARAMETERS FromFile
station = GETENV('STA')
RETURN SUBSTR(FromFile,1,AT('.',FromFile)) + ALLTRIM(station)
```

The advantage to this approach is that you can easily identify the contents of a temporary file given its filename. You may also be able to identify the owner of the file in the event of a system crash (if the user remains logged in to the network) since you know the STATION id of the user who created the file. The disadvantage is that you cannot use this approach if you have any memo fields in the file or if you will be creating a structural .cdx for the temporary file since FoxPro attempts to create a .fpt or .cdx file with the same name as the original.

Transaction Processing

In every network application, you must consider the possibility of a program terminating abnormally before it completes its processing. This could be the result of a program failure or a hardware failure. If this happens, will you be left with partial updates and database files out of sync? This is entirely possible unless you make use of a transaction processing facility.

In addition, there are times when you will have a series of related database updates that should either be made as a set or not made at all. If you successfully complete several of the updates and then are unable to complete one or more, perhaps because of the unavailability of a record lock, you need to be able to "undo" the related updates you already completed in order to leave the database in a consistent state. What you need is a way to abort your transaction.

In database terms, a transaction is a logical unit of work. It may be a single database operation or a series of update operations as defined by the application. These database operations must be made as a set in order to leave the database in a consistent state, maintaining data integrity. For example, a banking transaction may be made up of two operations: one to debit an account and one to credit another account.

Transaction processing ensures that a transaction is either completed in its entirety or is completely canceled. In the banking example, if the debit to one account is completed and then the system fails before the credit can take place, the transaction processing facility is responsible for undoing the debit, thus leaving the database in a consistent state. A transaction may be "rolled back," or aborted, before it completes, thereby restoring the database to the state it was in prior to the start of the updates. In addition to providing recovery from a hardware failure, a rollback feature allows an application to cancel a set of related updates that have already been made before they are written to disk.

FoxPro, unlike dBASE IV, does not provide a transaction processing facility. Therefore you must consider the alternatives of using a network-provided transaction tracking service or writing your own if you wish to implement transaction processing. Novell, for example, provides TTS (Transaction Tracking Services) on some of its NetWare operating systems. This section explores transaction processing alternatives in greater detail.

NetWare Transaction Tracking Services

NetWare TTS has a set of functions that can provide transaction processing to an application system such as one developed in FoxPro. Actually, two types of transaction tracking are available in NetWare TTS: explicit and implicit.

Implicit transaction tracking does not require any calls to the NetWare TTS functions; it works in connection with multiuser software that performs record locking. To enable implicit transaction tracking, the database files are simply flagged as Transactional.

Although this method is very easy to implement because it does not require any programming, it does not allow the developer to specify the beginning and end of a transaction. By default, NetWare starts a transaction when the first record is locked and ends the transaction when all records are unlocked. A utility is available to specify the number of locks required to start and end an implicit transaction. However, this will probably not provide enough flexibility to be used in a multiuser FoxPro application. In addition, the Novell documentation states that implicit transactions are not guaranteed to work with all multiuser applications. For these reasons, we do not recommend implicit TTS.

Explicit transaction processing, on the other hand, requires calls to NetWare functions defining the beginning and end of a transaction. This allows a developer to make the appropriate calls from anywhere within an application. Although it requires additional programming, it is the recommended approach. The function calls that pertain to explicit transaction processing are as follows:

Function Call	Description
TTS Begin Transaction	Signals the start of a transaction. The transaction remains open until either TTS Abort Transaction or TTS End Transaction is called.
TTS Abort Transaction	Backs out the transaction and returns the file to the state it was in prior to the beginning of the transaction.

Function Call	Description
TTS End Transaction	Signals the end of a transaction and writes the updates to disk. (If the file server fails before all updates are written to disk, the transaction is backed out when the server is rebooted.)

The remainder of this section addresses only the explicit transaction tracking functions.

You can take advantage of these functions by writing assembly language programs that place specific NetWare calls. You then either convert the executable files to .bin files that can be LOADed and CALLed from within FoxPro or integrate the functions into your application by taking advantage of the FoxPro APIs. Platinum Software's FPNet product implements TTS and other Novell functions through the FoxPro API facility. Three routines are needed: one to signal the beginning of a transaction, one to "commit" the transaction (write all updates to disk and make the update final), and one to "roll back," or undo, the transaction.

For example, in the banking transaction described earlier, you would implement transaction processing with .bin routines as follows:

1. LOAD the .bin files.
2. CALL the TTS Begin Transaction .bin file.
3. Perform the updates associated with debiting an account.
4. Perform the updates associated with crediting an account.
5. If all updates were successful, call the TTS End Transaction .bin file; otherwise, call the TTS Abort Transaction .bin file.

This sequence of events ensures that the database is left in a consistent state at the completion of the update cycle. In other words, either all the updates have been successfully applied to the database or none of the updates have been applied.

TTS Considerations If you decide to add transaction processing to your FoxPro application with NetWare TTS, you should consider several factors. First, there is the location of your transaction work files. These are the files that store your original data during an update. They are used to restore your database in the event that an update is incomplete and must be rolled back.

During NetWare installation, you specify the volume on which transaction work files will be stored. Novell recommends that the volume have sufficient disk space and that it be located on a separate disk channel from the database files. This allows the transaction data to be written simultaneously with database updates.

Record locks applied within a defined transaction are not released until the transaction is completed. This means that even if you issue an UNLOCK, the network operating system keeps the locks in place. This prevents other users from updating data within a transaction that is not yet complete, an important aspect since a transaction can always be "rolled back" before it completes. Be aware of this when defining a transaction because record locks may remain in force longer than you think. Also, since all record locks are held until the transaction completes, the possibility of deadlock increases. Refer to Chapter 14 for more details about deadlock and how to avoid it.

Be aware that a TTS Abort Transaction call is not the only way to roll back a transaction. The network will back out a transaction in any of several different circumstances. For example, if a workstation is rebooted or the application hangs in the middle of a transaction, the transaction will be backed out automatically. Also, there is the chance that even after a TTS End Transaction has been executed, the transaction will still be backed out. This happens if any of the disk updates associated with the transaction cannot be completed due to a system failure. Under this circumstance, the application thinks that the transaction completed normally, but the network actually backs out the entire transaction to avoid a partial update. When this happens, a message is displayed on the file server console.

Transactions may consist of as many updates as you want. However, you should keep your transactions as small as possible to make the sizes of the transaction work files manageable. Although transaction work files are reused after the transactions that belong to them are completed, a transaction work file continues to grow as long as updates take place and the transaction has not completed.

Any file flagged as Transactional cannot be deleted or renamed. Since all database files involved in a transaction must be flagged as Transactional, applications must be aware of this limitation. If it is necessary to delete or rename a file flagged as Transactional, you should first flag it as Non-transactional before attempting the rename or delete action.

Finally, remember that implementing the NetWare TTS functions slows down any application because each update requires two separate writes: one to the database and one to the transaction work file.

Implementing Your Own Transaction Processing

If a transaction tracking feature is not available on your network operating system, you can devise your own. Generally any transaction processing scheme you implement will be somewhat less effective than one that is provided by the operating system, but it can still offer improved data integrity.

The Simplest Approach: Make Updates to a Temporary File One very simple approach to transaction processing involves the use of temporary work files that you create. Once a record is locked, the contents of the record are copied to a separate temporary .dbf file. If several updates are involved in a transaction, each record is copied to its own file. All updates are applied to the temporary files while the database remains intact. Upon completion of all updates, the contents of the files are written to the database.

This approach allows you to abort a transaction (as defined by the application) and provides protection against a hardware crash. If the workstation or file server goes down while the updates are taking place, none of the updates are written to the database, and the database is left in a consistent state. The only risk of a partially updated database exists when the system fails (hardware or software) while the temporary files are being written to the permanent database.

The disadvantage to this approach is the overhead required by all of the writes to and from the temporary files. If quick response times are critical, this approach may not be feasible.

Another Alternative: Write Backup Data to a Temporary File Another approach to transaction processing is to store your data into temporary .dbf files prior to beginning the updates and to apply the updates directly to the database. This way, you only need to write the data from the temporary file to the database in the event of an aborted transaction. This alternative is a little more complex than the previous one.

The first requirement is that a field be added to each .dbf that will be involved in transaction tracking. This field should be able to hold at least 12 characters and is used to store the name of the temporary file while a transaction takes place. If desired, the field can be longer in order to hold additional information such as user name, module name, date/time of lock, and so on. We'll call this field Trans for our example.

In your program code, you execute an update or series of updates related to a transaction as follows:

1. Lock the required record(s).
2. Check the Trans field in each record to ensure that it is blank.
    a) If it is not blank, notify the user that the database is corrupted, release the record locks, and terminate the transaction. The database must be restored by a separate program, usually executed by a system administrator. This normally indicates that a system failure occurred while processing a transaction.
    b) If it is blank, continue to Step 3.

3. Copy the contents of each record involved in the update to its own temporary file. Write the name of the temporary file associated with the record into the Trans field.
4. Write the updates to the database.
5. Delete the temporary files when all the updates are complete.
6. Clear the Trans field in each record by overwriting it with spaces.

Although some processing overhead is still incurred with this approach, it is considerably less than with the previous alternative. Like the previous method, this method allows the application to abort a transaction as well as to back out a transaction in the event of system failure.

If an application needs to abort a transaction, the database updates are undone by reading the Trans field for each record to obtain the temporary filename and by copying the contents of that file back into the record. The Trans field should then be cleared by the application.

If a system failure occurs, the fact that the database is corrupted will be found the next time a user attempts to update one of the records involved in the failed transaction. As described earlier, if a record can be locked and yet it still contains Trans data, corrupted data is indicated.

A separate program is required to recover from a system failure and to resynchronize the database. This program must search each record in each .dbf looking for a nonblank value in the Trans field. When such a value is found, the program determines whether the record can be locked. If so, this record is part of the failed transaction and is restored from the data in the temporary file. If the record cannot be locked, we know that another user currently has the record locked and that the record is part of an active transaction. We do not need to concern ourselves with this record.

If you implement a transaction tracking procedure requiring the use of temporary files, you must ensure that your filenames are unique. (Network conventions for assigning unique filenames were discussed earlier in this chapter.)

This transaction processing technique can be modified slightly if your .dbf files do not contain memo fields. In this case, you do not need temporary files, but rather you add a memo field to each .dbf in your system—this memo field will be used to store the data prior to the update. This approach eliminates the need for a field in the .dbf to contain the name of the temporary file (the Trans field), since the data is stored right in the record. The data is cleared from the memo field when the update completes successfully. Thus the application checks whether the memo field (rather than the Trans field) is empty before starting a transaction. This approach is somewhat simpler than using an external temporary file, but cannot be used if any of the .dbf files already contain memo fields.

ON ERROR Processing

When you run a multiuser application, there is always a chance that a resource you need is unavailable. The application should handle these situations with an ON ERROR procedure.

Upon entering an application system, perhaps in the main menu routine, you should set an ON ERROR DO <procedure> statement, where <procedure> is the name of the error handling procedure. (We discussed the ON ERROR routine in some detail in Chapter 4.) Here we will look at multiuser specific error handling that should be included.

In handling errors in a multiuser environment, you should be most concerned with three situations: when a file is required for exclusive use, when a file is unavailable, and when a record is unavailable. Table 15-1 shows the three error messages (and codes) that are returned from FoxPro related to these error situations.

Table 15-1. Important Multiuser Error Messages in the Programming Environment

Error Message	Code	Description
Exclusive open of file is required.	110	Occurs when a command that requires exclusive use of a file is executed on a .dbf that was opened for shared use. Examples of commands requiring exclusive use of the .dbf are PACK, REINDEX, and ZAP.
File is in use by another.	108	Occurs if a user attempts to USE a file that is in EXCLUSIVE use by another user, if a user attempts to USE EXCLUSIVEly a file that is in use by another, or if a user cannot obtain a file lock because someone else has the file (or records in the file) locked.
Record is in use by another.	109	Occurs when a user cannot obtain a needed record lock, either because someone else has the record locked or because another user has the file locked.

Your users should not receive error 110 (Exclusive open of file is required) once your application is debugged; however, you may want to account for the possibility of this error while debugging.

The other two errors, 108 and 109, can happen anytime. The following code fragment demonstrates a way to handle these errors from within your ON ERROR procedure:

```
YN = .F.
DO CASE
CASE err = 108  && File is in use
        @20,1 SAY "File is in use by another"
        @21,1 SAY "Do you want to retry opening the file?" ;
              GET YN PICTURE 'Y'
        READ
        IF YN
                RETRY
        ELSE
                * Execute your close-out routine
                RETURN TO MASTER
        ENDIF
CASE err = 109  &&Record is locked by another
        @20,1 SAY "Record is currently in use by another"
        @21,1 SAY "Do you want to retry locking the record?" ;
              GET YN PICTURE 'Y'
        READ
        IF YN
                RETRY
        ELSE
                * Execute your close-out routine
                RETURN TO MASTER
        ENDIF
... (more CASE statements)
ENDCASE
```

Keep in mind that the ON ERROR procedure is called only after the system has retried to obtain the record or file for the duration specified by your SET REPROCESS value. If your user elects to retry the lock, the system again attempts to obtain the record or file lock until either it gets the lock or the SET REPROCESS period expires.

Maintaining a System Audit Trail

At times you might want to know who accessed what data or when and where errors were generated within your application. In these cases, you may want to maintain an audit trail that your programs write to during critical updates and/or as part of the error handling procedure.

If you have sensitive data or critical updates in your application, you may wish to record user access into a .dbf file. A sample structure used to record application name, module number, user name, date, time, and update indicator is shown in Figure 15-1. A simple library procedure can be written that is called from any application module for which you wish to monitor user activity. The calling procedure should pass the module number, user name, and whether updates were made; the library routine can determine the remaining values and simply add a record with the information. You can then use the Audit.dbf file by browsing it, or you can develop a set of reports to run against it based on your specific criteria.

You may also want to establish a file for recording error information. You can automatically call a procedure from your ON ERROR procedure to write pertinent error information such as the calling module, the line causing the error, user information, date, time, and so on. This makes it easier for you to debug your system and may help your end users by not making them solely responsible for reporting error information. It also allows you to collect statistics for errors by module.

```
Structure for database: D:\FOXCODE\AUDIT.DBF
Number of data records:          0
Date of last update     : 01/13/90
Field  Field Name   Type        Width    Dec
    1  AUD_APPLNM   Character      20
    2  AUD_MODNUM   Numeric         4
    3  AUD_USER     Character      12
    4  AUD_DATE     Date            8
    5  AUD_TIME     Character       8
    6  AUD_UPDATE   Logical         1
** Total **                        54
```

Figure 15-1. Audit.dbf structure for maintaining system audit trail.

Listing 15-1. Program to create a .bin file that can be LOADed and CALLed to write to the NetWare Net$Log.Msg file.

```
* Program to create the netmsg.bin file
* netmsg.bin is called to write to the NetWare Net$Log.Msg file

SET PRINTER TO FILE netmsg.bin
SET PRINT ON
???"{235}Z{2}{0}{13}{0}{0}{0}{0}{0}{0}{0}{0}{0}{0}{0}{0}{0}{0}{0}{0}{0}{0}"
???"{0}{0}{0}{0}{0}{0}{0}{0}{0}{0}{0}{0}{0}{0}{0}{0}{0}{0}{0}{0}{0}{0}{0}"
???"{0}{0}{0}{0}{0}{0}{0}{0}{0}{0}{0}{0}{0}{0}{0}{0}{0}{0}{0}{0}{0}{0}{0}"
???"{0}{0}{0}{0}{0}{0}{0}{0}{0}{0}{0}{0}{0}{0}{0}{0}{0}{0}{0}{0}{0}{0}{0}"
???"PSQRVW{30}{6}{139}{243}{14}{7}{191}{6}{0}{38}{198}{6}{5}{0}{0}{185}P"
???"{0}{172}{10}{192}t{13}{170}{38}{254}{6}{5}{0}{38}{255}{6}{2}{0}{226}"
???"{238}{14}{31}{190}{2}{0}{191}Z{0}{180}{227}{205}!{7}{31}_^ZY[X{203}"
SET PRINT OFF
SET PRINTER TO
```

An alternative to recording this information to a .dbf file is to write to a network message file, if one is available to you. On NetWare LANs, the Net$Log.Msg file is a text file available to application programs for recording system information. This file is stored in the SYS:SYSTEM directory so it is ordinarily accessible only to the system administrator. However, by taking advantage of a NetWare function call (E3H, Log Function 13), any user can write to this file. This function allows you to append a message (maximum 79 characters, plus the null terminator) to the file. NetWare precedes the message with the date, time, and STATION id. A sample Net$Log.Msg file was shown in Figure 13-1.

To create a .bin file that will execute the function call and permit you to write to the Net$Log.Msg file, run the program shown in Listing 15-1. This program uses the ??? command, which allows you to write directly to the printer. Once you have created the .bin file, you may LOAD and CALL it from any module from which you wish to write to the log file. You may want to record user access and/or error messages in this file.

For example, you can load and call the NetMsg.Bin file to store a test message in the Net$Log.Msg file as follows:

```
LOAD NetMsg
Testmsg = "Testing the NetMsg.Bin file"
```

```
CALL NetMsg WITH Testmsg
RELEASE NetMsg
```

If you run this example and then examine your Net$Log.Msg file, you will see that an entry has been added to the file containing your message.

You could also use the FoxPro APIs to write and directly call a function similar to NetMsg. For an example of a routine that takes advantage of one of the NetWare services and is called using FoxPro's APIs, see Chapter 16.

Other Multiuser Considerations

Offloading I/O Intensive Tasks

Running an application in a multiuser environment has one advantage that is often overlooked—the ability to offload time-consuming activities to another workstation. A good example of this is a print job server to which lengthy report runs can be offloaded. Using such a server, a user's request for a particular report is noted in a special print job database (maintained by the application), the user is notified that the request has been placed in a queue, and the workstation is then free to return to normal application processing. In the meantime, one or more dedicated workstations (the print job servers) are constantly monitoring the print job database for entries. When a new entry is found, the dedicated print job server reads the information about the requested report and calls the appropriate report generation module.

Depending on the complexity of the reports in your application and on the nature of the selection criteria available to the user, you can set up the print job database in either one or two .dbf files. Our example uses one .dbf, where the job parameters are passed as a character string (of up to 254 bytes). The report program is responsible for parsing the parameter string, if necessary. The alternative is to store report parameters in a separate database, with one record per parameter. Our sample .dbf is shown in Figure 15-2. The fields stored in this database are as follows:

Field	Description
ReportID	The name of the report program (.prg) to be called.
Parms	A string containing the report parameters. Parameters could be separated by commas or with AND or OR conjunctions, depending on the nature of the report.

Field	Description
Requester	The id of the user making the request (could be the network userid).
Req_Date	Date of the request (useful if you are maintaining an audit trail).
Req_Time	Time of the request.
Proc_Date	The date the request is processed by the print job server.
Proc_Time	The time the request is processed.

The print job server deletes the records after they are processed.

In a typical application, when a user requests a report, a program is called to prompt him or her for any selection criteria (for example, a date range or customer number). A program such as the one shown in Listing 15-2 can then be called to store the report information in the print job database and notify the user that the report request has been placed on a queue. At this point, control would be returned to the calling procedure (probably a menu), and the user could continue processing.

A program such as the one shown in Listing 15-3 would be run on each workstation designated as a print job server. This program constantly monitors the .dbf until it finds a new request, and then it processes the request by calling the appropriate report program with the report parameters. The report programs have to be able to accept the passed parameter string and process it accordingly. As mentioned earlier, special processing is required if your users

```
Structure for database: F:\APPL\FOXPRO\PRINTJOB.DBF
Number of data records:       57
Date of last update   : 04/30/91
Field  Field Name  Type        Width    Dec    Index
    1  REPORTID    Character       8
    2  PARMS       Character     254
    3  REQUESTER   Character      10
    4  REQ_DATE    Date            8
    5  REQ_TIME    Character       8
    6  PROC_DATE   Date            8
    7  PROC_TIME   Character       8
** Total **                      305
```

Figure 15-2. The print job database structure.

Listing 15-2. AddPrnJob.prg, a program to add a print job to the queue.

```
PROCEDURE AddPrnJob
*********************************************************************
* Program:  AddPrnJob.prg
* Author :  P.L. Olympia & Kathy Cea
* Purpose:  Adds a report request record to the Print Job database
*        :
* Syntax :  Do AddPrnJob WITH <mReport>, <mParmStr>, <mUser>
*        :  Where <mReport> is the name of the report .prg to be
*        :  called, <mParmStr> is the string containing report
*        :  selection criteria, and <mUser> is the requesting user's id.
*********************************************************************
PARAMETERS mReport, mParmStr, mUser
SELECT 1
USE PrintJob
APPEND BLANK
IF RLOCK()
     REPLACE ReportID WITH mReport, ;
               Parms WITH mParmStr, ;
               Requester WITH mUser, ;
               Req_Date WITH DATE(), ;
               Req_Time WITH TIME()
ENDIF
USE
@23,1 SAY "Your report request has been placed on the queue.  Press
any key to return..."
WAIT ""
RETURN
```

can choose AND and OR options. An example of this would be if your users can issue a request to print a report for all records for customer number 123 AND orders placed since 5/1/91 as compared to a request for customer number 123 OR orders placed since 5/1/91. In our example, you could choose to embed the AND or OR conjunction in the parameter string and have the report program parse for these conditions.

Aside from the obvious advantage of freeing up user workstations from lengthy report generation, this option also can provide an audit trail of report

Listing 15-3. PrnServ.prg, the program that runs on the print job server. It monitors the print job database for new jobs and processes them in order.

```
PROCEDURE PrnServ
**********************************************************************
* Program:  PrnServ.prg
* Author :  P.L. Olympia & Kathy Cea
* Purpose:  Monitors the print job database and processes jobs
*        :  in order.
*        :
* Syntax :  Do PrnServ
*
**********************************************************************
SET ESCAPE ON        &&Want to be able to break it when no report in
                     &&progress
SET DELETED ON       &&Make sure we don't process a job already completed
SET REPROCESS TO 1   &&Don't retry locks
SELECT 1
USE PrintJob
CLEAR
DEFINE WINDOW PrnMsg FROM 6,20 TO 12,60 TITLE "Print Job Server"
ACTIVATE WINDOW PrnMsg
DO WHILE .T.
    GO TOP               &&Make sure we process in order
    IF .NOT. EOF()       &&There's a new record
        IF RLOCK()
*-- FoxPro gets a fresh copy of the record from disk during an RLOCK
*-- So now we double check that the record hasn't already been
    processed
                IF EMPTY(Proc_Date)
                    @2,1 SAY PADC("Processing a report request",40)
                    REPLACE Proc_Date WITH DATE()
                    REPLACE Proc_Time WITH TIME()
                    DELETE
                    UNLOCK
                    ParmStr = PrintJob->Parms
                    IF LEN(ParmStr) > 0
                        DO (PrintJob->ReportID) WITH ParmStr
```

(continued)

Listing 15-3. Continued

```
                    ELSE
                        DO (PrintJob->ReportID)
                    ENDIF
                ELSE
                    UNLOCK
                ENDIF
        ENDIF
    ELSE
        @2,1 SAY PADC("Waiting for a report request",40)
    ENDIF
ENDDO
```

requests. A maintenance procedure could take the report request records that have been processed (those that have been marked deleted) and copy them to an audit trail file prior to packing the .dbf. Note that the technique shown is not limited to just report programs, but could be used to offload any lengthy I/O-intensive task.

Old, slower PCs around your office that no one wants are good candidates for a print job server. Although an 8088-based machine may be too slow for your users, it would be adequate as a print job server. You may also select to have workstations that are already serving as nondedicated, remote printer servers (using software like LANSpool or PS-Print) double as application print job servers.

Limiting Access to Reindexing Facilities

Special attention must be paid to rebuilding indexes in a multiuser environment. Since you should USE your .dbf EXCLUSIVEly before attempting to build an index, you can monopolize your database resources while a major reindex is underway. Therefore, it is not a good idea to let all of your end users have access to a reindex facility. Under most circumstances, a reindex program should be provided only to the system administrator on a separate maintenance menu. This prevents users from unknowingly tying up database files and indexes for long periods of time while reindexing. The administrator should schedule this maintenance activity as necessary and notify users accordingly.

The USE NOUPDATE Option

FoxPro has an option for its USE statement that prevents accidental changes when a module is intended to provide read-only access to .dbf files. Any attempted modifications to the data are denied when the file is opened with the NOUPDATE option. The syntax of this command is as follows:

```
USE <file> NOUPDATE
```

All the other options (such as IN and INDEX) are still available with the NOUPDATE option.

Chapter Summary

This chapter presented some additional considerations and approaches for programming in FoxPro/LAN. When a report must be run against an unchanging database, special processing is required. We presented three alternatives for ensuring that data does not change: lock all .dbf files for the duration of the report run, copy the .dbf files to temporary files, and create temporary files by selectively copying records. We also presented a method for assigning unique filenames in the network environment.

Transaction processing is an important issue in multiuser programming. Without a transaction tracking facility, a database may be left in an inconsistent or invalid state. FoxPro does not currently provide a transaction tracking service, but you can still incorporate one into your application by taking advantage of a network transaction tracking service or implementing your own. We discussed TTS, the transaction tracking service offered by some Novell NetWare operating systems, and presented two general approaches for writing your own transaction tracking facility.

An ON ERROR procedure is particularly important in a multiuser application, and we presented a multiuser-specific code fragment. We also looked at maintaining audit trails and where you write your audit/error information on a network. Finally, we reviewed some other multiuser considerations such as the ability to offload I/O-intensive tasks to another workstation.

Chapter 16

Application Program Interface

One of the cornerstones of FoxPro 2.0's open architecture philosophy is its Application Program Interface (API) facility. Heretofore programmers have relied on .bin routines to extend the capabilities of the Dbase language. Unfortunately .bin routines have several disadvantages, including the inability to allocate their own memory, an awkward way of passing parameters between the routine and Dbase, and a limit to the number of .bins that can be active at one time. Moreover, to use .bin routines properly in a Dbase program involves three commands: LOAD, CALL, and RELEASE MODULE.

For the first time, FoxPro's external routine APIs allow developers to extend the Dbase language completely and seamlessly without the disadvantages inherent in using .bin routines. With API routines, developers have access to almost every internal FoxPro feature. For example, an external routine API can intercept FoxPro events and manipulate objects such as database fields, memory variables, and windows.

In this chapter, we discuss how to create and use API routines coded in Watcom C. We also show some practical examples of routines you can use directly in your own applications. To fully follow the discussions in this chapter, you should have a working knowledge of the C programming language.

FoxPro API Basics

An API can be coded in either Watcom C or assembly language. The product of the compilation and link step is a .plb file. You activate the .plb file from your program using the SET LIBRARY TO <plb_file> command. Any function included in the .plb then becomes, for all intents and purposes, a FoxPro internal function except that the function name cannot be abbreviated to the usual four characters. With the Extended Version of FoxPro, the SET LIBRARY TO command loads the Proapi16.exe file from disk. Therefore you should make sure that the file, along with your .plb file, is accessible to the FoxPro program.

APIs require specific data types and structures. In a function definition, a data type shown in all capital letters is a C typedef, which is specific to the FoxPro API. One such example is MHANDLE, which is an identifier used to reference dynamically allocated memory. A common example of an API-specific data structure is ParamBlk, which is a parameter block structure that the API uses to obtain data from FoxPro. The structure consists of an integer that holds the number of parameters passed, followed immediately by an array of parameter unions. We discuss the ParamBlk structure in more detail later in this chapter in the section "Obtaining Parameters From FoxPro."

FoxPro calls routines that are linked into a .plb file as FAR code, and any pointers passed to or from FoxPro must be FAR pointers. We recommend that you use the Watcom C large memory model to compile your API routines.

FoxInfo and FoxTable Structures

Your API library routine should include two data structures, namely, FoxInfo and FoxTable. The FoxInfo structure defines all the functions in the library, whereas the FoxTable structure defines the linked list of libraries and the number of functions in the library. Assuming that your library contains three functions, say, PDOBJECT, PDDOCST, and PDDOCEND, your FoxInfo structure might look something like this:

```
FoxInfo MyDriver[] = {    /* MyDriver is user-selected data name */
  {"PDOBJECT",pdobject,2,"C","C"},
  {"PDDOCST",pddocst,2,"I","I"},
  {"PDDOCEND",pddocend,0,""}
};
```

Note that each entry in the structure table begins with the name of the function, enclosed in quotes and typed in capital letters. Following that is the actual function address, then the number of parameters required by the function (or a flag value), and finally the data type of the parameters. Thus the last entry in the structure means that your .c routine has a function that looks something like this:

```
FAR pddocend()
{
  .. statements ...
}
```

Since this particular function does not require a parameter, its entry in the table ends with 0 and a null string. On the other hand, the pdobject( ) function requires two character parameters, so its entry ends with 2, followed by two C's enclosed in quotes.

The FoxTable structure corresponding to the MyDriver example might look something like this:

```
FoxTable _FoxTable = {
  (FoxTable FAR *)0,
   sizeof(MyDriver)/sizeof(FoxInfo),
   MyDriver
}
```

API Rules Summary

You should observe the following rules when you write API routines:

- Leave all registers unchanged when your routine exits except for the AX register and registers used to pass parameters. Routines that execute callbacks (that is, documented routines requesting FoxPro service from within the external routine) must use the stack provided by FoxPro and should not change the SS register.
- Minimize the use of memory in your routine even if it allocates memory dynamically. Remember that the FoxPro environment has no memory protection.
- Always check your routine results. Remember that a stray pointer could destroy FoxPro's internal data structure, which could cause your application to hang the machine immediately.
- Free all handles your routines allocate except those returned in the standard API function _RetVal( ). Do not free any handles passed to your routine by FoxPro in the ParamBlk data structure.

Compiling and Linking API Routines

To create an external library of API routines with the large memory model of Watcom C, you would need, in addition to Watcom C, the following files from the FoxPro distribution disk:

File	Description
Pro_ext.h	Header file for the API routines.
Api_l.Obj	Large memory model startup code.
Proapi_l.Lib	Large memory model library of FoxPro API functions.

Assuming that you have installed the FoxPro 2.0 API files in the D:\FP2\API subdirectory and that you have installed Watcom C in the E:\WC directory following that program's install procedure, you may want to include the following lines in your Autoexec.Bat file:

```
SET include=e:\wc\h;d:\fp2\api
SET lib=e:\wc\lib286\dos;e:\wc\lib286;d:\fp2\api
PATH %path%;e:\wc\bin;e:\wc\binb
```

The first SET statement defines an environment variable INCLUDE that tells Watcom C where to find the header (.h) files used by the C routines. The second SET statement defines an environment variable LIB that tells Watcom C where to find the appropriate C libraries. The last statement in the file simply adds to the search path the Watcom C subdirectories containing the compiler (Wcc.Exe) and the linker (Wlink.Exe).

You may want to create a batch file, say, Wccl.Bat, to handle compiling and linking your API .C routines. An example of such a batch file is as follows:

```
WCC  /oals /s /zu /ml /zW %1.c
IF ERRORLEVEL 1 GOTO END
WLINK file d:\fp2\api\api_l,%1 lib proapi_l,clibl name %1.plb
DEL %1.obj
:end
```

The first line invokes the compiler with the following switches:

Switch	**Description**
`/oals`	Control optimization by assuming no aliasing (a), enabling loop optimization (l), and favoring small code size (s).
`/s`	Suppress stack checking.
`/zu`	Unlink stack and data segments.
`/ml`	Use large memory model.
`/zW`	Use windows stack linkage conventions.

Remember that the switch parameters are case sensitive and should be typed as shown.

If your API routine is called Super.c, invoke the batch file with the command

```
Wccl super
```

Note that you do not supply the .c extension when invoking the batch file. If everything works correctly, you should have the API library file named Super.Plb when the batch file terminates.

Obtaining Parameters From FoxPro

As mentioned before, your API routine obtains parameters from FoxPro by way of the ParamBlk structure. This structure contains the number of parameters that FoxPro passes to your routine, followed immediately by an array of Parameter unions. The Parameter is a union of two additional structures called the Value structure and the Locator structure.

Briefly, the Value structure defines the data types and characteristics (for instance, the length or width) of the fields being passed. On the other hand, the Locator structure defines whether the passed parameter is a memvar or a database field (and if so, its location within the database). How do you tell if the Parameter structure is a Value or Locator structure? You can tell from the first byte in the structure. If the first byte is an “R,” the Parameter is a Locator structure; otherwise, it is a Value structure.

All data structures are defined in the Pro_ext.h file supplied with FoxPro 2.0. For the sake of completeness, Listing 16-1 shows the structures of ParamBlk, Parameter, Value, and Locator.

Tables 16-1 and 16-2 briefly describe each of the fields in the Locator and Value structures, respectively.

To illustrate how you would use ParamBlk and Value structures in your API routine, consider the printer driver procedure PDDOCST described in Chapter 11. Recall that this procedure receives two integers from FoxPro, namely, the documents's page height and page width. Thus the printer driver program coded as a procedure in the FoxPro language begins with the following lines:

```
PROCEDURE pddocst
PARAMETER doc_height, doc_width
```

Were you to code the printer driver as an API routine in .c, the relevant portion of the library routine would look like this:

```
FAR pddocst(ParamBlk FAR *pblk)
{
  static long doc_height, doc_width;
  doc_height = pblk->p[0].val.ev_long;
  doc_width  = pblk->p[1].val.ev_long;
  ... additional statements ...
 }
```

Parameters by Value or Reference

Your API routine can obtain parameters from FoxPro either by value or by reference. By default, memory variables are passed according to the current setting of UDFPARMS, whereas other variables and expressions are passed by value.

API routines follow the usual FoxPro rules of parameter passing. You can force a variable to be passed by value by enclosing it in parentheses. For instance, if you have an API routine called DoIt and you want to pass to it a variable called MVar by value, the appropriate call is simply

```
Doit((MVar))
```

Listing 16-1. Data structures used by FoxPro to pass parameters to an API library routine.

```
/*----------------------------------------------*
 *           1. PARAMBLK Structure              *
 *     A parameter list to a library function.  *
 *----------------------------------------------*/
typedef struct {
    short int   pCount;     /* Number of Parameters PASSED.          */
    Parameter   p[1];       /* pCount Parameters.                    */
}ParamBlk;

/*----------------------------------------------*
 *           2. PARAMETER Structure             *
 *        A parameter to a library function.    *
 *----------------------------------------------*/
typedef union {
    Value       val;
    Locator     loc;          /* An 'R' in l_type means the Locator  */
                                /* part of this union is in use.     */
} Parameter;

/*----------------------------------------------*
 *             3. LOCATOR Structure             *
 *  A reference to a database or memory variable.*
 *----------------------------------------------*/
typedef struct {
    char    l_type;
    short   l_where,          /* Database number or -1 for memory    */
            l_NTI,            /* Variable name table offset          */
            l_offset,         /* Index into database                 */
            l_subs,           /* # subscripts specified 0 <= x <= 2  */
            l_sub1, l_sub2; /* subscript integral values           */
} Locator;

/*----------------------------------------------*
 *              4. VALUE Structure              *
 *            An expression's value.            *
 *----------------------------------------------*/
```

(continued)

Listing 16-1. Continued

```
typedef struct {
    char            ev_type;
    char            ev_padding;
    short           ev_width;
    unsigned short  ev_length;
    long            ev_long;
    double          ev_real;
    MHANDLE         ev_handle;
} Value;
```

To pass MVar by reference, precede the name with the @ symbol. Thus the appropriate call now becomes

```
Doit(@MVar)
```

Note that an individual array element is always passed by value, so you would need to precede the name with @ if you wanted to pass it by reference.

Table 16-1. Contents of Locator Structure Fields

Field	Contents/Description
l_type	Always contains "R."
l_where	The number of the database containing the field, or –1 if the variable is a memvar.
l_NTI	Name Table Index. FoxPro internal use.
l_offset	Field number within the database.
l_subs	The number of subscripts (0–2) if the variable is a memvar.
l_sub1	First memvar subscript if l_subs is 1 or 2.
l_sub2	Second memvar subscript if l_subs is 2.

Table 16-2. Contents of Value Structure Fields

Field	Contents/Description
ev_type	Parameter data type. One of the following: "C", "N", "I", "D", "L."
ev_width	Display width if ev_type is N or I.
ev_length	Number of decimal places if ev_type is N or the length of the string if ev_type is C. This is the only true indicator of the string length because the string is never null terminated.
ev_long	Long integer number if ev_type is I.
ev_real	Double precision number if ev_type is N or D.
ev_handle	MHANDLE if ev_type is C.

Returning Results to FoxPro

The FoxPro API library provides several functions for returning data from your API routine to FoxPro. In general, there is a return value routine designated for passing back each data type. For example, the _RetChar( ) function returns a null-terminated string, whereas the _RetInt( ) functions returns a long integer value.

Table 16-3 summarizes the API return value functions. You are likely to use the generic _RetVal( ) function most often because it can return any data type (except memo) since it passes a complete Value structure back to FoxPro. You must use _RetVal( ) instead of _RetChar( ) to return a character string containing embedded nulls, for instance, printer control code sequences.

All return value functions are of type Void. Invoking these functions does not automatically exit the routine and return to FoxPro. To relinquish control to FoxPro, follow the usual programming convention—either code an explicit return or let the program reach the end of the function.

Table 16-3. API Return Value Functions

Function	Description
_RetVal(Value FAR *val)	Returns any data type except memo because it can pass a complete Value structure. Use this to return a string with embedded nulls.
_RetChar(char FAR *string)	Returns a null-terminated string.
_RetInt(long ival, int width)	Returns a long integer value. Width is the number of columns that FoxPro should use to display the value. If in doubt, use 10 for this number.
_RetDateStr(char FAR *string)	Returns a date specified as a string value in the MM/DD/YEAR format where YEAR may either be two or four digits.
_RetLogical(int flag)	Returns a logical value. Zero is False; any nonzero value is True.

Here is a code fragment that shows how to return the status of the keyboard CAPS LOCK key:

```
FAR IsCapsLock()
 {
   _RetLogical(_bios_keybrd(_KEYBRD_SHIFTSTATUS) & 0x0040 ? 1 : 0);
    return;
  }
```

In this example, we use _RetLogical( ) because the function returns True or False, depending on whether or not CAPS LOCK is on. Note that the keywords _bios_keybrd and _KEYBRD_SHIFTSTATUS are defined in the Watcom C header file called Bios.h.

Summary of API Routines

The API routines supplied with FoxPro 2.0 fall into several categories, which this section describes. Appendix D describes the actual function calls, including the parameters that each routine requires. Note that the API functions are subject to change from time to time. For an up-to-date list of supported functions, you should always consult the prototype definitions contained in the Pro_ext.h file of your distribution disk.

Memory Management Routines

Memory management routines include those for allocating memory, allocating stack space for temporary storage, moving strings to and from memory, comparing contents of memory units, and manipulating memory variables and arrays.

In FoxPro you manage memory by using memory allocation units assigned to MHANDLEs. An MHANDLE is simply an identifier for referring to dynamically allocated memory; it does not represent a physical address. However, the API set includes the _HandToPtr( ) function for translating an MHANDLE to a FAR pointer. Note that the FoxPro API facility does not support the usual C memory allocation routines such as malloc( ) and free( ).

You can change the amount of memory allocated to MHANDLE. You can also lock and unlock MHANDLE to disallow or permit it to move during memory reorganization.

Your API routines can create public or private memory variables and arrays following standard FoxPro variable naming conventions, and then change their values or release them.

Input/Output Routines

API routines that handle input/output can be further classified into three major categories: File, Database, and Memo.

API file I/O routines are similar to the low-level file I/O functions in conventional FoxPro. Thus you have the equivalent routines to such functions as fopen( ), fcreate( ), fread( ), and fwrite( ).

Database I/O routines let you access the FoxPro database engine directly. The currently selected workarea number is represented by the number -1. You have all the functions to manipulate database records, including reading and writing fields and records.

Memo field I/O routines allow you direct access to memo fields, for such purposes as replacing the value of a specified memo field containing a string that is longer than about 64K bytes. For memo fields with string values under 64K bytes, you can use the _DBReplace( ) database I/O function.

User Interface Routines

User interface API routines let you install event handlers that can either modify the event before it is reported to FoxPro, or else handle the event itself. The user interface routines also include those for manipulating the entire FoxPro windowing environment and screen I/O. FoxPro uses WHANDLE as the basic identifier for a window.

Other Routines

The API set includes routines to execute a null-terminated statement that normally can be executed from the FoxPro command window, evaluate and execute an expression, intercept and report errors, and help debug API routines.

Example 1: A Bios API Library

Let us put everything together now and look at a simple example of how we would go about building an API library. In this example, we want to have three functions that can be called from a FoxPro application. These functions are as follows:

Function	Description
IsNumLock( )	Returns True if NUM LOCK key is on.
GetTimer( )	Returns the value of the system timer.
PrtPortAvail( )	Returns the base I/O address of a printer port given a port number.

The first two examples do not require any input parameters, but the third one does. The examples also show how to use _RetInt( ) and _RetLogical( ) to return values to FoxPro.

To build and use the library, follow these steps:

1. Write the API routines and compile them in the large memory model of Watcom C. The program is BiosApi.c shown in Listing 16-2.
2. Using the batch file Wccl.Bat we saw earlier, compile and link the API routines and turn them into BiosApi.Plb.

3. Write the actual FoxPro program that uses the API functions. This program is BiosShow.Prg, shown in Listing 16-3. The hook to the API library is established with the SET LIBRARY command.

Listing 16-2. BiosApi.c shows an API library of PC bios functions.

```
/*************************************************************
   BiosApi.c -- Simple example of a FoxPro API routine Library

                       by P. L. Olympia and Kathy Cea
                    Platinum Software International, 6/91

   This library consists of three functions that return various
   Bios states and values to the FoxPro program, BiosShow.Prg.

   Portions derived from KybdScan.c by David Ninheiser, Silverware, Inc.
 *************************************************************/
#include <stdlib.h>
#include <dos.h>
#include <string.h>
#include <bios.h>
#include "pro_ext.h"        /* From FoxPro API set */

/**************************************************
   The API .c function name is C_NumLock()
   The FoxPro function name is IsNumLock().
   Function returns 0 (False) if NUM LOCK key is off.
   It returns 1 (TRUE) otherwise
 **************************************************/
FAR C_NumLock()
{
    _RetLogical(_bios_keybrd(_KEYBRD_SHIFTSTATUS) & 0x0020 ? 1: 0);
     return;
}
```

(continued)

Listing 16-2. Continued

```
/*****************************************************
   The API .c function name is C_GetSysTimer()
   The FoxPro function name is GetTimer().
   Function returns the system time as a long value.
 *****************************************************/
FAR C_GetSysTimer()
{
    unsigned long far *SysTimer=(unsigned long far *)0x0040006c;
    _RetInt((long)*SysTimer, 10);     /* 10 is the display width */
}

/*****************************************************
   The API .c function name is C_LptAddress()
   The FoxPro function name is PrtPortAdr().
   Function returns the base I/O address of a
   specified printer port (0 = LPT1, 1 = LPT2, etc) if
   available. Otherwise, it returns 0.
 *****************************************************/
FAR C_LptAddress(ParamBlk FAR *parm)
{
    unsigned short far *PrtPort=(unsigned short far *)0x00400008;
    _RetInt(((long)PrtPort[(unsigned short)
    parm->p[0].val.ev_long]&0x0000ffff),10);
}

// Here are the usual FoxPro API Structure Tables, FoxInfo & FoxTable
FoxInfo _BiosPO[] = {
    {"ISNUMLOCK",  C_NumLock,      0, ""  },
    {"GETTIMER",   C_GetSysTimer,  0, ""  },
    {"PRTPORTADR", C_LptAddress,   1, "I" },
};

FoxTable _FoxTable = {
    (FoxTable FAR *)0,
    sizeof(_BiosPO)/sizeof(FoxInfo),
    _BiosPO
};
```

Listing 16-3. BiosShow.Prg is a sample FoxPro driver program that shows how to use the functions in the BiosApi library.

```
*************************************************************
* Program ...: BiosShow.Prg
* Author ....: P. L. Olympia & Kathy Cea
* Purpose....: Driver program to illustrate Bios calls through
*            : FoxPro 2.0's new API facility. Uses BiosApi.Plb
*            : compiled from BiosApi.c using Watcom C large model
* Notes .....: Make sure BiosApi.Plb and Proapi16.exe are
*            : accessible to this program
*************************************************************
SET TALK OFF
SET LIBRARY TO BiosApi.Plb   && Activates API library

*-- The library contains the following FoxPro extended functions:
*     IsNumLock(), GetTimer(), and PrtPortAdr()

DO WHILE .T.
   CLEAR

   ? "The NumLock key is  ",  IIF(IsNumLock(), "ON", "OFF")
   ? "System Time",    GetTimer()
   ? "LPT1 Address", PrtPortAdr(0)
   ? "LPT2 Address", PrtPortAdr(1)
   ? "LPT3 Address", PrtPortAdr(2)
   ? "LPT4 Address", PrtPortAdr(3)
   WAIT "<Esc> to abort. Any other key to continue ..."
ENDDO
SET TALK ON
RETURN
```

Example 2: An API Library Containing Novell Netware Services

Most multiuser business applications in FoxPro and other Dbase dialects require services and information from the network operating system. For instance, a typical requirement of a multiuser application running on a Novell network is to obtain the station number and name of the Netware workstation. Such data can be used to formulate unique names for network temporary files and to track application usage.

Novell Netware has always provided its developers with an extensive set of API library functions with which to access the internals of the network operating system. The Netware APIs are available as C libraries for the most common compilers, including Watcom C. Heretofore, the usual way to tap network services from a FoxPro or Dbase application was to create .bin routines in either assembly or C language. FPNet is one example of a product that uses FoxPro's API facility to provide an extensive set of Novell NetWare functions to a multiuser program. With FoxPro's API facility, incorporating network functions in an application now is easily within reach of an experienced programmer.

Listing 16-4 shows one example of a C language routine that returns an integer that contains the station number of a Netware workstation. The program, Novlsta.c, uses API functions and hooks provided by both FoxPro and Novell. Specifically it uses just one Novell API function called GetConnectionNumber( ). You can use the value returned by this function to get additional information about the workstation, including workstation name and login time.

To compile the program, you need to be pathed to the directory containing the Novell API C header files, and to the API library Lnit.Lib. Include the switch /zp1 in your Watcom C compiler invocation command in order to force data structures to be packed in one-byte boundaries. A sample batch file to compile and link the program is as follows:

```
REM Use to compile FP2 API with Netware
WCC /zp1 /oals /s /zu /ml /zW novlsta.c
IF errorlevel 1 GOTO end
WLINK file api_l, novlsta.c lib proapi_l,clibl,LNIT name novlsta.plb
:end
```

Additional Example

One excellent application of FoxPro APIs would be a program that directly displays pictures stored as graphic files in a FoxPro memo field. Traditionally this task requires copying the stored picture to a DOS file by way of the COPY MEMO command, and then RUNning an external viewer program to display the picture file. Clearly this approach is slow and cumbersome.

With an API routine and some knowledge of the workstation's graphic hardware, you can access the memo field data and show the picture directly without the aid of an external viewer program. A sample routine for this type

Listing 16-4. NovlSta.c shows how to tap Netware Services from a FoxPro API.

```
/************************************************************
  NovlSta.c -- Example of a FoxPro API routine Library

                  by P. L. Olympia and Kathy Cea
                 Platinum Software International


  This example returns the station number of a Novell Workstation.


  Sample FoxPro program usage:


     SET LIBRARY TO NovlSta.Plb
     ? "Your Novell workstation ID is ", staid()

************************************************************/
#include <stdio.h>
#include "pro_ext.h"       /* From FoxPro API set */

// These next two includes are from Novell
#include <nit.h>
#include <niterror.h>

/****************************************************
   The API .c function name is C_GetStaID()
   The FoxPro function name is StaID().
   Function returns a workstation ID number
 ****************************************************/
FAR C_GetStaID()
{
   _RetInt( GetConnectionNumber(), 10);
       return;
}

// Here are the usual FoxPro API Structure Tables, FoxInfo & FoxTable

FoxInfo _NovlPO[] = {
    {"STAID",  C_GetStaID,    0, ""  },
};
```

(continued)

Listing 16-4. Continued

```
FoxTable _FoxTable = {
     (FoxTable FAR *)0,
     sizeof(_NovlPO)/sizeof(FoxInfo),
     _NovlPO
};
```

of application is too long to be included in this chapter. Consequently the program, including all support files such as a database with preloaded picture images, is provided with the disk for this book.

Chapter Summary

The API facility allows developers to extend FoxPro's power indefinitely without the inherent limitations of .bin routines. API routines can be coded in assembly language or Watcom C. After an API library is assembled into a .plb file, its functions become available to a FoxPro program through the SET LIBRARY command. Functions provided by the API library behave just like FoxPro built-in functions for all intents and purposes.

With API routines you have direct access to virtually all FoxPro internals, including the ability to intercept events, allocate memory, and manipulate objects such as database fields, which include memos, arrays, memory variables, menus, and windows. Appendix D briefly describes most of the API function calls provided with FoxPro.

Your API routine obtains parameters from FoxPro by way of the ParamBlk structure. The parameters may be passed either by value or by reference. To return values to FoxPro, your API program can use one of several return value routines, depending on the data type of the return parameter.

In this chapter we discussed how you would code, assemble, and use a library of API routines. We showed an example of a library of bios functions. We also showed how you would use FoxPro's APIs, together with Novell Netware's API facility to tap network services and use the information in your multiuser database applications. Additionally this book's disk contains a sample API program that accesses graphic images stored in memo fields, and then displays the pictures directly.

Chapter 17

Building and Distributing an Application

During the development and maintenance cycle of any project, you must track and coordinate the location and status of each individual file that will constitute your final application. Under FoxPro 2.0, this task has become considerably simpler if you use the project management facilities. In this final chapter, we introduce the Project Manager and discuss some of the things you can do to make application distribution and turnover easier. This includes ensuring that your programs will perform optimally, providing or limiting access to certain system functions, protecting your investment by encrypting it, and creating an effective yet simple installation procedure. Here we pull together many of the performance issues addressed throughout the book and discuss a few more techniques for successfully distributing applications.

Project Management

FoxPro 2.0's Project Manager is a facility that lets you manage and distribute your application in an organized fashion. It can control all elements of your application, including programs, screens, menus, reports, labels, queries, libraries, and database files. The Project Manager maintains references to all the files that are defined within an application, including references to file locations (directories and paths), and it maintains a date and time stamp for all generated and compiled code so that it knows when regeneration/recompilation is necessary. Using the Project Manager, you can also build your application, specifying one of several different types of executable files. As discussed later, you can now generate an application (.app) file, a compact executable (.exe) file, or a standalone executable (.exe) file. Aside from the obvious advantage of maintaining all the component pieces of your application during development, the Project Manager greatly simplifies the distribution of applications.

Defining and Maintaining a Project

You will usually want to define a project at the initiation of an application and keep it up to date throughout the development cycle. You can define a project by either accessing the Project window (using the CREATE PROJECT command) or using the BUILD PROJECT command. BUILD PROJECT is useful if you need to create a project from within a program, without involving the user. CREATE PROJECT is far more powerful, however, and offers many more optional features. You will normally want to use the interactive Project window when creating a project.

You maintain your project with the MODIFY PROJECT command. Executing this command displays the Project window with your previously defined project components. You can add, delete, or modify file references at any time. You can also edit any file directly from the Project window. When you build a project, FoxPro generates source code for screens and menus and compiles all program files. Whenever you rebuild a project by selecting the Rebuild Project option in the Project window, all the files with a source time stamp later than the time stamp in the project file are refreshed (regenerated and/or recompiled). You can optionally have FoxPro refresh all files in the project, regardless of the time stamp of the file. Object code for an application is stored right in the project (.pjx and .pjt) database.

Important Project Considerations

When you assemble your project files, you do not necessarily need to identify each individual program file. If you include a program that calls other programs, those other programs will be included automatically in the project when you build it. There are several exceptions to this, however. If you use indirect file referencing or macro substitution with any filename, that filename must be referenced in the calling program with the EXTERNAL command in order for it to be included in the project. Also, there are certain circumstances under which you must identify an array as EXTERNAL. If you define an array in a program and then reference it in a lower level program, that array must be identified with the EXTERNAL ARRAY command. When an array is passed to a UDF or procedure, the array must be identified to the Project Manager with the EXTERNAL ARRAY command.

FoxPro designates nonexecutable files that are included in a project as read-only files. This includes database files, report (.frx) files, and label (.lbx) files. When you build an application for distribution, you need to exclude those files that your end users need to be able to modify. At a minimum, you will want to exclude database and index files that your user can update. If you have other files such as report or label forms that your end user can modify, these must be excluded as well. Note that excluding a file from a project is not the same as removing it; excluding a file leaves a file reference in the project but omits the file from the application. Removing a file from a project deletes the record, eliminating all references to the file in the project.

Files that are marked as excluded in a project remain as a reference in the project (.pjx) file but are not included in the generated application. The advantage to including a reference to an excluded file in your project is that at the time you build your application for final distribution, it serves as a handy reminder of the files that you need to assemble together with the .app or .exe file. To designate a file as excluded, choose the Exclude option on the Project menu popup while in the Project window.

Building an Application

When you are ready to assemble the application, take one of the following steps:

- Issue a MODIFY PROJECT <project name> command and select the BUILD option.
- Issue a BUILD APP <.app file name> FROM <project name> command from the command window to build a .app file.
- Issue a BUILD EXE <.exe file name> FROM <project name> [STANDALONE | EXTENDED] command from the command window to build a .exe file.

When you build an application, you can generate one of three types of executable files:

1. An application (.app) file. An .app file can be run with the FoxPro Runtime environment using the FoxR loader file. It requires the presence of the FoxPro Executable Support Library file(s) to execute.

2. A compact executable (.exe) file. Although it is executable from DOS (not requiring the FoxR loader file), a compact executable file still requires the presence of the Executable Support Library file(s).
3. A standalone executable (.exe) file. Note that you must have installed the required components from the FoxPro Distribution Kit before you can build a standalone or standalone extended .exe file. When you build a standalone .exe file, FoxPro must find the following files on your DOS path:

   Foxpro.lib
   Foxpros.lib
   Foxclibm.lib
   Foxmathm.lib

   When you build a standalone extended .exe file, FoxPro must find the following files on your DOS path:

   Foxprox.lib
   Foxprosx.lib
   Foxclibr.lib
   Foxmathr.lib
   Foxldr.exe

Project Alternatives

FoxPro does not require that you maintain your application files in a project. You can still manage your application yourself, just as you had to under FoxPro 1.x and FoxBASE+. If you choose not to maintain your application with the Project Manager, you should at least combine most or all of your individual .prg files into one procedure file. This can be accomplished with the FoxBind utility. Using a procedure file improves processing time over calling separate program files since it minimizes the number of files that FoxPro opens and closes.

Using the ENCRYPT and NODEBUG Options

Whether you build your application through the Project Manager or compile your .prg files into .fxp files, you should include the ENCRYPT and NODEBUG options when preparing to distribute your application. If you are using the Project window, these options are accessible on the Project menu under the Options selection.

To select encryption, check the Encrypt option. To select the NODEBUG option, make sure the Debugging Information option is not checked. Note that if you are including in your project any .fxp files that have already been encrypted, you must encrypt the project when you build it. If you are compiling your programs to .fxp files, you can include the ENCRYPT and NODEBUG clauses in the COMPILE command. These options perform the following functions:

Option	**Description**
ENCRYPT	Encrypts your compiled code, providing additional protection against a user who might try to decode your application's code.
NODEBUG	Reduces the size of your compiled code by 2 bytes per source program line by removing source code cross-references. Once compiled with this option, the Trace and Debug facilities and the DOHISTORY option are no longer accessible, but you should not need such access in your production compiled code. Executing this option reduces the size of your program files for distribution, thus saving disk space and copying time.

Optimizing Performance

Even though you may have an efficient program design (for example, normalized database, modular program design, use of arrays where appropriate, and effective use of indexes), there may still be room for improvement in your application. Specifically there are final considerations relating to the application's environment that can impact performance.

Programming Techniques

In this book we have covered many techniques for improving application performance and for simplifying long-term maintenance. We do not attempt to list these here, but rather we emphasize a few last-minute code checks you should make.

1. Make sure you SET DOHISTORY OFF. Although this is the default setting, you should ensure that it is not left turned ON from your debugging activities. Leaving DOHISTORY ON will significantly slow program execution, as discussed in Chapter 4.
2. Ensure that you have removed any SET TALK ON commands that may have been left over from a debugging session. Clearly, setting TALK ON not only slows processing, but it may compromise your source code by allowing a knowledgeable user to reconstruct your program based on screen output.
3. Keep the use of macro substitution to a minimum. It is a good idea to search through your code for all occurrences of the macro character (&) and determine whether macro substitution can be replaced with something else such as indirect file referencing or the EVALUATE( ) function. For instance, a command such as USE &dbf is slower than the alternative command USE (dbf).
4. Check your SYSMENU setting. If you decide to permit access to the system bar menu during a READ, make sure SET SYSMENU is ON; otherwise, set it OFF.
5. Don't go overboard with your index files and tags. Although you would normally want all index files for a database to be open so they remain updated, remember that keeping each one updated exacts a performance price. Index files that are used only rarely (for a sorted report, for example) may be better built as needed.
6. To minimize the cost of maintaining and supporting your application, consider including as part of your ON ERROR processing procedure a routine to record into a file every bit of information that will help you diagnose the source of the error. This includes a dump of the screen at the moment of error, the error message from FoxPro's MESSAGE( ) function, and the program nesting at the time, which you can get with the help of the SYS(16) or PROGRAM( ) function. You would also want to include the data provided by the LIST STATUS and LIST MEMORY commands. Chapter 4 demonstrates the use of many of these commands in a sample ON ERROR routine.

Using Files Exclusively in a Multiuser Environment

In Chapters 14 and 15, we discussed the implications of exclusive versus shared file use. Although it is not generally desirable to open a file for exclusive use, it can improve application performance and is an acceptable option when only one user will be running the application. For example, consider a nightly batch or reporting process. If the process is left running on just one network workstation, opening the files exclusively eliminates the overhead of checking file and record availability and improves performance.

Location of Temporary Files

If you are familiar with your client's hardware environment, you should be able to determine what options are available for alternate locations for overlay and temporary files. As we discussed in Chapter 4, the following configuration parameters in the Config.fp file specify the location of FoxPro overlay and temporary files:

Parameter	**Use**
OVERLAY	For FoxPro overlay file (standard FoxPro only).
EDITWORK	For temporary files created by the editor.
SORTWORK	For temporary sorting and indexing work files.
PROGWORK	For the FoxPro cache file.
TMPFILES	For EDITWORK, SORTWORK, and PROGWORK files if not otherwise specified.

As discussed in Chapter 4, performance can be improved by specifying an alternative drive for the location of the overlay and temporary files. This is especially true in a multiuser environment, where many users contend for access to the network hard drives. In these cases, OVERLAY, EDITWORK, SORTWORK, PROGWORK, and TMPFILES should specify local drives whenever possible.

Obviously you cannot specify alternate locations if you do not know the client's environment. Even so, you can provide instructions with your program documentation to include these statements in the Config.fp file where sufficient hard disk space is available.

Added Hardware

Overall performance can be improved by executing the FoxPro application on equipment that has LIM 4.0 expanded memory. FoxPro can take advantage of as much EMS as it can get. The Extended Version of FoxPro can take advantage of all available extended memory.

A RAM disk is the ideal location for FoxPro's PROGWORK (cache file), which does not grow as large as the sort work files. Of course, since a FoxPro application, like any other DBMS application, tends to be I/O bound, a hard disk with a fast access time is always a good investment. You may also encourage your clients to use a disk defragmenting utility on their local hard disks as part of their application maintenance routine.

Writing an Application Config.fp File

Every application should be distributed with a Config.fp file in order to ensure that your programs behave the way you intend them to. Even if all your settings are the FoxPro default settings, include this file to be sure that an extraneous Config.fp residing on your client's hard drive is not accidentally used.

In our discussion of optimizing performance earlier in this chapter, we mentioned several important settings that control application performance. It is a good idea to include every SET command that can potentially impact your application. This includes SET commands that affect screen display (SET COLOR, SET BORDER, and SET BLINK), date and time presentation (SET DATE, SET HOURS) as well as settings that control program functionality such as SET COMPATIBLE, SET EXACT, SET NEAR, SET HELP, SET RESOURCE, and SET UNIQUE. We recommend that you include all the settings, even if yours match the default, to ensure a correct setup. At a minimum, however, you should include those settings that are required for consistent and correct application execution.

Also note several settings that, if not assigned properly, can cause your programs to fail. These include SET INDEX, SET MVARSIZ, SET MVCOUNT, and SET REPORT. Refer to Appendix B for a complete listing and description of the configuration settings.

In addition to creating a Config.fp file for your application, you should consider any special requirements for the DOS Config.sys file. This includes the BUFFERS and FILES statements in the Config.sys file. The BUFFERS setting should be between 20 and 40 for optimal performance. The FILES statement should contain a number at least 10 greater than the maximum number of files open in your application at any one time. A minimum of 40 is recommended. If your clients do not have a Config.sys on their machines or if you are uncertain about the settings, you should supply one with your application.

Note that the FoxPro SYS(2010) function returns, as a character string, the FILES parameter in the Config.sys file or the files setting in effect. Thus your

FoxPro installation or initial checkout program can determine whether this number should be raised and even modify the current configuration file. Note also that on a network such as Novell, the FILE HANDLES setting in the Shell.cfg file overrides the FILES parameter in the Config.sys file.

Compressing Files for Distribution

Your application distribution disk(s) likely will consist of system files and application files. System files may include any or all of the FoxPro support files (Foxpro.esl, Foxpro.eso, Foxprox.esl, and Foxr.exe), the resource files (Foxuser.dbf and Foxuser.fpt), and configuration files (Config.fp and Config.sys).

The application files consist of the appropriate data (.dbf and .fpt) files, help, index, report form, format, or label files, along with the application (.app or .exe) file or compiled (.fxp) programs.

Together, these files can take up a lot of room. You will be doing yourself and your clients a favor by minimizing the number of disks that you need to distribute. You can easily do this using a file compression program that not only compresses files to 50 percent or better of their original sizes but also puts related files together to ensure that your users get all the required files. Of all compression programs in use to date, the one that we consider to be best suited for the job is LHarc, written by Haruyasu Yoshizaki.

LHarc is a completely free program and has one of the most efficient compression ratios among programs of its type. It also is a small (31K) program that is a complete compression/archiving utility. You use the same program to compress files, decompress files, list the contents of an archived file, and produce a self-extracting file out of the archive. Because LHarc can produce self-extracting files (either .com or .exe), your entire application can be distributed, if you wish, as one self-installing .exe file that does not require LHarc or anything else for decompression. The complete LHarc package, along with the C and Assembly language source, is available from many electronic bulletin boards in the United States. It is also included in the program disk for this book for the convenience of its readers.

Ideally you would want to have at least two self-extracting .exe files produced by LHarc on your distribution disk. One .exe consists of the system files, and the other consists of the application files. To build the self-extracting .exe of system files for a standard FoxPro application (.app) file, for example, the appropriate commands are as follows:

```
LHARC a sysfile foxpro.es? foxr.exe foxuser.* config.sys config.fp
LHARC s /x sysfile
```

These commands create a compressed executable archive file, Sysfile.exe, containing the FoxPro runtime loader, the standard FoxPro .EXE Support Library, the resource file, and the DOS and FoxPro configuration files. It assumes that all files are on the default drive. If they are not, simply add the appropriate path to the file. As described in the next section, the /x switch used in the second command specifies a large memory model, self-extracting archive.

Copy the Sysfile.exe file to your distribution disk. Your install program or batch file can then invoke Sysfile.exe to extract the individual files and store them in the appropriate subdirectory of your client's disk. A code fragment from a sample installation batch file is shown in the next section.

Follow a similar procedure for compressing the data and program files of your application. Depending on the size of your application, you may want to create separate self-extracting .exe files for program, data, and support files (including documentation, if any). Note that .dbf and text files compress very well with LHarc, sometimes up to 90 percent or better of their original sizes.

If any of the .exe files becomes too large to fit on one disk, you have two choices. You can reinvoke LHarc and create two or more files out of the large .exe, or you can use one of the many public domain programs such as Chop or Slice that split a file so they fit on a floppy disk and reassemble them later on your client's hard disk.

A Few Notes About LHarc

LHarc can create small and large self-extracting archive files. A small model archive is either a .com file (64K in size or smaller) or an .exe file, which theoretically can be as large as DOS's memory space of 640K, but ideally should not be much larger than 400K. A small model archive must be able to run (self-extract) within the machine's available RAM. So, creating a small model archive of 500K or more may fail to self-extract because a typical DOS machine's transient program area will probably be smaller than this. (Memory-resident programs such as a network shell, screen blanker, and others reduce the amount of memory available to the transient program.)

A large memory model self-extracting archive is limited only by available disk space. It is always an .exe file that runs under currently available RAM. Such a file can self-extract without regard for available RAM. To create a large memory model archive requires only the /x switch in the LHarc command line, for instance,

```
LHARC s /x sysfile
```

A large model archive has several additional features that facilitate the installation of its member files. If the archive is created with a "keyword," and if the archive contains a file named AutoLarc.bat, invoking the archive with the keyword causes the archive to self-extract and automatically executes AutoLarc.bat. For instance, if the keyword provided when the self-extracting file was built is "go", as in

```
LHARC s /x /kgo sysfile
```

then, giving the command

```
SYSFILE go
```

causes Sysfile.exe to self-extract and run AutoLarc.bat.

With a large model archive, you may also specify the target directory where the files should be restored. For example,

```
SYSFILE /ef:\myapp
```

restores all files in the Sysfile.exe archive to the F:\MYAPP subdirectory.

LHarc can also store full path information of the files in the archive and restore the files on the target machine to the appropriate subdirectories, creating the subdirectories as needed.

Installing Your Application

Your application should be "self-installing" in the sense that your clients need not have any intimate knowledge of computers to install the application from the distribution disks. Installation is greatly facilitated by having your applications in self-extracting files as we discussed in the previous section. The following code fragment is from an installation batch file that installs all the files in Sysfile.exe to your client's C:\ Sysfile subdirectory:

```
echo off
REM Log into the directory where system files will be stored
C:
CD\SYSFILE
Echo Place Disk #1 on the A: drive
Pause
A:sysfile
```

Of course, if you are providing Config.sys, you should copy Config.sys to the boot drive and remind your users that the machine has to be rebooted after installation. In a multiuser environment, the resource files probably should also be copied to users' home directories.

One perennial issue during installation and one that affects the speed with which your application runs is where the files should be stored and how your search paths should be set. Given that DOS slows down the more files there are on a subdirectory, it is a mistake to place all the files that an application needs, including the system files, into one subdirectory. At the very least, consider placing system files into one subdirectory, the compiled application programs in another, and the application data files into a third subdirectory. This arrangement is particularly advantageous in a network because users normally should have read-only access to the subdirectories containing program and system files.

On a network, you may also consider altering the search path so that the subdirectories containing your application data and program files are searched ahead of the network system subdirectories. Your application should then restore the original search path before it terminates.

Application Adhoc Reports and Database Security

Like most applications, yours probably contains a report module consisting of a number of canned reports which users can select from a menu. The set of reports in the module likely were determined during the systems analysis phase when users communicated to you the standard reports they expected from the application. No matter how thorough you have been during the analysis and design phases of the application development work, it is virtually impossible to come up with a complete list of all the reports that your users would want. Thus your application should allow users to query the databases or create adhoc reports.

Since your users only have a runtime version of FoxPro, they cannot create their own query programs. Naturally you would not want them to have the FoxPro development package to access the application data files directly because that could easily compromise the integrity of the data. That would also be an undesirable option in a multiuser implementation because one user conceivably can monopolize all the data files of the application rendering them inaccessible by others for extended periods.

One solution is to provide users with a third-party query product that simply accesses data files without modifying them. Another solution is for you to supply, as part of the application, an adhoc query program that simulates an interactive FoxPro command session or a FoxBASE+ dot prompt. This would be a compiled program that FoxPro-literate users can use to issue database queries and other commands as though they were using the full FoxPro development package in an interactive session. To preserve the integrity of the application's data, the program has the responsibility for filtering out destructive commands such as ZAP, DELETE, or PACK and modifying certain commands so they no longer contain any clauses or options that would alter the data. For instance, the program could accept the BROWSE command but would automatically add the NOMODIFY option to it before the command is issued. Luckily, in FoxPro this problem is trivial because the USE command's NOUPDATE clause bars any modification to the .dbf file.

Listing 17-1 shows Adhoc.prg, a rudimentary program that simulates a Dbase-style dot prompt that accepts commands from a user but filters out any destructive commands or command options. It does not include all the commands that a full query package should have, but it can be easily modified so that the program will recognize additional commands. It is intended to allow users, knowledgeable in both FoxPro and the application's data dictionary, to compose adhoc queries. Note that the program still alters the BROWSE command to add the NOMODIFY, NOAPPEND, and NODELETE options even though it always appends the NOUPDATE clause to the USE command. This is necessary because the program allows the CREATE REPORT command which, when invoked when no .dbf file is in use, activates FILER that can open a file for unrestricted use.

You can modify the program to include additional commands that you are willing to accept as long as you ensure that the commands will not modify data in any way. The INDEX command is a good example of one that requires scrutiny. On the one hand, you don't want to filter it out because users need it for a sorted report. On the other hand, because the command creates a file, there is a possibility that users could use an index filename used by the application in a production environment. One solution is to adopt a convention that the query program will only allow index filenames that begin with a standard set of letters. Another solution is to enforce the rule that any files created by the query program can only be written in the user's home directory.

Adhoc.prg has the added feature of storing the last 20 commands issued by the user. Like the Dbase-style dot prompt facility, the program allows the recall and reexecution of previously issued commands with the up and down arrow keys. You must include your own ON ERROR and ON ESCAPE routines with Adhoc.prg.

Listing 17-1. Adhoc.prg allows user adhoc queries by simulating a Dbase-style dot prompt that filters out commands that modify data files.

```
*****************************************************************
* PROGRAM ......... : Adhoc.prg
* AUTHOR .......... : Original by Emmanuel Sigler
*                   : Mangled substantially by P. L. Olympia & K. Cea
* PURPOSE ......... : Provides a limited command line capability with
*                   : the FoxPro Runtime module. Permits
*                   : nondestructive query of databases
* NOTES ........... : The program keeps track of the last 20 commands,
*                   : recallable using the up and down arrow keys.
*                   :
**********************************************************************
*-- Save the view
CREATE VIEW BAdHoc

CLEAR ALL
CLOSE ALL

*-- Define your own Error/Escape routine
*ON ERROR DO Adhoc_Err
*ON ESCAPE DO Adhoc_Esc
SET ESCAPE ON
SET SYSMENU OFF
CLEAR

DIMENSION ComList(20)
ComList = SPACE(10)
LastCom = 1
ComPtr = 1
CurIntense = 'ON'
CurTalk = SYS(103)
PromptLine = '24'
Miss =  'Missing phrase/keyword in command.'
Playdumb =  'Unrecognized phrase/keyword in command.'

DEFINE WINDOW remind FROM 1,40 TO 3,79
ACTIVATE WINDOW remind
```

(continued)

Listing 17-1. Continued

```
@ 0,0 SAY PADC ("Type QUIT to exit Adhoc", WCOLS())
ACTIVATE SCREEN

DO WHILE .T.
   SET TALK OFF
   SET INTENSITY OFF
   UNLOCK
   ExitKey = 0
   NoError = .T.
   ComLine = SPACE(250)
   PrevPtr = LastCom
   CurDevice = SYS(101)
   SET DEVICE TO SCREEN
   @ EVALUATE(PromptLine),0 SAY '.'          && Give 'em Mrs. Dot
   SET DEVICE TO &CurDevice

   DO WHILE ExitKey <> 271 .AND. ExitKey <> 15
      @ EVALUATE(PromptLine),2 GET ComLine PICTURE '@S78'
      READ
      ExitKey = READKEY()
      IF ExitKey = 260 .OR. ExitKey = 4       && Pressed the up arrow key
         IF ComList(PrevPtr) <> SPACE(10)     && Not yet top of list
            ComPtr = PrevPtr
            PrevPtr = IIF(ComPtr = 1, 20, ComPtr - 1)
            ComLine = ComList(ComPtr) +;
            SPACE(250 - LEN(ComList(ComPtr)))
         ENDIF
      ELSE
         IF ExitKey = 261 .OR. ExitKey = 5    && Pressed the down arrow key
            IF ComPtr <> LastCom
               PrevPtr = ComPtr
               ComPtr = IIF(ComPtr = 20, 1, ComPtr + 1)
               ComLine = ComList(ComPtr) +;
               SPACE(250 - LEN(ComList(ComPtr)))
            ELSE
               ComLine = SPACE(250)
               PrevPtr = LastCom
            ENDIF
```

(continued)

Listing 17-1. Continued

```
            ENDIF
         ENDIF
      ENDDO                 && while ExitKey

      IF ComLine = SPACE(250)
         ? ''
         LOOP
      ELSE
         LastCom = IIF(LastCom = 20, 1, LastCom + 1)
         ComList(LastCom) = TRIM(ComLine)
         ComList(IIF(LastCom = 20, 1, LastCom + 1)) = SPACE(10)
      ENDIF

      ModComLine = UPPER(LTRIM(RTRIM(ComLine)))
      SET INTENSITY &CurIntense
      SET TALK &CurTalk
      ? ''

    DO CASE

      CASE LEFT(ModComLine,MIN(4, LEN(ModComLine))) $
  'AVER,CONT,COPY,COUN,DIME,DIR;
  ,DISP,EJEC,EXIT,FIND,LIST,LOCA,QUIT,REPO,REST,SAVE,SEEK,SKIP,SUM;
  ,TOTA,TYPE' .OR. ModComLine = 'GO'
            IF ModComLine = 'QUIT'
               CLEAR WINDOW remind
               EXIT
            ELSE
               IF ModComLine = 'REST'
                  ComLine = TRIM(ModComLine) + ' Additive'
               ENDIF
               &ComLine
            ENDIF

       CASE LEFT(ModComLine,MIN(4, LEN(ModComLine))) $ 'USE ,SET '
            IF AT('EXCL',ModComLine) <> 0 .OR. AT('PROC',ModComLine) <> 0
            ELSE
               SET TALK OFF
```

(continued)

Listing 17-1. Continued

```
            ComClause = SUBSTR(ModComLine, MIN(5, LEN(ModComLine)), ;
              MIN(4, LEN(ModComLine)))
            SET TALK &CurTalk
            IF ModComLine = 'SET' .AND. ;
                 (LEN(ModComLine) = 3 .OR. ComClause $;
'ESCA,ECHO,PROC')
                        ? Playdumb
               RELEASE ComClause
            ELSE
               IF ModComLine = 'USE'
                  &ModComLine NOUPDATE
               ELSE
                  &ComLine
               ENDIF
            ENDIF
         ENDIF

     CASE ModComLine = 'BROW'
         &ModComLine NOMODIFY NOAPPEND NODELETE

     CASE LEFT(ModComLine,4) $ 'CLEA,CLOS'
         IF AT('ALL',ModComLine)=0 .AND. AT('PRO',ModComLine)=0 .AND.;
AT('MEMO',ModComLine)=0
            &ComLine
         ELSE
            ? Playdumb
         ENDIF

     CASE LEFT(ModComLine,4) $  'MODI,CREA'
         ClausePos = AT(' ',ModComLine)
         DO WHILE SUBSTR(ModComLine,ClausePos,1) = ' '
            ClausePos = ClausePos + 1
         ENDDO
         IF SUBSTR(ModComLine,ClausePos,4) <> 'REPO'
            ? 'Unrecognized command.'
         ELSE
            IF AT(' ', SUBSTR(ModComLine,ClausePos)) = 0
               ? Miss
```

(continued)

Listing 17-1. Continued

```
            ELSE
               &ComLine
            ENDIF
         ENDIF
         RELEASE ClausePos

     CASE ModComLine = 'SELE'
            &ComLine

     CASE ModComLine = 'INDE'
         SET TALK OFF
         ClausePos = AT(' TO ', ModComLine)
         ClausePos = ClausePos + 3
         DO WHILE SUBSTR(ModComLine, ClausePos, 1) = ' '
            ClausePos = ClausePos + 1
         ENDDO
         SET TALK &CurTalk
         &ComLine
         SET TALK OFF
         CurIndex = NDX(1)
         SET INDEX TO
         SET INDEX TO &CurIndex
         SET TALK &CurTalk
         RELEASE ClausePos, CurIndex

     *-- We're going to allow DO and RUN
     CASE ModComLine = 'DO' .OR. ModComLine = '!'
         &ModComLine
         SET EXACT OFF
    ENDCASE

    IF ModComLine = 'SET' .AND. NoError
       DO CASE
          CASE LTRIM(SUBSTR(ModComLine,MIN(4, LEN(ModComLine)))) = 'STAT'
             SET TALK OFF
             PromptLine = IIF (RIGHT(ModComLine,2) = 'ON', '21', '24')
             SET TALK &CurTalk
          CASE LTRIM(SUBSTR(ModComLine,MIN(4, LEN(ModComLine)))) = 'INTE'
```

(continued)

Listing 17-1. Continued

```
            SET TALK OFF
            CurIntense = RIGHT(ModComLine,3)
            SET TALK &CurTalk
         CASE LTRIM(SUBSTR(ModComLine,MIN(4, LEN(ModComLine)))) = 'TALK'
            CurTalk = SYS(103)
      ENDCASE
   ENDIF
   IF (AT(' GET ',ModComLine) = 0 .AND. AT('@',ComLine) = 0) .OR. '' =
TRIM(ComLine)
      ? ''
   ELSE
      @24,0 CLEAR TO 24,79
   ENDIF
ENDDO

* Sets the environment back to where it was before
* ON ERROR DO L_ERROR
* ON ESCAPE DO L_ESC
SET VIEW TO BAdhoc
RETURN
```

Chapter Summary

FoxPro 2.0's project management facilities ease the burden of application file maintenance and streamline distribution procedures. Using the facility, file references for all of your application files, including programs, screens, menus, reports, labels, queries, libraries, and database files, can be stored in a project (.pjx) database. Whenever you rebuild a project, FoxPro automatically refreshes (regenerates and/or recompiles) any files that have been modified since the last build. Creating an application from a project is simple and greatly reduces the number of files that must be distributed to your end users. Be aware, however, that you will still need to distribute separately any files, such as database, index, report, or label files, that end users can modify.

Before you distribute your application, review your program code one last time. During this last pass, make sure that your code is optimized and that extraneous code and settings (such as those used for debugging) have been removed. Then, either build your application using the Project Manager or combine your separate procedures and functions into one procedure file and compile the procedure file. Be sure to include the ENCRYPT and NODEBUG options, regardless of how you assemble your application.

Also review your client's hardware setup and, if appropriate, recommend the particular equipment that is best suited to host your FoxPro application. We summarized the hardware options that offer the most gain in performance. Also consider assigning alternate locations for FoxPro's overlay and temporary files if the hardware is available.

Write a Config.fp file that supports correct and consistent operation of your programs, and distribute it with the rest of your files. It is also a good idea to include a standard DOS Config.sys file in your distribution. Use a file compression utility such as LHarc to package your application into one or more self-extracting files. This minimizes the number of disks required to distribute the application and helps ensure that all required files are distributed together. It also facilitates the installation of your application significantly. An easy-to-use installation program is absolutely necessary to ensure that your end users form a positive "first impression" of your application, and to minimize training and support requirements.

These final activities are well worth your time and effort because they can make the difference between a satisfied and dissatisfied client and ultimately define the success of your FoxPro application.

Appendix A

FoxPro 2.0 New and Modified Commands and Functions

A. New Operator

%	Modulus operator. Like MOD( ), the % operator returns the remainder resulting from dividing two numbers.

B. New Commands

\ | \\	Sends a text line to the current output device.
@...EDIT; Text Editing Regions	Creates a rectangular text editing region for a character variable, which may be a database field, a memo field, memory variable, or array.
@...GET; Check Boxes	Creates a check box, which appears on the screen as a pair of square brackets next to a prompt describing what the box controls.
@...GET; Invisible Buttons	Creates "invisible" buttons, which are rectangular regions of the screen that can be selected.
@...GET; Lists	Creates a list, which contains a set of options that can be selected.
@...GET; Popups	Creates a popup, which appears on the screen as a rectangle with double right and bottom lines.

B. New Commands *(continued)*

@...GET; Push Buttons	Creates a push button, which appears on the screen as a string between left and right angle brackets.
@...GET; Radio Buttons	Creates a radio button, which appears on the screen as a pair of parentheses beside which is a prompt describing the button.
BUILD APP	Creates an application (.fxp), typically for runtime distribution, from a project file.
BUILD PROJECT	Creates a project database (.pjx) that tracks all files required to create an application as well as their interdependencies or connections.
CLEAR READ	Terminates READ on the current level and returns control to the previous level. (READs may be nested up to 4 levels.)
COPY INDEXES	Copies single-entry index files to a compound index file.
COPY TAG	Creates a single-entry index file from a tag in a compound index file.
CREATE COLOR SET	Creates a new color set from the color settings of the current environment.
CREATE MENU	Creates user-defined menus and popups by activating FoxPro's menu creation facility.
CREATE PROJECT	Opens a project window and lets you create a project database.
CREATE QUERY	Opens a RQBE window and lets you create a query file interactively.
CREATE SCREEN	Opens a screen layout window and lets you create a screen file with the screen builder.
CREATE SCREEN - Quick Screen	Creates a screen file from parameters passed to the command without opening a screen layout window.
CREATE TABLE - SQL	Creates a database from data specified in an array or the command line.
DELETE TAG	Removes a tag from a compound index file.

B. New Commands *(continued)*

EXPORT	Transfers data from a FoxPro database to a file with different format.
EXTERNAL	Tells the project manager about an undefined reference to a file that is part of a project.
IMPORT	Transfers data from a different file to a new FoxPro database.
INSERT - SQL	Appends a record to a database from values contained in an array or provided in the command line.
MODIFY MENU	Lets you modify or create menus and popups.
MODIFY PROJECT	Opens a project window so you can edit or create a project interactively.
MODIFY QUERY	Opens an RQBE window so you can edit or create a query file interactively.
MODIFY SCREEN	Opens a screen layout window to let you edit or create a screen file.
MOVE POPUP	Moves a user-defined popup to a different location.
ON BAR	Activates a menu popup or menu bar when a menu popup option is selected.
ON SELECTION BAR	Assigns a routine to a menu popup option.
ON SELECTION MENU	Assigns a routine to a menu bar.
POP KEY	Restores ON KEY LABEL commands placed on a stack in memory.
POP MENU	Removes a menu bar from a stack of menus.
POP POPUP	Removes a popup from a stack of menus.
PUSH KEY	Places all current ON KEY LABEL commands on a stack in memory.
PUSH MENU	Places a menu in a stack of menus.
PUSH POPUP	Places a popup in a stack of popups.
REGIONAL	Creates memory variables or arrays that are local to a “region.”
RELEASE BAR	Removes options from popups.

B. New Commands *(continued)*

RELEASE PAD	Removes pads from menu bars.
SELECT - SQL	Retrieves data from one or more databases.
SET ANSI	Specifies if the shorter of two SQL strings is padded with blanks during a string compare.
SET HELPFILTER	Defines a subset of Help topics that should be displayed in the Help window.
SET LIBRARY	Opens the specified external API routine library.
SET MARK OF	Defines the character used as a check mark for a menu pad or menu popup option.
SET OPTIMIZE	Enables or disables Rushmore technology.
SET PDSETUP	Loads or clears a printer driver setup.
SET SKIP	Defines a one-to-many relationship between one record in the parent database and multiple records in the child database.
SET SKIP OF BAR	Enables or disables a specific option in a popup.
SET SKIP OF MENU	Enables or disables a menu bar.
SET SKIP OF PAD	Enables or disables a specific pad of a menu bar.
SET SKIP OF POPUP	Enables or disables a popup.
SET TEXTMERGE	Enables or disables evaluation of database fields, expressions, functions, and memory variables during text merge (template processing).
SET TEXTMERGE DELIMITERS	Defines the set of delimiters for use during text merge.
SET TRBETWEEN	Enables or disables tracing between breakpoints in the Trace window.
SHOW GET	Redisplays a single GET object, referenced by name, optionally enabling or disabling it.
SHOW GETS	Redisplays all GET objects, optionally enabling or disabling them.

B. New Commands *(continued)*

SHOW OBJECT	Redisplays a single GET object, referenced by object number, optionally enabling or disabling it.
SIZE POPUP	Changes the size of a user-defined popup.
ZOOM WINDOW	Changes the size of user-defined or system windows.

C. New Functions

ACOPY( )	Copies elements from one array to another.
ADEL( )	Deletes an element, row, or column from an array.
ADIR( )	Places into an array the name, size, date/time of creation, and DOS attributes of all files matching a file mask, and returns the number of files that match the file mask.
AELEMENT( )	Returns an array element's number given its row and column subscripts.
AFIELDS( )	Places database structure information (field name, field type, field length, and number of decimal places) in an array and returns the number of fields in the database.
AINS( )	Inserts an element into a one-dimensional array or a row or column into a two-dimensional array.
ALEN( )	Returns the number of elements, rows, or columns in an array.
ASCAN( )	Returns the number of the array element that matches a given expression.
ASORT( )	Sorts an array in ascending or descending order.
ASUBSCRIPT( )	Returns an array row or column subscript given its element number.
CDX( )	Returns the names of open compound index files.

C. New Functions *(continued)*

CNTBAR( )	Returns the number of bars, or items, in a menu popup.
CNTPAD( )	Returns the number of menu pads in a menu bar.
EVALUATE( )	Evaluates a character expression and returns the result instead of just returning the type of the result as does the TYPE( ) function.
GETBAR( )	Returns the number of a bar in a popup position.
GETPAD( )	Returns the name of a menu pad from its position in a menu bar.
LOCFILE( )	Locates a file on disk and returns the name with a fully qualified path.
LOOKUP( )	Searches a database for the first occurrence of a specified expression in a specified field.
MDX( )	Returns the names of open compound index files, just like CDX( ).
MRKBAR( )	Returns .T. if a popup bar is marked (by SET MARK).
MRKPAD( )	Returns .T. if a menu bar pad is marked (by SET MARK).
OBJNUM( )	Returns the number of a GET object, which in turn is determined by the object's order of creation.
ON( )	Returns the name of the command currently assigned to an event handler.
ONKEY( )	Returns the command assigned by ON KEY LABEL to a key or key combination.
PRMBAR( )	Returns the text from the PROMPT clause of a DEFINE BAR command.
PRMPAD( )	Returns the text from the PROMPT clause of a DEFINE PAD command.
RDLEVEL( )	Returns the current READ level (0 – 4).

C. New Functions *(continued)*

SKPBAR( )	Returns .T. if a popup bar is enabled.
SKPPAD( )	Returns .T. if a menu pad in a menu bar is enabled.
SYS(2011)	Returns, as a string, the current record or file lock status for the current work area.
SYS(2012)	Returns the memo field blocksize of a database.
SYS(2013)	Returns the names of the System menu bar, menu bar pads, menu popups, and each option in the menu popups.
SYS(2014)	Returns the minimum path between a file and the current directory, or between a file and a specified directory.
SYS(2015)	Returns a unique 10-character procedure name starting with an underscore.
SYS(2016)	Returns the window name included in the last SHOW GETS WINDOW command.
SYS(2017)	Displays the FoxPro sign-on screen.
SYS(2018)	Returns the error message parameter containing additional information about an error.
SYS(2019)	Returns the name and location of the FoxPro configuration file.
SYS(2020)	Returns the disk capacity of the default disk in number of bytes.
SYS(2021)	Returns the filter expression of an open .idx file, or the filter expressions of tags in an open .cdx file.
TAG( )	Returns the tag names from compound index files or the names of .idx index files.
WBORDER( )	Returns .T. if a window has a border.
WCHILD( )	Returns the number of child windows or their names in the order in which they are stacked in a parent window.

C. New Functions *(continued)*

WLAST( )	Returns .T. if the specified window was active prior to the current window.
WPARENT( )	Returns the name of a child window's parent window.
WMAXIMUM( )	Returns .T. if the named window is maximized.
WMINIMUM( )	Returns .T. if the named window is minimized.
WREAD( )	Returns .T. if the named window participates in the current READ.

D. New System Memory Variables

_CUROBJ	Returns the current GET field or GET object number, or selects a GET field or object.
_GENMENU	Stores the name of the program (and its location) that FoxPro uses to generate menu code from the .mnx database.
_GENPD	Specifies a printer driver interface program.
_GENSCRN	Stores the name of the program (and its location) that FoxPro uses to generate screen code from the .scx database.
_MLINE	Stores the memo field offset; can be used as the second argument of MLINE( ) function.
_PDSETUP	Loads or clears a printer driver setup.
_PRETEXT	Defines a character expression to precede text merge lines.
_TALLY	Stores the number of records processed by the last database command.
_TEXT	Directs output from text merge commands (\\, \\\\, and TEXT...ENDTEXT) to a low-level file.
_THROTTLE	Specifies the delay after executing a program line when the Trace window is open.

E. Modified Commands

?/??	STYLE clause.
@...SAY/GET	SIZE clause, K PICTURE code.
ACTIVATE MENU	NOWAIT option.
ACTIVATE POPUP	AT, BAR, REST, and NOWAIT clauses.
APPEND FROM	Additional file types, different date formats are available in delimited files.
AVERAGE	If the destination array does not exist, it is automatically created.
BROWSE	FOR clause; NOLINK, NOLGRID, NOOPTIMIZE, NORGRID, LEDIT, LPARTITION, and REDIT keywords; PARTITION, WHEN, VALID, NOREFRESH, and REST clauses; support for SET SKIP, ROW( ), and COL( ).
CALCULATE	If the destination array does not exist, it is automatically created.
CHANGE	FOR clause; NOLINK, NOOPTIMIZE, LEDIT, LPARTITION, and REDIT keywords, PARTITION, WHEN, and VALID clauses; support for SET SKIP, ROW( ), and COL( ).
COPY STRUCTURE	CDX and PRODUCTION clauses.
COPY TO	Additional file types.
CREATE REPORT	Programmatic Quick Report capability with the FROM <file2>, FORM, COLUMN, FIELDS, ALIAS, NOOVERWRITE, and WIDTH clauses.
DEFINE BAR	BEFORE, AFTER, KEY, COLOR, and MARK clauses.
DEFINE MENU	BAR, AT LINE, IN WINDOW, KEY, MARK, and NOMARGIN clauses.
DEFINE PAD	BEFORE, AFTER, KEY, and MARK clauses.

E. Modified Commands *(continued)*

DEFINE POPUP	IN WINDOW, FOOTER, KEY, MARGIN, MARK, MOVER, MULTI, RELATIVE, SCROLL, TITLE, and PROMPT FIELD clauses.
DEFINE WINDOW	FOOTER, MINIMIZE, and FILL clauses.
DIMENSION/DECLARE	Arrays may be redimensioned without data loss.
DISPLAY/LIST STATUS	Provide additional information.
DO	IN <file> clause.
EDIT	FOR clause; NOLINK, NOOPTIMIZE, LEDIT, LPARTITION, and REDIT keywords, PARTITION, WHEN, and VALID clauses; support for SET SKIP, ROW( ), and COL( ).
GATHER	Supports memo fields.
INDEX	ADDITIVE, TAG, COMPACT, ASCENDING, and DESCENDING clauses; index expression may contain a user-defined function.
KEYBOARD	Stuffed expression can be a set of key labels or a UDF which returns a character expression.
LABEL	PREVIEW and NOCONSOLE options.
MODIFY LABEL	NOENVIRONMENT clause; NOWAIT option.
MODIFY REPORT	NOENVIRONMENT clause; NOWAIT option.
ON KEY LABEL	LBRACE and RBRACE key labels.
ON PAD	ACTIVATE MENU clause.
PACK	MEMO and DBF options; may be interrupted by pressing Esc.
PARAMETERS	Entire arrays may be passed.

E. Modified Commands *(continued)*

READ	ACTIVATE, CYCLE, DEACTIVATE, OBJECT, SHOW, VALID, WHEN, COLOR, MODAL, LOCK, and NOLOCK clauses.
REINDEX	COMPACT option.
RELEASE MENUS	EXTENDED option.
RELEASE POPUPS	EXTENDED option.
REPORT	PREVIEW and NOCONSOLE options.
RETURN	Omitting RETURN in a procedure or UDF automatically returns a logical true (.T.) value.
SCATTER	Supports memo fields.
SCROLL	Horizontal scrolling.
SET INDEX	ADDITIVE, ORDER, ASCENDING, and DESCENDING clauses.
SET MESSAGE	WINDOW clause.
SET OPTIMIZE	New, NOOPTIMIZE option in other commands.
SET ORDER	TAG, IN <work area	alias>, ASCENDING, and DESCENDING clauses.
SET PRINTER	Supports network server and queue.
SET SYSMENU	AUTOMATIC and DEFAULT clauses; FoxPro System menu control.
SET TALK	WINDOW clause.
SHOW WINDOW	REFRESH option.
SUM	If the destination array does not exist, it is automatically created.
TEXT...ENDTEXT	Text merge capabilities.
TYPE	AUTO and WRAP keywords.
USE	AGAIN, ORDER, ASCENDING, and DESCENDING clauses.
WAIT	NOWAIT option for the WINDOW clause, WAIT CLEAR.

F. Modified Functions

FULLPATH( )	Relative path between two files can be returned.
KEY( )	Compound index support.
LINENO( )	Optional 1 argument gives line number relative to the start of the current procedure.
MLINE( )	New clause for memo line offset.
NDX( )	Compound index support.
ORDER( )	Compound index support.
READKEY	Can indicate how the last READ was terminated.
SELECT( )	0 and 1 options.
SET( )	Can return the procedure specified by the SET PROCEDURE command.
UDFs	May be used in FOR and WHILE clauses and INDEX expressions; no longer requires a RETURN statement.

Appendix B

SET Commands

Table B-1. SET Commands That Can Be Defined in Config.fp

SET Command	Values	Description
ALTERNATE	<filename>	Direct screen or window output to a file.
ALTERNATE	**OFF**/ON	Disable or enable output to an ALTERNATE file.
ANSI	**OFF**/ON	Specify how SQL string comparisons are made.
AUTOSAVE	**OFF**/ON	Disable or enable periodic flushing of buffers to disk.
BELL	**ON**/OFF	Enable or disable sounding of the bell when a field is filled or when data entered is invalid.
BELL	<19 to 10000, 2 to 19>	Set the tone and duration of the bell. Default is 512,2.
BLINK	**ON**/OFF	Specify screen attributes and colors.
BLOCKSIZE	<expN>	Specify disk space allocation for memo fields. Default is 64.

(continued)

Table B-1. Continued

SET Command	Values	Description
BORDER	<attribute>	Define the border of menus, popups, windows and boxes created with the @...TO command. Default is SINGLE.
BRSTATUS	**OFF**/ON	Disable or enable the display of the status bar in a Browse window.
CARRY	**OFF**/ON	Disable or enable the ability to CARRY data forward to appended records.
CENTURY	**OFF**/ON	Disable or enable display of the century portion of dates.
CLEAR	**ON**/OFF	Enable or disable clearing of the screen when the SET FORMAT TO command is issued or when you QUIT FoxPro.
CLOCK	**OFF**/ON	Turn the system clock off or on.
CLOCK	<coord>	Specify the location of the system clock. Default is 0,69.
COLOR	<color attrib>	Define the colors for selected screen elements.
COLOR OF NORMAL| MESSAGES|TITLES| BOX|HIGHLIGHT| INFORMATION| FIELDS	<color attrib>	Define colors for various screen elements.
COLOR OF SCHEME <expN>	<ColorPairList>	Specify the colors of a color scheme.
COLOR SET	<ColorSetName>	Load a previously defined color set. Default is DEFAULT.
COMPATIBLE	**OFF**/ON (**FOXPLUS**/DB4)	Specify FoxBASE+ compatibility.
CONFIRM	**OFF**/ON	Disable or enable the requirement to press a key to exit a field during editing.

(continued)

Table B-1. Continued

SET Command	Values	Description
CONSOLE	**ON**/OFF	Enable or disable screen output.
CURRENCY	<char>	Specify the currency symbol. Default is "$".
CURRENCY	<position>	Position the currency symbol to the left or right of the currency value. Default is LEFT.
CURSOR	**ON**/OFF	Turn the cursor on or off.
DATE	<format>	Specify the date format. Default is AMERICAN.
DEBUG	**ON**/OFF	Enable or disable access to the Trace and Debug windows.
DECIMALS	<0 to 18>	Set the number of decimal places displayed in numeric results. Default is 2.
DEFAULT	<drive/dir>	Set the drive and/or directory for disk operations.
DELETED	**OFF**/ON	Disable or enable access or display of records marked for deletion.
DELIMITERS	**OFF**/ON	Disable or enable the display of field delimiters.
DELIMITERS	<expC>/DEFAULT	Specify field delimiter characters. Default is ":".
DEVELOPMENT	**ON**/OFF	Compare the creation date and time of a source program and its object file.
DEVICE	**SCREEN**/PRINT/ FILE <file>	Direct output of @...SAYs to the screen, printer, or a file.
DISPLAY	<type>	Specify a display mode. Default is Installed.
ECHO	**OFF**/ON	Deactivate or activate the Trace window for program debugging.
ESCAPE	**ON**/OFF	Enable or disable trapping for pressing of the Esc key.

(continued)

Table B-1. Continued

SET Command	Values	Description
EXACT	**OFF**/ON	Specify whether two strings must be of equal length in order to match when they are compared.
EXCLUSIVE	**ON**/OFF	Specifies whether database files will be opened for exclusive or shared use.
FULLPATH	**ON**/OFF	Specify whether a full pathname is included when a file name is returned from a command or function.
FUNCTION <num>	<char_str>	Assign a character string to a Function key(s).
HEADING	**ON**/OFF	Enable or disable the display of column titles for each field in the AVERAGE, CALCULATE, DISPLAY, LIST and SUM commands.
HELP	**ON**/OFF	Enable or disable the FoxPro online Help facility.
HELP	<filename>	Specify a Help file to be used when the FoxPro online Help facility is invoked. Default is FoxHelp.
HOURS	**12**/24	Specify a 12 or 24 hour format for time functions and the system clock.
INTENSITY	**ON**/OFF	Enable or disable highlighting of input fields.
LOGERRORS	**ON**/OFF	Specify whether compilation errors will be sent to a file.
MACKEY	<key>	Specify a key(s) that displays the Keyboard Macros dialog. Default is F10.
MARGIN	<**0** to 254>	Set the left printer margin.
MARK	<char>	Specify the date separator character. Default is "/ ".

(continued)

Table B-1. Continued

SET Command	Values	Description
MEMOWIDTH	<8 to 256>	Specify the width of memo field output and values returned by ATLINE( ), ATCLINE( ), MEMLINE( ), RATLINE( ), and MLINE( ) functions. Default is 50.
MOUSE	<1 to 10>	Specify the sensitivity of the mouse. Default is 5.
NEAR	**OFF**/ON	Specify placement of the record pointer after an unsuccessful database search.
NOTIFY	**ON**/OFF	Enable or disable the display of certain system messages.
ODOMETER	<1 to 32,767>	Specify the reporting interval for commands that return status information. Default is 100.
OPTIMIZE	**ON**/OFF	Enable or disable Rushmore.
PATH	<path>	Specify a list of directories for FoxPro to search for files not in the working directory.
PDSETUP	<printer driver setup>	Specify a printer driver setup.
POINT	<char>	Specify the character to be used as a decimal point. Default is ".".
PRINTER	**ON**/OFF	Enable or disable output to the printer.
RESOURCE	**ON**/OFF	Enable or disable use of the FoxPro Resource file.
RESOURCE	<filename>	Specify a Resource file. Default is FoxUser.
SAFETY	**ON**/OFF	Enable or disable file overwrite protection.
SCOREBOARD	**OFF**/ON	Specify display of NumLock, CapsLock, and Insert keys.
SEPARATOR	<char>	Specify the character used as a numeric separator. Default is ",".

(continued)

Table B-1. Continued

SET Command	Values	Description
SPACE	**ON**/OFF	Specify if a space will separate fields or expressions in the ? and ?? commands.
STATUS	**OFF**/ON	Disable or enable display of the status bar.
STEP	**OFF**/ON	Specify whether to execute a program without pausing or to single step with pauses.
STICKY	**ON**/OFF	Specify the display of menus in the FoxPro menu system. Only mouse users are affected.
SYSMENU	**ON**/OFF/ AUTOMATIC/ TO...	Control access to the system menu bar during program execution.
TALK	**ON**/OFF/ WINDOW/ NOWINDOW	Enable or disable display of command results to the screen or to a window.
TEXTMERGE	**OFF**/ON [TO[<file>] [ADDITIVE]] [WINDOW <window name>] [SHOW/NO SHOW]	Control text merge processing.
TRBETWEEN	**ON**/OFF	Enable or disable tracing between breakpoints in the Trace window.
TYPEAHEAD	<0 to 128>	Specify the number of characters to be stored in the typeahead buffer. Default is 20.
UDFPARMS	VALUE/ REFERENCE	Specify whether variables are passed to a UDF by value or by reference.
UNIQUE	**OFF**/ON	Specify whether records with duplicate keys will be included in the index file.

Table B-2. SET Commands That Can Be Defined Only in Config.fp

SET Command	Values	Description
COMMAND	<command>	Executes a FoxPro command after all other configuration settings are established.
DOSMEM	**OFF**/ON/<expN>	Specifies whether DOS memory is available to FoxPro. Used only with the Extended version.
EDITWORK	<dir>	Specifies where the text editor should place its work files.
EMS	**ON**/OFF/<expN>	Determines whether or not FoxPro will take advantage of EMS, or limits the amount of EMS for FoxPro's use.
EMS64	**ON**/OFF	Specifies whether FoxPro should use the first 64K of expanded memory as general purpose memory.
F11F12	**ON**/OFF	Specifies whether FoxPro should attempt to use the F11 and F12 keys.
INDEX	<extension>	Specifies the extension for FoxPro index files. Default is IDX.
LABEL	<extension>	Specifies the extension for FoxPro label definition files. Default is LBX.
MVARSIZ	<1 to 64>	Establishes the amount of memory, in K bytes, that is allocated for character strings stored in memory variables. Default is 6.
MVCOUNT	<128 to 3600> <128 to 65,000> FoxPro(x)	Defines the maximum number of FoxPro memory variables. Default is 256.
OUTSHOW	**ON**/OFF	Enables or disables the Shift+Ctrl+Alt feature.
OVERLAY	<dir>	Specifies where FoxPro should place its .OVL (overlay) and .RSC files.
PROGWORK	<dir>	Specifies where the program cache file will be placed.

(continued)

Table B-2. Continued

SET Command	Values	Description
REPORT	<extension>	Specifies the extension for FoxPro report definition files. Default is FRX.
RESOURCE	<pathname>	Specifies where the FoxUser resource file will be placed.
SORTWORK	<dir>	Specifies where SORT and INDEX operations will place their temporary work files.
TEDIT	<exp | expN>	Specifies the external text editor that is used when the MODIFY COMMAND command is issued.
TIME	<1 to 1,000,000>	Establishes the amount of time that FoxPro waits for the print device to accept a character. Default is 6000.
TMPFILES	<drive:>	Specifies a location (drive) for the EDITWORK, SORTWORK, and PROGWORK files if not otherwise specified.

Table B-3. Other SET Commands

SET CARRY TO [<field list> [ADDITIVE]]
SET DOHISTORY ON|OFF
SET FIELDS ON|OFF
SET FIELDS TO [[<field1>,<field2>...]]| ALL]
SET FILTER TO [<expr>]
SET FIXED ON|OFF
SET FORMAT TO [<file>| ?]
SET HELPFILTER [AUTOMATIC] TO [<expr>]

(continued)

Table B-3. Continued

SET INDEX TO [<file list>| ? [ORDER <expN> | <.idx file> | [TAG] <tag name>
    [OF <.cdx file>]] [ASCENDING | DESCENDING]] [ADDITIVE]
SET LIBRARY TO [<file name> [ADDITIVE]]
SET LOCK OFF|ON
SET MARK OF...
SET MESSAGE TO [<expC>]
SET MESSAGE TO [<expn> [LEFT|CENTER|RIGHT]]
    [WINDOW [<window name>]]
SET MOUSE ON|OFF
SET MULTILOCKS OFF|ON
SET ORDER TO [<expN> | <.idx file> | [TAG] <tag name> [OF <.cdx file>]
    [IN <work area | alias>] [ASCENDING | DESCENDING]] [ADDITIVE]
SET PRINTER TO [<file> [ADDITIVE]|<port>]
SET PRINTER TO [\\<machine name>\<printer name>=<dest>]
SET PRINTER TO [\\SPOOLER [\NB] [\F=<expN>]
    [\B=<expC>] [\C=<expN>] [\P=<expN>]
    [\S=<expC>] [\Q=<expC>]]
SET PROCEDURE TO [<file>]
SET REFRESH TO <expN>
SET RELATION OFF INTO <alias>
SET RELATION TO [<expr1> INTO <alias> [ADDITIVE]]
    [,<expr2> INTO <alias> [ADDITIVE]] ...
SET REPROCESS TO AUTOMATIC | TO <expN> [SECONDS]
SET SHADOWS ON|OFF
SET SKIP OF...
SET SKIP TO [[<alias1>[, <alias2>]...]
SET TEXTMERGE DELIMITERS [TO] [<expC1>[, <expC2>]]
SET TOPIC TO [<expC>|<expL>]
SET VIEW ON|OFF
SET VIEW TO <file> | ?
SET WINDOW OF MEMO TO [<window name>]

Appendix C

FoxPro Colors

Setting Colors

Three concepts are central to FoxPro's color system: color pairs, color schemes, and color sets. The concept of color pairs should be familiar to anyone who has programmed in FoxBase+; however, color schemes and color sets are new in FoxPro and are often confusing.

Colors may be defined for both color monitors and monochrome monitors. On monochrome monitors, the various color options control the intensity of the contrast of the screen display. If you are developing an application for use on both color and monochrome monitors, check the screen presentation on both types of monitors to be sure that it displays correctly.

Color Pairs

A color pair defines the foreground and background colors for an individual screen attribute. Examples of screen attributes are normal text, text box, and border. Retained from FoxBase+, the command

```
SET COLOR TO [[<standard>] [,/[<enhanced>] [,[<border>]
[,[<background>]]]]]
```

allows you to define foreground and background colors for the standard and enhanced display, and to define a color for the border.

The "standard" screen element is the area where your text will appear, such as @<row>,<col> SAY text. The "enhanced" elements are the data entry fields, such as are defined by your GET statements. Border is simply the screen border.

Colors are defined with the following codes:

Color	Code	Color	Code
Black	N	Green	G
Blank	X	Magenta	RB
Blue	B	Red	R
Brown	GR	White	W
Cyan	BG	Yellow	GR+

An asterisk (*) is used to indicate blinking (if SET BLINK is ON) or bright. A plus sign (+) indicates high intensity. On monochrome monitors, the only colors available are:

Black (N)
Inverse video (I)
Underlined (U)
White (W)

Color Schemes

A color scheme is a set of up to ten color pairs, with each pair defining a screen attribute and each scheme defining the colors for related attributes. Examples of schemes are windows, menu popups, and the Browse window. A total of 24 schemes are available. FoxPro uses Schemes 1 through 12 as shown in Table C-1. Schemes 13 through 16, although theoretically available, are reserved for future use, so you should resist using these schemes in an application. Schemes 17 through 24 are designated specifically for application customization, although actually any of the schemes may be redefined.

Although as many as ten color pairs may be assigned to each scheme, some schemes, such as the Menu Bar scheme, use considerably fewer than ten color pairs. For example, the Windows scheme (Scheme 8) has color pairs assigned for the following screen attributes:

Normal text
Text box
Border
Active title
Idle title
Selected text
Hot keys
Shadow
Enabled control
Disabled control

Table C-1. FoxPro Color Schemes

Scheme	Description
1	User windows
2	User menus
3	System menu bar
4	Menu popups
5	Dialogs and system messages
6	Scrollable lists and menu popups within dialogs
7	Alerts
8	System windows (e.g., Command window, Debug)
9	Window popups
10	Browse window
11	Report layout
12	Alert popups
13–16	Reserved (use colors of Scheme 1 by default)
17–24	For application use (use colors of Scheme 1 by default)

The Menu Bar scheme (Scheme 3) has color pairs designated for the following screen attributes:

Disabled pads
Enabled pads
Selected pads
Hot keys

Table C-2 defines the color pairs used for each scheme.

Table C-2. Color Pairs for Each Color Scheme

	Color Scheme					
Color Pair	**Scheme 1**	**Scheme 2**	**Scheme 3**	**Scheme 4**	**Scheme 5**	**Scheme 6**
Color Pair 1	SAY field	Disabled option	Disabled pads	Disabled option	Normal text	Disabled option
Color Pair 2	GET field	Enabled option	Enabled pads	Enabled option	Text box	Enabled option
Color Pair 3	Border	Border		Border	Border	Border
Color Pair 4	Title, active	Menu titles				
Color Pair 5	Title, idle	Message				
Color Pair 6	Selected item	Selected option	Selected pad	Selected option	Selected item	Selected option
Color Pair 7	Clock	Hot keys	Hot keys	Hot keys	Hot keys	Hot keys
Color Pair 8	Shadow	Shadow		Shadow	Shadow	Shadow
Color Pair 9	Enabled Control				Enabled Control	
Color Pair 10	Disabled Control	Disabled Control			Disabled Control	Disabled Control

(continued)

Table C-2. Continued

Color Pair	Color Scheme					
	Scheme 7	Scheme 8	Scheme 9	Scheme 10	Scheme 11	Scheme 12
Color Pair 1	Normal text	Normal text	Disabled option	Other records	Text & B full	Disabled option
Color Pair 2	Text box	Text box	Enabled option	Current field	Report field	Enabled option
Color Pair 3	Border	Border	Border	Border	Border	Border
Color Pair 4		Title, active		Title, active	Title, active	
Color Pair 5		Titles, idle		Title, idle	Title, idle	
Color Pair 6	Selected item	Selected text	Selected option	Selected text	Selected item	Selected option
Color Pair 7	Hot keys	Hot keys		Current record	Band A, empty	Hot keys
Color Pair 8	Shadow	Shadow	Shadow	Shadow	Shadow	Shadow
Color Pair 9	Enabled Control	Enabled Control			Band A, full	
Color Pair 10	Disabled Control	Disabled Control			Band B, empty	Disabled Control

Color Sets

A color set is a group of 24 color schemes. It defines colors for virtually every screen attribute available. Fortunately FoxPro comes preconfigured with a large selection of color sets. You can easily select a predefined color set with the SET COLOR SET TO [<ColorSetName>] command, or in the Config.fp file with the COLOR SET = <ColorSetName> statement. You can also define your own color set in the Color Picker dialog, discussed in the next section. When you define your own color set, you can assemble a group of predefined color schemes, define your own color schemes, or use a combination of both.

In summary, a color set can be defined as follows:

1 Color Set = 24 Color Schemes
1 Color Scheme = (Up to) 10 Color Pairs
1 Color Pair = 1 Foreground + 1 Background Color Code

The Color Picker

The Color Picker dialog is a completely integrated facility for defining color schemes and color sets. It is available from the Window menu. It allows you to view existing color combinations and change various color pairs for any of the color schemes. It also gives you the ability to assemble your own color set, and to try out a different color set by "loading" it for experimentation. The best way to define a set of custom colors is to define the desired combinations in the Color Picker, try them out, and make any necessary modifications. Then, when you are satisfied, you can save your changes for use within your application.

To define your own color settings, select the scheme to be modified by selecting the pop-up control in the upper right corner of the screen. You are presented a list of schemes from which to choose. When you have selected a scheme, each screen attribute associated with the scheme will be listed on a "radio button," a set of parentheses followed by text that describes the attribute. Only one radio button may be selected at a time. To change the colors for a particular attribute (for the selected scheme), select the appropriate radio button. All available color pairs are presented in the lower left corner of the screen. The X indicates the foreground color, and the box behind it shows the background color.

You can continue defining color pairs for each radio button for as many schemes as you like. When you are finished, you can test out your color selections by selecting "Load." Once you are happy with the color set, save the set by selecting "Save." It is a good idea to save a custom color set under a new name, rather than overwriting an existing color set, so just type a name for the color set you have defined. You can use the color set in an application by either issuing a SET COLOR SET TO command or including a COLOR SET = statement in the Config.fp file. Remember that changes made in the Color Picker dialog are lost unless you save them to a particular color set.

Using Colors in Applications

Although the Color Picker dialog is very effective for defining colors interactively, an application developer often needs to be able to control color presentation programmatically. Many commands contain an optional clause for defining color pairs or selecting a color scheme. In addition, a number of commands and functions are available for specifying color defaults within an application.

Color pairs or colors schemes may be specified as an optional clause with the following commands:

@...SAY/GET
@...GET—Check Boxes
@...GET—Invisible Buttons
@...GET—Lists
@...GET—Popups
@...GET—Push Buttons
@...GET—Radio Buttons
@...EDIT—Text Edit Regions
@...FILL
@...TO
BROWSE
CHANGE
DEFINE BAR
DEFINE MENU
DEFINE PAD
DEFINE POPUP
DEFINE WINDOW
EDIT
READ
SHOW GET
SHOW GETS
SHOW OBJECT

Colors can be controlled with the following commands and functions:

Command/Function	Description
CREATE COLOR SET	Creates a color set from the current color settings.
ISCOLOR( )	Returns a logical value indicating whether a color monitor is being used.
SCHEME( )	Returns a color pair or color pair list for the specified scheme.
SET BLINK	Determines whether screen attributes can be made to blink on EGA and VGA monitors.
SET COLOR OF	Sets colors for specific screen attributes of Schemes 1 and 2.
SET COLOR OF SCHEME	Assigns a color pair list to a particular color scheme.
SET COLOR SET	Loads the specified color set.
SET COLOR TO	Specifies the colors for user-defined menus and windows. This command is compatible with the FoxBase+ SET COLOR TO command.
SET DISPLAY	Specifies the monitor display mode.
SYS(2006)	Returns the type of graphics card and monitor in use.

Appendix D

API Library Routines

The list of API library routines is subject to change from time to time. For an up-to-date list of supported functions, always consult the prototype definitions contained in the Pro_ext.h file of your distribution disk.

Memory Management Routines

General-Purpose Memory

```
MHANDLE _AllocHand(unsigned int hsize)
```

Returns a new MHANDLE of size hsize. Returns a null when there is insufficient memory to satisfy the request.

```
void _FreeHand(MHANDLE hand)
```

Releases an MHANDLE previously allocated by _AllocHand.

```
void FAR *_HandToPtr(MHANDLE hand)
```

Translates an MHANDLE to a FAR (32-bit) pointer, which points to the memory allocated to MHANDLE.

```
int_MemAvail(unsigned int size)
```

Returns available memory.

```
unsigned int _GetHandSize(MHANDLE hand)
```

Returns the actual usable number of bytes associated with an MHANDLE.

```
int _SetHandSize(MHANDLE hand, unsigned int size)
```

Changes the amount of memory allocated to MHANDLE, returning TRUE if the reallocation is successful.

```
void _HLock(MHANDLE hand)
```

Locks an MHANDLE, preventing it from moving during FoxPro memory reorganization.

```
void _HUnlock(MHANDLE hand)
```

Unlocks an MHandle.

Stack Space for Temporary Storage

```
void FAR *_Alloca(unsigned int size)
```

Allocates a block of stack space, returning a pointer to the block if the operation is successful.

```
unsigned int _StackAvail(void)
```

Returns the number of free bytes on the stack.

Memory and String Handling

```
void _StrCpy(char FAR *dest, char FAR *src)
```

Copies a null-terminated string from src to dest. Use _MemMove if overlapping moves are required.

```
int _StrLen(char FAR *string)
```

Returns the number of bytes of a null-terminated string.

```
int _StrCmp(char FAR *string1, char FAR *string2)
```

Compares two null-terminated strings, returning 0 if they match. Returns a positive number if string1 is greater than string2; otherwise, returns a negative number.

```
void _MemMove(void FAR *dest, void FAR *src, unsigned int length)
```

Copies length bytes from src to dest, accommodating overlapping moves if necessary.

```
int _MemCmp(void FAR *ptr1, void FAR *ptr2, unsigned int length)
```

Compares two length byte memory areas, returning 0 if the areas match. Returns a positive number if the first area is greater than the second; otherwise, returns a negative number.

```
void _MemFill(void FAR *ptr, int character, unsigned int length)
```

Fills a memory area starting at the location pointed to by ptr with length copies of the byte in character.

Memory Variables and Arrays

```
int _NewVar(char FAR *name, Locator FAR *loc, int flag)
```

Creates a variable or array. Locator field l_subs determines the variable or array type. The flag may be NV_PUBLIC or NV_PRIVATE. The new variable is initialized to logical FALSE.

```
int _Release(NTI n)
```

Frees a memvar or array, returning 0 if the operation is successful.

```
int _Store(Locator FAR *loc, Value FAR *val)
```

Replaces the memvar specified by loc with the value val, returning 0 if the operation is successful.

```
int _Load(Locator FAR *loc, Value FAR *val)
```

Retrieves the value of the variable in loc and places it into val.

Input/Output Routines

File

```
FCHAN _FOpen(char *filename, int mode)
```

Assigns a FoxPro channel to an existing file, returning -1 if it cannot open the file. The mode options include FO_READONLY, FO_WRITEONLY, and FO_READWRITE.

```
FCHAN _FCreate(char *filename, int mode)
```

Assigns a FoxPro channel to a new file, deleting one with the same name if it exists, and returning -1 if the file cannot be created. The mode options include FC_READONLY, FC_SYSTEM, FC_HIDDEN, FC_TEMPORARY, and FC_NORMAL.

```
int _FClose(FCHAN chan)
```

Closes a file and ends access to it. Deletes the file if it was created with the FC_TEMPORARY attribute.

```
int _FCHSize(FCHAN chan, long length)
```

Changes the size of the file to the specified length, extending or truncating the file as necessary.

```
int _FEOF(FCHAN chan)
```

Returns TRUE if the file is currently at the end of file.

```
int _FError(void)
```

Returns the last file operation error recorded for any channel.

```
int _FFlush(FCHAN chan)
```

Flushes all modified buffers in memory to disk, returning 0 if the operation is successful.

```
int _FGets(FCHAN chan, char FAR *buffer, int maxlen)
```

Reads a single line delimited with a carriage return, and stores it in the buffer after translating the carriage return to a null terminator. Returns the number of bytes copied to the buffer.

```
int _FPuts(FCHAN chan, char FAR *buffer)
```

Writes a null-terminated string to a file, followed by a carriage return and linefeed pair. Returns the total number of bytes written to the file.

```
int _FRead(FCHAN chan, char FAR *buffer, int length)
```

Reads exactly length bytes from a file into the buffer without translation or addition of terminating characters. Returns the actual number of bytes read.

```
long _FSeek(FCHAN chan, long position, int mode)
```

Moves the file pointer to a new location as specified by position and mode. Returns the new value of the file pointer. The mode options include 0, 1 or 2, respectively, relative to the beginning of the file, current file pointer, or end of file.

```
int _FWrite(FCHAN chan, char FAR *buffer, int length)
```

Writes exactly length bytes from buffer to a file, returning the actual number of bytes written.

```
int _FCopy(FCHAN dc, long dpos, FCHAN sc, long spos, long len)
```

Copies len bytes from position spos in file sc to position dpos in file dc, returning TRUE if the copy is successful.

Database

```
long _DBRecNo(int workarea)
```

Returns the current record number in the database in the specified workarea.

```
long _DBRecCount(int workarea)
```

Returns the total number of records in the database open in the specified workarea.

```
int _DBStatus(int workarea)
```

Returns status flags for the specified workarea. The status flags include DB_BOF, DB_EOF, DB_RLOCKED, DB_FLOCKED, DB_EXCLUSIVE, and DB_READONLY.

```
int _DBRead(int workarea, long record)
```

Moves the record pointer to the specified record and workarea, returning 0 if the operation is successful.

```
int _DBWrite(int workarea)
```

Writes the current record in the specified workarea and updates any affected indexes, returning 0 if the operation is successful.

```
int _DBAppend(int workarea, int carryflag)
```

Appends a new record to the database open in the specified workarea. A carryflag value of 0 appends a blank record, whereas a value of 1 carries data from the previous record. A carryflag value of -1 uses the setting of SET CARRY to determine whether or not data from the previous record is to be applied to the appended record.

```
long _DBRewind(int workarea)
```

Performs a GOTO TOP in the specified workarea and returns the resultant record number.

```
long _DBSkip(int workarea, long distance)
```

Performs a skip in the specified workarea covering the specified distance.

```
long _DBUnwind(int workarea)
```

Performs a GOTO BOTTOM in the specified workarea and returns the resulting record number.

```
int _DBReplace(Locator FAR *fld, Value FAR *val)
```

Places a new value in the database field.

```
int _DBLock(int workarea, int whatobj)
```

Attempts to lock the current record or file, depending on whether whatobj is DBL_RECORD or DBL_FILE, respectively.

```
void _DBUnlock(int workarea)
```

Releases all user-obtained locks on records or files.

Memo Field

```
FCHAN _MemoChan(int workarea)
```

Returns the FoxPro channel of the memo file open in the specified workarea.

```
long _AllocMemo(Locator FAR *fld, long size)
```

Allocates size bytes of space in the memo file open in the workarea.

```
long _FindMemo(Locator FAR *fld)
```

Returns the location in the memo file where direct access is desired.

```
long _MemoSize(Locator FAR *fld)
```

Returns the length of the specified memo field.

User Interface Routines

General

```
unsigned int _ActivateHandler(FPFI handler)
```

Adds a function handler to the end of the list of event handlers. Returns an integer identifier for the handler.

```
void _DeActivateHandler(unsigned int)
```

Removes the specified handler from the event processor list.

```
unsigned int _ActivateIdle(FPFI handler)
```

Adds a routine to the list of routines called when FoxPro is waiting for user input or for an event to time out. Returns an integer identifier for this routine.

```
void _DeActivateIdle(unsigned int)
```

Removes the specified routine from the idle loop.

```
int _GetNextEvent(EventRec FAR *event)
```

Reads the next event into the EventRec. Returns the event type.

```
void _DefaultProcess(EventRec FAR *event)
```

Provides the default event processing for an event returned by _GetNextEvent when the event does not need special handling.

```
int _MousePos(Point FAR *pt)
```

Fills in **pt** with the current position of the mouse. Returns TRUE if the left mouse button is down when the function is called; returns FALSE if the left mouse button is not down.

```
int _InKey(int timeout, int flag)
```

Returns the next key typed during a timeout period.

```
int _FindWindow(WHANDLE *wh, Point pt)
```

Places the WHANDLE of the window to which point **pt** belongs into **wh**. Returns an integer indicating the portion of the window where the point is located.

```
WHANDLE _WOnTop(void)
```

Returns the WHANDLE of the frontmost window.

```
void _GlobalToLocal(Point FAR *pt, WHANDLE wh)
```

Translates a point in screen-relative coordinates to window-relative coordinates.

```
WHANDLE _WOpen(int top, int left, int bottom, int right, int flag,
int scheme_num, Scheme FAR *scheme, char FAR *bord)
```

Creates a new window at the coordinates specified by top, left, bottom, and right.

```
void _WClose(WHANDLE wh)
```

Closes a window and releases all memory associated with that window.

```
void _WHide(WHANDLE wh)
```

Removes a window from the screen but keeps track of its contents.

```
void _WShow(WHANDLE wh)
```

Redisplays a hidden window on the screen.

```
void _WZoom(WHANDLE wh, int newstate)
```

Zooms a window to a new state.

```
void _WSelect(WHANDLE wh)
```

Brings the specified window to the frontmost position on the screen.

```
void _WSendBehind(WHANDLE wh)
```

Sends the specified window to the rearmost position on the screen.

```
WHANDLE _WGetPort(void)
```

Returns the WHANDLE of the window that is currently selected for user output.

```
WHANDLE _WSetPort(WHANDLE wh)
```

Changes the user output window to be the specified window. Returns the previous user output window.

```
void _WMove(WHANDLE wh, Point pt)
```

Moves the specified window to a new location specified by **pt**.

```
void _WSize(WHANDLE wh, Point pt)
```

Sets the new dimensions of the window to the height and width specified by h and v in **pt**.

```
int _WTop(WHANDLE wh)
```

Returns the row on the screen where the top of the window is located.

```
int _WBottom(WHANDLE wh)
```

Returns the row on the screen where the bottom of the window is located.

```
int _WLeft(WHANDLE wh)
```

Returns the column on the screen where the left edge of the window is located.

```
int _WRight(WHANDLE wh)
```

Returns the column on the screen where the right edge of the window is located.

```
int _WHeight(WHANDLE wh)
```

Returns the number of rows in the content area of the window.

```
int _WWidth(WHANDLE wh)
```

Returns the number of columns in the content area of the window.

```
MHANDLE _WTitle(WHANDLE wh)
```

Returns an MHANDLE containing the null-terminated title of the window. Returns 0 if no title is specified for the window.

```
void _WSetTitle(WHANDLE wh, char FAR *title)
```

Changes the title of a window.

Window Output

```
void _WClear(WHANDLE wh)
```

Erases the contents of the specified window by changing the content area to the default background color.

```
void _WClearRect(WHANDLE wh, Rect r)
```

Erases a rectangular area of a window by changing it to the default background color.

```
void _WPosCursor(WHANDLE wh, Point pt)
```

Positions the logical cursor of the specified window at the location specified by **pt**.

```
Point _WGetCursor(WHANDLE wh)
```

Returns the position of the logical cursor in the specified window.

```
int _WAttr(WHANDLE wh, int color)
```

Returns the attribute byte for the color index in the specified window's color scheme.

```
void _WSetAttr(WHANDLE wh, int color, int attr)
```

Changes the attribute for the specified color scheme index in the indicated window's color scheme to the new attribute **attr**.

```
void _WPutChr(WHANDLE wh, int char)
```

Writes one character **char** to the specified window in the current color.

```
void _WPutStr(WHANDLE wh, char FAR *str)
```

Writes a null-terminated string to the specified window in the current color.

```
void _RefreshDisplay(void)
```

Redraws the entire screen, including all windows.

Streaming Output

```
void _PutChr(int char)
```

Writes one character **char** to the current output window in its normal attribute (color 0).

```
void _PutStr(char FAR *str)
```

Writes a null-terminated string to the current output window in its normal attribute (color 0).

```
void _PutValue(Value FAR *val)
```

Formats the value **val** and writes it to the current output window.

Dialog

```
int _Dialog(int scheme, char FAR *body_text, char FAR *button1,
char FAR *button2, char FAR *button3, int default, int escape)
```

Presents a dialog to the user that is the specified color scheme number **scheme** and contains the specified body text and button text. Returns the number of the button the user has chosen.

Menu

```
MENUID _MenuId(int literal)
```

Returns the actual menu id that corresponds to the system-defined literal for the system menu pad or popup.

```
MENUID _GetNewMenuId(void)
```

Returns an id that is available for use as a menu id.

```
ITEMID/ _GetNewItemId(MENUID menuid)
```

Returns an id that is currently available for use as an item id in the specified menu.

```
int _NewMenu(int mtype, MENUID menuid)
```

Creates a new menu of the specified menu type. If the routine succeeds, it returns 0; otherwise, it returns a negative integer whose absolute value is a FoxPro error number.

```
void _DisposeMenu(MENUID menuid)
```

Releases the specified menu and all its items and frees all storage associated with the menu.

```
int NewItem(MENUID menuid, ITEMID itemid, ITEMID beforeid, char
FAR *prompt)
```

Adds an item with the specified **itemid** to the menu specified by **menuid**. Returns 0 upon success, or -1 upon failure.

```
void _DisposeItem(MENUID menuid, ITEMID itemid)
```

Releases the specified menu item and frees all storage associated with the item.

```
void _SetMenuPoint(MENUID menuid, Point loc)
```

Specifies the upper left corner, **loc**, of a menu.

```
void _SetMenuColor(MENUID menuid, int scheme)
```

Sets the color scheme for an entire menu and for any menu items that do not specifically have a color scheme set.

```
void _SetItemColor(MENUID menuid, ITEMID itemid, int scheme)
```

Sets the color of a menu item individually.

```
void _SetItemSubMenu(MENUID menuid, ITEMID itemid, MENUID submenuid)
```

Assigns a submenu to a menu item.

```
void _GetItemText(MENUID menuid, ITEMID itemid, char FAR *text)
```

Copies the text of a menu bar or pad to the buffer pointed to by **text**.

```
void _SetItemText(MENUID menuid, ITEMID itemid, char FAR *text)
```

Changes the displayed text for a menu item.

```
int _GetItemCmdKey(MENUID menuid, ITEMID itemid, char FAR *text)
```

Copies the displayed keyboard shortcut string for the specified menu item to the buffer pointed to by the **text** parameter. Returns the internal keyboard code for the keyboard shortcut; returns 0 if there is no keyboard shortcut.

```
int _SetItemCmdKey(MENUID menuid, ITEMID itemid, int key, char FAR
*text)
```

Sets the keyboard shortcut for the specified menu item as well as the displayed text for the keyboard shortcut.

```
int _CountItems(MENUID menuid)
```

Returns the number of pads or bars on the specified menu.

```
int _GetItemId(MENUID menuid, int index)
```

Returns the item id of the **index** item in the specified menu. Returns 0 when **index** exceeds the number of items in the menu.

```
void _ActivateMenu (MENUID menuid)
```

Displays the specified menu on the screen and immediately returns control to the calling routine.

```
int _MenuInteract(MENUID FAR *menuid, ITEMID FAR *itemid)
```

Returns the item id for the selected menu item. If no item was selected from the menu, returns a negative integer whose absolute value is a FoxPro error number.

```
void _DeActivateMenu(MENUID menuid)
```

Removes a menu from the screen.

```
void _OnSelection(MENUID menuid, ITEMID itemid, FPFI routine)
```

Specifies a routine to execute when the specified menu and item are selected.

Other Routines

Statements and Expressions

```
int _Execute(char FAR *stmt)
```

Compiles and executes the null-terminated statement in **stmt**. Returns 0 if no error occurred, or the FoxPro internal error code for any error.

```
int _Evaluate(Value FAR *res, char FAR *expr)
```

Compiles and executes a FoxPro expression contained in **expr**, placing the result in **res**. Returns 0 if no errors occurred, or the FoxPro internal error code for any error.

Error Handling

```
void _Error(int code)
```

Signals the error specified by the value in **code** to the FoxPro runtime.

```
void _UserError(char FAR *message)
```

Reports an error with the text message specified in **message**.

```
int _ErrorInfo(int code, char FAR *message)
```

Returns the external error number that reflects the FoxPro internal error number specified by **code**.

Debugging

```
void _BreakPoint(void)
```

Transfers control to your debugger.

Appendix E

FoxPro Standard Index (.Idx) File Structure

A FoxPro standard .idx file consists of a header record and one or more node records. Each record type is 512 bytes long. The structure of the header record is shown in Table E-1 while the structure of a node record is shown in Table E-2.

The header record contains information about the root node, next available node, the length of the key, index options, the key expression and the index FOR expression (if used). Unlike dBASE IV, FoxPro does not store the type of the index key (for example, numeric) in the header record; FoxPro determines the index key type from the expression. When used as a key, numbers undergo an internal conversion process so they can be sorted using the same ASCII collating sequence as characters. FoxPro uses the following conversion algorithm for numeric keys:

1. Convert the number to IEEE floating-point format.
2. Swap the order of the bytes from Intel 8086 order to left-to-right order.
3. If the number is negative, take the logical compliment of the number (swap all 64 bits, 1 to 0 and 0 to 1); else invert only the leftmost bit.

A node record contains information about the node type, the number of keys in the node, pointers to the left and right of the node, and the characters encompassing the key value. A node record may be a root, leaf, or index node. The root node is the top node in the tree, where a search begins. Leaf nodes are the bottom nodes of the tree and point to database records. Index nodes are indexes into other nodes, narrowing down the set of nodes to be searched as they are traversed.

Table E-1. The Structure of a FoxPro Standard Index Header Record

Byte	Description
00–03	Pointer to root node. This value points to the entry location of the index file.
04–07	Pointer to free node list (-1 if not present). This value points to the next available 512-byte block in the index file.
08–11	Pointer to end of file (file size).
12–13	Length of the index key.
14	Index options (may be one of the following, neither, or the sum of both): 1 A UNIQUE index 8 FOR clause used
15	Index signature (reserved for future use).
16–235	Key expression (in ASCII).
236–455	FOR expression (in ASCII; ends with null byte).
456–511	Unused.

Table E-2. The Structure of a FoxPro Standard Index Node Record

Byte	Description
00–01	Node type or attribute (may be one of the following or their sums): 0 Index node 1 Root node 2 Leaf node
02–03	Number of keys present (0, 1, or many).
04–07	Pointer to the node directly to the left of the current node on the same level (-1, if not present).
08–11	Pointer to the node directly to the right of the current node on the same level (-1, if not present).
12–511	Group of characters containing the key value for the length of the key, along with a four-byte hexadecimal number. The number contains the actual database record number if the node is a leaf node; otherwise, it contains a pointer to another block which contains either the actual pointers into the file or pointers to a lower node. The key value/hexadecimal number pair occurs as many times as there are keys in the node record as defined in bytes 02–03.

References

Barkakati, Nabajyoti, *The Waite Group's Turbo C Bible*, Howard W. Sams & Company, Indianapolis, IN, 1989.

Date, C.J., *An Introduction to Database Systems*, Volume I, Addison-Wesley Publishing Company, Reading, MA, 1987.

Freeland, R. Russell, "Binary Output," *Data Based Advisor*, Volume 7, Number 4, May, 1987.

Kernighan, Brian W. and Dennis M. Ritchie, *The C Programming Language*, Prentice-Hall Inc., New Jersey, 1978.

Novell NetWare Application Programming Interface (API) manuals, 1989.

Olympia, P.L., R. Russell Freeland, and Randy Wallin, *dBASE Power: Building and Using Programming Tools*, Ashton-Tate Publishing, California, 1988.

Russell, Craig, "Printing Labels in Snaked Columns," *Ashton-Tate Technotes*, March, 1989.

Schulman, Andrew, "Inside dBASE," *Data Based Advisor*, Volume 5, Number 5, May, 1987.

Tenenbaum, Aaron M. and Moshe J. Augenstein, *Data Structures Using Pascal*, Prentice-Hall Inc., New Jersey, 1986.

White, Chris, ed., *Secrets of dBASE*, Ashton-Tate Publishing, California, 1987.

Index

ACHOICE( ) function, 197
ACOPY( ) function, 14–15, 199, 409
ACTIVATE MENU command, 413
ACTIVATE POPUP command, 413
ADEL( ) function, 14–15, 199, 409
ADIR( ) function, 14–15, 198–202, 219, 301, 409
AELEMENT( ) function, 14–15, 194, 199, 409
AFIELDS( ) function, 14–15, 199, 200, 202, 219, 409
AINS( ) function, 14–15, 199, 409
ALEN( ) function, 14–15, 198, 199, 409
Animation, string, 184–185
ANSI (American Standards Institute), 275
API (Application Program Interface), 2, 4–5, 16, 17, 62, 268, 344, 361
  basics, 367–369
  libraries, examples of, 378–384
  return value functions, 376
  routines, compiling and linking of, 270–271
  routines, summary of, 376–378
  rules, summary of, 369
  use of, 64–66
APPEND command, 58, 145, 150
  and deleting records, 326
  and implicit locking, 324
APPEND BLANK command, 324, 326
APPEND FROM command, 14, 15, 134, 143, 324, 413
APPEND FROM ARRAY command, 204, 205, 209, 219
APPEND FROM...DELIMITED command, 133, 134, 140, 181
APPEND FROM SDF command, 181
APPEND MEMO command, 145, 159, 161, 164–165, 175
Arithmetic operations, 137
Array(s), 14–15, 18, 66, 193–219
  before/after values in, 328, 338–339
  Clipper, 196–197
  commands involving, 202–204
  functions, built-in, 198–202
  initialization of, 195–196
  and memo fields, 165
  and memory variables, 437–438
  moving data to/from, and database fields, 204–209
  passing of, to procedures, 197–198
  and the Project Manager, 386–387
  and SCATTER/GATHER vs. COPY/APPEND commands, 209
  and sorting data, 209–218
ASC( ) function, 182

ASCAN( ) function, 14–15, 199, 409
ASCII, 129, 142, 154, 181–182, 452
  and printing, 262, 263
  and sorting, 209
ASORT( ) function, 14–15, 200, 210, 409
Assembly language, 4, 61, 62, 99, 393
  and API, 367
  and binary routines, 64
ASUBSCRIPT( ) function, 14–15, 194, 200, 409
AT clause, 145
AT( ) function, 174, 180
@ (at symbol), 64, 374
ATC( ) function, 161, 174, 175
ATCLINE( ) and ATLINE( ) functions, 145, 152, 174
AVERAGE command, 226, 324, 413
AVG( ) function, 286, 287

BETWEEN( ) function, 118, 174
Binary files, 309–317
BIN files, 61, 64–65, 264
BOE (basic optimizable expression), 2–3
Borland Turbo C compiler, 299
BROWSE command, 145, 150, 323, 413
  and color, 433
  and implicit locking, 324
  and Rushmore, 226
Bubble sort, 211, 219
BUILD EXE FROM command, 4
BUILD PROJECT command, 386

Calendar system, 117
C language, 3, 4, 5, 61, 62, 99, 382, 393
  and binary routines, 64
  and I/O functions, 297, 299
  and template language processing, 102
CALCULATE command, 226, 413
CALL command, 9, 64–66
CAPTURE command, 266
CDOW( ) function, 118
CDX( ) function, 6, 224–225, 241, 409
CDX files, 223, 239, 241, 244
CHANGE command, 58, 145, 150, 334, 335, 338, 413
  and color, 433
  and implicit locking, 324
  and Rushmore, 226
Character data, 171–192
  conversion of, 171–173
  and searching character strings, 173–176
Character fields, 237–238
ChkFptPO utility, 168
CHR( ) function, 182, 262
CHRTRAN( ) function, 179, 180–181, 182, 191
CLEAR ALL command, 145, 202
CLEAR MEMORY command, 202, 252, 272
CLEAR READ command, 10, 406
Clipper, arrays, 193, 197, 218, 219
CLOSE INDEX command, 224
Closing files, and library routines, 67
CLOSE MEMO command, 145, 151–152
CMONTH( )CTOD( ) function, 119
CNTBAR( ) function, 13, 410
CNTPAD( ) function, 410
Colors, 67, 97, 98
  and color pairs, 427–438
  and the color picker, 427, 432–433
  and color schemes, 428–431
  and color sets, 427, 431–432
  and the SET COLOR command, 94
  setting of, 427–433
  use of, in applications, 433–434
COMMAND statement, 94
COMPILE command, 389
Compilers, 46, 299
Compression, of files, for distribution, 393–395

Configuration, custom, 93–99
    and the FoxUser resource file, 97–99
    and the SET EMS option, 96
    settings, multiuser, 94–97
CONTINUE command, 235
Conversion, of string and character data, 171–173
CONVERT command, 334–338
COPY command, 65, 143, 222, 324, 348
COPY INDEXES command, 224, 406
Copying
    of .dbf files, 348–349
    and temporary files, creation of, 349–350
COPY MEMO command, 146, 159, 382
COPY STRUCTURE command, 324, 413
COPY STRUCTURE EXTENDED command, 48
COPY TAG command, 6, 224, 406
COPY TO command, 17, 14, 15, 146, 156, 226, 349, 413
COPY TO ARRAY command, 204, 205, 208, 209, 219, 226, 327
COPY TO DELIMITED command, 253
COUNT command, 226, 324
COUNT( ) function, 287, 335
CREATE command, 25, 48, 49, 50, 52, 58
CREATE FROM command, 59
CREATE/MODIFY LABEL command, 153, 414
CREATE/MODIFY PROJECT command, 4, 386, 387, 406
CREATE/MODIFY REPORT command, 153, 245, 247, 250, 397, 413, 414
CREATE/MODIFY SCREEN command, 7
CREATE TABLE command, 202, 275, 291–292, 295 406
CTOD( ) function, 123, 134, 172
Culprit, 46–47
Customization
    of applications, 61–99
    and calling other program modules, 61–66
    and custom configuration, 93–99
    and debugging facilities, 86–93
    and error handling, 86
    and establishing a set of library routines, 66–68
    and implementing your own help facility, 74–85
    and performing data validation, 68–74

Data
    character, 171–192
    conversion of, 108–115, 116, 171–73, 328, 334–338
    entry of, word wrapping with, 176
    integrity of, 26–28, 42
    security for, 67
    sorting of, 209–219
    validation of, 24, 47–49, 67–74, 81–85, 99, 117, 118
Data dictionary, 45–60
    advantages of, 47–48
    and the cross-reference field, 57
    the data element dictionary, 55–57
    and the data source, 57
    and default or initial value, 56
    definition of, 46–47
    dependent, 46
    and extending the dictionary concept, 57
    facility, Recital, 58–59
    and field description, 55
    files, 51–55
    implementation, in the DBase family, 57–58
    and the picture clause, 56

primitive, setting up a, 48–50
and the required field, 56
standalone, 46
steps to design and implement, 50–51
system, functional, 50–51
and the Valid clause and Range, 56
Database design, 19–44
creation of the database, 25–26
eight steps to, 19–25
example of, 34–42
and normalization, 28–34
and the relational integrity rules, 26–27
and requirements analysis, 19–20, 42
Datamanager (Manager Software Products), 47
Date, C. J., 22, 26
DATE( ) function, 87, 119
Date(s), 117–140
data, appendage of, from a delimited file, 133–34
averaging of, 134
comparisons, 125
fields, indexing on, 237–238
formats, 125–127, 128–129
FoxPro base, 129–132
indexing on, 134–135
and leap years, 135–136
and letter templates, 256
and months and years, days remaining in, 136
and null dates, 127–128
and the number of workdays, computation of, 137–139
operations, 123–125
packing of, 132–133
and random numbers and the system clock, 133
storage format, 128–129
DAY( ) function, 119
DBase, 1, 16, 17, 59, 250, 451
and arrays, 197
and .bin routines, 367
and the data dictionary, 45–46, 48, 55
and memo fields, 151, 154, 157, 163, 166, 168
and printing, 262
and string and character data, 171, 176
and template language processing, 101
and UI2, 58, 60. *See also* dBASE III PLUS and dBASE IV
dBASE III PLUS, 118, 123, 127, 131, 142–143, 153, 155, 157, 158, 167, 181–182
and printing, 261, 262, 264, 265, 272
and reports, 252
dBASE IV, 5–6, 8
and arrays, 218
Convert utility, 328, 334–338
and dates, 118, 123, 124, 125, 128, 131, 133, 135, 139
and deleting records, 327
and implicit locking, 322, 323
and memo fields, 142–143, 150, 153, 155, 158, 163
and printing, 268
and reports, 245, 246, 247
and square brackets, 193
and transaction processing, 351–352
DBASELOCK field, 334–335
DBF files, 2, 51–55, 59, 69, 71, 72, 98, 99, 133, 141, 154–158, 244
and arrays, 198
and auditing, 359
copying of, 348–349
and deleting records on a network, 326
and flagging records in use, 329
and Help, 74, 75, 79, 81, 82
and indexing, 222
and I/O functions, 300, 312
locking of, 348

and memo fields, 143, 150, 165, 167, 168, 169
and offloading I/O intensive tasks, 361
and ON ERROR processing, 357
and reporting, 347
and RQBE, 290, 293
and SQL, 276
and template language processing, 105, 113
and temporary files, 355
and work areas, 324
DBMS software, 46, 47, 392
Deadlock, 339–345
Debugging, 86–93, 99, 128, 389, 403, 450
and dates, 128
and monitoring program values, 92
and the set DOHISTORY option, 92–93
setting breakpoints, 92
DECLARE command, 193, 202, 414
Default definitions, global, 58
DEFINE BAR command, 12, 413, 433
DEFINE MENU command, 12, 433
DEFINE PAD command, 12, 413, 433
DEFINE POPUP command, 12, 414, 433
DEFINE WINDOW command, 9, 15, 144, 150, 151, 414, 433
DELETE command, 226, 324, 326, 397, 406
DELETE RECORD command, 324
DELETE TAG command, 6, 224
Deleting
records on a network, 326–328
and the referential integrity rule, 27–28
Dialogs, 247, 249, 447
Diary data, 97
DIF files, 15
DIFFERENCE( ) function, 174, 242–243
DIMENSION command, 193, 202, 414
DISKSPACE( ) function, 200, 222
DISPLAY command, 9, 152, 226
DISPLAY/LIST command, 146
DISPLAY/LIST STATUS command, 156, 414
DISPLAY MEMORY command, 195, 301
Distribution, 393–395
DMY( ) function, 119, 127
DO command, 414
DOS, 65, 99, 133, 165, 169, 191, 382, 388, 393, 396, 404
and arrays, 199
command, 94
DIR command, 301
and memory, 394
MODE command, 318
SHARE program, 95
DOW( ) function, 120, 137
DrawAxis procedure, 185
DrawBar procedure, 185
DTOC( ) function, 118, 120, 132, 139, 172, 173, 237
DTOS( ) function, 120, 123, 134, 172, 173

EDIT command, 58, 145, 150, 414
and color, 433
and implicit locking, 324
and Rushmore, 226
@...EDIT command, 12, 143, 144
EJECT PAGE command, 246, 272
EMPTY( ) function, 120, 125, 146
EMS (expanded memory), 94, 96, 391
ENCRYPT option, 388–389, 404
ENDFOR statement, 184
English system of measurement, 117
Entities
example of, 35
identification of, 20, 42
integrity of, 26–27
relationships among, identification of, 20, 21, 36
EOF (end of file), 298, 326
EOF( ) function, 164, 231
Epson, 263

ERR files, 93
Error(s), 86, 87, 99, 450
 and the API library, 5
 and .dbf files, 85
 and the data dictionary, 47, 58
 and library routines, 67, 68, 69, 70
 and the ON ERROR command, 86–93, 344, 357–359
EVALUATE ( ) function, 8, 9, 390, 410
EXE files, 3–4, 386, 388, 393–394
EXPORT command, 14, 15, 226, 407
EXTERNAL command, 4, 407
EXTERNAL ARRAY command, 387

F1 key, 75, 82
FCHSIZE( ) function, 298
FCLOSE( ) function, 297–298
FCREATE( ) function, 104, 297–298
FERROR( ) function, 298
FFLUSH( ) function, 298
FGETS( ) function, 298, 299
Field(s)
 and the AFIELDS( ) function, 14–15, 199, 219, 200, 202, 409
 character, 237–338
 cross-reference, 57
 database, 204–209
 and data dictionaries, 56–57
 date, 237–238
 DBASELOCK, 334–335
 description, 55
 logical, 38
 types, 41–42. *See also* Memo field techniques
Files
 binary, 309–317
 closing, 67
 compatibility, 392
 compression of, 393–395
 copying of, 348–350
 corruption, 167–168
 for data dictionaries, 51–55
 delimited, 133–134
 exclusive, 95, 321–322, 328
 locking of, 67, 322–28, 339–45
 opening, 67, 328, 341–342
 preassigning, 324
 resource, 97–99
 report form, 248–49
 shared, 321–322
 text, manipulation, 300–317
 temporary, 355
File formats
 .cdx, 223, 239, 241, 244
 .dbf, 2, 51–55, 59, 69, 71, 72, 98, 99, 133, 141, 154–58, 244, 348–349
  and arrays, 198
  and auditing, 359
  copying of, 348–349
  and deleting records on a network, 326
  and errors, 85
  and flagging records in use, 329
  and Help, 74, 75, 79, 81, 82
  and indexing, 222
  and I/O functions, 300, 312
  locking of, 348
  and memo fields, 143, 150, 165, 167, 168, 169
  and offloading I/O intensive tasks, 361
  and ON ERROR processing, 357
  and reporting, 347
  and RQBE, 290, 293
  and SQL, 276
  and template language processing, 105, 113
  and temporary files, 355
  and work areas, 324
 .exe, 3–4, 386, 388, 393–394
 .fpt, 141, 154–58, 165, 167, 168, 169
 .frm, 245
 .frx, 387, 245, 248, 250

.idx, 222, 228–229, 451–453
.lbx, 387
@...FILL command, 184
FIND command, 224, 226, 229–31, 232, 235, 242, 244
FLOCK( ) function, 242, 322
FOPEN( ) function, 104, 297–298, 299, 318
Foreign keys, 24, 26, 42
definition of, 20, 22–23, 37
null, 27
and relational integrity, 26–27, 28
FOUND( ) function, 230, 231
FoxBASE and FoxBASE+, 9, 101, 323, 397
and arrays, 218
and color, 427
command, 9
and dates, 118, 123, 127, 128
and deleting records, 326
and indexing, 222, 223
and memo fields, 142, 143, 154, 155, 158, 159, 167
and parentheses, 193
and printing, 261, 263, 264, 272
and reports, 245, 247, 252
FoxCode, 9, 101
FoxGen, 9
FoxInfo, 368–369
FoxPro (standard), 1
FoxPro (extended), 1, 14, 18, 153, 194, 223, 391
and API, 368
and work areas, 324
FoxPro 1.x, 1, 4, 8, 12, 16–17, 101, 197
and indexing, 222, 223
and memo fields, 164
and the Project Manager, 388
and reports, 248
and the SYS(3) function, 133
template language, 9
FoxReport, 13–14. *See also* Reports
FoxTable, 368–369
FoxView, 9, 101
FPT files, 154–158, 165, 167, 168, 169
FPUTS( ) function, 298, 299
FREAD( ) function, 298, 299
Freeland, Russ, 264
FRM files, 245
FRX files, 387, 245, 248, 250
Frx2Prg program, 250
FSEEK( ) function, 298, 299
FULLPATH( ) function, 416
FUNCTION formats, 10–11
FUNCTION statement, 62
FW2 file type, 15
FWRITE( ) function, 298, 299
FXP files, 4, 388–389

GATHER command, 146, 166, 204, 209, 219, 327, 328, 339, 414
GENMENU utility program, 105
GENSCRN utility program, 105
@...GET command, 59, 10–12, 151, 405–406
and implicit locking, 56, 58, 59, 323
and word wrapping, 176
GET statement, 176
GETBAR( ) function, 13, 410
GETPAD( ) function, 13, 410
GET/READ command, 150, 151
Goldengate, 46–47
GOMONTH( ) function, 120, 123
Graphs, 185, 187

HEADER( ) function, 222
Heapsort, 216–217, 219
Help, 74–85, 99
advantages and disadvantages of, 79–80
and the data dictionary, 50, 59
file database, 17
and library routines, 67, 70
use of, 74–79
writing your own, help system, 80–85

I/O, 5, 392
- and accessing communications ports, 317–318
- and binary files, 309–317
- buffered vs. unbuffered, 297, 298–299
- and copying .dbf files, 348
- functions, and character strings, 173
- intensive tasks, offloading of, 361–363, 366
- low-level file, 297–319
- and manipulating text files, 300–317
- and memo fields, 158
- routines, 377, 378, 438–441
- and the SET EMS option, 96
- uses of, 299–318

IBM box drawing symbols, 182
IDX files, 451–453
IEEE (Institute of Electrical and Electronic Engineers) format, 128, 139, 451
IIF( ) function, 172, 173, 238
IMPORT command, 14, 15, 407
INDEX command, 6, 135, 146, 227–228, 235, 238, 349, 397, 414
- and implicit locking, 323, 324
- and Rushmore, 226

Indexing, 221–244, 451–252
- and .cdx files, 223, 239, 241, 244
- on a character expression, 236–237
- commands and functions for, table of, 224–226
- and conditional indexes, 238
- and database searches, 229–235
- and descending indexes, 238–239
- and formulating index expressions, 236–239
- and .idx files, 222, 228–229
- and index expression length, 239
- and index file formats, 227–229
- and indexing options, 227–228
- and limiting access to reindexing facilities, 365–366
- on mixed data types, 237–238
- in a multiuser environment, 241–242
- and opening indexes and index order, 239–241
- and reindexing, 241
- and searching for close matches, 242–243
- and searching for multiple records, 231–232

INDEX ON command, 224, 241, 242, 244, 312
Initialization, of arrays, 195–196
INLIST( ) function, 121, 174
INSERT command, 275, 324
INSERT INTO command, 293–294, 295
Inserts, and the referential integrity rule, 27–28
Integrated Data Dictionary (Cullinet Software), 46–47
Integrity, 42
Invisible buttons, 10, 11
ISCOLOR( ) function, 434
ISDIGIT( ) function, 172
ISLEAP( ) function, 135–136

Japanese date format, 118, 126
JOIN command, 226, 323, 324
Julian calendar, 130–131, 132, 139–140

KEY( ) function, 224, 240, 317, 416
KEYBOARD command, 176, 191, 414

LABEL command, 226, 414
LABEL FORM command, 13, 152
Label forms, 108–115, 116
LABEL statement, 94
LAN (Local Area Network), 1, 65, 301, 321, 322, 345–346, 360, 366
- and NetWare semaphores, 332–334

and network conventions, 350
and the SET REPROCESS option, 343–344
LBX files, 387
LEFT( ) function, 146
LEN( ) function, 146
Letter templates, 256–259
LHarc, 393, 394–395, 404
Libraries, 66–68, 99, 370–384, 387, 388, 394, 435–450
LIKE( ) function, 174, 175, 243
LINENO( ) function, 87
LIST command, 9, 152, 164, 226
LIST MEMORY command, 88, 390
LIST STATUS command, 88, 390
LKSYS( ) function, 334, 335, 338–339
LOAD command, 64–66
LOCATE command, 226, 235, 236
LOCK( ) function, 323
Locking
implicit, 322–328
record and file, and library routines, 67
Logical fields, 238
LOOKUP( ) function, 410
Low level file I/O. *See* I/O

Macros, 8–9, 197
MailMerge, 247, 253–261
driver program, 259
and the letter template, 256–59
routine, generic, 259
MAKEMEM, 300–301
MAX( ) function, 287
MDX( ) function, 6, 121, 123, 126, 224, 241, 410
Measurement systems, 117
MEMLINES function, 146, 152, 250
Memo field techniques, 141–169
alternative methods for displaying, 152–153
and APPEND MEMO and the phantom record, 164–165
and creating and accessing memo fields, 150–152
and .dbf and .fpt files, 141, 154–158
and importing and exporting memo field data, 158–164
and managing memo field space, 158
and memo field length, 153
and memo fields as filing cabinets, 165–167
and memo file corruption, 167–168
and missing memos, 167
printing of, 250–252
reasons for using, 141–142
summary of, 142–150
MemoPlus Program, 168
Memory, 1, 18, 66, 394, 437–438
and APIs, 66, 368
and arrays, 208
expanded (EMS), 94, 96, 391
and FoxReport, 249, 252
general-purpose, 435–436
and layout windows, 14
LIM 4.0 expanded, 391
and MailMerge, 259
and MAKEMEM, 301
management, 2, 377, 435–438
and memo fields, 142–143, 165
and reports, 245–246
and the SCATTER Memvars, 273, 327–328
and stack space for temporary storage, 436
and strings, 182, 436–437
variables, 7, 153, 196, 412–413
MEMOWIDTH clause, 146
Menus, 7–8, 12–13, 197
and the ACTIVATE MENU command, 413
and the DEFINE MENU command, 12, 433

and the GENMENU utility program, 105
and the ON SELECTIONMENU command, 13, 407
popups, 7, 10, 11, 13, 14
and the READ MENU command, 206
and the RELEASE MENUS command, 415
System, 12–13
and user interface routines, 447–449
MESSAGE( ) function, 87
Metric system, 117
Microsoft, 128, 299
MIN( ) function, 287
MLINE function, 147, 152, 161, 416
MOD file type, 15
MODIFY LABEL command. *See* CREATE/MODIFY LABEL command
MODIFY MEMO command, 82, 145, 147, 150, 151, 161
MODIFY PROJECT command. *See* CREATE/MODIFY PROJECT command
MODIFY REPORT command. *See* CREATE/MODIFY REPORT command
MODIFY STRUCTURE command, 46, 50, 324
MONTH(d) function, 121
Mouse, 249
MOVE POPUP command, 13, 407
MRKBAR( ) function, 13, 410
MRKPAD( ) function, 13, 410
Multiuser procedures and techniques, 1, 67, 321–366, 390–391
and controlling concurrent updates, 328–339
and deadlock, 339–345
and deleting records on a network, 326–328
and flag records in use, 329–332
and implementing NetWare synchronization services, 344–345
and implicit locking, 322–328
and limiting access to reindexing facilities, 365–366
and locking all files and records needed at program initiation, 342–343
and maintaining a system audit trail, 359–361
and offloading I/O intensive tasks, 361–365
and ON ERROR processing, 344, 357–359, 366
and opening files in a prescribed order, 341–342
and opening files exclusively, 328
and preassigning files to specific work areas, 324
and reporting, 347–351
and the SET REPROCESS option, 343–344
and shared files, 321–322
and transaction processing, 351–356
and the USE NOUPDATE option, 366

Names
Array, 197
file, network conventions for, 350–351
temporary file, and library routines, 67
NDX( ) function, 224, 241, 416
NODEBUG option, 388–389, 404
Nonkey fields, 20, 23–24, 37–38, 42
Normalization, 24, 28–34, 38, 44
First normal form (1NF), 29–30, 38
Second normal form (2NF), 30–32, 38

Third normal form (3NF), 32–34, 38
Novell Netware, 266, 301, 302, 332, 343, 344–345, 346, 350, 352–354, 360, 381–82, 384

OBJNUM( ) function, 410
OCCURS( ) function, 174, 175
Okidata, 263
ON BAR command, 13, 407
ON ERROR processing, 86–93, 344, 357–359, 366, 390
ONKEY( ) function, 410
ON KEY LABEL command, 414
ON PAD command, 414
ON PAGE command, 246, 253, 272
ON SELECTION BAR command, 13, 407
ON SELECTION MENU command, 13, 407
Open architecture, 2, 7
Opening files, and library routines, 67
OR logical operator, 3
ORDER function, 224, 416

PACK command, 16, 17, 324, 326, 357, 397, 414
PACK DBF command, 17
PACK MEMO command, 17, 143, 147
PADC( ) function, 185
Page handler, 252–253
Parameters, 62, 371–375, 391, 393, 414
Pascal, 102
Passwords, 67, 98
PDDOCEND procedure, 368
PDDOCST procedure, 368, 372
PDOBJECT procedure, 368–369
PDOX file type, 15
PJX files, 387
Platinum Software, 168, 250
PLAY MACRO command, 151
PLB files, 367–368
PRG files, 245, 268
Primary keys, 23, 24, 25–26, 42, 39, 40
definition of, 20, 21–22, 36–37
and normalization, 32–33
and relational integrity, 26–27, 28
Printing, 16, 67, 166–167, 245–273
of memo fields, 250–252
on a network, 265–267
and offloading I/O intensive tasks, 361–365
and printer drivers, 268–272
and printjob and endprintjob, 267–268
and redirecting printer output to a file, 265
and sending commands directly to the printer, 261–262
and sending null to a printer, 262–264
PRINTJOB-ENDPRINTJOB command, 246, 266, 267–268
PRINTSTATUS( ) function, 265, 272
PRMBAR( ) function, 13, 410
PRMPAD( ) function, 13, 410
Procedures, definition of, 62
PROGRAM( ) function, 87, 390
Program interface application, 367–384
and API Basics, 367–369
and API libraries, example of, 378–384
and compiling and linking API routines, 270–271
and obtaining parameters, 371–375
and returning results to FoxPro, 375–376
and summarizing API routines, 376–378. *See also* APS
Project Manager, 4, 385–388

QPX files, 291
Quicksilver, 328
Quicksort, 212–216, 219

Radio buttons, 7, 10, 11, 14, 432
RAND( ) function, 133
RAT( ) function, 147, 174, 175–76, 191, 255
RATLINE( ) function, 148, 152, 174
RDLEVEL( ) function, 10, 410
READ command, 10, 74, 151, 323, 415, 433
READ/GET command, 10–11
READKEY( ) function, 416
READ MENU command, 206
READ MENUBAR TO command, 206
RECALL command, 226, 324
RECCOUNT( ) function, 222
Recital, 47, 55, 57, 59–60
RECSIZE( ) function, 222
Records
  and the CHANGE RECORD command, 324, 326, 327
  deletion of, 324, 326–28
  and the EDIT RECORD command, 324
  flagging of, 329, 329–32
  locking of, 67
  needed at program initiation, 342–343
  phantom, 164–65
  and the RECALL RECORD command, 324
  and the REPLACE RECORD command, 324
  and searching for multiple records, 231–32
Redundancy, 24, 42, 44
  and the data dictionary, 47
  and normalization, 28–34
Referential integrity, 26–27
REGIONAL command, 193, 407
REINDEX command, 54, 241, 224, 244, 357, 415
  and implicit locking, 324
Relational integrity rules, 26–27, 42
RELEASE command, 202, 252, 272
RELEASE MENUS command, 415
RELEASE MODULE command, 66
RELEASE POPUPS command, 415
REPLACE command, 148, 163, 164, 172, 173, 335
  and implicit locking, 324
  and Rushmore, 226
REPLICATE( ) function, 185–190
Report Expression Dialog, 247
REPORT FORM command, 13, 152, 153, 226, 247, 248, 249, 250, 253, 415
Reports, 245–273, 347–351
  and FoxReport features, summary of, 246–248
  and individual percentages in reports, 249
  and MailMerge, 253–259
  and page handler, 252–253
  and printing memo fields, 250–253
  and report enhancements, 248–249
  and the report form file, 250
  and report writing facilities, 245–246
  snaked column, 259–261
  and system memory variables, 245–246, 252
Requirements analysis, 34–35, 42
RESTORE FROM command, 148, 202
RESTORE MACROS command, 148
RESTORE WINDOW command, 148
RETRY command, 88
RETURN command, 63, 88, 415
RIGHT( ) command, 149
RLOCK( ) function, 322, 323
RPD files, 15
RQBE (Relational Query-By-Example), 6, 18, 290–291
Rules
  API, summary of, 369
  AUTOMATIC, 27
  CASCADE, 28
  DEPENDENT, 27
  NULLIFY, 27, 28
  relational integrity, 26–27

RESTRICT, 28
validation, 47, 48, 49
RUN command, 64–66, 65, 66, 99, 198
Rushmore technology, 2–3, 17, 226

SAVE MACROS command, 149
SAVE...MEMO command, 165
SAVE SCREEN command, 206
SAVE TO command, 149, 202
SAVE TO MEMO command, 164, 167
SAVE WINDOW command, 149
Saving, of screens, and memo fields, 165–166
@...SAY command, 245, 246, 265, 272
@...SAY/GET command, 69, 72–74, 82, 117, 144, 413, 433
Scaliger, Joseph, 132, 139
SCAN...ENDSCAN command, 226, 236
SCATTER command, 149, 166, 204–205, 208–209, 219, 327–328, 338–339, 415
SCATTER MEMVAR command, 327–328
SCHEME( ) function, 434
Schulman, Andrew, 300
Screen Builder, and screen painter objects, 7–8
Screen displays, and library routines, 67
Screen painter objects, listing of, 7–8
SCROLL command, 415
Scrollable lists, 7, 10, 11
Searching
for close matches, 242–43
of databases, 229–35
for multiple records, 231–32
of strings, 173–76
an unordered file, 235
SECONDS( ) function, 121, 133
Security measures, 67
SEEK command, 81, 224–226, 229–232, 234, 235, 242, 244
SEEK( ) function, 229, 231, 232, 244, 259
SELECT command, 6, 275–290
SELECT( ) function, 416
Semaphore functions, 328, 332–334
SET command, 94, 152, 392, 408, 415
and color, 434
listing of, 417–426
SET BLINK command, 392
SET BLOCKSIZE command, 149
SET BORDER command, 392
SET CENTURY ON command, 126
SET COLOR command, 94, 184, 392, 431
SET COMPATIBLE command, 392
SET DATE command, 392
SET DESCRIPTIONS OFF command, 58
SET DEVICE TO command, 246, 272
SET DOHISTORY option, 92–93
SET ECHO ON command, 86
SET EXACT command, 242–243, 392
SET EXCLUSIVE command, 95, 321, 322
SET FILTER command, 235, 236, 236
SET( ) function, 156, 416
SET HELP command, 75, 105, 392
SET HELPFILTER command, 17, 78, 79
SET HOURS command, 392
SET INDEX command, 225, 241
SET LIBRARY command, 4, 368, 379, 384
SET MARK OF command, 13
SET MEMOWIDTH command, 149
SET NEAR command, 242–243, 392
SET OPTIMIZE command, 3
SET ORDER TO command, 6, 135, 225, 227, 236, 238–240, 241, 349

SET PDSETUP command, 271–272, 272
SET PRINTER TO command, 246, 266, 272
SET RELATION command, 26, 222, 223, 225, 244
SET RESOURCE command, 97, 98, 392
SET STEP ON command, 86
SET TALK command, 17, 390
SET TEXTMERGE command, 9, 10, 102, 104
SET TOPIC TO command, 75, 77, 75, 79, 81
SET UNIQUE command, 225, 392
SET WINDOW command, 149, 150, 151
Shells, 69, 70, 211–212, 219
SHOW GET command, 10, 408, 433
SHOW GETS command, 408, 433
SHOW OBJECT command, 409, 433
SHOW WINDOW command, 415
SIZE POPUP command, 13, 409
SKPBAR( ) function, 411
SKPPAD( ) function, 411
SORT command, 221–222, 242, 348, 349
  and implicit locking, 324
  and Rushmore, 226
Sorting, 221–244
  and arrays, 209–218, 219
  and searching for multiple records, 231–232
  and searching a sorted database, 232–235
  and searching an unordered file, 235
SORT statement, 221
SOUNDEX function, 175, 242, 243
SPOOL command, 266
Spreadsheet file type, 15
SQL (Structured Query Language), 179–180, 191
  and the basic SELECT statement, 277–278
  and compound subqueries, 285–286
  and the CREATE TABLE command, 291–292
  and executing a subquery, 284–285
  functions, table of, 286–287
  and grouping results, 284
  and the INSERT INTO command, 293–294
  introduction to, 275–276
  and joining a table with itself, 283–284
  and obtaining unique values, 279
  and ordering the results and specifying column headings, 281–282
  and RQBE, 290–291
  relationality with, 275–295
  and repeating subqueries, 286
  and Rushmore, 226
  and the SELECT command, 3, 6, 18, 276–290
  and selecting rows that satisfy multiple conditions, 281
  and selecting rows that satisfy one of several conditions, 280
  and selecting specific rows, 279–280
  and specifying output columns, 278–279
  and WHERE clause filter conditions, 287–289
  and writing query results to an alternate destination, 289–290
STORE command, 207
STR function, 172, 185, 237
String(s), 56, 67, 171–192, 375
  animation, 184–185
  character, searching of, 173–176

comparison of, 176–180
and data type conversion, 171–173
encrypting and decrypting of, 182–184
and printing, 263
replacement of, 180–182
and the REPLICATE( ) function, 185–190
variable, and memo fields, 153
STRTRAN( ) function, 179, 191
STU function, 179
SUBSTR( ) function, 150, 180
SUM command, 226, 249, 324, 415
SUM( ) function, 287
SYLK file type, 15
Symmetry IV (Symmetry Software), 57, 58, 60
SYS(1) function, 121
SYS(2) function, 122
SYS(3) function, 133, 350
SYS(10) function, 122, 129
SYS(11) function, 122, 123, 129, 131
SYS(13) function, 265
SYS (14) function, 225, 240, 317
SYS(15) function, 179, 182
SYS(16) function, 87, 390
SYS(18) function, 76, 79, 82, 87
SYS(22) function, 225
SYS(2006) function, 434
SYS(2011) function, 323
SYS(2012) function, 150, 156, 411
SYS(2015) function, 133, 411
System audit trail, 359–361
System menu, 12–13
System 2000, 47

TAG( ) function, 6, 225, 241, 411
Target files, specification of, 104
TEDIT statement, 94
Template language processing, 9–10, 101–117
applications, 105–107
and converting a label form into source code, 108–115, 116
outputting generated lines, 104–105
and specification of target files, 104
steps to, 105
Temporary files, 67, 348–350, 355–356, 391
Text buttons, 7, 10, 11
TEXT...ENDTEXT command, 415
TEXTMERGE delimiters, 9
Time, 117–140. *See also* Date(s)
TIME( ) function, 87, 122
TMPFILES statement, 94
TOTAL command, 226, 324
Transaction processing, 351–356
TTS (Transaction Tracking Services), 352–354, 366
TYPE command, 415
TYPE( ) function, 9, 196–197, 218

UDFs (user-defined functions), 5, 4, 227, 278
and calling program modules, 61, 62–64
and data customization, 69, 72–74
and encrypting and decrypting strings, 183–184
and Field Objects, 7
and strings, 171, 176
UI2 Programmer (Wallsoft), 55, 56, 57–58
UNIX, 47, 173
UNLOCK command, 322, 323
UNLOCK ALL command, 322, 342–343
UPDATE command, 324
Updates, 27–28
UPPER( ) function, 175
USE command, 9, 227, 240, 322, 390, 397, 415
USE...AGAIN command, 105

USE NOUPDATE option, 366
USE...ORDER command, 240
User interface routines, 378, 442–449

VAL( ) function, 171, 172, 236
Validation, 24, 81, 82–85, 99
  date, 117, 118
  and library routines, 67, 68–74
  rules, and the data dictionary, 47, 48, 49
Variables
  and memo fields, 153
  memory, 7, 153, 196, 412–13, 437–38
  string, 153
  system memory variables, 245–46, 252
VARREAD( ) function, 69, 76, 79, 82, 87, 176
VERSION( ) function, 87

WAIT command, 415
Watcom C, 367, 370, 382, 384
WBORDER( ) function, 411
WCHILD( ) function, 16, 411
Window(s), 15–16, 18
  Browse, 97
  child, 16
  Command, 92, 97, 98
  and the FoxUser resource file, 97
  and library routines, 67
  memo, 55
  output, 445–446
  RQBE (Relational Query-By-Example), 290–291
  Trace, 91–92
WK1 files, 15
WK2 files, 15
WKS files 15
WLAST( ) function, 412
WMAXIMUM( ) function, 412
WMINIMUM( ) function, 412
WordPerfect, 102, 268
Word wrapping, 176
WPARENT( ) function, 16, 412
WR1 file type, 15
WREAD( ) function, 412
WRK file type, 15
WYSIWYG, 272

XLS file type, 15

YEAR( ) function, 122
Yoshizaki, Haruyasu, 393

ZAP command, 324, 357, 397
ZOOM, 16, 409

Developing FoxPro 2.0 Applications
Program Disk

Order Form

The Program Disk for this book contains: (1) all program listings shown, for example, Lbx2Prg.Prg and the API C routines, (2) programs that are too lengthy for the book, for example, the graphics/memo field APIs, (3) utility programs for FoxPro 2.0 written by the authors, for example, new structure and index list programs, and (4) outstanding free utilities for use in developing applications, for example, Lharc.

Enclose a check or money order for U. S. $21.00 for the disk. Foreign orders outside North America, add $4.00 shipping and handling.

____
Name

____
Address

____________________ __________ __________
City State Zip

____
Country

____
Daytime Phone (with Area Code)

☐ 5.25-inch disk

☐ 3.5-inch disk

Please make your check payable to Platinum Software International and send it along with this order form to:

Platinum Software International
FoxPro 2.0 Applications Disk
17 Thorburn Road
North Potomac, MD 20878